ALSO BY GEORGE BLACK

On the Ganges: Encounters with Saints and Sinners Along India's Mythic River

Empire of Shadows: The Epic Story of Yellowstone

Casting a Spell: The Bamboo Fly Rod and the American Pursuit of Perfection

The Trout Pool Paradox: The American Lives of Three Rivers

Genocide in Iraq: The Anfal Campaign Against the Kurds

Black Hands of Beijing: Lives of Defiance in China's Democracy Movement
(with Robin Munro)

*The Good Neighbor: How the United States Wrote the History
of Central America and the Caribbean*

THE LONG RECKONING

THE LONG RECKONING

A STORY OF WAR, PEACE, AND REDEMPTION IN VIETNAM

George Black

 ALFRED A. KNOPF | NEW YORK | 2023

THIS IS A BORZOI BOOK
PUBLISHED BY ALFRED A. KNOPF

Copyright © 2023 by George Black

Library of Congress Cataloging-in-Publication Data

Names: Black, George, [date] author.
Title: The long reckoning: a story of war, peace, and redemption in Vietnam / George Black.
Description: First edition. | New York: Alfred A. Knopf, 2023. | "This is a Borzoi book." |
Includes bibliographical references and index.
Identifiers: LCCN 2022023618 (print) | LCCN 2022023619 (ebook) |
ISBN 9780593534106 (hardcover) | ISBN 9780593534113 (ebook)
Subjects: LCSH: Agent Orange—Health aspects—Vietnam. | Agent Orange—Environmental
aspects—Vietnam. | Vietnam War, 1961–1975—Health aspects—Vietnam. | Vietnam War,
1961–1975—Environmental aspects—Vietnam. | War victims—Services for—Vietnam. |
Unexploded ordnance—Vietnam. | Land mines—Vietnam. | United States—Foreign
relations—Vietnam. | Vietnam—Foreign relations—United States.
Classification: LCC DS559.8.C5 B53 2023 (print) | LCC DS559.8.C5 (ebook) |
DDC 959.704/31—dc23/eng/20220810
LC record available at https://lccn.loc.gov/2022023618
LC ebook record available at https://lccn.loc.gov/2022023619

Jacket photograph by Eddie Adams/AP/Shutterstock
Jacket design by Chip Kidd
Maps by Joe LeMonnier

Manufactured in the United States of America
1st Printing

For Hien, Hong, Lai, Linh, Phu, Toan, and Trung,

who grew up under the long shadow of war

and have done so much to lighten it.

For Ngo Thien Khiet, in memoriam.

And for Yen Ly

The evils of war are great in their endurance, and have a long reckoning for ages to come.

—THOMAS JEFFERSON,
letter to the Young Republicans of Pittsburg,
December 2, 1808

Contents

THE LONG RECKONING

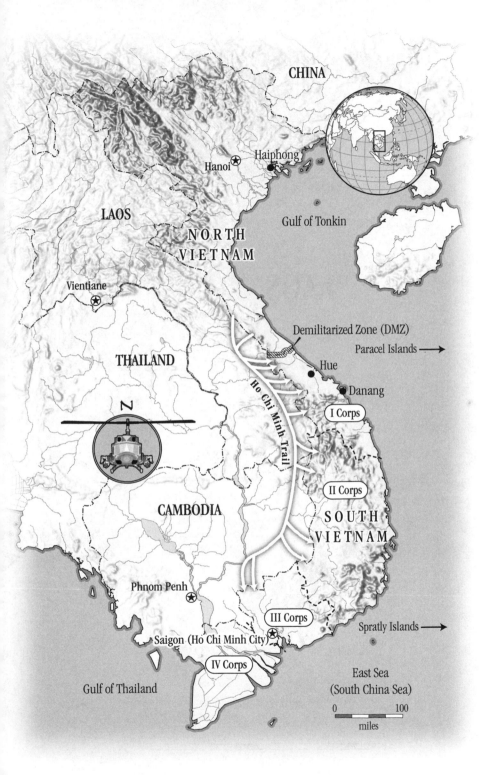

The Ho Chi Minh Trail ran almost all the way from Hanoi to Saigon, with a "Sea Trail"
that carried supplies from the port of Haiphong. This map shows the main axis of
the Trail in Laos and Cambodia and the principal infiltration routes into South Vietnam.

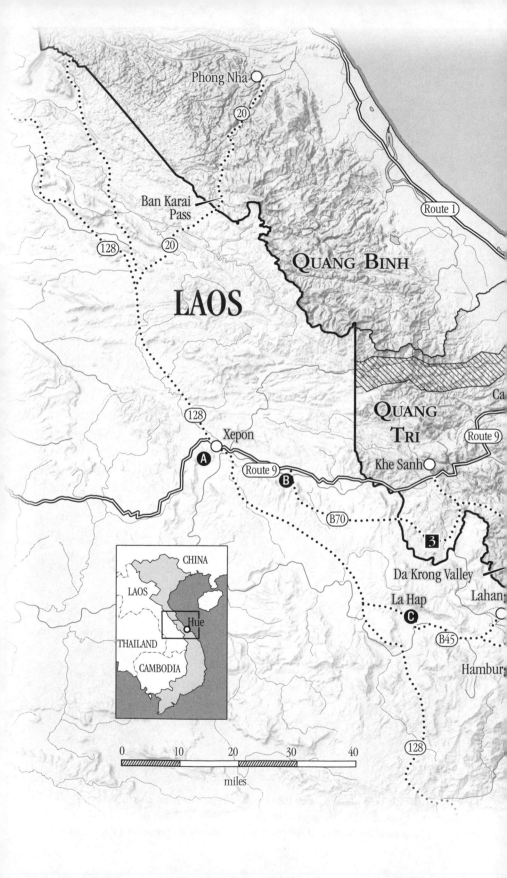

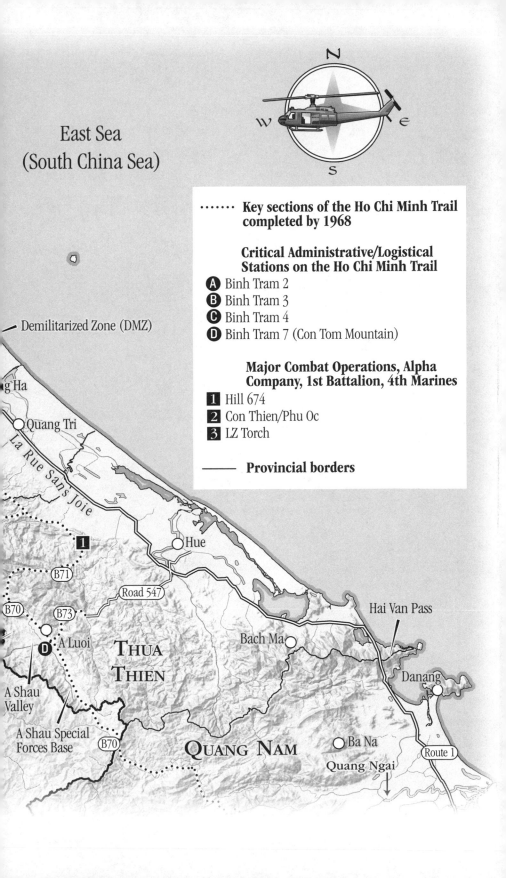

East Sea
(South China Sea)

**⋯⋯ Key sections of the Ho Chi Minh Trail
completed by 1968**

**Critical Administrative/Logistical
Stations on the Ho Chi Minh Trail**
Ⓐ Binh Tram 2
Ⓑ Binh Tram 3
Ⓒ Binh Tram 4
Ⓓ Binh Tram 7 (Con Tom Mountain)

**Major Combat Operations, Alpha
Company, 1st Battalion, 4th Marines**
🄁 Hill 674
🄂 Con Thien/Phu Oc
🄃 LZ Torch

—— **Provincial borders**

Demilitarized Zone (DMZ)

g Ha

Quang Tri

La Rue Sans Joie

🄁

Hue

B71

Road 547

B70

B73

A Luoi

Ⓓ

THUA
THIEN

Bach Ma

Hai Van Pass

Danang

A Shau
Valley

A Shau Special
Forces Base

B70

QUANG NAM

Ba Na

Route 1

Quang Ngai

Prologue

HER NAME IS KIEU. There are thousands like her.
She had seen many different kinds of airplanes in the year since the Americans arrived. There were tiny ones with only one man inside that circled almost soundlessly overhead like a hawk searching for some small field creature. There were fast, terrifying ones that swooped down from the sky like birds that had spotted their prey. Some of these had short, stubby wings, and some had wings that were swept back like the point of an arrow. Both kinds threw down a curtain of red fire and black smoke that consumed long lines of banana trees and bamboo thickets and stuck to people's bodies and burned off all their flesh. Sometimes these airplanes fired rockets that made the houses explode and burst into flames.

She had also seen many different kinds of bombs. Some came in big containers that opened up before they hit the ground and shot out hundreds of little round bombs in all directions, small enough to fit into your hand. They reminded her of the ball she sometimes saw the Americans tossing around when they were off duty. Some of these little bombs thudded to the ground but did not explode, lying half-buried in the dirt. They seemed to be harmless, but Kieu's mother warned her not to pick them up. Not every child in the village heeded that warning, and they paid dearly for it. There were also shells that were bigger than her baby brother, and her father told her that these came from the big guns on wheels that the Americans had placed on a hilltop west of the town. They made a whistling, roaring sound as they streaked overhead, and sometimes you could see the puff of smoke that rose when they struck their faraway targets. But the worst bombs of all fell from airplanes that flew so high no one could see them, and these shook the ground for many kilometers around and left rows of large deep holes in the rice fields that filled with water when the rains came.

There was also another kind of airplane that whirred like a dragon-fly, and like a dragonfly, it could stop in midair and hover motionless. Mr. Tuan, who spoke the language of the Americans and helped them when they wanted to talk to local people, told Kieu that the soldiers gave these planes a special name: Huey. Once she had seen them firing their weapons at a patch of forest on the outskirts of her village, and then one of the fast planes came and set fire to all the trees. Then the dragonfly planes landed nearby, and all the men inside climbed out and hurried away, ducking their heads in the wind that gusted from the part on top that spun around in circles, flattening the grass.

Once Kieu was so close to one of the dragonfly planes that she could see the face of a soldier who sat in the open doorway holding a big gun. Somehow that made these hovering airplanes less frightening; you could look at him and hope he might look back and see that you were not his enemy. It was very different in this way from the silvery shapes in the sky that seemed to fly by themselves without human assistance.

Many of the soldiers lived at the base the Americans had built at the edge of the nearby town, on the road that led to the border between Vietnam and Laos. You would see them every day in the market, toss-ing coins to the women who squatted on the ground with their meager piles of fruit and vegetables for sale. Most of the men were friendly, although the ones from the government army who helped them could be rude and insulting. Some young women had come to live in the town when the Americans arrived, and they often waited at the gates of the camp and went for long walks with them and did not come back for a long time. Occasionally a soldier unwrapped a bar of sweet brown chocolate from its silvery paper and gave Kieu a square or two that she kept on her tongue until it melted.

After the soldiers went out to fight, she often saw them bringing back their dead on trucks or strapped to the back of a tank. Sometimes they were wrapped up in big green bags.

About a year later, when Kieu was twelve, a new kind of airplane came, very different from all the others. It was big and slow and ugly, with a fat engine slung under each wing and a high tail. Usually three of them flew so close together that their wings almost touched. They made a harsh, steady drone that grew louder as they approached and put her in mind of a big, lumbering water buffalo. Often a fast plane came ahead of them and dropped many of the little round bombs. These planes were called *ma*, the Phantom, Mr. Tuan said, and Kieu was always frightened when she saw one coming like an angry spirit.

The big airplanes came in the still of the early morning, from the direction of the East Sea, on days when there was no wind. They dipped low over the forest, barely high enough to clear the tallest trees, and a fine white mist streamed out behind them for some distance, then drifted to the ground like gentle summer rain.

The first time she saw these planes, they passed a few kilometers to the north of her village, where most of the fighting was, but later she saw them heading to the west, toward the Day Truong Son, the high mountains that ran along the border. Once they flew right over the fields next to her village, and people who were working there that morning got wet from the spray that came down on them. It made their eyes sting, and it smelled bad. After that the vegetables had a bad taste, and all the trees died.

The planes took off from the big air base in Danang, Mr. Tuan said. That was where the first American soldiers had come ashore from boats at the start of the war. He said that there had been a big celebration when they arrived. Schoolgirls had waited on the beach to greet them with garlands of flowers. Kieu had never been to the city herself; it was too far away. Mr. Tuan told her that even though the planes flew slowly, they could get here in less than an hour, which she found impossible to believe.

One day government soldiers came with guns and told everyone they had to walk into the town, which was four kilometers away. This was where they would live now, in small huts that they had to make from things that the Americans at the base had thrown away. They were surrounded by a fence made of curls of wire with sharp spikes. From the time the sun went down until it came up again the next morning, people were ordered not to leave their huts. A few days after they arrived, the soldiers burned Kieu's village to the ground.

Despite the many hardships, Kieu made new friends in the town. Her parents got to know a family from a nearby village, whose eldest son, Thao, was sixteen years old. Her parents often said how much they liked the boy, how respectful he was, how devout his family were in worshipping their ancestors. At least once a week, Thao and his parents visited their graves, which were in one of the rice fields by the river that were still undisturbed. Kieu caught Thao glancing at her out of the corner of his eye; she had the impression that he liked her very much.

But then suddenly one morning he was gone. Kieu heard rumors that the Americans had come looking for him, and he had run away to the mountains with some of the other young men.

By the time peace came to her village, Kieu was a grown woman of twenty. She helped her parents and her two younger brothers rebuild their house and replant their fields. One day her father stepped on one of the little round bombs that had lain concealed for years in the mud of an irrigation ditch. It blew his left leg off below the knee and blinded him. After that, it was impossible for him to go on working.

About two years later, Kieu learned to her surprise and delight that Thao had returned to his ancestral village to visit his family. She went there to see him. He told her stories of the experiences he had had as a soldier. Many young men in his regiment had died, and he wondered if their bodies would ever be found and given a proper burial, or whether they would become wandering ghosts. He had seen the strange spray planes many times, he said, and twice, on the secret border trails, they had soaked him. Later he had watched the leaves on the nearby trees turn yellow and fall to the ground, and it was no longer safe to use those parts of the trail because now the bomber planes could see them from the air. But by that time the army from the North had big guns that were powerful enough to shoot down aircraft, and he watched several of them crash in flames, deep in the mountains.

Thao told Kieu that he had been living in the capital since the war ended. He now wore the uniform of the People's Army, which made him look very handsome, and one day he asked his parents and Kieu's if they would look well on his wish to join their families together.

After their marriage, Kieu and Thao moved to a small town near the ancient city of Hue, where Thao's battalion was stationed. Their first child was born less than a year later. He was a strong, healthy boy, and they named him Hieu, choosing the name because it signified that he would be an honorable person and show respect to his parents.

A girl came next, and they called her Phuc, because she brought them happiness and good fortune. But this happiness did not last, because the child refused to nurse and was no more than skin and bone. She had only three fingers on one hand and dragged one very thin leg behind her when she learned to walk. Sometimes her whole body seemed to tremble, and she would fall to the ground.

Another brother followed, and his problems were of a different kind. He didn't understand things well, and he never learned to speak properly. There was no question of sending him to school. Phuc sometimes went, but often she stayed home because she suffered from bad headaches, and her classmates made fun of her whenever she fell down.

A doctor from the city came to examine the two malformed children, but he had no explanation for these strange maladies. Kieu was not the only mother in the commune to have this experience. Several other families had two children who were sick in different ways, and one even had three. Kieu and her husband wondered if perhaps the villagers had done something to offend their ancestors and thereby aroused vengeful spirits. One morning when her younger son was ten, he did not wake up. Kieu was ashamed to admit it, but it came almost as a relief.

Many years passed. The government gave the family a little money because Thao was considered a hero of the war and Phuc was sick, but Kieu found it hard to look after their daughter alone. When Phuc reached the age at which a girl begins to think of marriage, Kieu knew that such a thing could never happen for her daughter. Though she herself had not even reached her forty-fifth birthday, she felt old before her time.

One day Mr. Tuan announced that some honored guests would be visiting the commune. He was the chairman of the people's committee now, and it was only after the war that people learned that the whole time he had seemed to be working for the Americans, he had really been spying on them and passing along their secrets.

The guests were from America, Tuan said, which startled Kieu, because she had seen no Americans since the war ended. The villagers who had sick children, or who had been hurt by stepping on one of the little bombs, were invited to attend a special meeting with the visitors. Kieu went with Phuc. They sat next to their neighbor, Grandmother Huong, who came in her wheelchair, and Ong Khanh brought along his son, who had no arms.

Four Americans with graying hair, all a little older than Kieu, arrived in a small white van. She had forgotten how big Americans were. Mr. Tuan told the villagers that the men had fought here during the war, and two of them had even been in the big battle in Hue city, which had left so many people dead. The tallest of the guests, who seemed to be their leader, said that it had been very hard for them to come back, because their army had lost the war, even though it was so big and powerful. But they wanted to see the places where they had served their country, and to honor their fallen comrades.

Phuc grew restless as the man talked, and although Kieu told her to sit still and listen respectfully, she got up and began to walk around, dragging her misshapen leg behind her and making the strange little noises she made when her head hurt. The leader of the Americans stopped talking and watched Phuc with a sad expression on his face. He turned to Mr. Tuan and spoke softly to him. When he had finished, Mr. Tuan translated what he had said: "Is there anything we can do to help?"

PART I

WAR

Even the finest sword plunged into salt water

will eventually rust.

—SUN TZU, *The Art of War*

1

Going to B

HANOI REMEMBERS THE WAR, but mainly Hanoi forgets. There seems to be no end to the construction boom. In the city's upscale neighborhoods, Vietnam's nouveaux riches build themselves gaudy mansions with Roman balconies, Doric and Corinthian pillars, and classical fountains and statuary. Luxury high-rise apartment buildings spring up overnight. Many of these monuments to the new prosperity have English names—the Lancaster, the Gardenia, Goldmark City, the Skylake. Towering over a cloverleaf intersection by the rust-brown crawl of the Red River is the Sunshine Riverside, the name revolving in rainbow colors on a giant LED display at penthouse level. Other complexes, like the D'Le Roi Soleil, pay oblique homage to Vietnam's French colonial heritage.

By the end of the second decade of the twenty-first century, the politburo of the Vietnamese Communist Party had designated tourism a "spearhead industry," and Vietnam was welcoming close to 18 million foreign visitors a year. About half come from East Asia. Among the Westerners, two groups predominate: twentysomething backpackers and retirees, most of them old enough to remember the war. They come to see Vietnam, the country, and to look for echoes of Vietnam, the war.

Sometimes it can seem that on any given day most of them are strolling around Hanoi's Hoan Kiem Lake, the Lake of the Restored Sword, the beautiful though polluted heart of the city's tourist district, stopping in at the Temple of the Jade Mountain and taking photos of the elderly ladies doing their morning tai chi exercises. Dodging the motorbikes in the labyrinthine "36 Streets" of the Old Quarter, they book package tours to the beautiful karst archipelago of Ha Long Bay and homestays in the stilt-house villages of the ethnic minorities whom the French and the Americans called the Montagnards, the mountain people. They squat on blue plastic stools beneath the caged songbirds to slurp up *pho*, Vietnam's classic noodle soup, and shop for silks and silver and revolutionary kitsch—Ho Chi Minh T-shirts and refrigerator magnets, faux Zippo lighters and dog tags, reproductions of wartime propaganda posters.

Some of the tourists take a cyclo ride for a couple of miles to join the early morning throngs of uniformed soldiers and schoolchildren and young pioneers in red neckerchiefs lined up to visit the monolithic granite mausoleum of Ho Chi Minh on Ba Dinh Square, which is ringed by the elegant colonial-era buildings, painted mustard yellow and salmon pink, that house the offices of party and government. Inside, they shuffle around the icy crypt for a brief glimpse of the waxy corpse of the iconic leader of the Vietnamese revolution, preserved thanks to the skills of Soviet embalmers, who had perfected their art on Lenin. The spectacle would have appalled Uncle Ho, a frugal man who left written instructions that his body should be cremated, his ashes divided into three parts and scattered in the north, south, and center of the country, but with neither monument nor grave marker.

Some visitors take a short walk to the Museum of Military History, with its totemic display of crashed American airplanes and the antiaircraft guns that brought them down. Nearby, running parallel to a stretch of the main north-south railroad where the modest houses and shops crowd in close enough to the tracks for residents to reach out and shake hands with the passengers, is a long street called Ly Nam De, named for a sixth-century emperor who is regarded as one of the earliest champions of Vietnam's independence.

For the most part, Ly Nam De looks much like countless other streets in modern Hanoi. The tree-shaded sidewalks are an obstacle course of parked motorbikes. The Ficus Suites offer luxury rental apartments for expats. Farther down the block are Annie's Lingerie and the Laura Beauty Spa. But Ly Nam De is also a military enclave, resonant with history. There are two barracks of the People's Army of Viet Nam, the

PAVN, and the offices of the Army Publishing House. Gen. Nguyen Chi Thanh, who commanded military operations in the South from September 1964 until his death in July 1967, lived at number 34, which is now home to the Viet Nam War Veterans Association. Number 83 houses the Military Library, and while there is no public monument or memorial plaque, the building was the setting for one of the most consequential events in Vietnam's history, a secretive meeting in May 1959, convened on orders from the politburo, that prefigured the entire logic of what Vietnamese call the American War.

For many years after the fall of Saigon, the conventional wisdom was that the success of the Vietnamese revolution could be attributed primarily to two men, each with his own distinctive charisma and legend. Ho Chi Minh, "He Who Enlightens," founder of the Indochinese Communist Party, with his wispy chin-beard, benign smile, and avuncular manner, was its inspiration. Gen. Vo Nguyen Giap was the military genius who had engineered the decisive victory over the French at Dien Bien Phu in 1954 and who, for decades until his death in 2013, at the age of 102, charmed foreign visitors with his urbane manners and impeccable French. But the story is more complicated and in many ways much darker. By 1959, other powerful voices had risen to prominence in the Vietnamese Workers Party—known after reunification as the Vietnamese Communist Party—contesting and eventually eclipsing the paramount authority of Ho and Giap.

Two men were central to this less visible power structure. The senior of the two was Le Duan, a member of the politburo, a gaunt and dogmatic figure distinctly lacking in charisma. On the military side, there was his close political ally and fellow politburo member Nguyen Chi Thanh, the head of the PAVN's general political department and the only general promoted to share Giap's five-star rank.

Following the Leninist precepts of democratic centralism, the party took great pains to present a unified public face that masked its internal debates and the often brutal silencing of dissent. American policy makers, and the first generation of postwar historians, were generally aware of two camps that could be classified, at the risk of oversimplification, as moderates and hard-liners. The faction headed by Ho and Giap favored a protracted armed struggle combined with patient diplomacy and negotiations; the other, headed by Le Duan, advocated bold acts of revolutionary violence that would trigger mass uprisings as the key to national liberation. Sometimes these factions were respectively categorized as pro-Soviet and pro-Chinese, though those allegiances shifted at different times, and in general the party as a whole succeeded in holding on to the support of both Communist powers while never allowing them to dictate Vietnam's war strategy.

The two factions were defined by differences of temperament and ideology, each camp reading in its own way the shifting currents of global politics in the Cold War. But the clashes were also deeply rooted in geography and above all in the personal experiences and local loyalties of Le Duan and Thanh during the war against the French.

The first signs of friction had been apparent as early as 1951, and they grew bitter with the 1954 Geneva Accords, which split Vietnam in two after the collapse of French colonial rule in Indochina. There was fierce argument in Geneva about where the country should be divided. Negotiators for the North—the Democratic Republic of Viet Nam—initially demanded the thirteenth parallel, which would have given them control over two-thirds of the country. Ho Chi Minh was prepared to settle for the sixteenth. But both the Soviet Union, emerging at the time from the darkness of Stalinism, and China, still reeling from the Korean War, pressed him to make further concessions, anxious to prevent the hostilities in Vietnam from triggering a wider conflict. In the end, Ho was forced to accept the seventeenth parallel, which split the country into two more or less equal halves. The demilitarized zone between them, the DMZ, would roughly track this line of latitude, extending for five kilometers on either side of the meandering Ben Hai River at the northern edge of Quang Tri province.

The distance between two lines of latitude is only fifty-nine miles, but these particular miles had enormous significance for how the American war in Vietnam would be fought. Drawing the line at the seventeenth parallel ceded to the southern government of Ngo Dinh Diem the ancient imperial capital of Hue as well as the city of Danang, with its deepwater harbor. It also gave Diem control of the vital east-west highway, Route 9, which ran parallel to the southern edge of the DMZ. Completed by the French in 1930, it was the only direct connection between the Mekong River on the Thai-Lao border and the South China Sea, which Vietnamese call the East Sea.

Vietnam is a long, skinny S-shaped country, and Route 9 crossed it at its narrowest point and thus the easiest for the South to defend against incursions. In places, the mountainous Lao border is not much more than thirty miles from the ocean, and the coastal plain, the fertile rice-growing area that is home to most of the population, is sometimes only ten or fifteen miles wide, which made it uniquely vulnerable to attack from the western mountains of Quang Tri and its neighbor to the south, Thua Thien.

The location of the DMZ was a stinging personal affront both to Le Duan and to Nguyen Chi Thanh, because these were their home provinces, and they had commanded local revolutionary forces there during the war against the French. Both men had humble origins. Le Duan was from the outskirts of the town of Dong Ha, in Quang Tri, just below the DMZ and close to the point where Route 9 intersected with Route 1, the north-south coastal highway linking Hanoi and Saigon. A railway worker like his father, he was often disdained by other senior party officials for his rough manners; it was as if a hick from Appalachia had insinuated himself into the Ivy League circles of Washington, D.C. That only fed his grievances against the French-educated elite, leaders like Giap, who was the son of a Confucian scholar, went to law school, and played Beethoven and Mozart on the piano. Le Duan also considered imprisonment a sign of revolutionary virtue, a prime reason for ascent within the party, and he made a point of stressing that he had spent ten years in jail. (Giap had been jailed for thirteen months.)

Nguyen Chi Thanh was born in a village just outside Hue, forty-five miles south of Dong Ha in the province of Thua Thien. The stretch of Highway 1 separating the two men's birthplaces was infamous to the French as the Rue Sans Joie—the Street Without Joy—with dozens of small villages strung out like pearls on a necklace, separated from the ocean by a bleak ribbon of salt marshes and sand dunes, and all teeming with revolutionary fighters who were indistinguishable, to both the French and the Americans, from the rest of the population.

Thanh was celebrated for his modesty and austerity, but also for his insistence on Marxist-Leninist orthodoxy and the eradication of bourgeois individualism among his troops. They called him the "General of the Peasants," and in that respect, though he aligned ideologically with Le Duan, he had something in common with Giap, who called his soldiers Brother and Sister and was addressed by them in turn as Elder Brother.

Hardened by their years of leadership in one of the most brutal theaters of the French War, Le Duan and Thanh bitterly resented the terms of the Geneva agreement, which forced southern fighters to "regroup" to the North. Some 26,000 of these "regroupees" were from Quang Tri and Thua Thien, about a third of the total. Their forced departure from the old battlefields, coupled with Ho Chi Minh's insistence on the primacy of building socialism in the North, Giap's reluctance to commit his war-weary PAVN to a new round of fighting, and the demand from both the Soviet Union and China to refrain from armed aggression that might provoke American intervention, all combined to put an end to active resistance below the DMZ. This left the southern revolutionaries, in Le Duan's view, at the mercy of Diem's new government in Saigon.

After the Geneva Accords, the plan had been to hold nationwide elections in 1956, but Diem refused to go ahead with them, fearing with good reason that Ho Chi Minh would win a landslide victory. Instead, he set about crushing his political opponents, expanding his Army of the Republic of Vietnam (ARVN) to 150,000 men, thanks to stepped-up military aid from the Eisenhower administration. After a secret tour of inspection of the South in late 1958, Le Duan saw his worst fears materializing, and though he held his rhetorical fire, his sympathies became clear as fissures opened between the two great Communist powers, with Khrushchev preaching peaceful coexistence with the West and Mao Zedong's China now in the throes of the radical Great Leap Forward.

If any one thing tilted the intraparty dispute in Le Duan's favor, it may have been Fidel Castro's triumphant entry into Havana on January 8, 1959. By coincidence, the fifteenth plenum of the party's Central Committee was scheduled to begin just eight days later, and Le Duan's arguments in favor of a more militant line prevailed, with a formal decision in May to prepare for war in the South. By the end of 1961, Thanh had his fifth star, and the Third Party Congress had named

Le Duan general secretary—at the same time expanding the powers of the office—and head of the politburo. Hanoi created the National Liberation Front (NLF) and its armed wing, the People's Liberation Armed Forces (PLAF), to carry forward the revolution in the South, though Diem and the Americans had little interest in these acronyms; to them, the enemy, not all of whom were Communists, were simply lumped together as the Viet Cong, the sense of which can be roughly rendered as traitorous Vietnamese Commies.

Once the political decision had been made to prepare the ground for armed revolution south of the DMZ, Hanoi had to determine how this was to be done, and that brought in a third important figure, Col. Vo Bam, who was charged with executing the politburo's orders. Cut from the same cloth as Le Duan and Thanh, he was a native of impoverished Quang Ngai province, which, like Quang Tri and Thua Thien, was part of what the Americans called I ("Eye") Corps, the northernmost of the four tactical military zones in South Vietnam. His village was called Son My, though Americans would later come to know it as the site of the 1968 My Lai massacre.

On May 19, 1959—with the streets of Hanoi bedecked with flags and banners to celebrate Ho Chi Minh's sixty-ninth birthday and the anniversary of the foundation of the Viet Minh, the Communist-led independence movement that he had founded in 1941—Vo Bam was ordered to put together a trusted group of planners to work out the mechanics. He gathered eight officers together at 83 Ly Nam De, the nucleus of what would become the 559th Transportation Group of the PAVN, named for the month and year of its creation.

Group 559's assignment was to turn the pathways of the forested Truong Son range—the Annamese or Annamite Cordillera, in French and American parlance—into something much more substantial, a clandestine transportation route along the border between Vietnam and Laos that would funnel men, weapons, and supplies into the South. As a commander of local forces during the anticolonial war against the French, Vo Bam was more than familiar with these secretive trails. Many of them were centuries old, starting life as pathways for warriors and rebels or hacked out of the forest by the ethnic minority people of the highlands to plant their upland rice and hunt wild animals. During the French War, fighters had opened new cross-border paths to the north and south of what would later be the DMZ, as well as a connective tissue of trails linking their mountain bases with the coastal plain to the east. One group of fighters had made the trek as far south as Cambodia. All this added up to a rough but coherent first draft of what Americans would later call the Ho Chi Minh Trail.

In keeping with the PAVN's long-standing practice, Vo Bam was ordered to cloak the project in absolute secrecy: "It must not be allowed to become a beaten path—that is, not a single footprint, cigarette butt, or broken twig must be left on it after the men's passage." Forbidden to take notes, he had to memorize his instructions. No more than five hundred men would be involved at first, handpicked for their revolutionary zeal and fighting spirit. All of them would be regroupees, and General Thanh took the lead in selecting them. They would carry only arms captured from the French, nothing that would indicate support from the Soviet bloc or from China. They would wear black pajamas and sandals to blend in with the local peasants. If challenged, they were to pass themselves off as local woodcutters, and as natives of the central provinces they had the accent to back this up.

The first targets for infiltration were the two provinces immediately below the DMZ, Quang Tri and Thua Thien, which the PAVN would later designate the Tri-Thien Military District. Their mountains could provide a safe refuge for the beleaguered southern revolutionaries, and become a staging point for the support of the struggle farther south, all the way to the critical war zones around Saigon. The two provinces were a unique prize, but they also presented a singular challenge. The biggest question facing the builders of the Ho Chi Minh Trail was how infiltrators from the North were to get across the DMZ and Route 9. Since the departure of the French, much of the road had degenerated into an overgrown cart track, although it was heavily patrolled by South Vietnamese forces. Just across the border, the Royal Lao Army maintained a base on Route 9 in the small town of Xepon, a location that would play a huge role in the course of the war.

If Vo Bam's team could crack the problem, the rewards would be enormous. Just south of Route 9 on the Vietnamese side, beyond an ethnic minority village called Khe Sanh, home to the Bru-Van Kieu people and a small community of French coffee planters, were two heavily forested valleys that the Viet Minh had used earlier as transit routes and sanctuary. The first was the watershed of the sinuous Da Krong River, and beyond that was Vo Bam's most important strategic objective, the A So or A Shau Valley, a long, narrow refuge snugged up against the Vietnamese side of the Truong Son Mountains, hemmed in by towering peaks, some twenty-eight miles from north to south, and no more than a couple of hundred yards wide at its northern bottle-neck. Control of the A Shau would give the PAVN a secure base for launching attacks on Hue and Danang. American military strategists would come to see the valley as the most threatening place in central Vietnam, perhaps in the entire country, and those who had the misfortune to fight there would find it the most terrifying.

Vo Bam set out on the 350-mile journey from Hanoi to the DMZ right after the meeting at 83 Ly Nam De. At the Ben Hai River, he met with clandestine leaders of the southern resistance, and together they plotted a route through Quang Tri, crossing briefly into a small salient of Laos, until they reached a handover point for weapons at the head of the A Shau Valley. This was remote and rugged country, sparsely populated by small ethnic minority groups. Quang Tri was home to the Bru-Van Kieu ("the people who live in the woods"). Farther south, on both sides of the border, were the Pacoh ("those who live behind the mountains") and their close relatives, the Ta Oi and the Katu, originally an insulting term coined by French colonialists, with the connotation of "savages."

The first infiltrators set out on foot in small groups of twenty-five or thirty, guided by a Bru-Van Kieu hunter with a crossbow and poison-tipped arrows, carrying weapons wrapped in layers of oilcloth and nylon in woven rattan back-baskets like those still used today. Evading South Vietnamese patrols, they struck out along forest paths that paralleled the DMZ to the north, skirting Khe Sanh. Finding a promising place to cross Route 9, they unrolled a length of nylon sheeting and walked across it in obedience to the no-footprint rule. Later they found a better crossing point, crawling through a muddy, rat-infested culvert and reaching a small river where a sampan would be waiting. On August 20, 1959, they sent a brief message back to Hanoi: "All goods delivered safely."

The infiltrators sustained their first casualty in April 1960, a young lieutenant betrayed by a defector and killed by ARVN Special Forces, who cut off his ears as trophies. Diem flooded western Quang Tri with troops and civil guards, killing hundreds of infiltrators and their supporters. Hanoi's response was to circumvent the DMZ altogether by driving the main Trail through the relative safety of neighboring Laos.

The timing was good, because the ostensibly neutral country was in political chaos. Government troops rarely set foot in the mountainous east of the country, where the Communist Pathet Lao had its strongholds, with support from the PAVN. President Eisenhower warned his successor, John F. Kennedy, that Laos was the most urgent test of what he had labeled the domino theory. However, when the CIA launched a secret war in 1961 to support ethnic Hmong rebels, its focus was on the more heavily populated northern region of the country. The fighting there had little direct bearing on the remote southern panhandle, on which Vo Bam now set his sights.

As soon as the rainy season ended that October, Group 559 started work on a new section of the Trail that would "jump the gap" over Route 9 in Laos. It was rough, roadless country, negotiable only by bicycle or on foot. Nonetheless, in a matter of months, the Trail was extended for about thirty miles south of Route 9, as far as the village of La Hap. Vo Bam decided that this small settlement, nestled in a protective bowl of hills, would be its pivotal point. From there, a new spur could be cut due east for another twenty miles or so to the border village of A Tuc, at the head of the A Shau Valley. The first PAVN troops arrived there in 1961.

Ho and Giap continued to argue against provoking an American intervention. But Le Duan, over and above his deep-rooted belief in revolutionary violence and the almost sacramental value of bloodshed, saw it as a distinct possibility, regardless of what Hanoi did. He could back up his argument by pointing to the flood of U.S. military aid and advisers to Diem, whom Vice President Lyndon Johnson was now hailing as "the Winston Churchill of Asia." For Le Duan, this was part of a worldwide wave of imperialist aggression, from the Bay of Pigs invasion to the secret war in Laos, from the crisis in Berlin to the military coup in South Korea.

Each side interpreted these events in its own way. The party's moderate faction cautioned that the PAVN was not ready to confront the United States, especially when it was in such a belligerent mood. Le Duan argued that North Vietnamese regular units and their southern allies should seize the opportunity to launch full-scale attacks on ARVN units, destroying them before the Americans had time to send in significant numbers of ground troops. With the United States already preoccupied by crises on three continents, its energies might be spread too thin for it to act quickly in South Vietnam. If the politburo needed proof of the enemy's weakness, it needed to look no further than the ARVN's humiliation in the rice paddies of Ap Bac in the Mekong Delta on New Year's Day of 1963, when two thousand South Vietnamese troops, backed by American helicopters and advisers, were routed by a much smaller force of NLF fighters. Introducing the highly trained and better equipped troops of the PAVN could further tip the balance, Le Duan insisted.

The debate continued through 1963, until events unfolding on the ground forced the issue. Diem's control of the country was steadily unraveling. The "Buddhist crisis" of that spring and summer, provoked by the killing of unarmed protesters in Hue, precipitated a chain of events that included the self-immolation of the monk Thich Quang Duc in Saigon in June and culminated in the overthrow of Diem in November, tacitly endorsed by the Kennedy administration and quickly followed by his assassination.

Now firmly ascendant, Le Duan and his supporters waged a "rectification" campaign against more moderate party leaders, many of whom were jailed or sent into exile. Nguyen Chi Thanh published a broadside against "revisionism and right opportunism" in the party journal, *Hoc Tap*. "Some comrades tremble before the fierce struggle in South Vietnam," he wrote, in a thinly veiled attack on Giap and his supporters, "manifesting their lack of revolutionary consciousness."

When the next plenum of the Central Committee convened in December, it approved Resolution 9, endorsing Le Duan's vision of a "General Offensive, General Uprising" in the South. Massed attacks would shatter the ARVN's main forces, leaving them in no position to suppress a mass urban uprising. Khrushchev strenuously opposed these radical new strategies; China praised them. It was the high point of Le Duan's open support for the Chinese line. "It is the CCP headed by Comrade Mao Zedong which has carried out most satisfactorily the instructions of the great Lenin," he told the plenum.

Giap kept his formal titles—minister of defense and supreme commander of the PAVN—but his influence was diminished, and there were even efforts to remove him from the politburo. Even Ho Chi Minh was sidelined, still an inspirational figurehead but no longer an architect of policy.

Despite his radicalism, Le Duan never lost sight of the importance of the political and diplomatic struggle, and the party still hedged on just how much violence it would support in the South. It would be used "to a greater or lesser degree depending on the situation." But Resolution 9 was an authorization in principle to wage all-out war, and in July 1964, a combined force of NLF and PAVN regulars laid siege to a remote U.S. Special Forces base in Nam Dong, close to the A Shau Valley. Even without large-scale support from the North, the NLF had regained virtually all the territory that had been lost since the end of the French War. The ARVN appeared close to collapse, and after two military coups in two months, and with a third in the offing, the government in Saigon was in disarray. In Washington, there was what could only be described as a state of near-panic.

On August 7, President Lyndon Johnson was given carte blanche to wage war after two alleged torpedo attacks by North Vietnamese patrol boats on American warships in the Gulf of Tonkin—the second of which never in fact happened. Armed with a congressional resolution, he responded by ordering retaliatory bombing raids on the North, starting with the city of Vinh, where supplies were offloaded on their way to the Ho Chi Minh Trail.

The wheels of mutual escalation were now in motion. In September, Thanh was given command of R Base, the Central Office for South Vietnam (COSVN), and the following month, as soon as the dry season began in Laos, units massed to move south down the Ho Chi Minh Trail. By the following February, the PAVN's elite 325th Division, made up largely of regroupees, was in position across the border from the Central Highlands, part of the preparations for an eventual attack on Saigon. Le Duan called this Plan X—the first draft, as it were, of the "General Offensive, General Uprising" strategy that finally came to fruition during Tet, the celebration of the Lunar New Year, in 1968.

In a series of letters to Thanh in early 1965, he shrugged off the possibility of failure. If the planned offensive didn't work this time, well, North Vietnamese forces would withdraw, regroup, and try again. After all, he reminded his colleagues, it took Castro three attempts to conquer Havana. When fainter hearts in the party warned that the plan was too risky, Le Duan's retort was, "Let's act, then see"—a line variously attributed to Lenin and Napoleon.

By August 1964, Col. Vo Bam had installed his forward headquarters at La Hap, and by the end of that year, the basic shape of the Trail was in place. There were more than one hundred miles of new road as far south as the "tri-border area" where Laos, Cambodia, and Vietnam meet, although this stretch was still little more than a dirt track. Two-ton Soviet trucks could manage the first thirty miles or so south of La Hap, but most of the rest was suitable only for the specially reinforced bicycles that had been used earlier during the attack on Dien Bien Phu, each capable of carrying more than a quarter-ton of supplies. During the rainy season the whole Trail washed out. The spur to A Tuc was still not passable for vehicles, and there was no way to infiltrate supplies into the A Shau other than for porters to pick their way through ravines and along streambeds, staggering under the weight of hundred-pound backpacks.

This was no way to win a war. To achieve the goals of Resolution 9, the whole concept of the Trail required a strategic upgrade, and Group 559 brought in heavy road-grading equipment, opening a new phase in the southward advance, the start of what would eventually become a brutal war of airplanes against trucks. The road between La Hap and the border rapidly took shape. It was designated Road B45, although the Americans would call it Route 922. In time there would be many trails both large and small from Laos into the A Shau, but for U.S. intelligence this was Avenue Alpha. "The Americans were most afraid of road B45, as it was a knife thrust" at northern I Corps, a report by the PAVN's military science committee said later.

On March 2, 1965, the U.S. Air Force launched Operation Rolling Thunder, the intensive bombing of the provinces north of the DMZ. Six days later, the first Marines waded ashore to provide security for the air base at Danang. By the end of the year, there were 184,000 American troops in the country. In Laos, convoys of PAVN trucks loaded with men, weapons, and supplies rolled down the Ho Chi Minh Trail, with hundreds of miles of new dirt roads to carry them, and the Democratic Republic of Viet Nam instituted the draft for all males aged eighteen to forty, with the exception of only sons.

The party used a simple key to designate the different battlefronts in the widening war. A was the North; B was the South; C was Laos. Cambodia was either D or K (for Kampuchea). All pretense at secrecy was now abandoned, and by the last quarter of 1965, it seemed that everyone in the North had a son or knew a young neighbor who had pricked his finger to sign up in blood and was "going to B."

Of Mountains and Machines

THE AMERICAN WAR is memorialized in Vietnam in countless ways, in statues and monuments, graveyards and museums. The most famous to foreign visitors is the War Remnants Museum in Ho Chi Minh City, which for many years before diplomatic relations were restored in 1995 was known as the Exhibition House for U.S. and Puppet Crimes. But few tourists visit the Ho Chi Minh Trail Museum, which is far off the beaten track in the nondescript southwestern suburbs of Hanoi.

A large poster at the entrance says, HOC TAP VA LAM THEO TAM GUONG DAO DUC HO CHI MINH. "Study and Follow the Moral Example of Ho Chi Minh." A sign displays the name of the museum in English, a concession to foreigners, since Vietnamese themselves never called it the Ho Chi Minh Trail; for them it was the Duong Truong Son—the Long Mountain Road. Inside, a huge bronze bas-relief presents an idealized montage of workers, soldiers, and peasants, stonebreakers hacking out the Trail, others humping heavy boxes of munitions on their shoulders, someone playing a guitar, bare-breasted women volunteers bathing in a stream, a B-52 ominous overhead, Uncle Ho in his central place of honor, hand raised in benediction.

On a scorching afternoon in mid-April, two American veterans were visiting the museum. I'd known them both for several years, seeing their hair shade from gray to white—or silver, as the Vietnamese would say. They had served in Vietnam at the same time as each other, almost to the week, from the summer of 1967 to the summer of 1968, the most savage period of the war. The Tet Offensive, which marked the turning point of the conflict, had come midway through their tours of duty.

The younger of the two was a former Marine grunt from Bayonne, New Jersey, named Manus Campbell, who had endured the horrors of combat in "the bush," first on the back roads that led east from the A Shau Valley to the city of Hue, then along the edge of the DMZ, and finally on a section of the Ho Chi Minh Trail where it crossed from Laos into Quang Tri province. Chuck Searcy was three years older than Campbell; tall, thin, and stooped, he had just turned seventy-four, though Vietnamese friends who helped him celebrate his birthday said seventy-five, since in Vietnam you count the time spent in the womb. He still spoke with the soft cadences of his native Athens, Georgia, and he had an effortless, low-key, almost courtly charm that seemed entirely without artifice.

Searcy's war had been very different from Campbell's. He had worked in military intelligence in the clamor of Saigon, one of the 80 percent of Americans in Vietnam—REMFs, or rear-echelon motherfuckers—who never fired a shot in combat. But both men, for their separate reasons, had come back to Vietnam after the war and resolved to stay, and over the years they had become fast friends.

Searcy returned to live in Vietnam in November 1994, just eight months before full diplomatic relations were restored, and for the past twenty years he had dedicated himself mainly to cleaning up the legacy of the war in Quang Tri, the most heavily bombed province in Vietnam, where only a handful of villages had been left standing. He had quickly become the acknowledged leader of the small community of resident veterans; people sometimes jokingly referred to him as the shadow U.S. ambassador. Campbell, meanwhile, had struggled for decades with the traumatic aftermath of the conflict and had returned to Quang Tri's neighboring province, Thua Thien-Hue, as it was now called, to confront his inner demons and help in modest ways to aid those he called the invisible victims of war—disabled kids and orphans, including those presumed to have been sickened by the toxic defoliant known as Agent Orange. In 2010 Searcy and others had founded a Vietnam chapter of an organization called Veterans for Peace. Campbell was one of the first to join and acted, in the words of a mutual friend, as the "ballast" of the sometimes fractious group.

The two Americans paused to study a large map above the desk in the museum lobby, picking out some of the places where Campbell had seen combat. The map showed how completely Col. Vo Bam's vision had been realized by the time the war ended. Western renderings of the Ho Chi Minh Trail are invariably schematic, showing a thick north-south line and half a dozen arrows crossing the border into Vietnam from Laos and Cambodia, as if it were an interstate highway system. But the map made it clear that the Trail, which eventually stretched all the way to the outskirts of Saigon, was actually a vast spiderweb of all-weather roads and primary and secondary trails, some just wide enough for a man leading a pack animal or wheeling a reinforced bicycle. One legendary porter had broken all records by transporting 420 kilograms—925 pounds—on his "steel horse." Color-coded symbols on the map showed bypasses, river crossings, tunnel complexes, repaired bridges, bridges that could be hidden underwater in the daytime, storage areas, truck depots, wireless relay stations, and switchboards spaced at intervals along a continuous telephone line that linked together the binh tram, the administrative and logistical hubs of each section of the Trail.

The shape of the Trail is often compared to a ladder, the side rails formed by two north-south truck roads running parallel to each other through Laos, with extended rungs that led eastward to infiltration points along the border, connecting to more trails and roads inside South Vietnam. Vietnamese military historians estimate that by the time the system was completed, it covered 16,800 kilometers—more than 10,000 miles—of drivable roads, about 10 percent of them paved with cobblestone or asphalt by the last two years of the war, after the American bombing ended. Eight hundred kilometers were K roads— K for *kin,* meaning "covered" or "secret," designed for daytime use, concealed from prying eyes by overhanging trees woven into an elaborate trelliswork. By 1971, there was even an oil and diesel pipeline.

In the sixteen years between the creation of the Trail and the final assault on Saigon, Vo Bam's Group 559 grew from a nucleus of eight men to a force of 30,000, the equivalent of a full-fledged military corps, supported by thousands of youth volunteers. About 33,000 people are thought to have died on the Trail, from accidents, starvation, snake-bites, or animal attacks, but above all from malaria and aerial bombing.

There were only a handful of other visitors to the museum that after-noon, all of them Vietnamese, and Campbell and Searcy took their time browsing display cases that held relics from the Trail—rusted weapons, cracked leather boots, field telephones, diaries, a Russian-made 16mm projector, a Chinese record player, an accordion. Eventu-ally they came to a small exhibit that two older Vietnamese women were studying with special interest, trailed by a TV cameraman and a young reporter with a microphone. The women wore impeccably pressed dark-green military uniforms, each adorned with medals. They were raucous and funny, and they spent several minutes pump-ing the Americans' hands and clapping them on the back and singing the praises of Vietnamese-American friendship and insisting that they pose for group photos and talk to the TV interviewer, which Searcy did in his more than passable Vietnamese. It was always like this when you ran into Vietnamese veterans, Campbell said. Soldiers were soldiers, joined by common experience.

Both women had risen to the rank of first lieutenant in the PAVN, but they'd first become friends as teenagers, working around the clock to build a celebrated section of the Trail that was commemorated in the exhibit. Designated Duong 20 Quyet Thang—translated on the wall plaque as "Road 20 Determined to Win"—it was one of the most critical elements in Vo Bam's grand plan.

The national highway connecting Hanoi and Saigon runs through flat, open country, rarely straying more than a few miles from the coast. Once the aerial bombing campaign began, it made an easy target. The alternative for the Communists was to drive new roads to the Lao border across Quang Binh province, immediately north of the DMZ, through some of the most challenging landscapes in Vietnam.

From a logistical point of view, the true point of origin of the Trail was the port of Vinh, 170 miles north of the DMZ, where military sup-plies arriving by rail or ship were offloaded onto trucks. From here, the PAVN built two new roads leading to the southwest, crossing the bor-der through a pair of narrow gaps in the Truong Son Mountains. The Ban Karai Pass, which entered Laos through a tightly constricted area that American bomber pilots called the Chokes, had two advantages over the initial route. It was the shorter of the two, and large amounts of weaponry and supplies could be stored along the way in the limestone karst caves of Phong Nha, safe from the reach of bombs. Today Phong Nha is one of Vietnam's eight UNESCO World Heritage Sites, a floodlit labyrinth of caverns and underground rivers that has become a magnet for adventurous backpackers.

The road from Phong Nha to Ban Karai was given the number 20 because that was the average age of the soldier-engineers and the volunteers, the Shock Youth Brigades Against U.S. Aggression for National Salvation, who built it. More than 70 percent of these volunteers were women, like the two at the museum. The French had once planned a road here but abandoned it, defeated by the mountainous terrain. The Japanese had the same idea during their World War II occupation of Vietnam, but they too had given up. The young volunteers on Road 20 began work in January 1966. They had no maps; they traced parts of their route by following the notches that Japanese surveyors had cut into the trees. They counted ten hairpin bends for each kilometer of progress. When the food ran out, they dug for wild turnips. Many died of malaria, which they called the "Truong Son tax," or drowned in floods or were buried in rockfalls. A doctor was eaten by an Indochinese tiger.

The skies over Road 20 came alive with American aircraft: F-4 Phantoms out of Danang and Saigon's Tan Son Nhut air base, F-105 Thunderchiefs operating from bases in Thailand, A-1 Skyraiders launched from carriers in the South China Sea. At night the Trail workers watched in awe as the flares drifted down on their tiny parachutes to illuminate targets, lighting up the sky as if there were a city out there in the mountains. They slept in A-shaped shelters cut into the hillsides and topped with layers of earth, which shielded them from the bombs but did little to keep out venomous snakes, scorpions, and giant centipedes.

Road 20 ran for 120 kilometers, all the way to the Lao section of Route 9. It was completed in four months, an astonishing accomplishment given the circumstances. One of the women pointed to the sign that described the exhibit, with the famous motto of those who worked to build Road 20: THE ENEMY DESTROYS 1 KM, WE CONSTRUCT 10 KM.

On the second floor of the museum, a large diorama illustrated the most critical section of the Trail. Small red and yellow flags showed the location of North Vietnamese forces. Red arrows probed for gaps in the steep green wall of the mountains. A pennant planted in the hills near Route 9 marked the critical PAVN facilities close to Xepon, a small town that was obliterated in 1971 by a South Vietnamese invasion, Operation Lam Son 719, backed by American airpower. The first name on the Vietnamese side was Khe Sanh. What was missing was any kind of marking to indicate the border. The demarcation line had shifted repeatedly, until the French drew one between Xepon and Khe Sanh in 1916. To the ethnic minority people of the mountains, it had little meaning, and for decades they had moved back and forth across this fictive division to escape whoever happened to be oppressing them at the time, whether with taxes, conscription, or corvée labor.

Vo Bam's system became an ever more intricate cat's cradle of braided trails that wound their way for another thirty miles or so to the southeast as far as his headquarters at La Hap, where Road B45 made its sharp dogleg turn toward the A Shau Valley. This was the heart of what the North Vietnamese called the "Pocket of Fire"; years of aerial bombing reduced La Hap to a moonscape, but it was never conquered, and the command facilities remained intact.

Another cluster of arrows indicated smaller concealed pathways that twisted across the jungled border, following ravines and streambeds, into the A Shau and Da Krong valleys. Straddling the border was the formidable PAVN stronghold designated Base Area 611.

By late 1965, the "expeditionary" phase of combat was over; this was now all-out war. The movement of men and equipment into this section of the Trail in the final months of that year, combined with their buildup along the northern edge of the DMZ and the first incursions from Laos farther south in the Central Highlands, unnerved American military strategists. Until now the enemy in the South had almost exclusively been the Viet Cong—the VC, or "Charlie," although usually the dehumanizing *gooks* was name enough. But the troops converging on the DMZ and the A Shau were regular units of the PAVN, including several of the North's six original "Steel and Iron" divisions. These were disciplined and well-drilled troops, ferocious in combat, and in deference to their superior fighting qualities, the Marines upgraded their nickname to "Mister Charles." They also appeared willing to absorb limitless casualties, and for the first time in modern warfare, the index of success on the American side was not the amount of territory gained, but the number of enemy dead: the body count.

The wall map had made it clear why many historians prefer to speak of the Second Indochina War rather than the Vietnam War. (To Vietnamese, it is the American War.) The borderlands of Vietnam, Laos, and Cambodia, pierced at intervals by spurs of the Trail, were the spinal column of the conflict. Together, General Giap said, the area formed "a strategic unity, a single military theater of operations," and in practice that was how the Americans treated it too, although they did not always say so, given the inconvenient fact that Laos was officially a neutral country.

The rhythms of warfare are always determined by the geography of the battlefield, be it the tree lines at Gettysburg, the open fields of Flanders, or the bleak, rocky wastes of Afghanistan. Here it was the mountains and their cloak of rain forest. "To seize and control the mountains is to solve the whole problem of Vietnam," Giap said. The map had shown the logic of this in two dimensions; the diorama showed it in three.

The border between Laos and Vietnam was defined by some of the most remote and forbidding terrain on the planet. The Trail snaked invisibly through valleys and gorges, crossing rushing streams that carved out deep limestone caves, hemmed in by pillars of karst, vertical rock faces, and towering, misty peaks that rose to six thousand feet or more. The higher elevations were carpeted with layers of double- and triple-canopy rain forest, with trees that soared as high as two hundred feet, and the lower slopes were an impenetrable thicket of bamboo, rattan, and ferns, hung with entangling "wait-a-minute" vines that grabbed at you like steel cables.

Filled with hidden dangers and physical discomforts, the mountains could be as nightmarish for the Vietnamese fighters as they were for their American counterparts. But the terrain was also the PAVN's greatest ally, and they used it to dictate the terms of engagement. They called the mountains their "killing zone."

American war planners sought to offset the disadvantages of geography with the assets of technology and machinery that only they possessed. "War is death and destruction," said Gen. Frederick Weyand, who commanded the final U.S. military operations in Vietnam. "We believe in using 'things'—artillery, bombs, massive firepower—in order to conserve our soldiers' lives. The enemy, on the other hand, made up for his lack of 'things' by expending men instead of machines."

There were access roads to be bulldozed, hundreds of helicopter landing zones and firebases for field artillery to be blasted out of the hills by giant Rome plows and ten-thousand-pound "daisy cutter" bombs shoved out of the loading door of cargo planes, the vegetation cleared by napalm, incendiaries, and chemical herbicides. There were thousands of helicopters to ferry the troops into battle and myriad airplanes loaded with every conceivable kind of bomb, rocket, and missile. There were battleships and aircraft carriers and amphibious landing crafts, eight-engined B-52 Stratofortresses, U2 spy planes that flew seventy thousand feet above the earth, forward air controllers and aircraft equipped with infrared cameras, electronic sensor fields, and in Thailand a complex of the most powerful computers in the world to process the flood of data that these gizmos sent back from the Ho Chi Minh Trail.

Yet all this technological dominance was too often thwarted by something more elemental: the weather, which in turn was a function of the topography. Two separate monsoon systems collide in central Vietnam. From October to April, when the northeast monsoon brought burning heat to the Trail in Laos, troops might be shivering in torrential rain on the Vietnamese side of the mountains. The city of Hue got 128 inches of rain a year, almost twice as much as humid, tropical Saigon. From May through September, the months of the southwest monsoon, the pattern was reversed. Quang Tri and Thua Thien, the two northernmost provinces in I Corps, had a particularly freakish microclimate, boxed in as they were by a spur of the Truong Son Mountains. Rising to five thousand feet, this range runs from the Lao border all the way to the South China Sea, separating Hue from Danang and broken only by the twisting Hai Van Pass, which the French called the Col des Nuages, the Pass of the Clouds. This quirk of geology created a unique strategic problem for American commanders, raising the specter that these two provinces could be severed from the rest of South Vietnam, with Hue as the prospective capital of liberated territory.

Hard against the Lao border, the A Shau Valley was subject to both monsoons, and it was especially notorious for its foul weather. As often as not, the surrounding peaks were shrouded in fog, regardless of the season, grounding the helicopters and bombers and leaving the spy planes blind. The early months of the year were made more miserable still by what the French called the *crachin,* a long, dreary spell of drizzle and low-hanging clouds. During the weeks of street fighting in Hue during the Tet Offensive, wrote the young CBS News correspondent John Laurence, the city was "enveloped in a wet gloom," even as the sun beat down on nearby Danang.

On their way out of the museum, Searcy and Campbell stopped in the lobby for a last look at the wall map. The greater part of their adult lives had been defined by the war in Quang Tri and Thua Thien and its bitter aftermath. Yet it was startling to see how small an area these two provinces embraced. Bounded to the west by the Ho Chi Minh Trail, they formed a rough parallelogram, less than a hundred miles long and nowhere much more than forty miles wide.

Understanding how past and present were intertwined here involved what an epidemiologist might call backward contact tracing, seeing how the extreme brutality of the war in northern I Corps grew out of its singular geography, the dictates of ideology and strategy, and the personal choices of political and military leaders on both sides. The names of its battlefields became synonyms for hell: Hue, the DMZ, Khe Sanh, Con Thien, Hamburger Hill. The heaviest bombing of the war fell on Quang Tri and the Lao borderlands, and millions of munitions failed to detonate, littering the land with unexploded ordnance. To deny food and shelter to the enemy, the forests and crop fields were blanketed by chemical defoliants laced with a deadly contaminant called Tetrachlorodibenzo-p-dioxin. The ferocious antiaircraft defenses that the PAVN built on the Trail and in the A Shau Valley meant that more planes were shot down here than anywhere else, and hundreds of American pilots and aircrew went missing in action. The Marines took by far their heaviest casualties in Quang Tri, and the survivors suffered from post-traumatic stress disorder at twice the rate of army veterans.

All the worst legacies of the war were concentrated here, in an area smaller than the state of Connecticut, and more than half a century later its shadow lay darker and heavier over this tiny patch of earth than anywhere else in Southeast Asia.

3

The Summer of Love

FOR THE THREE YEARS after the March 1965 landings at Danang, through to the Tet Offensive and the siege of Khe Sanh, I Corps was the territory of the Marines. They experienced every variety of terror there: feeling the earthquake of a B-52 strike; listening to the thump of mortars and the roar of incoming shells, like a First World War Tommy cowering in the trenches; stumbling into a perfectly laid ambush in the permanent claustrophobic twilight of the forest; seeing men with whom they had shared a bunker loaded into body bags and whisked away in a Huey; digging up North Vietnamese rotting in mass graves to check the body count.

And when it was all over and they returned to The World, what scars did it leave? And in the end, what had been the point of it all? Many of the Marines of I Corps asked those questions with special bitterness, coming to understand that the carnage inflicted on them was the consequence not only of the strategies of a ferocious and well-trained enemy but of the idées fixes of William Westmoreland, the commander of U.S. forces from 1964 to 1968, and Defense Secretary Robert McNamara. They struggled, too, with the knowledge of the carnage they themselves had inflicted, and wondered what on earth had happened to the teenage innocents they had been when they first set foot on Vietnamese soil.

If the Marines of I Corps saw the worst of the war, you could also make the case that they produced much of its finest literature. In

A Rumor of War, Philip Caputo, a Marine lieutenant who went on to become a distinguished journalist, drew on the great British memoirs of trench warfare in World War I by Robert Graves and Siegfried Sassoon to explore the futility of the conflict in Vietnam. Yet the book wasn't a conventional antiwar diatribe. His purpose, he wrote, was "to make people uncomfortable—in effect to blow them out of their smug polemical bunkers into the confusing, disturbing emotional and moral no-man's-land where we warriors dwelled."

W. D. Ehrhart entered the Marines as a private and left as a sergeant, fought on the DMZ at Con Thien, was wounded in the battle of Hue, and went on to become the unrivaled poet of the war. *Vietnam-Perkasie* was his unsparing confessional, the story of how an ordinary eighteen-year-old from a small town in Pennsylvania could be transformed by fear, adrenaline, and camaraderie into someone who could gun down an unarmed old woman because she was wearing black pajamas and running away, or yuk it up with the rest of his platoon after destroying an abandoned Buddhist temple just for the hell of it, or take his place in a line of Marines waiting for their turn with a starving woman who traded her body for a can of C-rations in the ruins of Hue. Caputo had written about the "precarious moral edge" of combat; Ehrhart showed what it was like to cross it.

Karl Marlantes, a Marine lieutenant like Caputo, took thirty-five years to produce *Matterhorn,* his astonishing novel of the harrowing grind of combat in the mountains of Quang Tri, taking a hill of no discernible strategic value only to abandon it again. Just as remarkable was his later volume of essays, *What It Is Like to Go to War.* Caputo asked his readers to visit the land where warriors dwell; Marlantes explored how that land is created, interspersing episodes from his time in Vietnam with his readings of the Grail legend, Viking mythology, Sophocles, the *Iliad,* the Bible, and the Mahabharata, to illuminate the enduring constants of war: killing, guilt, numbness, lying, loyalty, heroism, the innate human instinct for revenge.

Like Caputo's memoir, this was not comfortable reading for anyone living in a smug polemical bunker. War is this way because it has to be this way and it will always be this way. Warriors are not born but made, and it starts the day they shave off your hair. The function of a Marine infantryman is to kill people, as many of them as possible, and the purpose of basic training is to turn individuals into the interchange-able working parts in a machine of unfathomable dimensions and to weed out the "unsats." If you can't stand up to the tyranny of the drill sergeants at Parris Island, South Carolina, the thinking goes, you will crack under the much greater pressure of combat, and if that happens, you become a liability to others. Fear and incompetence are conta-gious. Few teenagers have a natural-born instinct to kill another per-son, so that person must be reduced to a lower order of being—a *gook* or a *dink*. Once this logic takes hold, those incinerated by a napalm strike can be laughed off as "crispy critters." This pseudospeciation, as Marlantes terms it, is not in itself evidence that Vietnam was a "bad war." *Gook* and *dink* were simply the Vietnamese equivalent of *huns* and *krauts, japs* and *nips* and *towelheads,* each a locally particular racist variant of the alien Other.

Every Marine understood the other lesson that Marlantes drew from his own experiences. However a man might feel about the morality of war in general, or of a particular war like Vietnam, it "blows away the illusion of safety from death. Some random projectile can kill you no matter how good a soldier you are. Escaping death and injury in modern warfare is much more a matter of luck—or grace—than skill." Blind chance, as Manus Campbell discovered many times, is the one great constant of war.

In those who were scarred by the brutalities of I Corps, the signs of how they process these events in memory never entirely fade. The evidence is there in the tone of voice, the choice of words, the facial expressions, and the body language, when they laugh nervously and when they break off midsentence and fall silent, even after so many years.

By the time of his visit to the Ho Chi Minh Trail Museum, Campbell had aged into a soft-spoken man with a neatly trimmed white goatee and a beret that he had the habit of wearing backward, giving him a puckish look. He had a gentle demeanor and an easy smile, with a cha-risma that crept up on you slowly. He'd become an accomplished ama-teur photographer, carrying his camera wherever he went. Yet there was also the sense in Campbell of an unfinished quest for something elusive, of someone who rarely rested comfortably in one place.

He was drafted in the fall of 1966, straight out of high school, a

Jersey boy from Bayonne, in the exurbs of New York City, brought up in a solid middle-class Catholic household just a couple of miles from the Statue of Liberty. Manus Campbell, Sr., the son of an Irish immigrant copper miner in Butte, Montana, had attended seminary with hopes of becoming a Columban missionary priest, but those ambitions were derailed by ill-health. Instead, he worked as a salesman for a local business—pipes, valves, and fittings—a job that kept his six kids decently provided for, with summers spent on the Jersey Shore.

Like so many teenage boys sent to war, what mattered most to Manus Jr. was how he would stand in his father's eyes. A quiet, reserved child, he bulked up and became a long-distance swim champion, a token of manliness. He enlisted in the Marines in preference to the army, because, he said, "my nature is to challenge myself; I've always had a hard time choosing the easy way." And that was the mystique of the Marine Corps: joining them was a passport to the gallery of heroes. The recruiter told Campbell that he could enlist for either two years or three, but the shorter time would increase his chances of being sent to Vietnam. Campbell opted for the worst of both worlds: three years *and* Vietnam. His father told him how proud this made him, and like many traditional fathers, he was not a man who bestowed praise easily.

Campbell arrived at boot camp on Parris Island on October 6, the quintessential grunt, one of hundreds of thousands who were processed there. On a good day, they might call you "Campbell, Private M.," but more often you and the others were worms, pigs, lowlifes, girls, ladies, pussies, scumbags, faggots, maggots.

Looking back on basic training, he quoted a paragraph from Remarque's *All Quiet on the Western Front*.

> We were put through every conceivable refinement of parade ground soldiering till we often howled with rage. . . . We became hard, pitiless, vicious, tough—and that was good; for these attributes were just what we lacked. Had we gone into the trenches without this period of training most of us would certainly have gone mad.

He learned how to handle an M-14, soon to be replaced by the lighter M-16, a weapon the grunts hated for its habit of jamming on them at the wrong moment. He was taught the honor code of the Marines, the submission of the individual to the unit, always having the next guy's back and knowing he had yours, and he was instructed in the fine points of killing another human being.

After the biting sand fleas and screaming drill sergeants of Parris Island, he was sent for a spell to Camp Lejeune in North Carolina, and then to Camp Pendleton in California. During the first eight months of his enlistment, the country had gone through convulsive changes. Hair was growing longer by the minute, and the smell of pot was in the air. There were new bands with bizarre names like the Grateful Dead. Campbell devoured these new sounds, the Doors and the Beatles and Cream, and he loved Motown—Marvin Gaye, the Temptations. Before leaving for Vietnam, he took in a Four Tops concert in Los Angeles.

On June 2, the Beatles released *Sgt. Pepper's Lonely Hearts Club Band*, with its exotic Indian instruments and surreal lyrics. Two weeks later a former paratrooper in the 101st Airborne Division named Jimi Hendrix set fire to his hand-painted Fender Stratocaster at the Monterey Pop Festival. And on June 11, sandwiched between those two seminal moments in that Summer of Love, Manus Campbell stepped out onto the tarmac in Danang, another FNG, a Fucking New Guy.

He was nineteen years, five months, and three weeks old. This left him still more than eighteen months short of being able to vote, but it was the average age for a Vietnam draftee; in World War II it had been twenty-six. The day after he arrived in Danang, he was shuttled fifty miles north to the Marine base at Phu Bai, just outside the city of Hue. On the airstrip he bumped into an old classmate, the captain of his high school football team. In his later years, Campbell came to believe that there was no such thing as coincidences in life, only unseen connections that revealed themselves in unexpected ways. He believed in dreams and omens, in hidden designs. "See you this time next year," the kid said. "If we get out of here." Like so many others, Campbell looked around and asked himself, *Where the hell am I?* and *What am I doing here?*

He was assigned to Alpha Company of the First Battalion of the Fourth Marines—Alpha 1/4, in military parlance, or the Alpha Raiders, which is what it said on their shoulder patches. Like every enlistee, he was given a booklet with the "nine simple rules," among them:

"Remember we are special guests here; we make no demands and seek no special treatment. Reflect honor upon yourself and the United States of America."

The Fourth Marines had a tainted reputation as a consequence of their surrender en masse to the Japanese on Corregidor Island in 1942. Legend said that as punishment for its dishonor, the regiment was cursed to wander the Pacific forever, like the *Flying Dutchman*. Campbell may not have wandered the Pacific, but his tour of duty encompassed the full trifecta of horrors of the war in the northernmost provinces of I Corps, each step reflecting the larger geographical logic of the war. It began on the treacherous roads and trails connecting the imperial city of Hue and the A Shau Valley to the west; continued at the Marine forward base of Con Thien, the most terrifying of the outposts along the southern edge of the DMZ; and ended up on the Ho Chi Minh Trail, in the forested mountains between Khe Sanh and the A Shau, three miles from the Lao border.

A photograph shows Campbell sitting bare-chested in a bunker at Con Thien with three other grunts, eating C-rations. To his left is a Latino from New York, whose name has faded in memory. To his right is a dark-skinned American Indian, one of three in the unit. They always hung together; their dominant member, predictably, was nicknamed "Chief." Farthest to the left is a tall, good-looking white man, grinning at the camera as if he is at a Fourth of July barbecue, or heading to the beach at Malibu with a surfboard. This guy loved to gamble and never lost, Campbell remembered. His name was Burke, so everyone called him Amos, for the dapper police investigator in the TV show *Burke's Law*.

Campbell himself is center-right in the frame. He is hunched slightly forward, eyes narrowed—he got those eyes from his mother, although in the photo they give the impression of a kid trying to look tough. He has thick black hair; somewhere along the way he has abandoned the Marine buzz cut. His bunk is behind him, the top one. He'd hung his Marine Corps ring on a nail, together with a pinkie ring he bought on R&R in Bangkok. Twenty years later he remembered he'd left them hanging there.

If you were in the army, you served for twelve months; for a Marine it was thirteen. This led to predictable jokes about bad luck, but in the case of those who served in I Corps, they had real justification. To add to the Marines' sense of inequity, army troops were rotated in and out of combat operations, withdrawn for spells to rearguard areas where they could catch their breath. Marines could remain in the hot zone for months on end.

By 1968, more than half of all the American troops in Vietnam were concentrated in I Corps. Of the 58,220 Americans who lost their lives in Vietnam, Marines made up more than a quarter—a casualty rate twice as high as that of the army. Well over 80 percent of them died in the four provinces closest to the DMZ, and the heaviest losses of all were in Quang Tri and Thua Thien. They hit their peak during the months Campbell spent there. It was his particular misfortune to serve in the most terrible combat zone in Vietnam, and at the worst possible time.

And then there were those who supported the combat troops in the field, the administrators and the bureaucrats, the warehousemen and construction crews, the engineers and economists, the demographers and mapmakers, the doctors and nurses and diplomats, those who served offshore in the Seventh Fleet, and the intelligence analysts, like Chuck Searcy, whose job was not to fight the war but to interpret it.

Born in Alabama in October 1944, Searcy had grown up in a conservative middle-class family in the small, rigidly segregated town of Thomson, Georgia, the Camelia Capital of the South, where his father was manager of the local Coca-Cola bottling plant. Chuck was the eldest of three children. A straight-arrow Georgia boy, a regular at the Presbyterian church, he enrolled in the University of Georgia in Athens to study music, played the euphonium, and joined the Dixie Redcoats Marching Band. Blessed with a good singing voice, he sang in the men's chorus. He'd always been interested in politics, and after a while he dropped out of school to volunteer on Barry Goldwater's 1964 election campaign, feeling that the Arizona Republican had good, commonsense ideas about how to fix the country's problems.

UGA had been desegregated three years earlier, leading to riots, and with some Southern Democrats betraying their white supremacist heritage by their alliance with the new civil rights movement, Georgia went heavily for Goldwater, one of only five states he carried, all of them in the Deep South. Despite this disappointment, Searcy fell into line behind the policies of Lyndon Johnson. He didn't question the idea that the United States had an obligation to stop the advance of international Communism, and Vietnam seemed like the right place to do it. When the government talked about something it called "the domino effect," it surely knew what it was doing.

Even so, there were subtle shifts in the way Searcy saw the world. He took a summer job at a camp in Maine that was populated by wealthy Jewish kids from New York, and he had long conversations with one of the older camp counselors, a man in his forties who had made a lot of money, lost it again, worked as a cab driver, lectured at the United Nations, and lived in bohemian Greenwich Village. Later he would become involved with a group in California called Course in Miracles, or the Foundation for Inner Peace. He forced Chuck, in a friendly but insistent way, to examine and defend the prejudices that had shaped his small-town upbringing.

When Chuck went back to UGA, he was unsettled. His grades were poor—girls and alcohol seemed like more pressing priorities. He got engaged, broke it off. By 1966 a few kids on the leafy old campus were discreetly smoking grass and growing their hair below the collar, and some even began to murmur misgivings about the war, but the school was still dominated by frats and football, and the South remained suffocatingly conservative. Georgia made national headlines that summer when a disc jockey on WAYX radio in Waycross, down close to the Florida line, urged teenagers to throw their Beatles LPs onto a giant bonfire—Georgia's response to John Lennon's comment that the four young men from Liverpool were more popular than Jesus Christ.

By that time, Chuck was feeling the hot breath of the draft board on his neck, and whatever fears he might have had about being thrown into the vortex of Vietnam, the forces conspiring to send him there were impossible to resist. His father, Hayes, was a proud veteran who had fought in the Battle of the Bulge and spent the last months of World War II as a POW. For a year his wife had had no idea if he was dead or alive. When Patton's forces liberated the camp, Hayes was a 120-pound skeleton. By tradition, all the Searcy boys went into the military. Chuck had joined both the army and air force ROTC in college, and his brother had already enlisted in the navy, signing up on the day he graduated from high school.

In October 1966, the same month Manus Campbell went to Parris Island, Chuck bowed to the inevitable. He was to have a good war, to the extent anyone did, in the sense that he never fired a shot in anger. The eleven weeks of basic training at Fort Benning, Georgia, were probably the worst of it, he said one morning, sitting in the coffee shop of the historic Saigon Morin Hotel in Hue, on the banks of the Perfume River, where the sign on the elevator still said *ascenseur.* The free movie on offer that evening was the Michael Caine remake of *The Quiet American.* It was raining outside, a typical February Hue drizzle, the kind of day when the Truong Son Mountains would be wreathed in the low cloud that forced pilots to abort their missions.

Countless young men went through the same routines at Fort Benning. In the words of a 1969 Pentagon film called *The Men from the Boys,* "They come from city and farm, from slum and mansion, and almost to a man they would rather be somewhere else." Recruits were dragged out of bed at five a.m. for rifle training, grenade training, bayonet training, hand-to-hand combat, obstacles to be wriggled under, and obstacles to be clambered over, hand-over-hand overhead ladders, thirty-six rungs in sixty seconds. There were classes on how to conduct yourself if you were captured by an enemy bent on destroying the American way of life. Drill sergeants like something out of Stanley Kubrick's *Full Metal Jacket* worked hard to turn Searcy against his quiet nature, teaching him to hate the faceless *gooks. The enemy is not a human being; he has no mother or father, no sister or brother.* "They screamed at us, and we had to scream back: *I'm a killer! I'm a killer! I'm a killer!,*" he said. All this was calculated and in its way rational, he came to believe. "It made us turn our anger and hatred against people we didn't even know, for they were the reason we were being put through this awful harassment."

After boot camp, he went to the U.S. Army Intelligence School at Fort Holabird in Baltimore. There were smart young men there from elite universities, much better read than Searcy, and some of them shared their doubts about what was happening in Vietnam in those early months of 1967, as the troop levels escalated, the battles along the DMZ grew hotter, and the Spring Mobilization to End the War, "the Mobe," brought hundreds of thousands into the streets of New York.

"A feeling is widely and strongly held that 'the Establishment' is out of its mind," wrote Assistant Secretary of Defense John T. McNaughton a couple of weeks after the huge protest. "The feeling is that we are trying to impose some U.S. image on distant peoples we cannot understand (any more than we can the younger generation here at home) and that we are carrying the thing to absurd lengths."

Assigned to the 519th Military Intelligence Battalion, Searcy got his first taste of the bureaucratic illogic of the war. When his superiors asked what language he'd like to learn, he said Vietnamese. They rejected the request. When he eventually got to Saigon, he found that none of the Americans in his unit spoke the language. Since their job was to gather intelligence about what was happening in the country, the reasoning behind this remained obscure to him.

In San Francisco, he boarded a charter flight on World Airways, stopping to refuel in Juneau, Alaska, and then switching in Manila to Philippine Airlines. The new recruits were pampered by beautiful cabin attendants who were both maternal and flirtatious and brought them coffee and pastries. It all seemed unreal. Everyone in the plane fell silent when the pilot announced that they had entered Vietnamese airspace, and the plane banked alarmingly over the mountains as he took evasive measures to avoid ground fire on the approach to Pleiku, the most important air base in the Central Highlands. The hostesses gave them long, wistful looks as they disembarked, knowing that many of them would come home in nylon bags.

Searcy could see lots of military traffic on the roads, all the now-familiar images of Vietnam that you saw on TV—people on bicycles, plodding water buffalo, farmers in conical hats. The base itself was a bleak expanse of red laterite backed by verdant mountains. Beyond them was Cambodia and the newest extension of the Ho Chi Minh Trail. The guards in the gun emplacements at the edge of the runway were ragged, dirty, and unshaven, bare-chested or wearing their sleeveless flak vests unzipped. Some leaned on their elbows with the thousand-yard stare. Others glanced at the newcomers in their neatly pressed uniforms and shook their heads. *You poor bastards, you have no idea.* Even before Searcy's platoon had formed up, the aircraft had turned around and was airborne again, taking another batch of soldiers back to The World. All of them were laughing.

A bellowing staff sergeant was waiting for the new kids. *If there's incoming, you get in that bunker as fast as you can. Forget about your orders, what's written on that paper, from now on you're all infantry.*

On that first night, Searcy was assigned to guard duty, with instructions to pop off a flare if he saw any movement. The man beside him in the dugout was jumpy, and within half an hour he had let one off by mistake, lighting up the night sky. The sergeant came crackling over the radio: *Who the fuck let off that flare?*

Back in the enlisted men's tent, there was no shortage of beer. The sergeant told them how happy it made him to be here. *This is what the army is for. I'm like a pig in shit.*

And then one day Searcy was given twenty minutes' notice to board one more flight, a two-hundred-mile jog in a C-130 transport to the Tan Son Nhut air base on the edge of Saigon. "It was the most desolate feeling I've ever had," he said. The rainy season had begun just a few weeks earlier, and while the highlands had been blessedly cool, getting off the plane at Tan Son Nhut thrust him into a wall of damp heat heavy with the stink of jet fuel.

A two-and-a-half-ton 6x6 truck, a deuce and a half, was waiting to pick up the new arrivals. The driver fancied himself a comedian. With the vehicle belching black diesel smoke, he decided to entertain his passengers by swerving into a deep mud puddle, drenching an old woman who was carrying two heavily laden baskets on a shoulder pole. As the truck lurched past, she looked up and met Searcy's eye. There was no anger or hatred in her expression, he remembered, just incomprehension at an action so capricious, so uncalled for. *Why did you do that?* As his year in Saigon wore on, Searcy found himself echoing her thoughts: *Why are we doing this?*

4

Socks on an Octopus

WHEN VIETNAMESE FIGHTERS marched down the Ho Chi Minh Trail—"going to B"—what they secretly hoped for was "Long B," which would take them to the Central Highlands, rather than "Short B," which exposed them to the singular horrors of Quang Tri and Thua Thien.

A journalist for the People's Liberation Armed Forces, Tran Mai Nam, was sent on Short B toward the end of 1966 and spent the next several months reporting on what he saw there. He called it "the country of the Apocalypse," a world of artillery shells and bomb craters, B-57s skulking behind the clouds "like masked gangsters," F-4 Phantoms with their "howl of death," dead trees, and abandoned villages. Worst of all were the B-52s, flying silent at thirty thousand feet. A formation of these could saturate a "box" two miles long and half a mile wide, the equivalent of bombing the National Mall from the Lincoln Memorial all the way to the back lawn of the White House.

"We march in the desolate gray of the forest," Nam wrote. "Around us, giant trees, their foliage stripped by poison chemicals, thrust their stark branches into the sky. Their ghostly silhouettes march across a low and cloudy sky, heavy like a soaked quilt. . . . Our eyes have become red from watching such devastation. . . . [O]n these mountains green with heavy growth, such a rage against nature seems insane. One finds himself thinking, 'But what do they want?' "

The diorama in the Ho Chi Minh Trail Museum had suggested

many of the reasons for the unique intensity of the destruction in these two provinces by the time Manus Campbell arrived. It grew out of the defense of the DMZ, the threat to the cities of Hue and Danang, and the pivotal importance of the A Shau Valley to the PAVN and of Khe Sanh to the Americans.

As General Giap said, control of the mountains was the key to the war, and this meant gaining the support of the ethnic minority people who lived there, the Montagnards—though the Americans simply called them the 'Yards. During the French War, as chairman of the underground provincial committee in Thua Thien, Gen. Nguyen Chi Thanh had organized base areas in the mountains, "cradles of the revolution" that served both as staging grounds for attacks on the coastal plain and secure refuges from reprisals. Le Duan himself traveled to the Lao border area in 1953, nurturing a special relationship with the local Katu people. Among the dozens of ethnic groups in the Truong Son Mountains, the PAVN would have no fiercer supporters.

Diem's policies contributed mightily to this. In 1955 he installed his younger brother, Ngo Dinh Can, as a kind of unelected warlord in Hue, where he ran a fearsome network of secret police, paramilitaries, and death squads. Starting in 1959, ARVN units roamed the hinterlands of Thua Thien with mobile guillotines and urged the Katu "savages" to abandon their traditional ways and take up sedentary farming. In response to the repression, the revolutionaries pulled back into the security of the A Shau Valley, and a number of young Katu were sent north for military training.

The CIA quickly saw the importance of winning over the ethnic minorities, creating a pilot program in 1961 among the Rhade people of the Central Highlands that was soon turned over to the Special Forces. Within two years, they established dozens of bases along the Lao and Cambodian borders, "pioneer fortresses set out in the badlands," as one veteran called them. "The Communist will find that a nation which produced Davy Crockett and Daniel Boone and Jim Bowie is afraid of no forest and no swamp and no game of fighting, however toughly it is played," said Vice President Lyndon Johnson, promising that the Green Berets would "nail the coonskins to the wall."

Their core purpose was to create Civilian Irregular Defense Groups (CIDGs), made up of local ethnic people and supported by mercenaries recruited mainly from the Nung, a group from the Chinese border provinces. Of all the border bases, none were more important than A Shau—the biggest of three in the valley—and Khe Sanh.

Winning the trust of the ethnic people meant that the Green Berets had to become amateur anthropologists, learning the idiosyncrasies of their culture. The ethnic groups practiced swidden or "slash and burn" agriculture, and they hunted with spears and crossbows. They had no source of loyalty or authority beyond their home villages, no sense of belonging to a larger nation. They spoke many different languages, mutually unintelligible and almost none having a written form. They believed that the course of human events was dictated by mountain, forest, village, and household spirits peculiar to each locality. They practiced animal sacrifice and shared a widespread belief in sorcery. Some believed in a python god who would return to earth after a great cataclysm. Dressed in little more than loincloths, the women sometimes going bare-breasted, they feasted on snakes and field rats, chewed betel nuts, and drank copious amounts of fiery alcohol. The women, and even the children, had a taste for pipe-smoking. Some groups filed their teeth into points as a guarantee of long life and prosperity. Others kept slaves, a habit they had learned from early Thai invaders, and sold them to markets in Bangkok and Phnom Penh.

The early French colonists in Indochina had debated where these people belonged in the hierarchy of humanity. They had recognizable religious beliefs and used tools for farming, and for military explorers that was enough to classify them as barbarians. But Catholic missionaries argued that their spirit-worship was not a true religion: it was mere superstition, conforming to the concept of "animism" recently established by the English anthropologist Sir Edward Tylor. This classified the Montagnards as savages, a lower rung on Monsieur Darwin's evolutionary ladder, making it easier to rationalize their subjugation.

Equipped with little handbooks culled from the works of French scholars and missionaries, the Green Berets ate the locals' food, drank their rice wine, took part in their ceremonies, brought them medical care for the first time, and schooled them in animal husbandry, as if the Special Forces were a branch of the Peace Corps.

The North Vietnamese didn't necessarily take the support of the ethnic minorities along the Trail for granted. Vo Bam's first infiltrators in Quang Tri were under strict instructions to avoid contact with the Bru-Van Kieu. But then they began to find food hung from the trees along the mountain pathways, a chicken or a bunch of bananas, and took these gifts as a sign that they were dealing with "revolutionary-minded people aroused by us and our friends"—meaning the Communist Pathet Lao. As work on the Trail progressed into the A Shau, the PAVN took pains to consult with village headmen to be sure the spirits would not object to the planned route.

Some ethnic minorities made good soldiers and enthusiastic allies for the Americans; others, obviously, didn't. Nothing antagonized them more than Diem's strategic hamlet program, which involved bulldozing small, scattered settlements and consolidating them into new villages ringed by ditches, barbed wire, and guard towers. The program advanced more rapidly in Quang Tri than in any other part of the country; 498 strategic hamlets were planned for the province, and by mid-1963, 441 of them had been built.

American policymakers saw these "protected villages" as a way of winning hearts and minds; for Diem, they were an instrument of coercion and population control. Either way the plan was a disaster, breeding either resentment or outright resistance. This was especially true in Thua Thien, where the policy of forced displacement to the lowlands around Hue, on top of the ARVN's earlier brutality, did more to drive the ethnic minorities into the arms of the Communists than any number of recruiters from the North. For any Vietnamese villagers, being severed from their rice fields and the tombs of their ancestors was anathema, but for the Ta Oi, Pacoh, and Katu, it was a special horror. How could you communicate with the local spirits and keep the world in balance if you were penned up in a barbed-wire enclosure twenty miles away?

Most had kin in Laos, and many sought refuge there, crossing an unmarked border that they saw as the puzzling creation of outsiders who drew lines on maps, a thing unknown to them. Once there, a good number set to work helping the PAVN build the Ho Chi Minh Trail.

The most formidable of these ethnic groups, and the most resistant to recruitment by the Americans, were the Katu. Their young men, their long, flowing hair adorned with boar tusks, had struck terror in the French authorities and the royal court in Hue with their murderous raids, in which they collected what they needed for their ceremonies of human blood sacrifice. The Royal Lao Army had a saying, wrote the North Vietnamese military historian Nguyen Viet Phuong: "The Katu eat our flesh like tigers."

In the A Shau Valley, most of the ethnic people had made their choice of loyalties long before the Green Berets arrived. There were few if any hearts and minds to be won, therefore few human intelligence sources and no reliable supply of CIDG recruits. A 1964 Army Intelligence analysis reported that the Special Forces "have tried to establish an advisory relationship, but, thus far, they have had trouble making contact. . . . Their leadership appears to be hard-core Viet Cong."

On Christmas Day of 1962, a twenty-five-year-old infantry captain from the South Bronx landed at Saigon's Tan Son Nhut air base, one of the eleven thousand U.S. personnel in South Vietnam by this time. His name was Colin Powell, and many years later he would become chairman of the Joint Chiefs of Staff and secretary of state. The conflict was not going well; an aide to JFK warned the war effort had "an absurd quality," based on "the most Micawberesque predictions" of progress.

Powell was there to advise the ARVN troops stationed at the A Shau camp. Briefed on conditions in I Corps, he was flown north to Quang Tri city, the provincial capital, where he waited impatiently for a break in the weather that would allow him to proceed to his destination. On January 17, 1963, he boarded a helicopter for the short flight, sharing the ride with a contingent of fresh recruits, some sacks of rice, and an assortment of live pigs and chickens. The chopper bounced and jolted its way through thunderheads and squalls of rain for half an hour before setting down on the base's planked-steel airstrip, where Powell had a surreal exchange with the South Vietnamese captain waiting to welcome him, a man with the demeanor of an amiable schoolteacher. The officer pointed to the looming wall of mountains less than two miles to the west and said with a grin, "Laos."

Powell asked why the base had been established in such a remote and forbidding location.

"Very important outpost," the captain answered.

"What's its mission?"

"Very important outpost."

"But why is it here?"

"Outpost is here to protect airfield."

"What's the airfield here for?"

"Airfield here to resupply outpost."

Recounting the conversation in his memoir, *My American Journey*, Powell wrote that it was his first hint of the absurd circularity of the war in Vietnam. "We're here because we're here, because we're . . ."

The camp was connected to the other two small bases in the valley by a boneshaking strip of washboard dirt or boot-sucking mud, according to the season. Officially this was designated Route 548, although later, as it was extended southward toward Danang, the Americans took to calling this section the Yellow Brick Road.

Daily life for the troops at A Shau consisted of hacking their way through thickets of vines and bamboo and double- and triple-canopy jungle, struggling against the heat and humidity or soaked by bone-chilling monsoon rains. In the valley bottom, the forests gave way to knife-sharp elephant grass, taller than a man, which inflicted deep cuts that invariably became infected. The ponds and streams and the soggy flatland teemed with leeches. Your assignment came with a travel advisory: There are a hundred kinds of snakes in the valley; ninety-seven are venomous, and the other three will eat you. If you managed to avoid these, there were fire ants, malarial mosquitos the size of houseflies, and all manner of other biting insects, four-hundred-pound Indochinese tigers with a taste for human flesh, and the threat of Charlie lurking invisible behind every tree.

Powell and his men patrolled the hills, engaging in occasional small firefights, taking casualties from an enemy they never saw, until one day in July he stepped into a trap, and a punji stick smeared with excrement pierced clear through his instep. A medevac helicopter whisked him off to Hue.

As for the Special Forces base at Khe Sanh, perched on its plateau above Route 9 in Quang Tri, sixty miles or so northwest of the A Shau camp, its most important function was to maintain a watch on the Ho Chi Minh Trail. By the time the base was established in August 1962, the

CIA had been running its secret war in northern Laos, supporting the Hmong in their fight against the Pathet Lao and the North Vietnamese, for more than a year. But it quickly took note of the new threat below the seventeenth parallel, as the Trail crept into the four border provinces of Laos's southern panhandle.

The agency set about secretly "teaching simple people how to defend themselves and protect their families against the Communists." It called this the Kha program, perhaps unaware that the term, in Lao, has the derogatory sense of "slaves." It recruited "trailwatch" teams of ethnic villagers, equipping them with cameras to capture evidence of infiltrators, which they often lost or couldn't figure out how to use. The program was a fiasco, but it was the first step in what would become a multifaceted clandestine war, much of it run out of Khe Sanh. The United States was not a signatory to the 1954 Geneva Accords, which affirmed the neutrality of Laos; it merely "noted" them.

Khe Sanh is usually thought of as Lyndon Johnson's obsession, but it was a much more enduring fixation of William Westmoreland, who was immediately impressed by the strategic position of the base, which blocked the most obvious path of attack on the coastal lowlands. Just a few minutes' flying time from the Lao border, its airstrip offered an ideal base for operations inside that country, a perfect jumping-off point for what in time became his most impassioned wish—an invasion of Laos by ground troops to cut the Trail. The Joint Chiefs of Staff supported the idea, but for political leaders it was always a bridge too far, which left two alternatives: continued clandestine operations and intensive aerial bombing.

"Watch this trail they're coming down," LBJ said to Sen. Richard Russell (D-GA) in 1964. "Try to bomb them out of there when they're coming in." Russell's reply, citing the failure of a comparable bombing campaign in the Korean War, was, "Oh hell! That ain't worth a hoot. That's impossible."

McNamara shared those doubts, but decided it was time to drop the restrictions on operating "over the fence," using Khe Sanh for airdrops into Laos of small intelligence and sabotage teams to identify bombing targets, and creating a new special operations command with a cumbersome but innocuous-sounding name, the Studies and Observations Group, or MACV-SOG, whose emblem was a grinning skull topped with a green beret. The first operation, conducted by ARVN Special Forces and Nung mercenaries, was another failure, with most of the participants either killed or captured, and in September 1965 MACV decided that future incursions had to be led by Americans.

The teams involved in the new operation were still small, and the Green Berets who commanded them were inserted by unmarked helicopters after being "sheep-dipped." They carried no ID, all identifying marks were erased from their weapons, and their uniforms bore no insignia. The prime minister of Laos was not informed, and as time went on the rules of engagement were progressively loosened until the Special Forces were remaining in Laos for weeks or months at a time, sabotaging North Vietnamese facilities, snatching enemy soldiers to be brought back to Khe Sanh for interrogation, training local "resistance cadre," and identifying "lucrative" bombing targets.

Operation Barrel Roll started in December 1964, bombing mountainous areas of Laos north of the seventeenth parallel. Three months later, as Rolling Thunder was beginning over North Vietnam, the campaign was extended southward into the Lao panhandle. Some of it was carried out by Lao pilots, though that brought its own challenges: they needed a lot of training, and the Royal Lao Air Force refused to use one plane because it was under a curse. Fortunately, U.S. advisers reported, "Buddhist monks were able to exorcise the bad spirits. The cost was $7.62, covering the cost of candles and herbs for the ceremony and Salem cigarettes, tooth paste and soap for the monks."

The bombing had limited impact, however, and in the last quarter of 1965, the CIA produced a series of urgent secret reports on the rapid expansion of the Trail. The binh tram were fully operational now, each with its contingent of engineers, infantry, medical teams, guides, workshops, truck depots, and storage areas. Col. Vo Bam himself had taken up full-time residence at La Hap, Binh Tram 4, his forward command headquarters.

Spy planes detected more than 140 miles of new north-south arterial roads, sections of which were graded and comparable to American logging roads, and there were at least four new truckable spurs leading east to the border. The most immediately menacing of these was a seventeen-mile all-weather stretch of Road B45 from La Hap, which connected to another eight miles of improved trails into the

A Shau Valley. There were large truck convoys and bulldozers; the first antiaircraft emplacements; new bypasses and alternate routes to avoid bottlenecks; timber bridges and ferry crossings; in time even Potemkin truck parks and troop camps to lure bombers away from their targets. It was like a living organism, less a trail than a maze, said one pilot, and to make matters worse, most of the Trail was invisible, even to spy planes. Bombing it was "like putting socks on an octopus."

As instructed, Colin Powell had kept a daily diary during his six-month-long stint in the A Shau Valley. On February 18, 1963, he noted, his patrol had come to an abandoned Katu village, where everyone fled at their approach except for one old woman who was too feeble to move. "We burned down the thatched huts, starting the blaze with Ronson and Zippo lighters," he wrote—an image that shocked Americans when they witnessed it on TV for the first time more than two years later in a report by Morley Safer of CBS News, who showed Marines doing the same thing in a village near Danang. This provoked a furious reaction by LBJ, who called the head of the network to accuse him of having "shat on the American flag."

"Sprayed two [hectares] sweet potatoes, manioc destroyed," Powell went on. "The ARVN troops slashed away with their bayonets at fields of corn, onions, and manioc. On later occasions the destruction became more sophisticated. Helicopters delivered fifty-five-gallon drums of a chemical herbicide to us, a forerunner of Agent Orange. From the drums, we filled two-and-a-half-gallon hand-pumped Hudson sprayers, which looked like fire extinguishers. Within minutes after we sprayed, the plants began to turn brown and wither." The chemical was called Herbicide Purple, and in the course of that week, according to declassified Air Force records, helicopters repeated the exercise eight times in the foothills above the A Shau base.

Washington had few qualms about the idea of using chemical herbicides to expose the enemy's hiding places, but destroying food crops was a different matter. How could you be sure you were starving the enemy and not local civilians, those you were pledged to protect? Would the military value be outweighed by the political cost? And what if the United States was accused of committing a war crime?

Policy makers had agonized over this moral dilemma before. When scientists proposed the destruction of Japan's rice crop in July 1944, FDR's chief of staff, Adm. William Leahy, vetoed the idea, saying it "would violate every Christian ethic I have ever heard of and all known laws of war."

President Kennedy formally authorized the defoliation campaign that would become known as Operation Ranch Hand on November 30, 1961, but he refused to endorse crop destruction—or "resource control," as the military called it. Each target had to be approved at the highest levels, and by the following July only a handful of missions had been flown, aimed at reducing the risk of ambush by stripping vegetation from the perimeter of highways, power lines, rivers and canals, the north-south railroad near Saigon, and the mangroves of the Mekong Delta and the Ca Mau Peninsula, at the southernmost tip of the country.

In that month, Westmoreland's predecessor, Gen. Paul D. Harkins, submitted a list of six new targets. One of them was the lines of communication between A Shau and the smaller A Luoi base, ten miles up the valley. It was the first time I Corps had been targeted, and the joint chiefs balked at the proposal. The location was too sensitive; the valley was right on the Lao border, and talks were under way in Geneva that same week that would reaffirm the country's neutrality. Harkins pushed back: the proximity of the Ho Chi Minh Trail in Laos was precisely the point.

On November 30, after four months of debate interrupted by the Cuban Missile Crisis, Kennedy authorized the other five targets on the list, but not the A Shau Valley. Harkins not only continued to push for the mission; he added a specific request for crop destruction. Washington finally yielded, but only if the operation was preceded by unspecified psychological operations to defuse local concerns. In fact, that didn't happen until 1964, long after Powell's troops carried out their mission, when civilians were given leaflets in advance of a herbicide run, telling them, "If you live with the Communists, you will suffer misery and diseases. If you return to the government, you will be well off." Of course these weren't much use in the A Shau, since the population, besides being uniformly hostile, had no written language and didn't speak Vietnamese.

As Washington feared, that first round of crop destruction in the valley provoked a storm of propaganda from Hanoi, with charges of chemical warfare and violations of the Geneva Accords, all serving to strengthen Le Duan's hard-line position within the politburo. In June 1963 General Giap even compared the crop destruction program to the Nazis' use of poison gas against the Jews. But once the door was cracked open, there was no turning back. A dozen areas of South Vietnam were secretly designated for crop destruction in 1964. Of these, the mountainous western half of Quang Tri, Thua Thien, and neighboring Quang Nam province was by far the largest target.

Conventional defoliation also accelerated, and again much of the escalation was spurred by the precarious security situation in the A Shau Valley. In April 1964, just two months after his arrival in Saigon, William Westmoreland flew north to inspect the bases at Khe Sanh and A Shau. The visit to A Shau almost cost him his life. When his plane prepared for takeoff at the end of his visit, gunfire raked it, ripping through the cockpit and cabin, wounding the pilot, the co-pilot, and a Green Beret officer, and missing Westmoreland by inches.

The narrow escape taught him two lessons. The first was the sobering one that every ordinary grunt learned: that survival was a matter of fine margins. The second infuriated him: overgrown areas like the one at the edge of the runway gave the enemy intolerable protection. He ordered immediate defoliation of the base perimeter, and more chemicals were stored there for future use. At the end of May, C-123 aircraft flying in formations of three or four at a time blanketed the valley floor between the A Shau and A Luoi bases with almost ten thousand gallons of Agent Purple, the first intensive defoliation in I Corps. By the time the campaign wound down six years later, more than half a million gallons of herbicides had rained down on the valley.

"Saddle Up, Cowboys!"

THE MARINE LANDINGS at Danang were only one of three thresholds that were crossed in March 1965, each embodying another facet of the escalating cycle of destruction. The bombing of the North, Operation Rolling Thunder, began on March 4, based out of Danang. The Marines came ashore four days later to protect the air base. And on March 29, the defoliation campaign, Operation Ranch Hand, moved from its initial phase of "program development" to full operational status.

Its official designation was Trail Dust, but Ranch Hand (with its signature departure call of "Saddle up, cowboys!") was the name that stuck. The radio call sign was Hades, which may have been the most apposite of all. The campaign was something without precedent in history, using all the tools of science, technology, and airpower to lay waste to a country's natural environment. To accomplish this, it employed a variety of chemical compounds that became known as the rainbow herbicides, for the three-inch-wide colored stripe painted on the fifty-five-gallon barrels in which they were shipped and stored.

Ranch Hand had begun with tiny amounts of defoliants called dinoxol and trinoxol, followed by slightly larger quantities of herbicides Pink and Green. (The air force disliked the word *agent*, arguing that it gave a sinister tinge to a benign operation designed to save American lives.) Powell's men at A Shau had sprayed Herbicide Purple, while Blue, a fast-acting desiccant, was used to destroy rice.

Initially, Purple was the most widely used defoliant, but after March 1965 the air force decided that the one it liked best was a new one with an orange stripe on the barrel. One factor in their choice was the rapid growth in demand, and Orange was a little cheaper. The last of the rainbow chemicals, introduced in 1966, was White, which worked well on broadleaf crops like manioc and sweet potato and had a longer-lasting effect than either Orange or Blue. Agent Orange became the heart of the campaign, however. Accounting for more than 60 percent of all the herbicides used, it became a lucrative business for big corporations like Monsanto, which also produced DDT, and Dow Chemical, whose other products included napalm.

In December 1964, Saigon saw the last in its apparently endless cycle of coups. This one installed ARVN Gen. Nguyen Van Thieu as head of a new military junta, and he was subsequently elected president with the flamboyant young Air Force chief, Nguyen Cao Ky, as prime minister. Ky affected an Errol Flynn mustache and caused ripples in Washington by declaring that Hitler was his only hero and that what Vietnam really needed was "four or five Hitlers to deal with subversive elements and unify the Vietnamese nation." He loved the Ranch Hand cowboys, who mirrored his own belief that pilots constituted a gung-ho elite among fighting men. He let them park their planes in his private section of the Tan Son Nhut air base and presented them with one of his own favorite violet neckscarves. "These are your colors," he said. "Wear them with pride." Westmoreland banned them, hating any kind of flamboyance, but the pilots ignored him, and he eventually backed down.

The workhorse of the herbicide campaign, the slow and ungainly Fairchild C-123, first produced in 1949, was dragged out of retirement and retrofitted with thousand-gallon defoliant tanks. It was an old-fashioned seat-of-the-pants beast to fly. "Flying the one-twenty-three is a lot like playing with yourself," one pilot said. "It's a hell of a lot of fun, but you're ashamed to admit you do it."

Each mission was planned by an interagency group, the 203 Committee—named for Room 203 at Tan Son Nhut, where the team met. The targets had to be approved by local government authorities and ARVN commanders, but the pilots were assured that this was a chummy formality: "Meetings usually terminate at a little social hour at the Province Chief's villa," one air force briefer told them.

Tan Son Nhut was their first command center, though Danang and Bien Hoa, twenty miles north of Saigon, soon became the twin operational hubs of the campaign. The flights usually lifted off in the cool of early morning, when thermal updrafts would not cause the spray to drift and dissipate. The pilots marked the starting point of the run with a white phosphorus rocket, and depending on the number of aircraft on a mission, they could lay down anything from a few hundred to several thousand gallons of herbicides along a strip 260 feet wide and as long as ten miles. Some targets had to be sprayed several times, because tropical and subtropical forests did not yield easily. The stink of the chemical was said to be like a mixture of DDT and fuel oil.

They came in low and slow over a target, 150 feet above the treetops at 130 knots. Crop-spraying, especially of upland rice in the mountains, was a particular challenge to a pilot's skills, since it might involve zigzagging among multiple locations in search of small plots of farmland under the constant threat of ground fire. This grew more intense as the PAVN built up its antiaircraft defenses in critical target areas like the A Shau Valley. In the course of the war, five of the twenty-five Ranch Hand planes were shot down. One celebrated C-123 was riddled with almost six hundred bullet holes, earning it the nickname "Patches."

Given these dangers, the spray runs were often preceded by a flight of fighter-bombers. Assured by forward air controllers that the target area was free of American troops—sometimes a dubious assertion—these planes suppressed the threat of ground fire by laying down napalm, cluster munitions, even larger bombs over especially hot targets. Cluster bomblets—*bom bi,* as the Vietnamese call them—were especially prone to failure, leaving heavily defoliated areas such as Quang Tri and Thua Thien strewn with unexploded ordnance.

The first time a plane was hit by ground fire was occasion for what the cowboys called a cherry party, a debauch "monumental in scope and damage," in the words of one pilot, from which they emerged soaked and staggering amid a litter of empty champagne bottles. "Only you can prevent forests" was their standing joke, a dark echo of Smokey the Bear. They called themselves the World's Wackiest Weed Wilters and composed parodies of antiwar songs: "Where have all the flowers gone? Sprayed by Ranch Hands every one."

They never gave any thought to the possible health risks. "I would like to emphasize that the defoliant is completely non-toxic and not harmful to any form of animal or human life," a briefer told one assembly of pilots. "The aircrews get slopped with it daily, and our ARVN loaders have been exposed to it for several years with no ill effects. For demonstration purposes, Ranch Hand personnel have actually drank [*sic*] the stuff." Some pilots tossed back a shot glass of Agent Orange as an initiation ritual, and ARVN troops smeared the chemicals on their bodies to prove the point to villagers, who were given cartoon leaflets to reassure them that these were "standard defoliants which are widely used throughout the world in controlling weeds and other vegetation." When the storage barrels were empty, soldiers often perforated them and turned them into showers, or cut them in half to make improvised barbecue pits. *Empty* wasn't quite the right word, however: there was generally a gallon or two left in the bottom, and that was just sluiced onto the ground.

Even scientists, with a few notable exceptions, had little concern at first. The first Earth Day, the federal Environmental Protection Agency, and laws like the Clean Air Act and the Clean Water Act were still several years away. Rachel Carson's book *Silent Spring* had drawn attention to the catastrophic effects of DDT on wildlife, but the main ingredients of the rainbow herbicides were assumed to be harmless, an embodiment of the old DuPont promise of "Better Living Through Chemistry." They were an indispensable tool for farmers keeping down weeds, and they kept American lawns and golf courses trim and green. A similar logic applied on the battlefield. "Vegetation control" was just another way for humans to demonstrate their mastery over nature, especially useful where elements of the natural world were as insubordinate as mangrove swamps and rain forests.

Each of the herbicides had a different chemical composition. Agent Blue combined dimethylarsenic acid and sodium cacodylate, dumping three and a half pounds of pure arsenic onto each acre sprayed. In this organic form, it was relatively harmless, but scientists later determined that in soil and water it could be transformed into *inorganic* arsenic, a known human carcinogen with no half-life. Agent White was a mix of 20 percent picloram—a proprietary product of Dow Chemical, which is now known to be associated with damage to the liver and central nervous system—and 80 percent 2,4-dichlorophenoxyacetic acid, normally abbreviated to 2,4-D. In Agents Orange and Purple, 2,4-D was combined with 2,4,5-trichlorophenoxyacetic acid, and it was the latter that proved to be the hidden menace.

Marketed under the name of Silvex, 2,4,5-T was highly effective against woody plants and broad-leafed weeds. The problem was that it contained a trace amount of a lethal toxin called 2,3,7,8-tetrochlorodibenzo-p-dioxin, or TCDD, and it was used in Vietnam in concentrations "at least an order of magnitude greater"—as much as ten times greater—than when applied to farm fields in the United States.

Although the manufacturers were aware of the trace amount of dioxin in 2,4,5-T, it didn't bother them much at first, because under carefully controlled conditions, the contamination was negligible. The problem arose under the relentless pressure of keeping up with demand from the Pentagon, with companies speeding up the chemical production process and failing to maintain proper temperature controls.

Dioxin is actually a family of more than four hundred compounds, and TCDD is the worst of them, one of the most toxic substances ever created, its presence measured in parts per trillion, or ppt. When the word *dioxin* is used in the context of the war in Vietnam, this is what it means, for TCDD is the unmistakable fingerprint of Agent Orange and Agent Purple. But still the public, like the Ranch Hand crews, was unworried. "TCDD?" said Jeanne Stellman, an occupational health specialist at Columbia University, who did more than anyone else after the war to document the magnitude of the herbicide campaign and its possible health effects on American veterans. "People would have sprinkled it on their breakfast cereal."

The Green Berets at A Shau had seen a lot of chemicals sprayed on the valley, but in the final weeks of 1965, they might have been startled to see some of the big C-123s flying in an unfamiliar direction, heading west across the Lao border.

In a November 1965 memo to the State Department, U.S. Ambassador to Laos William Sullivan—known as the "field marshal" for his assertive control over the secret war in that country—wrote from Vientiane, "I am convinced that our efforts in Laos, particularly along infiltration route [sic], are critical to U.S. forces engaged in South Vietnam."

You couldn't win the war in Vietnam and then turn your attention to Laos, because the Trail was what sustained the North's war effort.

The joint chiefs decided that "a weight of effort sufficient to strangle the determined infiltration [is] necessary." Attacks on the Trail would call for "a large spectrum of tactical air capability, equipment, and expertise," including B-52 Arc Light strikes flown out of Guam, carried out largely at night when most of the truck convoys were in motion.

The problem, as Sullivan pointed out after inspecting the Trail himself, was that most of it was concealed by an "impenetrable tree canopy which high-speed, high-flying jets literally cannot see through. . . . [N]owhere on this road, except for two limited areas, was it open to the sky. Even flying over it slowly in a helicopter, the road was not discernible from above."

The answer was to remove the forest cover, a flagrant breach of Laos's neutrality and one of the most closely guarded secrets of the war in Southeast Asia. "We can carry on these efforts only if we do not, repeat do not, talk about them," Sullivan wrote, "and when necessary, if we deny that they are taking place." The pilots took an oath of silence, and Prince Souvanna Phouma, the neutralist prime minister, averted his eyes.

The new campaign, a coordinated mix of defoliation and heavy aerial bombing, was called Tiger Hound, and Westmoreland himself was said to have come up with the name: Tiger, for its ferocity; Hound, because it would first sniff out the enemy. The C-123s would target the same area where the clandestine special operations teams were now operating—the mountainous strip east of a line drawn between Route 9 and the triborder area between Vietnam, Laos, and Cambodia. Their initial targets would be on Road B45, to cut the trail between La Hap and the A Shau Valley.

In essence, the spraying of Laos was a mapping exercise, laying bare the Trail so that it could be bombed. Sullivan thought this would take "massive amounts of defoliants," which meant "Washington discussion at high levels." His prediction was correct: the spraying of Laos was as intense an escalation of the herbicide campaign as anything seen thus far in South Vietnam. Only the notorious War Zone D, the NLF stronghold just north of Saigon, was hit as hard this early in the war.

An indiscreet source in Saigon let slip to the legendary *New York*

Times reporter R. W. "Johnny" Apple that "we're turning the Ho Chi Minh Trail brown," but the comment appeared only in a small sidebar to a longer story, and no one seems to have followed up on it at the time. The most secret part of a secret war remained forgotten.

The first Tiger Hound spray run hit the mountains on the border with the A Shau on December 5; the bombing began the next day; and two days after that, the Green Berets abandoned their two smaller bases in the valley, judging them to be indefensible, and consolidated their forces at A Shau.

The first wave of B-52s, a fleet of twenty-four aircraft, took off from Guam four days later, and by the end of the month, air force, navy, and Marine pilots had flown more than eight hundred bombing runs, with Sullivan personally approving the targets. Once the effects of the defoliation kicked in, and the roads became more visible, the rate increased to one hundred a day, and by the time the monsoon rains began in late April, that number had doubled again. The bombing of the Trail was so intense that missions had to be canceled at one point because of a shortage of ordnance.

An internal air force analysis of the first four months of the campaign reported, "The FACs [forward air controllers] were unanimous in praising this [defoliation] program, and state that it is the one thing that has helped them open up the area, to see the truck traffic and to locate where these trucks are parked." In May, Westmoreland and Sullivan agreed to expand the spraying of Road B45 to include destroying crops in the surrounding fields.

"The success of this campaign will weigh heavily in the outcome of the war in Vietnam," the report concluded. Success was elusive, however. Even with more sections of the Trail now visible, it took hundreds of airstrikes for every truck destroyed, and the Soviet Union quickly sent replacements. While the pressure did force the PAVN to switch more of its energies to breaking through the DMZ, its troops continued to pour down the Trail, headed for the A Shau and points south.

For all its strategic importance, the A Shau camp didn't look like much, just a collection of tin-roofed buildings and muddy trenches, flanked by the turbid A Sap River, with a triangular perimeter of minefields

and barbed wire that rusted in the constant rain and humidity—
"fortifications out of the Middle Ages," in the words of Gen. Harold
Johnson, the army chief of staff. There were seventeen members of the
Special Forces at the base, together with more than four hundred Vietnamese, a mixture of civilian irregulars, Nung mercenaries, an ARVN
platoon, and fifty-odd support staff.

Despite mounting antiwar protests at home, the Green Berets were
still seen as intrepid all-American heroes. The most famous of them
was Staff Sgt. Barry Sadler, who had served at a border base in the
Central Highlands until he, like Colin Powell, was invalided out after
stepping on a poisoned punji stick. Sadler was an unsavory character: a
heavy drinker, a brawler, and an admirer of Nazi Germany with a dim
view of Jews. He also fancied himself a singer-songwriter, and one day,
sitting in a whorehouse in Mexico, he wrote a patriotic number called
"Ballad of the Green Berets":

Silver wings upon their chest,
These are men, America's best.

On March 5, 1966, the song, which he performed on TV standing
square-jawed and ramrod-straight in full dress uniform, hit number
one on the *Billboard* charts. The very same day, two PAVN defectors
surrendered to the Special Forces at A Shau and told them that four
battalions of the elite 325B Division were closing in for an attack.

It began in the predawn hours of March 9, with a devastating mortar barrage. It resumed the next day with a human wave assault—
"grabbing the enemy by the belt," a tactic devised by General Thanh
the previous October in the Ia Drang Valley in the Central Highlands,
the first large-scale confrontation, at Thanh's urging, between American troops and PAVN regulars. "I would do anything to have 200 of
them under my command," said Special Forces Maj. Charles "Chargin'
Charlie" Beckwith when asked about the PAVN's performance in that
encounter. "They're the finest soldiers I've ever seen."

While 234 Americans died in the battle of Ia Drang, estimates of
the North Vietnamese dead ran to more than 3,500. "Ten to one is a
damn good exchange," Westmoreland told Morley Safer of CBS News.
The Vietnamese retort to that was exactly what Ho Chi Minh had told

the French twenty years earlier: "You will kill ten of my men while we will kill one of yours. But you will be the ones to end up exhausted." Ia Drang was a pivotal event in the war, cementing in place Westmoreland's fixation on the body count and the use of overwhelming force and providing a template for the mutual carnage that would follow.

By the end of the afternoon of March 10, the assault on the A Shau base was over. The buildings were reduced to rubble, the ruined barrels of defoliants in the storage area leaking their chemicals into the ground. The small force of Green Berets took 100 percent casualties: five dead and twelve wounded. Half of the camp's Vietnamese defenders fled or defected to the enemy, and 172 died, a further footnote to Westmoreland's theory of the body count: his 10-to-1 kill ratio never accounted for his South Vietnamese allies, who lost more men than the Americans in every year of the conflict from 1961 to 1975.

The weather was foul on the Lao side of the border that day, and one of the C-123s was forced to abort its mission and return to Danang with a full tank of chemicals. As the pilot flew low over the camp, he looked down and saw the attack in progress. Should he dump his unused load of Agent Orange on the attackers? No, he decided, that would only interfere with the relief operation. But that turned out to be a disaster. Another eight Americans died when a relief helicopter and two attack aircraft were shot down. Desperate local fighters mobbed the big choppers sent to evacuate the camp, and the retreating Americans opened fire on them, killing thirteen.

The bodies of the dead lay unburied and rotting in the sun and rain for two months before they were finally retrieved. The PAVN did nothing to clean up the battlefield, and the Ta Oi, Pacoh, and Katu refused to come near the place for fear of malignant ghosts. "It has been said that this is a strange and ugly war," said John Laurence of CBS News. "It has never been worse than at A Shau."

At first blush, the loss of a small, remote base like A Shau might have seemed insignificant. But Westmoreland realized its importance. Just weeks earlier, at a conference in Honolulu, LBJ had asked him what his top priority would be if he commanded the PAVN. The answer came without hesitation: he would capture Hue, the historic symbol of a united Vietnam, and declare Quang Tri and Thua Thien liberated territory. Control of the A Shau was the key to this, he understood, as the base for future attacks on Hue and Danang.

The PAVN never left the A Shau, turning it into their most important stronghold in South Vietnam. With the Special Forces gone, they set about mining and booby-trapping the valley, monitoring all potential landing zones and artillery sites, installing antiaircraft batteries in the surrounding hills, and developing their lines of communication with virtual impunity, driving new trails through the mountains in the direction of Hue and extending the Yellow Brick Road south toward Danang. None of this would have been possible without control of Road B45 in Laos, which they held no matter how many bombs and defoliants the Americans threw at it.

The fall of the base coincided with a fresh political crisis, with warring factions of ARVN in Danang threatening to turn their guns on each other. Taking advantage of the disarray in I Corps, the PAVN pushed more troops across the DMZ into Quang Tri, and Westmoreland responded by pouring yet more Marines into the wild borderlands. In September they took control of Khe Sanh, transforming the Green Beret base into a giant armed camp.

The A Shau Valley now had the most sinister reputation of any battlefield in Vietnam. When the grunts went back to The World, or kicked back over a cold one during R&R, they would sometimes compare notes on the scariest places you could be sent to fight. Some would say it was walking point in a flooded rice paddy in the delta, waiting for Charlie to put an AK-47 round through your head; others said it was cowering in a bunker under mortar fire at the edge of the DMZ; still others thought it was sitting in the open door of a Huey, pumped with adrenalin but knowing that half of all the helicopters in Vietnam went down in flames. "Choppers fell out of the sky like fat poisoned birds a hundred times a day," wrote Michael Herr in *Dispatches,* his hallucinatory account of the war in I Corps. "After a while I couldn't get on one without thinking that I must be out of my fucking mind."

But those who served in the A Shau, or merely knew of its dark associations, agreed that it was the most terrifying place of all. Even the toughest soldiers—and only the elite units would ever be sent to fight there—took to calling it the Ah Shit Valley, or the Valley of Death.

Even after raising his troop request to 542,000, Westmoreland knew that retaking the A Shau was beyond his means. "I simply lacked the forces . . . to hold the valley against determined attack," he wrote. Not until the summer of 1967 would he give any thought to crossing that fearful bridge. It was just as Manus Campbell arrived in Thua Thien that Westmoreland asked his Marine commanders to plan a fresh assault.

6

Grunt

BY JUNE 1967 both sides knew the war was at a stalemate that had been years in the making. *What are we doing here?* Chuck Searcy had wondered, and Robert McNamara, the chief architect of the war, was now asking himself the same question. On June 17, the very day Searcy's plane touched down in Vietnam, McNamara ordered a top-secret study of U.S. involvement in Indochina, giving his analysts free rein. "Let the chips fall where they may," he said, and four years later the chips did just that, in the form of thousands of classified documents leaked to *The New York Times* and published as the Pentagon Papers.

A new ambassador, Ellsworth Bunker, arrived in Saigon that same month. Yale class of '16, he arranged a dinner club at the request of his fellow Elis, on condition they could sing at least one verse of "The Whiffenpoof Song":

We are poor little lambs who have lost our way, baa-baa-baa,
We are little black sheep who have gone astray, baa-baa-baa.

Though patrician in his manners, Bunker was cold-eyed in his politics, nicknamed "the Refrigerator," a supporter of Westmoreland's insistent call for more ground troops so he could invade Laos, backed up if necessary, said the fiercest hawks in Washington, by the threat of chemical, nuclear, and bacteriological weapons. But the belief that yet more firepower would fix things only illustrated the core problem, which was an inability to think outside the cultural and political box. After more than two years, Operation Rolling Thunder had failed to bring North Vietnam to its knees. "Instead of rationally," wrote Barbara Tuchman in *The March of Folly*—in the American conception of rationality, that is—"Hanoi reacted humanly in anger and defiance, as the British had done under the German Blitz."

The leaders in Hanoi might be Marxist-Leninists, but that didn't necessarily mean they were bent on toppling dominoes all the way to the Philippines. The core of their fight was a crusade for national independence driven by a militant spirit of resistance to outside domination that long predated the arrival of the Americans and would long outlast them.

Le Duan, Nguyen Chi Thanh, and their followers were now firmly in control of the politburo, pushing their "big battle" plans, and preparing for their "General Offensive, General Uprising," though Giap continued to press the case for his favored tactic of depleting the enemy by hit-and-run attacks—"Quick Strikes, Quick Victories." The statistics tended to favor him, since at least 80 percent of military encounters were initiated by the PAVN and the NLF, almost always with an ambush, and they were now killing at least eight hundred Americans a month.

No matter how many battalions the Americans added, the PAVN matched them, both sides using the same rationale and language. "We'll just go on bleeding them until Hanoi wakes up to the fact that they have bled their country to the point of disaster," said Westmoreland. "We will entice the Americans close to the border and bleed them without mercy," said Giap. The Americans would not progress by throwing more troops at the problem. Adding another fifty thousand, he said, would be like "throwing salt into the sea."

Westmoreland was a man driven by metrics, a product not only of West Point but of an advanced management course at Harvard Business School. He demanded data on the tonnage of bombs dropped, sorties flown per truck destroyed, gallons of chemicals sprayed, acreage defoliated, tons of rice destroyed, number of villages pacified, number of Viet Cong neutralized, battalion-days and man-hours in the field, and the kill ratio, which gave young officers with thoughts of promotion every incentive to inflate the numbers. *If it's dead and it's*

Vietnamese, it's VC. The magnitude of the destruction was the main index of progress.

Entire areas below the DMZ were designated as free-fire zones, the villages razed, their inhabitants herded into squalid refugee camps like Cam Lo, on Route 9, severed from their homes, their rice fields, the tombs of their ancestors. Operation Ranch Hand hit its peak. In 1965 the C-123s had flown about 250 missions, including the first wave in Laos. The following year the number was well over one thousand, including the only two ever authorized inside North Vietnam—hitting the famous Road 20, the key portion of the Ho Chi Minh Trail from Phong Nha to the Lao border. Sorties doubled again in 1967, and the campaign was sustained at that level through 1969, with almost 5 million gallons of defoliants sprayed each year. The escalation in I Corps was especially intense. In Thua Thien alone, the volume increased almost fivefold from 1967 to 1968. In Quang Tri, the DMZ was off-limits until February 1967. But after PAVN troops continued to pound away at American defenses, pilots were authorized to spray the southern half of the DMZ for the first time. By August, all restrictions on spraying in the zone had been lifted.

"In effect, we are fighting a war of attrition," Westmoreland wrote, "and the only alternative is a war of annihilation." But public opinion, and for that matter world opinion, would never tolerate a war of annihilation, and the North Vietnamese would never be defeated by a more limited war of attrition: they were past masters of that form of warfare. On the American side, it was the Marines in I Corps who paid the highest price.

The worst of it was that Westmoreland's top Marine commanders never shared either his core assumptions or his ongoing fixations. A major rationale for bombing the North was that it would obviate the need to commit large numbers of ground troops. But the Danang air base, the main takeoff point in South Vietnam for Operation Rolling Thunder, obviously had to be secured. Since Westmoreland didn't trust the ARVN with the task, he brought in the Marines. He saw this, he wrote in his memoirs, "not as a first step in a growing American commitment, but as a way to secure a vital airfield and the air units using it."

But Marines were not known for sitting around passively waiting to be attacked. "You can't defend a place like that by sitting on your ditty box," said Marine Gen. Wallace M. Greene, Jr. And once they ventured out beyond the perimeter wire, into villages where anyone might be the enemy, the "enclave strategy" was a dead letter.

There were two battalions of Marines in Danang. Westmoreland added a third at Phu Bai, a secondary airfield just outside Hue. Another two arrived in early April 1965, with tanks and field artillery, hardly the kind of thing you needed for base perimeter defense. And then there were the two southernmost provinces of I Corps, Quang Tin (which was absorbed into Quang Nam after reunification) and Quang Ngai. Defending these meant building another base, at Chu Lai.

One of the most celebrated attributes of the Marine Corps was its mastery of amphibious operations, but there were no seaports north of the Hai Van Pass, which separated Hue from Danang. So the next requirement was a support facility for landing craft, which was built at the mouth of the Perfume River. This still left a big gap between Hue and the DMZ, so that led to another combat base in Dong Ha, and another in Quang Tri city. There's no such thing as being a little pregnant.

Westmoreland's memoir was at best disingenuous, for the decision to escalate had been made secretly within weeks. On April 1, LBJ had authorized the Marines to carry out offensive operations, approving the dispatch of another twenty thousand troops. The tactical area of operations around Danang had been limited to eight square miles; now it was extended to a fifty-mile radius, which meant the Marines could act as a strike force all the way to the Lao border.

The emblem of the war of attrition that Westmoreland pursued was the search-and-destroy mission, a term he hated for its insinuation of random brutality, preferring more neutral terms like *sweeping operation* or *reconnaissance in force*. The biggest problem with these missions was the *search* part, because the PAVN were nimble masters of concealment, evasion, ambush, and escape, and fighting them in the dense forests guaranteed high friendly casualties.

Westmoreland had no philosophical objection to the "spreading inkblot theory," the steady pacification of the towns and villages of the coastal plains, striving, in the words of then-ambassador Henry Cabot Lodge, "to improve the lot of the little man at the grassroots"—and many of the Marines in I Corps did just that, with dedication and sincerity, in the so-called combined action platoons. But Westmoreland thought pacification should mainly be the ARVN's job, once its spine was stiffened by the security shield and by training provided by its American mentors.

For Victor "Brute" Krulak, commanding general of the Fleet Marine Force Pacific, and Gen. Lew Walt, commander of the Third Marine Division in I Corps, sparsely populated places in the middle of nowhere, like Khe Sanh and the A Shau Valley, had no strategic value; committing so many troops there was a waste of limited resources. "Victories in the search-and-destroy operations were not relevant to the total outcome of the war," Krulak insisted, and Walt agreed. "The raw figure of VC killed . . . can be a dubious index of success," Walt said, "since, if their killing is accompanied by devastation of friendly areas, we may end up having done more harm than good."

In the end the Marines were asked to do both, with predictable results. The more they were stretched to fight on multiple fronts, the greater the demand for more boots on the ground. Sending more men into the mountains meant more body bags. The more deaths, the greater the need for reinforcements, the more qualms among the folks at home. It was war as conducted by the Sorcerer's Apprentice.

Events at Khe Sanh in the spring of 1967 convinced Westmoreland of the correctness of his methods. Walt had irritated him by reducing the size of the Marine battalion there, and by late April, PAVN units were dug into tunnels, bunker complexes, and mortar pits on three hills overlooking the base. According to the official Marine Corps account, the three weeks of fighting to regain these hilltops cost the Marines 155 men, but they killed an estimated one thousand North Vietnamese, so the operation could be accounted another success. On June 1, three weeks after the hill fights ended, Walt was relieved of command, removing a persistent thorn in Westmoreland's side. "Rigidity in doctrine is no virtue," he wrote in evaluating the general's two years at the helm of the Marines in I Corps.

What the hill fights mainly showed, however, was the dominance of Le Duan and Nguyen Chi Thanh in setting military strategy. The deployment of elite main-force units as the cutting edge of the war in Quang Tri and Thua Thien prefigured the all-out siege of Khe Sanh and the Tet Offensive, enticing another fifty thousand American troops into the mountains of northern I Corps to draw them away from the defense of urban areas farther south.

Like the U.S. government, the politburo in Hanoi was anxious to break the deadlock in the war, and all that spring it debated the best way of pushing for a decisive victory. The PAVN General Staff proposed to "annihilate" 150,000 American troops and liberate Dong Ha and Quang Tri city. Ho Chi Minh and Giap pushed back strongly, and the politburo agreed that it would be hard to achieve that level of success even against smaller company- and battalion-size forces. Le Duan proposed skipping this preliminary step altogether and going straight to an all-out offensive in the cities, risking everything on a single roll of the dice.

These debates were briefly derailed, however, by news on July 6 that Nguyen Chi Thanh was dead. There was much confusion about the circumstances. Westmoreland chose to believe a defector's story that he had died of wounds sustained during a B-52 raid on the Cambodian border. Some whispered that he had been poisoned by ideological rivals. But Giap, to whom that accusing finger was implicitly pointed, was said to be devastated by his fellow general's death. Only much later did it become clear that the official story was the correct one: Thanh had died of a massive heart attack at his home at 34 Ly Nam De in Hanoi. He was stricken after a send-off dinner at Giap's residence as he prepared to return to the battlefields of the South.

Though Giap was blameless, a purge of "revisionists" began almost as soon as Thanh was laid to rest. By the end of the year, moderate officials had been targeted with three waves of arrests and expulsions that reached deep into Giap's inner circle, reassuring Mao's China, now swept up in the radical excesses of the Cultural Revolution, that Vietnam would not backslide into the Soviet camp. Most shocking of all, the "Revisionist Anti-Party Affair" culminated in a failed assassination attempt that December on Ho Chi Minh himself.

With all dissent eliminated, the Central Committee approved the final plan for the offensive in January, with Ho abstaining from the vote and Giap out of the way in Hungary "for medical treatment." The most radical elements of the plan were scaled back in a bow to realism— with one important exception. Quang Tri and Thua Thien would see the full force of the PAVN's elite combat units. Here at least the strategy of "annihilation" would prevail.

Manus Campbell arrived at Phu Bai with the war deadlocked and the cycle of destruction approaching its climax. In the two years since it was built, the base had been transformed into the headquarters of the Third Marine Division. It was now the size of a small town, with serried rows of barracks and a long runway, flanked by Route 1 and the north-south railroad tracks. The Rue Sans Joie was as perilous as ever. Bernard Fall, who had made the name famous in his book about the French War, *Street Without Joy*, had himself been killed there in February while accompanying a Marine patrol.

Campbell's first assignment took his unit to a spot on the southern outskirts of Hue where war and history intersected. Engineers had laid a narrow pontoon bridge across a bend in the Perfume River, half a mile upstream from the grandest of the tombs of the Nguyen imperial dynasty, the nineteenth-century mausoleum of the emperor Minh Mang. Near the bridge was a quarry known as the Rock Crusher, a good source of gravel for roadbuilding. There was also a small base occupied by ARVN troops and a local unit of the Regional Forces and Popular Forces, or RF/PF, who accompanied the Marines in the combined action platoons and were known with unconcealed contempt as the Ruff-Puffs.

The real significance of the bridge was that it marked the junction of the coastal highway and Route 547, a rough track that twisted its way westward through the mountains, offering the most direct and threatening path of access to Hue from the A Shau Valley.

In the fifteen months since the fall of the Special Forces base, the Americans had kept their distance from the A Shau, except for bombing raids and the insertion of small reconnaissance and guerrilla teams, which tended only to result in more ambushes, shot-down helicopters, and MIAs, not much in the way of useful intelligence, and no lasting presence on the ground. Whenever there was discussion of a renewed assault on the valley, the idea was dismissed. It was "nothing but a place for disasters to occur," said Lt. Col. Arthur J. Sullivan, commanding officer of the First Marine Reconnaissance Battalion.

The PAVN had made excellent use of those fifteen months. Trucks were rolling down the Trail in Laos in convoys of as many as a hundred at a time, traveling sixty kilometers or more in a night, lighting their way with bicycle lamps mounted under the front fender. No matter how intense the bombing, it did little to stop them. Labor gangs worked around the clock to repair damage, rarely taking more than twenty-four hours to fill bomb craters or bypass road cuts. Concealed antiaircraft batteries took a brutal toll of American fighter jets and helicopters. In the caves and tunnels of Con Tom Mountain, in the heart of the A Shau, the PAVN continued to turn Binh Tram 7 into its most heavily fortified redoubt in South Vietnam, a formidable arms and logistics depot, and a forward operating base for attacks on Hue and the coastal plain.

By the spring of 1967, North Vietnamese engineers had completed the cross-border road from La Hap to the A Shau, where it now intersected with the road through the valley. This was the first solid connection between the Trail in Laos and the road network inside South Vietnam, and when Westmoreland reviewed the evidence from aerial photographs, it might have been the first time he grasped the full strategic significance of the A Shau.

The PAVN's next steps were to work on a southward extension of what the Americans called the "Yellow Brick Road" through the A Shau, moving steadily closer to Danang, and to build out the connecting trails through the wild mountains to the east of the A Shau. A new shortcut would join Route 547 halfway to Hue, while a narrower trail, a dizzying series of switchback turns, headed for an old Viet Minh stronghold in the hills northwest of the city.

When bombs and defoliants failed to stop this inexorable progress, the air force reached even deeper into its box of technological tricks. If the nasty weather in Laos and the A Shau impeded its operations, American ingenuity would find new solutions. In July 1967, big C-130 transport planes began to drop fifty-pound paper sacks of powdered chemicals on the A Shau and the twenty-mile stretch of the Trail from La Hap to the border. The compound, which the aircrews called "soap" or "detergent," was a proprietary product of Dow Chemical. Acting through a process called chelation—literally "grabbing," or "binding"— the idea was to turn the earth into a sticky, clinging gumbo. "Make mud, not war," said Ambassador Sullivan in Vientiane. But the two-week-long operation, Commando Lava II, turned out to be another technological blind alley.

So did another secret experiment, this one code-named Popeye, which targeted the same areas. This also aimed to turn the Trail into a swamp, using a technique that had been invented by Kurt Vonnegut's elder brother, Bernard, and became familiar during drought periods in the American farm states: firing silver iodide into the clouds to make rain. But there was no real way to judge the success of the operation, and when the air force owned up to the project at a Senate hearing seven years later, it admitted that the results were "limited and unverifiable."

During that summer of 1967, at least another twenty thousand North Vietnamese fighters infiltrated from Laos, and Marine reconnaissance patrols reported a sharp increase in enemy forces in the hills west of Hue. The A Shau had become an intolerable threat, and no matter what horrors it portended, or how stretched his forces were, Westmoreland's thoughts began to turn to a new offensive that would regain a foothold in the valley.

The first priority in preparing the assault was to head off any enemy advance on Hue, which meant controlling as much of Route 547 as possible. While PAVN engineers were busy improving its western half, Campbell's company of Marines moved into the section that began at the Perfume River, assigned as a security detail for a team of engineers grading the road. This would allow mechanized troops to move westward as well as giving access to new firebases for heavy artillery with sufficient range to target the A Shau. The convergence of the two armies on the road from the valley was oddly like the two teams racing to finish the transcontinental railroad.

The operation had been under way for just a few days when Campbell arrived. It was an uncomfortable if deceptively uneventful start to his tour of duty. Temperatures rose well above one hundred degrees, with stifling humidity; many men were incapacitated by heatstroke. But there was only light contact with the enemy, occasional sniper fire or a couple of mortar rounds, a few prisoners captured and interrogated, an abandoned bunker blown up, a cache of rice destroyed. Work advanced steadily, helped along by intermittent airstrikes and artillery fire, and by the end of July, the Marines had lost just one man, with another twenty-five wounded in action.

Sent to fight in the country of the Apocalypse, the grunt didn't think much about the big picture. He existed simultaneously in multiple realities. The first was the world of grand abstractions that determined where he was sent and why—the domino theory, international Communism, the Free World. The second was the giant chessboard on which both sides moved him around along with all the other pawns, the squares constantly shifting size, shape, and color in response to invisible forces and the changing rhythms of the conflict. The third reality, the only one of which he had much conscious awareness, was defined by the minutiae of survival: rats and snakes and mosquitoes, dysentery and crotch-rot, his entrenching tool and his weapon. *Charlie is two klicks west of that ridgeline. Did we lose anyone today? Can I trust my lieutenant, who is only a couple of years older than I am? Above all, how many days until my DEROS?* Date of Expected Return from Overseas was a number that many Marines scrawled on their helmets.

What delicacies will today's C-rations have in store? A four-pack of frankfurters, the four fingers of death? Ham and lima beans, with a shot of Tabasco to disguise the taste? Universally known as ham and motherfuckers, these were sometimes bartered with the local Vietnamese, who developed an unaccountable taste for the things. Perhaps there would be yet another care package of chocolate-chip cookies from the Daughters of the American Revolution, which arrived in such quantities that you grew sick of them. W. D. Ehrhart fantasized about loading them into a mortar tube and firing them at Charlie, but he feared that Charlie might fire them straight back again.

The geography of a grunt's life was vague. You knew where you were based—Danang, Chu Lai, Phu Bai, Dong Ha—all suffused by the stink of human waste burning in trash barrels. But all the other singsong place names were hard to remember, and even if you were told the name of an operation, you didn't think much about its geography or purpose. There were only three exceptions to this rule. The name Khe Sanh was on everyone's lips after the bloody hill fights that spring. Con Thien, under unremitting fire from North Vietnamese mortar and artillery crews, was dominating national headlines. And above all there was the gnawing anxiety that you might be sent into the Valley of

Death, and that was what now awaited Campbell's battalion, together with a company of the ARVN's elite Black Panthers. This operation would be code-named Cloud.

Lt. Gen. Robert Cushman, Lew Walt's successor as commander of the marines in I Corps, had grave misgivings. The weather forecast for the A Shau was lousy—as usual—and there were few helicopters to spare, with most already committed to fighting along the DMZ.

The mantra of a search-and-destroy operation was "Find, Fix, Fight, Finish," but Cloud didn't even get past the finding stage, the initial reconnaissance of the target area. The planned insertion point was at the narrow southern end of the valley, close to the abandoned village where Colin Powell had supervised the 1963 crop-destruction missions. Small advance recon parties, code-named Party Line One and Mono Type II, set off in two big Sea Knight helicopters on consecutive days, August 1 and 2, planning to land a mile apart from each other.

From the start, everything went wrong. The PAVN had booby-trapped all the possible landing zones, so Party Line One had to set down in ten-foot-high elephant grass, smashing it flat with the helicopter tailgate. The marines made their way downhill through a landscape torn apart by aerial bombing, and in the predawn darkness the earth shook with new B-52 Arc Light strikes. The enemy was invisible and unknowable, as always. Any civilians remaining in the area were presumed to be hostile. On the second morning, the Marines stumbled on a trail and came under fire, radioed for extraction, and took shelter in a deep bomb crater as fighter jets and helicopter gunships strafed the surrounding hills.

From their nearby place of concealment, the six men from Mono Type II listened impotently as the relief chopper was shot down, killing the crew chief. "It always twists the guts out of a Recon team to listen to another team's being shot to hell the way Party Line was," wrote a Marine officer in an account of the abortive mission. Now another helicopter was needed to pick up the survivors. This also came under fire, but it managed to lurch away, badly damaged, leaving three of the men from Party Line One dead on the ground. Four members of Mono Type II were wounded when they were finally evacuated under heavy fire on the third day, by which time Operation Cloud had been called off. The bodies of the Marines were never recovered, adding to

the growing number of MIAs in the A Shau, which remained nothing
but a place where disasters occurred.

By the start of August, Campbell's unit, Alpha 1/4, had lost twenty-
two men, but in much of Thua Thien, the next couple of months were
unnervingly quiet again, and the company suffered only one more
KIA. By October, the battalion had moved to Camp Evans, a newly
built Marine base north of Hue, but the worst of the action at this
point was up along the DMZ, especially at Con Thien, and that was
what filled TV screens at home, adding new fuel to the antiwar fires.
On October 21, seventy thousand protesters marched on Washington,
angrier and more confrontational than before, chanting "Hell no, we
won't go." Regular troops from the 82nd Airborne joined the phalanx
of cops and MPs to form a protective ring around the Pentagon. Some
of the potential draftees pissed on the building; Allen Ginsberg and
Abbie Hoffman tried to levitate it; other demonstrators stuck flowers
in the gun barrels of the soldiers. Four days later Manus Campbell's
battalion was ordered into action, against another threat to Hue that
emanated from the A Shau. The operation, code-named Granite, was a
full-scale, two-battalion search-and-destroy mission.

Vietnam was above all a war of the unexpected, of being suddenly
engulfed in the terrifying violence of an ambush. The date and place
of that first frontal encounter with the enemy were hazy in Campbell's
memory, but the details were indelible—the chaos, the slaughter, the
sounds, the jolting flashbacks and nightmares that lasted for decades.
The battalion's meticulous hour-by-hour after-action reports made it
clear, however, that only one incident in those months matched his
description.

For weeks, Alpha Company had been carrying out "reconnaissance
in force" in the Co Bi-Thanh Tan Valley, about fifteen miles west of
Hue. They searched caves, blew up sampans on the Song Bo, a navi-
gable tributary of the Perfume River. A lieutenant was shot in the head
when he made the cardinal error of moving the company under cover
of darkness.

The valley and the surrounding foothills were no ordinary target.
Connected to the A Shau by the primitive, twisting back trail that the

PAVN called B71, this was Base Area 114, one of the "cradles of the revolution" in the 1950s and now home to thousands of PAVN and NLF fighters. The battalion was headed for nothing less than the command headquarters for the two northernmost provinces of I Corps, the PAVN's Tri-Thien Military District.

The entire valley had been classified by this time as a free-fire zone, the local villagers corralled into internment camps. Over the previous eighteen months, B-52 strikes had left a trail of craters along the valley floor. The topography was forbidding. One side of the meandering Song Bo was flanked by low, brush-covered rises, rice paddies, and irrigation ditches; the other by vine-tangled hills, dense forests, and sharp ridgelines. The dominant feature of the landscape was Hill 674, a steep-sided saddleback cut by small streams that made convenient pathways for enemy forces. At the summit was a radio relay site that a Marine reconnaissance patrol had managed to install there a year earlier.

Operation Granite began in the early hours of October 26. Bravo, Charlie, and Delta companies went in first, and Alpha was choppered in to reinforce them two days later. The weather was cool, humid, drizzly, and overcast. As usual, each man went clanking along well supplied with rifle rounds and M-26 fragmentation grenades and pop-up flares and entrenching tools, the nooks and crannies of his pack stuffed with mosquito repellent, antimalaria pills, antifungal foot powder, Chapsticks, cans of C-rations, rain ponchos, halazone tablets to purify drinking water, salt pills to prevent dehydration, letters from home, photographs of high school girlfriends, good luck charms. You tended to dispense with underwear; if it didn't give you crotch-rot, it quickly stank of diarrhea.

There were signs of heavy foot traffic, but the company kept well clear of the beaten paths for fear of ambush. In the dense undergrowth, the going was muddy and treacherous, the sodden ground infested with leeches, and they made painfully slow progress. Yet there was something perversely idyllic about the surroundings, Campbell remembered. "We would walk through the jungle, with these streams that were so pure and refreshing, and I would wonder if anyone else had ever ventured here."

Their advance was backed by five batteries of artillery, tanks, helicopter gunships, and fixed-wing airstrikes, even the modified AC-47 aircraft that the soldiers called Spooky, or Puff the Magic Dragon. Introduced just a month earlier, its three Gatling guns could each fire six thousand rounds a minute. With all of them firing in unison, this was enough to saturate a football field. Vietnamese fighters on the Ho Chi Minh Trail said that the sound of Spooky in action was the most terrifying in the world, "like the long scream of a cow being slaughtered."

Bravo Company had run into a large PAVN force on the second day and taken heavy casualties, nine dead and more than thirty wounded. Delta Company lost two of its own coming to their aid. But October 28 was quiet, and Campbell hoped the next day, which dawned sunny and mild, would be the same. One platoon from the Alpha Raiders was sent out to begin a sweep of the lower slopes of Hill 674, while his was held in reserve, providing security for the company commander, Capt. Charles Thompson, who was well liked by the men after organizing the evacuation of two dozen wounded Marines at Con Thien a few months earlier.

Campbell was close to the radio that day, always a vulnerable target because of its long, waving antenna. A little more than an hour after the first platoon set off, the radio crackled with the sound of automatic weapons. As the Marines approached one of those pure, refreshing mountain streams, they had walked straight into a carefully planned ambush, a nest of bunkers, booby traps, and snipers perched in trees to create an efficient killing zone.

No one ever forgot the spitting, crackling sound of an AK-47. "You could hear it in stereo," Campbell said, "AK-47s and M-16s talking shit on the radio and in the distance at the same time. And a voice, not a calm voice, calling for help, medevacs, backup. They were pinned down. Oh, shit, the mind starts to race. *Backup.* That would be us." Later he would witness even worse scenes of carnage, but he would be haunted for decades by the sound of that first firefight and the image of the American bodies his platoon found piled up on the stream bank, the water running red with their blood. A North Vietnamese soldier was using the corpses as a breastwork, and when he popped his head up, Campbell and two other Marines opened fire on him simultaneously. It was the first time he had shot a man, though like a member of a firing squad, he could never be sure whether the fatal bullet was his. But he was no longer an FNG.

The staggering firepower supporting the Marines hindered the operation on Hill 674 more than it helped. "In some instances the support was not completely satisfactory," the after-action report said, a bland understatement. There were so many aircraft in the skies that they interfered with artillery strikes; helicopters flew into the line of fire without warning; bombs missed their targets; radios were knocked out; men were wounded by friendly fire; medevac choppers were delayed.

Arriving with stretchers for the wounded, Delta Company found bunkers around the site of the ambush that had been pulverized in earlier airstrikes, burying their occupants. As dusk fell, the normally dispassionate report noted, "a heavy odor of death prevailed."

When it was over, there was a kind of collective adrenal crash. "Nobody talked," Campbell said. "We cleared trees to make a landing zone for the helicopters to take out the dead and wounded. We set up a security perimeter for the night. Inside, it's shut down, closed off. You put on the lock and forget the combination. You don't go there, and I don't want anyone to know that I've been there. It's all locked away, the sights, the sounds, the feelings. My youth. The screams of the dying and the screams of my own dying."

Alpha 1/4 lost nine men in the ambush that afternoon on Hill 674, none of them older than twenty-one. The eldest, Lance Cpl. Larry Havers of Allegany, New York, had married his hometown sweetheart, a girl named Cindy, just before shipping out. William Dykes, a cherub-faced twenty-year-old from Kingsport, Tennessee, had loved science in high school and hero-worshipped Roy Rogers, with whom he shared a birthday. He took a bullet in the back of the head as he ran to help a wounded buddy. Two of those who died had arrived in Vietnam in the same week as Campbell. One of them, Earnest Hinsley, a boy from the flyspeck town of Blossom, Texas, up near the Oklahoma line, was eighteen years and nine months old, though his sweet, ingenuous features made him look even younger. He had already picked up two Purple Hearts. Now it looked as if he was in line for a third. But this time the medics couldn't save him.

The battle, such as it was, did nothing to inflect the course of the war. It was shattering, life-defining for those who were there, but it merited no more than a footnote in the official histories. Set-piece horrors like Ia Drang and Con Thien made headlines and TV specials, but with the exception of two-paragraph obituaries in countless small-town papers, incidents like the bloodbath on Hill 674 passed largely unnoticed. Yet they were a telling indicator that these battalion-size operations in hostile territory often amounted to little more than blundering into well-laid traps.

"The forests protect our soldiers and encircle the enemy," General Giap had said. The PAVN and the NLF knew every tree, every path, every streambed, every place of concealment, and armed with this knowledge, they continued to dictate the terms of battle. Twenty-five Americans died on and around Hill 674 over those four days, another two were dead on arrival when the medevac choppers unloaded them at Phu Bai, and two days later Earnest Hinsley was gone. That made twenty-eight Marines altogether, with more than one hundred wounded. The after-action reports recorded just seventeen confirmed deaths on the other side, with another nineteen marked down as "probable," a category that was always open to question.

In later years, it became an article of faith that while the United States might have lost the war in Vietnam, it never lost a battle. But that was far from the truth, at least if you counted actions like this one, as the grunts did, as a battle. If a 10-to-1 kill ratio was Westmoreland's metric of success, the body count from the fighting on Hill 674 could only mark it down as a shattering defeat.

Orphans of Creation

A S MANUS CAMPBELL was fighting the war, Chuck Searcy was analyzing it. A photograph taken in Saigon shows him standing by
the coiled razor wire of a perimeter fence, dressed in olive-drab army
fatigues with the sleeves rolled up. A strikingly good-looking twenty-
two-year-old, he looks entirely at ease with the world, with the hint of
a half-smile.

His home for the next year was the cavernous warehouse of a
French-owned blanket factory between the Tan Son Nhut air base and
the Binh Loi bridge over the Saigon River, which carried the highway
to Bien Hoa, now the headquarters of the defoliation campaign. The
factory had been converted into a three-story barracks, with a tin roof
that turned it into an oven and no air conditioning. A small tributary
ran next to the compound, and to deny cover to the enemy its banks
were regularly sprayed with Agent Orange by helicopters, leaving the
vegetation dead and brittle and coating everything with a fine chemical film. But otherwise it was a pleasant neighborhood of small houses
and cafés, interspersed with rice paddies and banana trees. Old men
with wispy Ho Chi Minh beards sat around smoking, kids played in the
street, chickens ran around in backyards.

Each morning the hundred men of Searcy's 519th Military Intelligence Battalion were bused into the city to the blessedly cool offices
of the Combined Intelligence Center of Vietnam, CICV—pronounced
sick-vee. Its motto was "Strength Through Intelligence." Searcy put in

twelve-hour days, bent over his desk under the buzzing fluorescent lights, with a half-day off each week thanks to a sympathetic captain who kept the arrangement quiet. Sometimes you'd see combat troops in the street, fresh from the battlefield, mud still on their boots. Kids greeted them with cries of "G.I. Number One!" Seductive young women in miniskirts with American-style bob cuts and beehives called out to them from doorways on Tu Do Street, Graham Greene's Rue Catinat.

At night, when the enlisted men went back to their steam bath, the officers repaired to hotel rooms with air-conditioning, obliging maids, and daily laundry service. Visiting dignitaries whizzed around the city in black limousines, hidden behind blue curtains. Reporters went through the ritual of the daily military briefing at the Rex Hotel, the Five O'Clock Follies, where, as Westmoreland himself admitted, they often knew more than the briefers. After that they could stroll three blocks for drinks at the rooftop bar of the Caravelle. As the evening progressed, you could get a great steak and a Bloody Mary at the Auberge Ramuntcho before venturing out into a fantasyland of desirable and available women.

Each of the CICV analysts had a South Vietnamese counterpart, but they worked separately and never saw each other outside the office, even though there was no official order against fraternizing. For Searcy, this was uncomfortably reminiscent of the segregation he'd grown up with, and he set out to make Vietnamese friends. One of them was a cyclo driver who worked the streets around Tan Son Nhut. About the same age as Searcy, he was planning to marry. One Saturday, Searcy was pondering his plans for the evening: drinks at the enlisted men's club, maybe a movie, or perhaps just catch up on some reading. Then there was the jangle of a cyclo bell and an invitation to dinner. Why not? He liked the guy; there seemed no harm in it.

They drove for a long time through unfamiliar neighborhoods until they reached the outskirts of the city. Finally the driver stopped and led Searcy down a wooden plank walkway to a collection of ramshackle stilt houses on the Saigon River. His whole family was there: parents, brothers and sisters, prospective wife. They sat on the bamboo floor and ate dinner, drank a few beers. Local kids clustered in the doorway to observe the spectacle.

Next morning Searcy ran into his captain. *So what did you end up doing last night, Searcy?* He'd had an invitation to dinner at a friend's house and met his family, he said.

The officer looked aghast. *You mean a Vietnamese? Where was it?* He'd never heard such an outlandish idea. He strode over to a wall map of the city and told Searcy to try and retrace the route he'd taken. *Jesus Christ, Searcy, are you crazy? That whole area is crawling with VC. Everyone there is a sympathizer. You could have been killed!*

The thought had never crossed Searcy's mind. But perhaps he was just another innocent abroad: that, after all, was exactly what had happened to Alden Pyle in *The Quiet American.*

Searcy was part of a five-man team that had a direct line to the CICV director, processing raw intelligence that came up the food chain from the hundreds of analysts, covering everything from projections of the next rice harvest to the selection of targets for B-52 strikes. Diligent young USAID officials and high-priced consultants from the RAND Corporation with degrees in history, psychology, and anthropology produced reports and monthly assessments of the order of battle—the size, location, and organization of enemy forces.

One of Searcy's first assignments was to produce a handbook called *What a Platoon Leader Should Know About the Enemy's Jungle Tactics,* which was issued on October 12, 1967, over the signature of Brig. Gen. Phillip Davidson, Westmoreland's chief of intelligence. "Jungle ambushes are normally established on natural routes of movement like trails and streams," Searcy wrote. He described several typical scenarios, illustrating them with his own drawings. In one, "The enemy will use snipers to draw friendly forces into ambushes." Just two weeks after his handbook was issued, Alpha 1/4 Marines walked straight into just such an ambush on Hill 674. Searcy's war, and Campbell's, were two faces of the same coin.

It was tacitly understood that CICV's reports were not to be tainted by negativity. You always knew what your superiors were looking for: omit this, massage that, revise and rewrite in order to reflect the war that Washington liked to imagine rather than the one that was actually being fought.

If the news was bad, it could always be finessed. A report that same October, for example, summarized a survey of residents in the new

Cam Lo Government Resettlement Camp in Quang Tri, which housed people displaced from villages in the free-fire zone below the DMZ. The responses were disheartening: "Over 95% of the refugees felt that their present situation was worse than that existing before they moved to Cam Lo. . . . 95% of the refugees feel that their present housing is less comfortable than their premigration living quarters." It wasn't hard, however, to spin such discouraging data. One way was to shift refugee numbers from the "resident in VC-controlled areas" column to the "resident in government-controlled areas." This allowed them to be tabulated as "friendlies," although after being burned out of their homes *friendly* was perhaps not quite the right word. Alternatively, their sufferings could be laid at the door of the enemy. There had been no option but to move them into the camp for their own protection.

For a while, Searcy maintained enough faith in the integrity of his government that he saw the stumbles of the war effort as a matter of good intentions gone awry rather than outright lies, which would have implied malice. Americans didn't do malice. But in those waning months of 1967, the dissonance between truth and fiction became harder to ignore. After Thieu's fraudulent "re-election" in September, for instance, how could anyone keep up the pretense that the United States was in Vietnam to defend a democratic government?

CICV's upbeat reporting on Operation Ranch Hand was especially egregious, since the RAND Corporation was now pointing up some of its worst failings. Did defoliation even work?, its analysts asked. A spray run over dense jungle normally killed only the top layer of foliage, so the operation had to be repeated, often more than once, and in the tropical and subtropical climate the trees, vines, and bamboo thickets grew back quickly.

An October 1967 RAND report on crop destruction was especially damning. It concluded that the herbicide campaign was directly undermining the pacification effort. A compensation program was in place, but it was a sick joke: how was a peasant, more than likely illiterate, supposed to fill out a claim form for his losses and provide supporting documentation—eight copies, please—and pay a hefty "fee" to a corrupt local official for handling the paperwork?

Most problematic of all was the accounting of enemy dead, which was becoming a fraught issue in Washington. "It almost seemed like we'd killed more people than had ever been born in Vietnam," Searcy said, "and our operation went into serious meltdown." One CICV analyst went over the after-action reports carefully and concluded that the numbers were cooked. He was ordered to go back and work on it some more: *I guess you made a mistake, lieutenant. Keep reviewing those reports until you get it right.* But each time the man came back and said he saw no reason to alter his findings. Eventually he was relieved of his duties. *You obviously can't handle the pressure, lieutenant.* The whispers said he'd been referred for psychiatric evaluation.

When the war was over, many of the postmortems argued that these brightly burnished intelligence reports had contributed to its worst setbacks. One textbook that was later taught at West Point said they had lulled military planners into a false sense of security in the weeks leading up to the Tet Offensive, leading to an intelligence failure comparable to Pearl Harbor.

In fact, American officials had a good deal of advance knowledge of what was coming. They knew the PAVN was building a new shortcut from the A Shau Valley to Hue at breakneck speed. They knew the politburo had approved a plan for a nationwide military offensive and mass uprising. They knew Ho Chi Minh and Vo Nguyen Giap had strong reservations, that Giap was in Hungary "for medical treatment" and Ho had been in Beijing, "convalescing from illness."

The real issue, General Davidson wrote later, was that the plans for Tet seemed too crazy to be taken seriously. Attack one hundred targets in all parts of the country simultaneously? Expose massed military units whose specialty was concealment to devastating American firepower? The idea was absurd.

Perhaps the most extraordinary thing about the misreading of Tet was that Westmoreland and his generals had ignored Sun Tzu's first lesson of warfare: "Know your enemy." For years, Le Duan had exercised a kind of stealth leadership in Hanoi, with none of the inspirational visibility of Ho or Giap. When Westmoreland published his postwar memoir, *A Soldier Reports,* he made not a single mention, in 425 densely printed pages, of the man who was actually guiding Vietnam's revolutionary strategy. In the minds of the American media, Giap and Tet were synonymous, and when Westmoreland famously remarked that "life is cheap in the Orient," the insinuation was that it was the legendary general who was responsible for this barbarous philosophy. Nothing could have been further from the truth.

The real problem with Tet was not the lack of military intelligence but the gulf between private anxieties and public deception. McNamara, who had been agonizing about the war for more than two years, wrote a memo to Lyndon Johnson on November 1—tantamount to a letter of resignation—telling him plainly that the war could not be won "through any reasonable military means" and without unacceptable costs. Westmoreland himself told LBJ of his private misgivings, but the president had no intention of letting him express these publicly. On the contrary, he ordered Westmoreland to come to Washington and tell the public that things were going well. The result was his celebrated address to the National Press Club on November 21, in which he announced, "We have reached the important point where the end begins to come into view." He assured the public that the United States had never been bested on the battlefield—with, he allowed, one single exception: the rout of the Special Forces base at A Shau in March 1966. And that, in terms of its lasting impact, might have been the most significant battle of all. When Westmoreland met with Johnson on the day of the speech, much of the discussion was devoted to the A Shau and fresh plans to attack the valley as part of his preparations for an imagined invasion of Laos. But that, Westmoreland said, would require another 200,000 troops.

The analysts at CICV were not privy to these high-level intrigues, but they were bright young men, college graduates like those Searcy had met in training at Fort Holabird. They read the 1954 Geneva Accords, the speeches of Ho Chi Minh, the same increasingly skeptical newspaper and magazine stories and editorials that people were reading at home, and while few of them were brave enough to rock the boat in public, they shared their unease after work over drinks at the club.

Otherwise life in Saigon followed its own mundane daily rhythms. The shooting war could seem distant, even abstract. You had a couple of beers, went to a movie, shopped at the PX, found a girlfriend. One of Searcy's friends had a portable battery-operated record player, and they sat around one day under the American flagpole on the banks of the Saigon River, drunk and stoned, listening to *Sgt. Pepper.* Other than that, as he reached the midpoint of his tour of duty, the only real excitement was the Christmas 1967 USO concert with Bob Hope and Raquel Welch. She wore a blue miniskirt and white go-go boots and sang, "You and I travel to the beat of a different drum," and upped the testosterone level by inviting soldiers up on stage to dance the frug and the jerk and the watusi.

The night of January 30, 1968, seemed much like any other, although like LBJ in the Situation Room, everyone at CICV was anxiously following reports of the siege of the Marine Corps base at Khe Sanh, which had now entered its eleventh day. There was a sign at the entrance to the CICV building that showed the daily threat level: green, yellow, or red. They'd switched it to yellow, though that wasn't enough to get agitated about. It was the start of the annual Tet holiday, when everything shut down, people went home to celebrate with their families, and it was understood that the traditional ceasefire would be in effect everywhere but up north in Quang Tri province. Searcy went to bed as usual. If you heard a pop and a crackle in the night, it was probably just the usual celebratory fireworks to usher in the Lunar New Year.

There was no onstage dancing with Raquel Welch in Quang Tri, which was where Manus Campbell found himself in the weeks following the ambush on Hill 674, briefly dropped into the Marines' original tasks of perimeter defense and pacification. He was assigned to the big new combat base just outside Quang Tri city, on Route 1 five miles from the coast, which was still under construction by Navy Seabees. It came under mortar fire every night, and in the daytime Marine patrols scoured the surrounding countryside looking for the source, crisscrossing a landscape of flooded paddy fields and muddy dikes, poking around in clusters of primitive thatched hooches inhabited by incomprehensible people speaking an incomprehensible language, surrounded by menacing tree lines and hedgerows, a thousand hiding places for an almost-always-invisible enemy. You were constantly on the alert for all the things Searcy's handbook had warned about—snipers, hidden tripwires and detonator cords, camouflaged pits with shit-smeared punji sticks of stiletto-pointed bamboo—constantly learning new lessons about the nature of this strange war in which there were no front lines.

What you dreaded most was walking point, when it was your responsibility to detect danger. If you screwed up, the rest of the platoon would never trust you again. The iron rule was that everyone had to follow exactly in your footsteps, maintaining a safe and even distance between one man and the next, since a single bullet or grenade could kill or wound in multiples.

The nighttime attacks on the base were so aggravating that patrols went out at full company strength, 180 or 200 men, often heading out in the predawn hours. On one occasion it was Campbell's turn to walk point through a village called Ai Tu ("loving children" in Vietnamese). On the western edge of the Quang Tri base, it was a mile or so from the birthplace of Le Duan. Despite the iron rule of patrolling, Campbell's platoon sergeant had his own ideas, moving to the head of the column and blundering into a tripwire that was rigged to trigger an unexploded five-hundred-pound bomb. Remarkably, it failed to go off for the second time. Campbell yelled bloody murder at the man's stupidity.

On they went, through the village, until they came to a narrow bamboo bridge over a stream. Campbell motioned for the column to stop. The bridge made him nervous; better to wade across. Again the sergeant preferred to trust his own judgment. This time the booby trap he tripped was a hand grenade, and it was too much to expect to be lucky twice. Four men were wounded, including the soldier walking next to Campbell.

There were two things a Marine learned quickly in Vietnam. One was that you could never take it for granted that your superiors knew what they were doing. *What's the difference between the Marine Corps and the Boy Scouts? The Boy Scouts have adult leadership.* The other lesson was delivered for a second time later that day. Approaching a low rise, Alpha Company came under fire from invisible snipers and then from automatic weapons. Campbell threw himself to the ground, his head pressed up against the foot of another Marine. There was a sudden jolting impact and a cry of pain; the man had taken a bullet through that foot. It might just as well have been Campbell's head. "I learned that day that life in wartime is a matter of inches," he said. "You haven't really lived until you've almost died: that was something a lot of the guys wrote on their helmets." Still a nominal Catholic, he might have had the same thought as Karl Marlantes: was it luck, or was it grace? "The one true god of modern warfare," Philip Caputo wrote, "is blind chance."

Alpha Company shuttled for a few weeks between Quang Tri city and the larger Marine base at Dong Ha, two or three miles away, the command-and-control center for operations along the DMZ. Dong Ha anchored the southeastern corner of what came to be known as Leatherneck Square, a rough quadrilateral of four Marine bases: the other three were Cam Lo, Gio Linh, and the most famous of them all, Con Thien, "the Hill of Angels," the only place whose reputation was now grim enough to rival that of the A Shau Valley. It was to Con Thien that Campbell's company was sent next, at the end of November, a month shy of his twentieth birthday.

Like Khe Sanh, the base had been built originally for the Green Berets, but the Marines had taken it over in the summer of 1966, after the PAVN infiltrated one of its formidable "Steel and Iron" divisions across the DMZ. Westmoreland's response was Operation Hastings, the biggest of the war to date, followed by Operation Prairie, a series of search-and-destroy missions that flooded Quang Tri with Marines and led to a relentless demand for body bags—1,419 by the time the campaign was over.

In February 1967, Westmoreland authorized the first shelling of the DMZ, using a "firing fan" of artillery led by the battery of huge 175-mm self-propelled guns at Camp Carroll, on a hilltop near Cam Lo. On March 30, Leatherneck Square was designated "Priority One Defoliation Task," and the C-123s began to saturate it with tens of thousands of gallons of chemicals. The entire area was turned into a free-fire zone, blasted by B-52 strikes and artillery barrages, the villages burned and their inhabitants shepherded, often at gunpoint and with no advance warning, into the wretched resettlement camp in Cam Lo town, where they were confined under curfew.

They started off in tents, then built huts from whatever castoffs they could scavenge from the dump at the American base. Some looked like mosaic billboards advertising Schlitz and Pabst and Budweiser. The grunts called the place Tin City. Some of the Marines found it an opportunity for a little comic relief, one recalled. Kids would line up along the road begging for food, and you'd collect your heaviest C-rat cans—spaghetti and meatballs, ham and motherfuckers—and sling them at their heads, or try to knock them off their bicycles.

On May 7, the thirteenth anniversary of the French defeat at Dien Bien Phu, Alpha and Delta companies of the 1/4 Marines moved in to strengthen the defense of Con Thien. At four a.m. the next day, following an artillery barrage, two PAVN battalions stormed the base, an attack that degenerated into savage hand-to-hand combat—"grabbing the enemy by the belt." Five hours later, forty-four Marines were dead. Westmoreland immediately lifted the prohibition on ground incursions into the southern half of the DMZ, but by August the PAVN had tightened the screw further, severing Route 9 east of Khe Sanh, seizing control of the western half of the road, all the way to the Lao border, cutting off the base from resupply by land and giving themselves breathing room to carve out new spurs of the Ho Chi Minh Trail.

Con Thien was a battlefield like no other in Vietnam. Less than two miles from the DMZ, and eight miles north of Cam Lo, the base was perched on three low, humpbacked hills that rose five hundred feet above the plain. It was essentially a human tripwire, designed to block further North Vietnamese incursions. Stripped bare by bulldozers, it offered an unobstructed view into North Vietnam, but while you looked out on the enemy through your binoculars, he was looking at you through his. Its exposed position meant that Con Thien was all but indefensible, and it became target practice for PAVN heavy artillery that could be rolled in and out of caves in the hills to the north before there was time to call in an airstrike. Visiting reporters, looking at the warren of bunkers and trenches and rusty barbed wire, separated from the enemy by a desolate no-man's-land, compared Con Thien to Verdun. The grunts called it Disneyland.

Marine commanders detested Con Thien. The base was anathema to the doctrines and traditions of the corps. Squatting in a hole in the ground under mortar fire was not how they had conquered the Halls of Montezuma or the Shores of Tripoli. But Westmoreland had little patience with their grumbling.

In September the siege intensified, and the onset of the fall rains turned the choking red dust of summer into squelching, ankle-deep muck that one Marine likened to melted Hershey bars. Reporters flocked to the base, telling the folks back home that Con Thien was the latest word for *hell* in Vietnamese. David Douglas Duncan's cover portrait for *Life* magazine of a Marine, eyes frozen in fear, became one of the war's most iconic images. CBS News suspended its regular programming for a half-hour special on the siege. Its baby-faced correspondent John Laurence, who looked young enough to be a grunt himself, reported that the new military doctrine known as Mobile Defense "seems to mean putting 3,000 men on the ground and allowing them to sit in the mud and wait for the shell with their name on it."

By the time Manus Campbell's contingent from Alpha 1/4 arrived at Con Thien in the chill, foggy damp of late November, part of Operation Kentucky V, the joke among the grunts they relieved was that the initials DMZ stood for "Dead Marine Zone." One of them scrawled a poem on the back of his flak jacket:

Born of indignation
Children of our time
We were orphans of creation
And dying in our prime.

8

"This Is Not a Practice"

THE MAIN RATIONALE for Con Thien's growth from a Green Beret outpost to a major Marine Corps installation was that the bluntest instrument of destruction, aerial bombing, had failed. It had neither bludgeoned North Vietnam into submission, nor blocked infiltration across the DMZ, nor prevented the trucks from rolling down the Ho Chi Minh Trail. In the summer of 1966, McNamara commissioned a secret seminar of forty-seven scientists, "the cream of the scholarly community in technical fields," to study the problem. Perhaps technology could provide the solution, they suggested, combined with more intensive defoliation and "area-denial weapons." Why not build a fence, part physical and part virtual, all the way across the DMZ and the Trail in Laos? Their "fence" not only threw Manus Campbell into the horrors of combat on the DMZ; it marked the birth of a whole new conception of warfare, the electronic battlefield.

Marine engineers began work on the project in April 1967. Informally it came to be known as "the McNamara Line," and in the end most people simply wrote it off as McNamara's Folly. Marine commanders could barely conceal their disdain for the plan, which tied down several precious battalions of infantry, two of which were deployed for the sole purpose of guarding two battalions of engineers charged with executing a project that probably wouldn't work anyway.

Along its eastern half, in the low, brushy farm country of Leatherneck Square, the McNamara Line relied on traditional technologies.

Bulldozers and chainsaws cleared a naked strip, between 600 and 1,000 meters wide, like the world's biggest golf fairway, dotted with watchtowers, minefields, barbed-wire barriers, and other obstructions. The Trace, as it was known, was fortified by the Strong Point Obstacle System, with fixed positions numbered from A-1 to A-6 and C-1 through C-4. Con Thien itself was A-4, with a command post near the perimeter wire that was designated "Yankee Station." For six months, the Trace would circumscribe the horizons of Manus Campbell's universe.

In the mountainous west of Quang Tri, and on the Lao side of the border, the rugged topography dictated a very different approach, based on electronic surveillance. Although Westmoreland was a creature of World War II and the conventions of armor and infantry, he became enamored of the idea, envisioning after his return from Vietnam a future army "built into and around an integrated area control system that exploits the advanced technology of communications, sensors, fire direction, and the required automatic data processing."

The imaginative powers of the project verged on science fiction. Aircraft dropped a jaw-dropping variety of state-of-the-art sensors, twenty thousand in all, along the DMZ and the Lao border. "We wire the Ho Chi Minh Trail like a drugstore pinball machine and we plug it in every night," said one air force officer. These sensors could "detect anything that perspires, moves, carries metal, makes a noise, or is hotter or colder than its surroundings." The information they collected was relayed to circling aircraft called Batcats and fed into IBM mainframe computers, the most powerful in the world, at a command and control center in Thailand. Complex algorithms translated raw electronic data into brute force. Operatives watching real-time movements on TV screens could call in airstrikes within five minutes of "target acquisition." Sometimes it was as little as two "from the beep to the boom."

Among the high-tech exotica was a sensor called the Acoubuoy, which hung up in the trees to eavesdrop on every hostile cough and sneeze. The Black Crow could pick up the rumble of a truck engine several miles away. The Turdsid was named for its shape. A "people-sniffer" homed in on the smell of sweat and urine, though the PAVN learned to use buckets as toilets and hang them in trees at a safe dis-

tance. The Marines joked that all these gizmos did a great job of locat-
ing and blowing up any wandering elephants and water buffalo, and
when the war was over, they left behind other piles of scrap metal on
top of the millions of unexploded bombs, shells, grenades, landmines,
and other munitions that already cluttered the landscape.

But the whole project had a basic conceptual flaw. Its purpose, like
that of the secret Green Beret incursions into Laos, was to find more
targets in order to unleash more bombs. Yet the whole rationale for the
McNamara Line had originated in his fear that no amount of bombing
could ever win the war. It could only drag it out for longer. And North
Vietnamese troops continued to surge down the Trail.

Alpha 1/4 was shunted around from one of McNamara's Strong Points
to another. You always seemed to be either in a fighting hole or in a
helicopter. You dug a hole, lived in a hole, and slept in a hole, which
you shared with rats that were two feet long from nose to tail tip. "We
had a real battle with the rats," said one Marine. "They'd keep you from
sleeping, they'd piss all over your gear, fight you when you confronted
them." Some of them carried bubonic plague, and that winter of 1967
brought an outbreak in Cam Ranh, home of the great American naval
base. You killed as many of the creatures as you could, and in the
morning you strung up the trophies outside your bunker. Campbell's
commanding officer organized competitions. Catch a rat, put it in a
cage, douse it with gasoline, set fire to it, open the cage door, see how
far it could run.

Campbell's first full month at Con Thien was a bad one, though
the same could have been said of most months there. On the cold,
rainy afternoon of December 6, out in the open at a perimeter line
they'd established a mile east of the base, his unit walked into a barrage
of mortars and rocket-propelled grenades. A big Choctaw medevac
helicopter was shot down. An A-6 Intruder, famed for its accuracy,
came streaking in over the battlefield and dropped its payload on
the Marine positions. Six men were killed that afternoon, and thirty-
seven wounded. One of the dead, hit in the chest by shrapnel, was
Staff Sgt. Junior Schriner from Lancaster, Ohio. "He was a prince,"
Campbell remembered. "Everyone loved him." He had only a few days

left to serve. The cause of death was recorded as "short round"—the official euphemism for friendly fire, which was something of a euphemism in itself.

On another day, word came that a PAVN advance unit had taken a nearby hilltop, and Alpha Company was given the order to storm it and drive them out. Expecting to come under fire, they reached the top without incident. They found nothing but some unoccupied fighting holes and dug in. All they had accomplished was to make themselves targets, and the barrage of artillery and mortars began. *Incoming* became the most important word in the vocabulary of the Marines at Con Thien. There was something uniquely unnerving about mortar attacks, because they were so arbitrary and unpredictable. You were always on edge, never knowing when the next one would come or where it would land. There was just the dull thump, and then the whistle, and you had only a few seconds to dive for cover. Hunkered down in his hole that night, Campbell had a silent conversation with God: *Please, Lord, let me live, and I will take down my Playboy centerfolds.* It was the last talk he had with God for many years.

Meanwhile the B-52s, invisible and inaudible, made the earth tremble from bombs that fell miles away. The C-123s droned low overhead in formation, trailing their white spray. In the raging postwar debate about the exposure of troops to the defoliants, the air force insisted that each mission was checked out in advance by a forward air controller to make sure no Americans were in the vicinity. Yet buried away in the papers of Col. Alvin Young, the air force's principal toxicologist, was a map showing four flights right over the fixed Marine positions on the McNamara Line between December 1967 and March 1968. Other declassified air force records showed at least two more on December 16 and 20, dumping a combined 5,700 gallons.

Campbell's twentieth birthday fell on the twenty-second, and that night, as he stood guard duty with two other men asleep beside him, a mortar round slammed into the sandbagged roof of their bunker. Two feet to the right, and it would have gone in through the open entrance, surely killing them all. It was the same lesson, endlessly repeated: survival in combat was a matter of inches and feet and usually just dumb luck. Early the next morning another Ranch Hand flight went over, a few hundred yards from Con Thien, three thousand gallons this time.

"A lot of racist shit went down in the war," Campbell said, especially during the long months at Con Thien. Southern whites favored country-and-western music and sometimes flew the battle flag of the Confederacy. Black Marines kept largely to their own bunkers, blasting out Otis Redding and Wilson Pickett and James Brown, with their own subculture, the dap and the Black Power handshake. After the assassination of Martin Luther King, Jr., on April 4, 1968, the tensions grew worse. A white officer in Quang Tri was shot dead after demanding that a group of Black soldiers turn down their stereo.

Occasionally a chopper took you back to Dong Ha for a day or two, where there were tents and cots to sleep in, and a mess hall with hot food and cold beer. When you fantasized about going back to The World, which you did constantly as the magic day approached, much of the talk was about what you planned to eat, how much beer you would drink, how many girls you would have, how many you had had already in Manila or Hong Kong or Bangkok during R&R, which some people called Rape and Run, although others preferred I&I, Intercourse and Inebriation. Sometimes you worried that the girls back home, knees clenched together as they waited for early marriage, could never measure up to the LBFMs, the Little Brown Fucking Machines, who could always be found hanging around the base perimeter. Others quietly read letters from wives or high school sweethearts, and as in any war, a lot of them were Dear Johns. You listened to tapes from your family, who never quite knew what to say, and passed around cookies and chocolate and birthday cakes that came in their care packages.

All-volunteer kill teams—"guys who had seen too many John Wayne movies," Campbell called them—sneaked out into the DMZ at night for quick hit-and-run raids. Alpha Company was sent out into the bush for days at a time, watching the hedgerows and ridgelines, wading through irrigation ditches, digging holes to sleep in, hunting for the elusive enemy. Sometimes you found him, and other times he found you first. You might locate a complex of bunkers and tunnels and blow it up, or come upon a mass grave of North Vietnamese soldiers and dig up the putrid bodies to count the confirmed KIAs. Often you saw more monkeys than men.

Eventually the men of Alpha 1/4 spent so much time in the bush that they got a unit citation for their powers of endurance. They heard the politicians talk about the light at the end of the tunnel, but to the Marines of I Corps, it was as convincing as the sign in the bar that always says Free Beer Tomorrow.

By early 1968, the horrors of Con Thien were the day before yesterday's news. TV viewers at home had learned new synonyms for *hell*: Hue and Khe Sanh.

On January 20, the PAVN launched the all-out assault on the huge Marine base that Westmoreland had been anticipating, even perversely looking forward to. A week later Soviet-supplied amphibious tanks crossed the Lao border and overran the Special Forces camp at Lang Vei on Route 9, seven miles from the Khe Sanh base.

The attack on Khe Sanh was a feint, designed to draw even more Marines away from the strategic coastal cities of I Corps. But for Westmoreland, it was the defining act in the drama, his opportunity to replay the siege of Dien Bien Phu. The enemy would throw their full weight against the base, and he would crush them. The French commanders, after all, had not had the benefit of B-52s or F-4 Phantoms or rainbow herbicides, let alone the arcane new technologies dreamed up by his scientists. If there was a serious threat that Khe Sanh might fall, he was prepared to resort to tactical nuclear weapons. "Although I recognized the controversial nature of the subject," he said—a strikingly understated choice of words—the willingness to use such extreme measures would "tell Hanoi something . . . just as the two atomic weapons had spoken convincingly to Japanese officials during World War II." Without informing the White House, he put together a secret plan, codenamed Operation Fracture Jaw, that included moving nuclear arms to South Vietnam so that they could be used at short notice. But National Security Adviser Walt Rostow got wind of it and fired off a memo to the president, who was infuriated, and the plan was quickly canceled.

As Tet approached, Quang Tri and Thua Thien were the only targets that really kept Westmoreland up at night, and with good reason. They turned out to be the only two provinces where the PAVN committed its own regular forces—elsewhere the NLF, the Viet Cong, took the lead. Khe Sanh and Hue were the defining encounters of Tet, and with five battalions of Marines now tied down at the base and more holding down the McNamara Line, there were none left over to block the advance on Hue by PAVN troops, the equivalent of a full division, who held uncontested control of the A Shau Valley. Others converged on the city from Base Area 114, where Campbell had endured the nightmare of the "stream fight" on Hill 674.

Yet in one of the stranger ironies of Campbell's thirteen months in Vietnam, the Tet Offensive was one of the quietest times he could remember. Con Thien itself was not a target. Alpha 1/4 was sent to Cam Lo for mopping-up operations after a suicidal North Vietnamese attack on the Marine headquarters there, but the slaughter was over by the time they arrived. His company heard news of the larger dramas unfolding at Khe Sanh and in Hue, but the grunts along the Trace were not touched by these events.

Paradoxically, Tet was the one time when Chuck Searcy personally experienced the violent reality of the war. He was awakened in the middle of the night by the alert siren at the blanket factory. There were the usual groans and complaints, because everyone knew the routine by now. You dragged yourself out of bed, pulled on all your gear, grabbed your heavy M-14, stumbled out to the perimeter for the practice drill, waited until the all-clear was sounded, and then went back to bed.

But this time was different. A captain in Searcy's battalion was zipping around the compound in a jeep, bellowing into a bullhorn, "This is not a practice, repeat, this is not a practice!" In the faint pre-dawn light, Searcy could see plumes of smoke rising in the distance. The war had come to Saigon.

The captain had his radio tuned to a channel that allowed him to communicate with the pilot of a helicopter that had appeared overhead, carrying relief troops from the 101st Airborne to resecure the U.S. embassy, which had been attacked by a squad of NLF commandos at a little before three a.m. The problem was that the pilot was lost. Half a million troops in Vietnam, and the relief of the embassy was in the hands of someone who had been in country for two weeks and had never been to Saigon. So the captain was marking instructions for him on the squawk box: *Do you see the church? Okay, then turn east from there, hang a right two blocks, maybe three, and you should see the embassy.* As soon as the chopper wheeled away, it started to take ground fire.

What remained with Searcy after Tet was not only these sometimes farcical aspects of military conduct, but the sheer scale of the destruction that was unleashed in response. His neighborhood was an escape route for Viet Cong fleeing Saigon, and for many days, he watched the spectacular lightshow over the city, the flash of fighter jets and the throb of helicopters, and listened to the deep *crump* of artillery, the chatter of heavy machine-guns, and the crackle of small-arms fire. Most of it bypassed the CICV compound and offices, although one of Searcy's fellow intelligence analysts took a direct hit from a rocket fired by an American helicopter when he volunteered to go into the field with a combat unit, lost both legs, and died in surgery. Searcy never got used to the sight of someone else sleeping in his vacated bed.

Although the compound itself was undamaged, little remained of the surrounding neighborhood but blackened rubble. Refugees flooded the streets, carrying their possessions on their backs like beasts of burden. An estimated 6,300 civilians died in Saigon in the reprisals that followed Tet. It was "in the nature of a reflex," Neil Sheehan wrote, "to turn loose on the urban centers the 'stomp-them-to-death' firepower that had brutalized the Vietnamese countryside."

After weeks of bloody street fighting, the NLF flag was finally torn down from the flagpole atop the citadel in Hue. By March 3, the last of the resistance had been overcome, though half the city and much of the citadel, which housed thousands of residents in its warren of streets and alleyways, lay in ruins.

It was another five weeks before Khe Sanh was at last relieved, though the pressure had long since relented as the battered PAVN forces pulled back to their sanctuaries. By that time, the B-52s alone had dropped almost 100,000 tons of ordnance on the surrounding hills, the biggest such campaign in history against a single tactical target. For its constant cascade of bombs, it was called Operation Niagara.

All parties delivered their own verdict on Tet. Westmoreland insisted that it was a resounding victory, which was true enough in a strictly military sense. Le Duan proclaimed a political triumph because the offensive had broken America's will to win, which was also accurate, but the revolutionary forces had suffered hideous losses, perhaps forty thousand dead, and the NLF never recovered from the battering it took.

The internal postmortems were devastating. As Ho and Giap had warned, there had been an excess of "subjectivity"—something close to reckless arrogance. The worst consequences of this had unfolded in the Tri-Thien Military District, where the regional party committees had balked at the orders from Hanoi, pleading for the offensive to be put off until the spring. "We did not have a firm grasp of the situation, our preparations had been cursory," the PAVN later acknowledged in its official history of the war. The expected mass uprisings had not materialized. In Quang Tri, wrote a CIA analyst with a purple pen, "The people, some of whom were mugwumps before, have hardened against [the enemy's] cynical and bloodthirsty visage."

On the American side, the true shock of Tet was not for the generals, who had at least half-expected the offensive, even if they didn't anticipate its full sweep. It was for the American public, who had been fed a steady diet of assurances about how well the war was going. "Populists like to speak of the 'wisdom of the people,'" wrote Barbara Tuchman. "The American people were not so much wise as fed up, which in certain cases is a kind of wisdom."

Henry Kissinger, still a Harvard professor, admitted privately that the war was hopeless and that no vital national interests were at stake—other than American credibility. In a conversation with Kenneth Waltz, a professor at Swarthmore College and a distinguished theorist of international relations, he said the United States could not cut and run. "If we get out of Vietnam, just withdraw, the McCarthy period in politics will pale into insignificance," he told Waltz. "American society will just blow up. There will be such recriminations, because we will be seen as having sold out."

But Tet was the beginning of the end of the American project in Vietnam, and that had to be explained. Right-wing military leaders came up with something akin to the *Dolchstoss* theory—the stab-in-the-back—that followed Germany's defeat in World War I. Faithless civilians, cowardly politicians, and treasonous journalists, exemplified by the CBS anchor Walter Cronkite, had forced the troops to fight with one hand tied behind their backs, even if the free hand wielded every tool technology could muster.

The loudest proponents of this thesis were bomber pilots operating out of Thailand, officers in the Green Berets and the airborne divisions and the clandestine MACV-SOG units—those whose wartime experience, in other words, had been focused on the Ho Chi Minh Trail and the border areas of Laos and Cambodia. If they had a godfather figure, it was Col. (later Maj. Gen.) Jack Singlaub, the overall commander of the secret war on the Trail. Their enduring bitterness and the conspiracy theories they fostered, crystallizing into a hatred of what they would call the Deep State and the Fake News, would infect American politics for decades.

Like everyone, Chuck Searcy and his fellow intelligence analysts at CICV saw Lyndon Johnson's televised speech on March 31, when he announced, "I shall not seek, nor will I accept" nomination for a second term as president. "The air seemed palpably cleaner in Saigon," Searcy recalled. "The sun was gentler, there were smiles and high-fives among the GIs in my unit. Even the officers were grinning."

But then, just four days later, came news of the assassination of Martin Luther King, Jr. In the weeks of riots that followed, Searcy wandered around in a daze, caught up in a bad movie and struggling to find the exit door. He went through the motions at work, counting down the days to his Date of Expected Return from Overseas, looking forward to completing the final year of his enlistment at U.S. Army headquarters in Germany, far from the war.

On June 6, with his DEROS nine days away, he found himself in a payroll center in downtown Saigon, surrounded by clerks tapping away at adding machines as lines of other GIs processed out, collecting their final cash payments or converting military scrip into real dollars. Transistor radios, as usual, were tuned to the Armed Forces Network, when the broadcast was interrupted by a news flash. Bobby Kennedy was dead in Los Angeles. Searcy felt his knees buckle. "Fuck," someone muttered, "what are we going back to?"

At that same moment, Manus Campbell was also absorbing the news, sitting on a hilltop six hundred miles away, gazing out over the beautiful, treacherous, impossibly green mountains on the Lao border. His reaction to the RFK assassination, he remembered, was almost identical, word for word: *What kind of country are we going back to?* But while Searcy was on his way out, the Marines had their thirteen-month curse, and Campbell still had another month to go. In some ways it would be the worst of them all.

"Tonight You Die, Marine"

THERE WAS ONE final respite from the alien hellscape of the war. Campbell had already had one spell of R&R, a couple of days in country in Danang, watching the drunken South Korean troops holding kung fu competitions on China Beach. Now he was entitled to another, making his choice, like all the other guys, on the basis of the swaggering reports brought back by others. He opted for Bangkok.

The shuttle buses were stacked high with cases of beer. Boom-boom with a girl from one of the go-go bars on Patpong Road cost twelve dollars. If you wanted more, you could head for a massage parlor and make your selection from the seated rows of beautiful and compliant young women in a glass-walled fishbowl. That would cost you twenty-five dollars for the whole day, a portion of which would go to feed a hungry family upcountry.

But Campbell was depressed and couldn't relax. He sat in his hotel room and watched the latest news from Vietnam on the black and white TV set, dreading his return. *A year down, a few more weeks to go, and here I am, deep in the shit.*

Even if you wanted to, it was impossible to put yourself in the shoes of those fighting on the other side, to imagine that they might feel the same way. The dehumanization of the Other in wartime is universal, and the PAVN were schooled to see American devils, imperialists, and puppets. But fear is also universal. Fighters on the Ho Chi Minh Trail were as terrified of bombing raids as the Marines were of sudden ambushes, and both sides feared the darkness above all. For Americans, the most nightmarish attacks were those that came silently before dawn, as they did at A Shau and Con Thien. On the Ho Chi Minh Trail, the night bombings were the worst, lit by the surreal glare of flares drifting down on their miniature parachutes and the streak of red tracer rounds. The ingenious new weapons devised by McNamara's scientists made each southward footstep a deadly risk—gravel mines that looked like teabags, "dragontooth" bombs shaped like butterfly wings, button bomblets disguised as animal droppings, tentacle mines that threw out snare lines twenty-five feet long.

For the Vietnamese, there was the additional dread of unquiet ghosts, the deep-seated belief that death had to be followed by a reverent funeral and a known place of rest. In Bao Ninh's classic antiwar novel, *The Sorrow of War,* his narrator, Kien, searches for those missing in action on the haunted battlefield, which he calls the Jungle of Screaming Souls. In the latter part of the war, the U.S. Army's Sixth Psychological Operations Battalion played on those fears, producing a "ghost tape" that helicopters broadcast at night over the jungle, with echoing haunted-house wails and screams and the weeping of children unable to give their fathers a proper burial. The operation was called Wandering Soul.

There was no lack of romantic idealism on the part of the young North Vietnamese fighters, and no shortage of wooden propaganda exalting martyrdom from the commissars attached to each unit. Westmoreland might have believed that "life is cheap in the Orient," but losing a friend was every bit as traumatic for a Vietnamese as it was for an American. Diaries from the Trail describe elaborate funeral services and weeping mourners. Name, date of birth, and hometown or village were written on a slip of paper, sealed up in an empty medicine vial and placed in the mouth to protect it from insects. The corpse was wrapped in a hammock and buried with the head facing east, to the sunrise and the homeland. Seven rifle shots were fired over the grave, a number that can be auspicious but is also associated with ghosts and spirits. The way stations on the Trail had their own cemeteries, the graves arranged in neat rows in the forest.

Other things were constants in any war. There were no go-go bars on the Trail, but there were thousands of young women volunteers, and despite the party's puritanical insistence on celibacy, people found love in the mountains, or just the heat of another body, and there were pregnancies. Abusive officers extracted sexual favors, and a small number of the young women sold their bodies—not so they could send money home to their families upcountry, or buy makeup and a hairdo like the bar girls of Patpong, but in exchange for food, although the monotonous diet of rice, powdered eggs, dried fish sauce, and canned meat was no more appealing than ham and motherfuckers were to the Marines.

To celebrate Tet there might be the luxury of fresh pork, and the fighters would strip off tree bark to make ornamental flowers for the festival. But hunger was the norm. Sometimes they were so desperate that they would barter weapons for rice or corn from local villagers, on condition that it could only be a weapon captured from the enemy. They dug wild roots, ate leaves and herbs, even scraped algae from the rocks. They fished and hunted. No minnow was too small to eat. A poet named Nguyen Xuan Duy remembered the vile taste of elephant meat. The only part worth eating was the heart, he wrote, and it was hard to get at: "The best way was to put a grenade inside its stomach and explode it."

The everyday physical hardships were often greater for fighters on the Trail than for the Marines. American soldiers labored under seventy- and eighty-pound packs, but those carried by the smaller Vietnamese were just as heavy. People were desperate to shed every ounce possible; some cut off pockets and zippers and belting, the sleeves of their shirts and the legs from their pants. Everything came from China—the rice, the hammocks, the walkie-talkies, the helmets with their red and gold star, the medicines and water-sterilization tablets, the masks they wore as protection against the spray planes, copies of Mao's *Little Red Book*. "It was the thoughts of Chairman Mao," Duy said, "but we threw away the thoughts and kept the cover as a purse."

Yet there were consolations, and it's not sentimental to say there were moments of sweetness and poignancy. One man who spent twelve years on the Trail and was wounded four times taught himself to whistle hundreds of birdsongs, a substitute for those that had been silenced by the bombing and spraying. One porter carried a copy of the poems of Walt Whitman in his rucksack and recited verses.

All goes onward and outward, nothing collapses,
And to die is different from what anyone supposed, and luckier.

He was excited when his unit captured an American prisoner near Khe Sanh. He asked the GI what he thought of "Song of Myself," but the man had never heard of Whitman.

Marching at ten or twelve kilometers a day, it was a long, hard slog from one binh tram to the next, with rest stops at the way stations, where you could get medicines and ginseng and vitamin pills. These could be welcoming places, even improbably bucolic. Sometimes they had a little bamboo gate with a hanging sign, and flat rocks for serving tea. Some had a resident bicycle repair expert, others a ferryman or an elephant trainer. For entertainment, there were theater troupes and musicians who performed under the bombs. The fighters would sometimes construct a dummy of President Thieu, string it up from a branch like a monstrous piñata, and hurl stones and shrapnel at it. The Trail had its own newspaper, *Truong Son Gang Thep* (Long Mountain Iron and Steel), with a special edition for troops in the A Shau Valley.

Above all there was boundless inventiveness. Truck drivers learned that they could patch a punctured tire with the skin of a frog or toad. Soldiers mastered the art of blacksmithing. They fashioned cookstoves from the wreckage of trucks. The wings of crashed American aircraft made good meeting tables. Flare tubes, which were made of flexible aluminum, became combs and glasses cases, spokes and mudguards for damaged bicycles. It was the birth of a cottage industry in scrap metal that sustained poor farmers in Quang Tri and Thua Thien for decades after the war. It still defines much of daily life in the ethnic minority villages of Laos.

The months after the Tet Offensive were the hardest. Even though the commissars lauded it as a political triumph, no amount of propaganda could conceal its devastating human consequences as the survivors retreated to the mountains to regroup. Rank-and-file troops openly criticized their commanders, and perhaps one in twenty deserted. Some were packed off to reeducation camps. "Rightist thoughts, pessimism, and hesitancy appeared among our forces," the PAVN wrote in its official history. The aerial bombing of the Trail intensified. Rice rations were reduced, and when the rainy season began in April, bringing incessant thunderstorms, it bred mosquitoes that carried a hideous strain of malaria that made all your hair fall out before it killed you. The medics had no remedy but the juice of boiled worms.

After the battering the PAVN had taken in February, it seemed inconceivable that it would come back for more. But at the end of April, despite the misgivings of some commanders, the politburo ordered a follow-up, hoping to strengthen Hanoi's hand in the recently started Paris peace talks. The new offensive went by various names: Mini-Tet, Little Tet, Tet Phase II. Again, the politburo underestimated the ferocity of the American response, and as before, the worst of the carnage was in northern I Corps.

On April 29 several battalions of the 320th Division surged across the DMZ in an attempt to take the Dong Ha combat base. After a ferocious three-day battle at Dai Do, just north of the base, in which the Marines lost 81 men and estimated that the PAVN lost at least 600, things seemed to quiet down again. But it was only a brief lull, and on the hot and dusty afternoon of May 22, Manus Campbell had his turn to encounter the 320th. Bravo Company, headed by eight tanks, set out along the Trace, looking to flush out enemy troops to the east of the road that led from Con Thien to Cam Lo. It took them to an especially grim part of Leatherneck Square, near the blackened ruins of a village named Phu Oc, where thirty-one Marines had died in an encounter the previous September. Some of the bodies had been mutilated; one had the Marine Corps tattoo cut from his chest. This was not something the PAVN did often, but it made Phu Oc a place that inspired not only fear but vengeful rage.

Bravo 1/4 ran into a lethal ambush that afternoon, and within twenty minutes dozens of men were down. One of the dead was the company's commanding officer, Capt. Robert Harris, who was shot in the back. The fragging of unpopular officers did not become widespread until later, but the bullets that killed Harris came from an M-16. It was the action of "some heartless psychopathic cretin," the tank platoon commander wrote in his memoir of Con Thien. "Such was the warped value system of a few highly trained teenage killers who had seen too much death and dying and who knew full well that they were also doomed."

Alpha Company was rushed to the scene as the fighter jets came in at treetop height, close enough that Campbell could feel the scorching heat from the scarlet poppy blossom of napalm and watch the soldiers of the 320th Division burst into flames, flesh melting off their bones, as they tried to escape across the open ground of the Trace. The two Marine companies lost seventeen men on that particular though not exceptional afternoon. The body count for the enemy was officially recorded as 142. Yet no matter how many died, more would follow, wave upon wave, relentless. For the Americans, May 1968 would be the bloodiest month of the year, with more than 2,300 dead.

After the turkey shoot near Phu Oc, Campbell had seven weeks left to serve, and his DEROS countdown became more insistent, though he knew that the only true short-timers were those who had already made it back safely to The World. His worst experiences had been dictated by the two sides' mutual strategies of attrition and Westmoreland's misbegotten doctrine of mobile defense. He had seen too many men cut to pieces, set on fire, nineteen-year-olds with missing limbs screaming for their mothers. Yet here he was still, wrestling with the cosmic mysteries of survival. The only injury he'd sustained was from diving into a fighting hole during a rocket attack on the Dong Ha base, when another man's elbow rammed into his eye socket. Although it required stitches, a small mishap like that didn't get you a Purple Heart or your father's acclaim as a hero: it just went into the book with amoebic dysentery and jungle rot, with rat bites and gonorrhea and FUO, fever unknown origin. So was this what people meant when they said you had a charmed life? Had God accepted the deal with the Playboy centerfolds? The arbitrariness of death, one army medic said, was the "root stem" of guilt among those who made it home.

U.S. forces had finally relieved the eleven-week siege of Khe Sanh on April 8, but the senior echelons of the Marine Corps were incensed by the manner of the operation. They had never bought into Westmoreland's vision of the importance of these remote border areas, and the final phase of the drama turned their misgivings into bitterness. The Marines had borne the brunt of the war in Quang Tri and fought for weeks to hold on to a base they'd never wanted in the first place. But when the time came to break the siege, Westmoreland turned things over to the First Cavalry (Airmobile), which had just swaggered god-like into I Corps. He dubbed the operation Pegasus—after the flying horse—which seemed a gratuitous insult, "the most unpardonable thing Saigon ever did," said Maj. Gen. Rathvon Tompkins, commander of the Third Marine Division.

By the time the Air Cav showed up at Khe Sanh, the Marines had made it clear that they had neither the desire nor the need to be rescued by what they pointedly called "outside forces." The siege had slackened off in March, and they felt more than capable of taking care of the problem themselves. In a meeting at Phu Bai, Westmoreland's Marine commanders requested permission to shut down the base, and he erupted in rage. The relief of Khe Sanh, he said, had been "a classic defeat of a numerically superior besieging force by coordinated application of firepower," and the PAVN still had to be driven out of their mountain fastnesses along the border.

This time at least, Marine commanders were more ready to agree with him. Jealousy between the arms of service ran deep, and if the First Air Cavalry had covered themselves in glory, hopscotching around the battlefields in their helicopters, the Marines were now happy to do the same, to put the static frustrations of Khe Sanh and McNamara's Folly behind them.

With the PAVN in temporary retreat, the Marines would attack the new section of the Ho Chi Minh Trail south of Khe Sanh that had been built in the weeks leading up to Tet. They assembled their forces as Campbell was drinking beer and watching the TV war in his Bangkok hotel room. Meanwhile, the Air Cav, taking advantage of a rare spell of good weather in the A Shau, would lead a fresh assault on the valley, going to the source of the attack on Hue that all of Westmoreland's plans had failed to prevent.

The airborne forces attacked from the north. One chopper after another went down in flames. A competition was under way by this time among the North Vietnamese gunners. When the 150th shoot-down of the war in the valley was confirmed, the unit responsible would win an "emulation prize" of cigarettes, tobacco, tea, and candy. If the pilot was captured alive, there was the additional reward of a Russian-made radio.

The Americans were wholly unprepared for what they found when they finally assaulted Con Tom Mountain, Binh Tram 7. They came away with the biggest intelligence haul of the war—more than ninety thousand documents that told them more than they had ever known about the structure of the Ho Chi Minh Trail, the full significance of the A Shau Valley, and the road from La Hap to the border. After ARVN translators had gone through the first tranche, U.S. intelligence analysts finally saw into the heart and hub of the North's military strategy. The A Shau was "the most important VC war zone in South Vietnam, even more important than War Zones C, D, or the Iron Triangle/Cu Chi"—the three strongholds that threatened the approaches to Saigon. The Valley of Death was not just the key to I Corps; it was pivotal to the whole war.

The clock ticked closer to June 11, the anniversary of Campbell's arrival at Danang. Just one more month before he could get back to The World. His fretful impatience was emblematic of another of the great flaws of American military strategy in Vietnam. North Vietnamese and NLF fighters often served for a decade or more, with no end in mind but victory. American army and Marine infantrymen served deliberately short tours that softened the public demand to "bring the boys home." Battalion commanders served for only six months, and company commanders, who bore the brunt of frontline combat, for only three, all punching their ticket to promotion. Those above the rank of major usually kept to the rearguard, where the beer was always cold. After Tet, most soldiers couldn't wait to get away from a war that seemed to make no sense and have no end and was increasingly unpopular at home. It all made for a fatal incoherence on the battlefield.

By coincidence, June 11 was also the day Westmoreland resigned his command and handed it over to his deputy, Gen. Creighton Abrams. But Westy was not finished with Campbell. He had fought on the trails to the A Shau, in Leatherneck Square and along the DMZ. Now he would face the last of the trifecta of horrors that awaited the Marines in I Corps: the Ho Chi Minh Trail and the mountains along the Lao border.

Everyone knew of the sinister mystique of the Truong Son, which had once been the hunting grounds for Annamese royalty in search of tigers. The mountains were "spooky, unbearably spooky, spooky beyond belief," Michael Herr wrote, cloaked in mist and six shades of green—seven perhaps, if your unit was lucky enough to have one of the new starlight scopes, the first generation of night-vision technology, whose phosphorescent green images helped to dispel the terrifying darkness by showing you that trees did not walk around and boulders were not the crouching shapes of enemy soldiers.

When the Marines arrived in the hills south of Khe Sanh, they were astounded by the sophistication of the new extension of the Trail, which ran for twenty miles or more to link up with the main road through the A Shau Valley. Protected by heavy artillery on the Lao side of the border, which could be trundled in and out of caves like the Guns of Navarone, it was an expertly camouflaged K road, undetectable from the air beneath its overhead cover of interwoven branches. There were stone bridges and culverts, field hospitals, kitchens, storage depots, bunker complexes, and fully equipped machine shops, spaced at intervals along a graded strip broad and flat enough for heavy trucks and tanks. The plan, a captured prisoner said, was to reach Hue by the end of July.

Alpha 1/4 arrived in the area on June 3, tasked with destroying all of this new infrastructure, after B-52 strikes and artillery barrages had prepared the ground for new helicopter landing zones. On June 7, the day Campbell heard the news of RFK's assassination, his company was choppered to a remote hilltop, with instructions to hack out a new LZ. In the daylight hours, while work went ahead on clearing what would be christened LZ Torch, they scoured the Trail, blowing up everything they could find and destroying hundreds of North Vietnamese bunkers. There were skirmishes and air strikes and singsong taunts in the velvet darkness: "Tonight you die, Marine."

By June 9, an intimidating battery of Marine artillery had been airlifted into LZ Torch, on what was clearly not a routine assignment. The next day, to general amazement, a helicopter touched down briefly with a VIP passenger, Maj. Gen. Raymond Davis, the newly appointed commanding officer of the Third Marine Division. Davis was a Marine's Marine, disgusted by the idea of tying his men down in fixed defensive positions like Con Thien. Flying them into LZ Torch to blow up the Ho Chi Minh Trail was his kind of fight.

Chuck Searcy stands at the perimeter wire of his compound in Saigon during the 1968 Tet Offensive, midway through his one-year tour with the 519th Military Intelligence Battalion.

In November 1967, Manus Campbell, center right, was assigned to the Marine base at Con Thien, on the edge of the Demilitarized Zone (DMZ) separating North and South Vietnam. The base was subjected to a constant barrage of artillery and mortar fire.

Vietnamese leader Ho Chi Minh and Le Duan, general secretary of the
Vietnamese Workers Party, visit Moscow for the annual congress
of the Communist Party of the Soviet Union, 1961. During the Sino-Soviet
split, Ho Chi Minh favored the Soviet Union, while Le Duan leaned toward
Mao Zedong's China.

Vo Nguyen Giap and Nguyen Chi Thanh, the only two five-star
generals in the People's Army of Vietnam (PAVN), review plans for
the Tet Offensive on July 3, 1967, just three days before Thanh's death
from a heart attack.

ABOVE Especially in the early 1960s, porters on the still-primitive Ho Chi Minh Trail used the specially reinforced bicycles employed earlier during for the 1954 siege of Dien Bien Phu, which ended French colonial rule in Vietnam.

LEFT The PAVN and the indigenous people of the Truong Son Mountains sometimes used elephants to carry supplies on the Ho Chi Minh Trail.

RIGHT PAVN soldiers march south on the Trail through the remote mountains of Quang Binh province, immediately north of the DMZ, in the typically overcast and rainy weather conditions that often shielded them from American bombers and spotter planes.

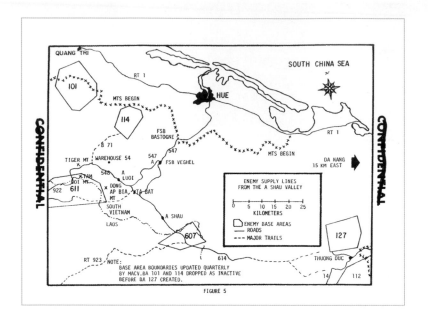

FIGURE 5

Quang Tri and Thua Thien, the two northernmost provinces of South Vietnam and the first target for infiltrators from the Ho Chi Minh Trail, housed several vital base areas of the PAVN and the National Liberation Front, commonly referred to as the Viet Cong.

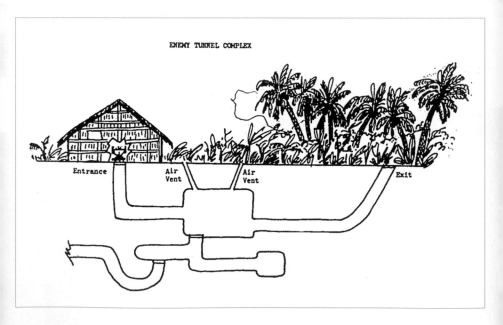

At the Combined Intelligence Center of Vietnam (CICV), Chuck Searcy produced a booklet in October 1967 on enemy ambush tactics, illustrated with his own drawings, like this one of a typical Viet Cong/PAVN tunnel system.

LEFT Most missions o
Operation Ranch Hand
the ten-year-long U.S.
defoliation campaign
in South Vietnam, were
conducted by specially
equipped C-123
"Provider" aircraft,
but some missions
were carried out by
helicopters.

GHT President Lyndon Johnson and Gen.
lliam Westmoreland, commander of U.S. forces
Vietnam, saw the siege of the Marine base of Khe
1h as a replay of the 1954 battle of Dien Bien Phu.
fact, it was a feint, designed to draw U.S. troops
ay from the defense of the coastal plain during the
8 Tet Offensive. This cartoon by PAVN Col. Pham
anh Tam mocked the Americans for the ease with
ich they had been lured into the trap.

enty-eight Marines died on Hill 674 in Thua Thien province in late October 1967, including nine
n from Manus Campbell's company. Three of them were, from left to right, William Dykes (20),
nest Hinsley (18), and Larry Havers (20).

From 1969 to 1971, Lady Borton worked with the American Friends Service Committee (AFSC) in Quang Ngai province. This photograph was taken on Buddha Mountain, close to the birthplace of PAVN Col. Vo Bam, the original architect of the Ho Chi Minh Trail.

In April 1971, Chuck Searcy joined the massive protest by veterans in Washington, D.C., that culminated in the "medal-throwing" on the steps of the U.S. Capitol. "Who are you going to believe," he asked the crowd, "the Vietnam veterans of America or Tricky Dick [Nixon]?"

hen Phan Thi Hanh and her husband returned to Dong Ha from Hanoi in late 1972, they found
town in ruins after carpet bombing by B-52s in response to the PAVN's Nguyen Hue, or Easter,
fensive earlier that year.

der the Paris Peace Accords of January 1973, the cease-fire allowed PAVN forces to remain in the
erated zone of Quang Tri. Under a portrait of Ho Chi Minh, a teacher uses the text of the agreement
his adult education class.

In the A Shau (A Luoi) Valley, Canadian scientists from Hatfield Consultants and their partners from Vietnam's 10-80 Committee carried out a comprehensive study of the lasting impact of dioxin, the toxic by-product of Agent Orange. Team leader Tom Boivin collected samples of soil, sediment, animal tissue, and human blood and breast milk for later analysis.

As part of the Hatfield/10-80 Committee survey, ethnic Katu villagers collected grass carp from fishponds in craters left by American bombing raids. Dioxin entered the human food chain when it accumulated in the liver and fatty tissue of fish.

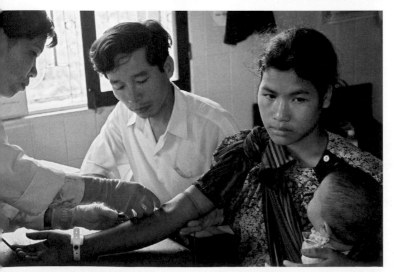

The Canadian scientists and Vietnamese health workers had to work hard to overcome the reluctance of the Katu, historically suspicious of outsiders, to give blood samples for dioxin analysis.

Campbell knew that he was on the Trail and surmised from this that he was in Laos. In fact, the new LZ was three miles inside Vietnam. It was a tough place to defend, a high ridge occupied by Marine infantry and a flat, narrow finger of land for six artillery guns. The crest of the hill was surrounded by deep-cut ravines, a little like the spokes of a wheel, thick with head-high elephant grass. The topography seemed like an open invitation for the enemy to creep up on the landing zone unseen, and that was exactly what happened.

At 2:15 a.m. on the hot, humid night of June 11, Campbell's one-year anniversary and the last day of Westmoreland's command, two full companies from the PAVN's elite 88th Infantry Regiment stormed the American lines. Being overrun in the night was a unique variant of terror, especially when near-suicidal PAVN sappers were involved. The most frightening thing about the unknowable Other was that they were invisible, until you either saw them dead or coming at you whites-of-the-eyes close in the darkness.

They attacked LZ Torch with mortar fire and rocket-propelled grenades and hurled themselves into the Marines' fighting holes with satchel charges—bags filled with explosives. An officer moved Campbell out of the hole he had just finished digging and occupied it himself with two other men; it promptly took a direct hit. The by-now-familiar riddle of survival: was it grace or was it luck? The firefight went on for hours, and like so many others, it was settled in the end by overwhelming firepower on the American side, including the terrifying aerial gunship, Puff the Magic Dragon, with its cow-slaughter scream. LZ Torch went into the books as another military victory.

When dawn broke, fourteen Marines were dead, ten of them from Alpha 1/4, and another twenty-three were wounded. At eight-thirty a.m. a renewed mortar barrage wounded another seventeen, including the company commander, Capt. Dick Mannila, who was hit in the back by red-hot shrapnel. But the last casualty of the day was the one that stuck in Campbell's memory. Early in the evening, one of the two lieutenants attached to his platoon walked up to his foxhole and said he was taking a toilet break. Campbell found it odd that he would make a point of broadcasting this. A minute or two later there was a gunshot, followed by a cry for help. The lieutenant had taken a bullet to the foot. The after-action report listed it as sniper fire, but the men wondered:

Was it self-inflicted? Such things were not infrequent. Was the lieutenant a coward? Getting yourself medevacked out in this way was a serious breach of the Marine Corps code of honor, although with night descending again on LZ Torch, anyone but a Marine might have hesitated to blame him.

There had been forty-two men in Campbell's platoon, and by the end of the attack, only eighteen were alive and uninjured. The landing zone had been occupied on June 7, fought over at terrible cost four days later, and then abandoned again a week after that—a story that was repeated time after time in Vietnam. Take the hill, hold the hill, abandon the hill. The most sobering statistic, an artillery lieutenant wrote, was that more Marines died in the operations that followed the relief of Khe Sanh than in the eleven weeks of the siege itself. The Marines had lost 205 men at the base; the death toll from the three months of obscure hill fights like LZ Torch was 326.

But the horror, like Hill 674, was in the end just another footnote, a single paragraph in the Marine Corps' eight-hundred-page official history of the war in 1968, *The Defining Year*. The operation that sent Alpha 1/4 to LZ Torch had redeployed the company from Operation Lancaster II to Robin South, which was an element of Robin, which was a spinoff from Scotland II, which in turn was a subset of Scotland, which grew out of Pegasus, in the endless, dizzying flowchart of destruction.

On June 17, six days after Westmoreland's departure, Creighton Abrams ordered the Khe Sanh base torn down. The buildings were dynamited, the bunkers filled in, and the airstrip destroyed—a conspicuous waste of energy, since the PAVN had no aircraft that could have used it. A sometimes unremarked feature of war is its many ironies: the B-52s, which had saturated the battle zone to ensure the survival of Khe Sanh, now returned to obliterate its last remnants. By October, even as other airplanes continued to drop their high-tech sensors on the Trail in Laos, the whole concept of the McNamara Line along the DMZ—what Marine Gen. Robert Cushman called "that stupid fence"—had been abandoned. The elephant grass grew lush again along the bald fairway of the Trace.

Campbell's war was all but done, though every remaining hour brought its own anxieties. Alpha Company had lost forty-two men during his thirteen months in Vietnam, and the simple law of averages meant that hundreds of the Americans who died there were killed in the final days of their tour of duty, like Staff Sergeant Schriner at Con Thien.

After LZ Torch was abandoned on June 18, Campbell spent three weeks at the big new Vandegrift Combat Base on Route 9, which had served as the jumping-off point for the April assault on the A Shau Valley. Finally there were three days back at Dong Ha, and then on July 13, one last chopper ride to Danang, where he boarded the Freedom Bird back to The World. John Michalsky, the star football player from his New Jersey high school, was on the same plane. Same day in, same day out, and both of them had made it through, although it would be too much to say that they had survived unscathed.

On June 15, while Campbell was still at LZ Torch, Chuck Searcy was already on his way home. Pan American Airways had a billboard outside the CICV blanket factory that said, "Welcome to Sunny Saigon." By the time his year was up, it had been replaced by another message that became a standing joke: "Pan Am Makes the Going Great."

A few days before he shipped out, one of his Vietnamese friends came to say goodbye, a good-natured ARVN soldier named Nguyen Kim Long, who had liked to hang out with the Americans, perfecting his English, allowing himself to be the butt of their jokes. After three years as a translator at CICV, he had been selected as one of ten men assigned to teach Vietnamese to GIs in Texas. When the authorities saw the list, they replaced all ten with the sons of high-ranking ARVN officers and government officials, a living illustration for Searcy of the pervasive corruption of the Saigon regime. When Long protested, he was sent back to the front, always given the most perilous assignments as point man with forward assault units.

Now he was briefly home on leave to see his wife and kids. "I will miss you," he told Searcy, "but I'm glad you're leaving. I wish you could take every American with you. I don't like Communism, but as long as the Americans are here we will never have peace."

As the Braniff charter flight lifted off, there were cheers and applause, with a second round when the pilot announced they had left Vietnamese airspace. "I settled into my seat and relaxed, totally," Searcy said. "It was as if I were immersed in a tank of cool water, with my eyes and nose just above the surface. Goodbye, Vietnam."

And yet even in those moments of suspension, he mused about the possibility of coming back when peace was restored, when people no longer lived in daily fear of death and destruction. He wondered if perhaps, after the most profound experience of his twenty-three-year-old life, he might even find a place for himself in that future Vietnam.

Manus Campbell had no such thoughts as the Freedom Bird headed out over the East Sea from Danang. He never wanted to see the place again, and the legacy of his thirteen months in Thua Thien and Quang Tri would endure for decades. There were multiple legacies, in truth. He left the visible ones behind him—the denuded forests and the poisoned fields, the unexploded ordnance, the burned-out villages and mass graves and crashed helicopters and the bodies of the missing, both American and Vietnamese, left unrecovered. The other legacies Campbell carried home inside him, though his wounds, other than the stitches from a careless elbow, were psychic and not physical.

Each of these legacies of the American war in Vietnam came to be known by an acronym: TCDD, for the poison; UXO, for the bombs; MIA, for the men lost; POW, for those supposedly still held captive; PTSD, for the trauma. Over the decades that followed, men like Campbell would find out whether these wounds could be healed, and to how imperfect an extent, since the truth of all wars is that they never really end; they cast a long shadow and have a long reckoning. It didn't occur to Campbell for a moment that he, like Searcy, might one day come back to be part of the equally long, slow process of healing.

PART II

PEACE

The stranger considers the years he has spent
wearing the weight of what he has done,
thinking his tiny part important.

—W. D. EHRHART, "The Distance We Travel"

10

Scavengers

WHEN A WAR ENDS, a baby boom begins. One of the first women to get pregnant in Quang Tri's Cam Lo district was a twenty-six-year-old former combatant named Phan Thi Hanh. Her father, a platoon leader in the Viet Minh, had been killed by the French when she was three years old. Her mother remarried in 1957, to another fighter, and the family moved to a new house near the fortified nineteenth-century citadel in Quang Tri city. As a teenager, Hanh was devoutly religious, and though money was short her stepfather had a generous nature and bought her the proper robes for her visits to the pagoda.

Hue, thirty-five miles to the south, was a historic center of Buddhist learning and worship, which often overlapped with Confucianism, nationalism, and political militancy. After missionaries arrived and the French made it the capital of their protectorate of Annam, Hue also became a hub of Vietnamese Catholicism, further strengthened by the arrival of many of the Catholic refugees who fled to the South after 1954. On May 4, 1963, Catholics decked out the city streets with the gold and white banners of the Vatican to celebrate the twenty-fifth anniversary of the elevation of Ngo Dinh Thuc, elder brother of President Ngo Dinh Diem, to the bishopric of Hue. Vesak, the annual celebration of the birth of the Buddha, happened to fall just four days later. The Catholic prelate, rigid and arrogant, was intensely disliked by the Buddhists of Hue, and on Vesak, thousands took to the streets in opposition to the bishop and the Diem regime. Police opened fire, killing a dozen protesters. Many more were arrested, including the sixteen-year-old Hanh.

They took her to Hue's notorious Chin Ham prison. For the next three years, her family made fruitless inquiries to the authorities, while she was repeatedly subjected to torture. They waterboarded her. They put snakes down the front of her dress, a scene depicted in Stanley Kubrick's *Full Metal Jacket*. When she was finally released, she returned home and joined the People's Liberation Armed Forces. She fought for the next three years, mainly in the southern part of Quang Tri province, where one of her duties was the clandestine transport of weapons to the battlefront.

One day her platoon ran into American soldiers as it made its way down a dry streambed. Trampled underfoot as her comrades ran for cover, she heard the whine of a bullet inches from her head. On another occasion, a helicopter hovered over the bunker where she was hiding, close enough for her to see the faces of the pilot and the door gunner. But instead of opening fire, they called in an airstrike, and by the time the fighter-bombers streaked in a few minutes later, Hanh had fled. Later, near a Green Beret camp, the fighter walking point ran into an enemy patrol. When Hanh's platoon returned to the spot, they found his severed head impaled on a stake and crowned with an American helmet.

She was wounded three times, decorated twice. The third time, her injuries were serious enough for her to be evacuated to Hanoi for medical treatment, which meant a two-month journey, much of it on foot, up the Ho Chi Minh Trail. Assigned a job at a temporary military museum, she met a man who was ten years her elder, a fellow native of Quang Tri, and in 1971 they married.

Life in wartime Hanoi was bleak. Many schools and markets were closed, clothing was rationed, and power outages lasted for weeks. Families were divided by mass evacuations to the countryside, and in May 1972 the city was bombed for the first time in four years. The fearsome secret police snuffed out any flicker of dissent.

Yet despite these grim conditions, Hanh and her husband had reason to feel optimism, starting with the phased withdrawal of American combat troops and the failure of the ARVN's February 1971 invasion of Laos, in which some 3,800 South Vietnamese died, as well as 353 Americans providing air support.

But this evidence of the ARVN's fragility led to overconfidence on the part of Le Duan's politburo. In the spring of 1972, North Vietnamese forces launched the Nguyen Hue, or Easter, Offensive, named in honor of the commander of an army that drove back a Chinese invasion in 1789. The goals were similar to those of the Tet Offensive four years earlier: to break the ARVN's resistance and trigger a general uprising that would bring down the Thieu government in Saigon. Again it was an election year in the United States, and the North was looking to strengthen its hand in peace talks, this time feeling squeezed by the twin shock of Nixon's overtures to China and new moves toward détente with the Soviet Union.

The new offensive would be "even more massive than [Tet]," said Le Duc Tho, Le Duan's closest ally on the politburo. This time the PAVN proposed to deploy Soviet-style mechanized divisions with tanks and heavy artillery, with the Tri-Thien Military District as the primary target. As in the months before Tet, there were bitter divisions within the politburo. The troops were not adequately trained to operate this sophisticated equipment, Giap argued. It would be a logistical nightmare; the PAVN's supply lines might easily become overstretched. As in 1967, he was outvoted.

At first all seemed to go according to plan. North Vietnamese forces advanced along all the same routes of attack they had used in earlier years, surging across the DMZ and moving eastward from Xepon, Khe Sanh, and the A Shau Valley. Quang Tri city fell. But then the offensive stalled, largely for the reasons Giap had predicted. Le Duan had again underestimated the ferocity of the enemy's response. The ARVN proved more resilient than expected, and the Americans escalated their reliance on firepower and technology to previously unheard-of levels, with forty B-52s dedicated to the Quang Tri theater, supplemented by massive naval bombardments and a new generation of laser-guided bombs. Forty thousand North Vietnamese soldiers died. After a decade of war, it might have seemed that there was nothing left to destroy in the province of Le Duan's birth, but the Easter Offensive was a mutual exercise in pure brute force that surpassed everything that had gone before. The provincial capital, one reporter said, was "no longer a city but a lake of masonry." Almost nothing remained but the bullet-ridden walls of a Catholic church, which still stands as a permanent memorial to the war.

With the fighting finally over, and the population of Quang Tri reduced to less than a quarter of its previous 320,000, Hanh and her husband returned home toward the end of 1972. The offensive had achieved few of Le Duan's larger goals, yet much of the province had been liberated, and the Paris Peace Accords the following January allowed the PAVN and NLF forces to remain in place in areas they controlled. The Quang Tri People's Committee took an inventory of the destruction: 96 of the 101 hamlets in Gio Linh district razed; 50 out of 83 in Cam Lo district, where the Provisional Revolutionary Government set up its foreign ministry and received visiting dignitaries like Fidel Castro. No doubt they saw what the PRG wanted them to see, but the first reporters to arrive were impressed by the speed of change: Dong Ha already had a branch of the state bank, a functioning 150-bed hospital, a rebuilt market, a bookstore, and a restaurant, even an ice cream factory. Schools were open in many villages, and adult literacy classes were using the Paris Accords as a text. Hanh and her husband were assigned an apartment in Dong Ha, and she was put to work as a tax collector. In 1974, she gave birth to her first child, a boy.

Over the next two years, work teams repaired roads and bridges, dikes and dams. The army cleared minefields, while civilian work crews removed 6 million pieces of unexploded ordnance, losing hundreds dead or injured in the process. Almost a quarter of the surface area of Quang Tri and Thua Thien had been contaminated by defoliants—perhaps 2 million gallons in all.

In March 1975, the PAVN began its inexorable southward advance, and on April 30 the Saigon government collapsed. Three decades of French and American wars were finally over, leaving 3 million dead. By September, Hanh was pregnant again, and in June 1976 she gave birth to a second son, Ngo Xuan Hien. His given name, Hien, means "gentle." His birth certificate was one of the last to be headed "Republic of South Vietnam." Two weeks later, the country was formally reunified.

The quirks of political geography made the task of reunification harder in Quang Tri than anywhere else in the former South Vietnam. In the sliver of the province north of the DMZ, as well as the neighboring province of Quang Binh, the economy had been collectivized for years.

The remainder of Quang Tri had remained under what the Communist Party called "the ruling yoke of neo-colonialism." Now the two systems had somehow to be reconciled, and Le Duan decided to accomplish this by amalgamating Quang Binh, Quang Tri, and Thua Thien into a single new province, which the government called Binh-Tri-Thien.

Under this interim arrangement, more than three-quarters of a million people returned home. Three cities, fifteen towns, and three-quarters of all the villages in Binh-Tri-Thien had been destroyed or severely damaged. On a forested rise near Cam Lo, the government began work on the monumental Truong Son National Martyrs Cemetery, with 33,000 graves to honor those who had fallen on the Ho Chi Minh Trail.

Much of the new makeshift housing was made of sheet metal stamped "Made in USA." The wreckage the Americans had left behind—"Ozymandias in camouflage paint," television reporter Morley Safer called it—fed a thriving scrap metal business. Eventually this trade in the detritus of war became a significant part of the national economy, though Vietnam had to sell much of the metal to foreign buyers at fire-sale prices, only to buy it back, reprocessed, at the full market rate.

By 1978 the transformation of Binh-Tri-Thien's economy was almost complete. One of the sixty-eight production collectives, in Cam Lo district, was an East German–sponsored black pepper plantation, and Ngo Xuan Hien's father found work there as head of construction, a job that gave the family a certain level of prestige and later entitled him to a trip to Berlin.

Harmonizing political loyalties was an additional challenge, and Communist Party reports warned that "100,000 puppet soldiers and government employees had not been transformed. . . . The vestiges of U.S. and puppet presence were still serious in every aspect of social activity." For many, this meant an arduous spell in a reeducation camp. There were three of these in Quang Tri, one of them in the village of Ai Tu, where Manus Campbell's headstrong sergeant had triggered a pair of booby traps.

Meanwhile divided families had to be reconciled. Lady Borton, who during the war had been an aid worker at a prosthetics clinic and childcare center operated by the Quaker American Friends Service Committee in Quang Ngai province, told of families living along the Ben Hai River in the middle of the DMZ who had hedged their bets by trading children. Say a family had six, she recalled. They would ferry three across the river in a sampan to a host family on the other bank and take three of theirs in return, hoping that at least some would survive. If there were two siblings of military age, one might be drafted into the army of each side, leaving bitter animosities to be healed when the war was over.

One divided family was that of Nguyen Thanh Phu. Like Hien, he was a native of Cam Lo district, born into a large family that had migrated from the North and could trace its lineage back through thirteen generations. In later years, the two young men would become firm friends and colleagues.

In 1967, Phu's father, like Hien's mother, had joined the People's Liberation Armed Forces, fighting in the area around his village, which was at the edge of Leatherneck Square. But he was seized in an American raid shortly after the Tet Offensive, taken to Danang, and from there to the Phu Quoc prison, on an island off the southern tip of Vietnam. Phu Quoc was notorious for the ingenious variety of its tortures, which included wrapping prisoners in sacks and laying them on top of a hot stove, gouging out their teeth, burning out their retinas by shining powerful lights in their eyes, and confining them in wire-mesh "tiger cages." Thousands died there, but Phu's father was released in 1973 as part of the prisoner exchange under the Paris Peace Accords, and he rejoined the armed struggle until the end of the war. Returning to Cam Lo, he found his village, like most, in ruins, and set about rebuilding. He named his firstborn son Phu, for the prison.

His brother, meanwhile, had been an ARVN draftee. The trauma of war was real for both men, but it was buried deep—post-traumatic stress disorder has never been recognized as a medical condition in Vietnam. It was years before Phu's father could speak about his prison experiences, finally opening up at family gatherings, where social conventions demanded harmony.

Phu's parents were peasant farmers, rising at three or four in the morning to labor in the rice fields. The yield was meager; fertilizers were in short supply. Rice was a luxury that parents set aside for the children. Roadside noodle stands kept their food warm in insulated

Mermite cans the GIs had left behind. Otherwise the staples were cassava and sweet potatoes. Sometimes people turned the cassava into tapioca; sometimes it made them sick. Chickens died of disease. If the fishermen came in with a good catch from a nearby lake or the Cam Lo River, Phu's mother and grandmother might put a little in a jar to ferment, eking out enough fish sauce to last for a few months. The taste of milk was unknown. In the communal market in Dong Ha, more than two hours distant on foot, they might find candy as a special treat. Once, Phu remembered, his father came back from Hue with a piece of meat and a single can of beer, which the whole family shared as if it were vintage Dom Pérignon.

The abundance of scrap metal allowed them to get by. As a child, five years older than Phu, Hien could see burned-out tanks and armored vehicles abandoned along Route 9. Bullets, both live and spent, were everywhere, washed out of the rocks and hedgerows whenever it rained, and kids picked them up and took them home to play with. Hien and his friends made their own amusements, cavorting in the bomb craters, splashing around in them during the monsoon season. They cut off the tips of bullets, sealing the mouth of the cartridge case, attaching it with rubber bands to a stalk of elephant grass, and tossing the whole contraption up into the air. During the annual Tet celebrations, regular firecrackers were feeble by comparison.

Sometimes they would hear a louder explosion. *Someone must be fishing.* But as often as not, it was an accident, Hien said, and people would rush to the scene to find a hand or a limb blown off, someone blinded, sometimes a death. Amputees puttered around in the fields, struggling to remain productive. Villagers became skilled in the search for larger troves of unexploded ordnance, thinking they might contain gold or other valuable metals. They might spot a patch of ground on a hillside where the vegetation had been burned off. When the topsoil was washed away after a heavy rain, it might expose the point of impact of an artillery shell. The real treasures came from excavating the largest craters, digging as deep as thirty feet or more, where the bigger bombs lay buried. As the local market in scrap metal grew, the scavengers would often hack off the fuses, thinking to prevent an explosion only to cause one.

For Phu's family, poorer than Hien's, searching for scrap metal was serious business. Their village was close to an airstrip on the old McNamara Line, and Phu went there often with his father, loading up a cart with metal that they used to build irrigation channels for their rice fields. Well into the late 1980s they could still find discarded rifles and caches of unused munitions. When Phu picked them up, his father would tell him sternly to put them down. Over time Phu learned to distinguish one kind from another: hand grenades, RPG rounds, mortar and artillery shells, and cluster bombs, *bom bi,* the most dangerous of them all.

Many of the older kids would spend half the day in the fields, planting, harvesting, searching for freshwater shrimp, or looking after the cows or water buffalo. The other half they would spend in school, trudging along dirt roads that turned to sucking red mud during the monsoon. One of Hien's classmates was disfigured by a cleft lip. Another drooled and fell to the ground in convulsions. The other children made fun of them. A neighbor boy in Phu's village, the son of a woman who had fought on the Ho Chi Minh Trail, had especially severe deformities. Eventually he went off to a nearby lake and drowned himself. A doctor from Hue, Dr. Nguyen Viet Nhan, came to Cam Lo district when Phu was a teenager and found an alarming number of children who suffered from birth defects. The health ministry in Hanoi set up an office, Committee 10-80, to study the problem, and villagers began to trade rumors: might all these disabilities have something to do with the chemicals the Americans had sprayed on Quang Tri during the war?

For the first postwar decade, Vietnam was one of the poorest countries on earth, and there was more than enough blame to go around for its hardships. Ho Chi Minh had died in 1969, and his successor, Le Duan, ran the peace in the same doctrinaire fashion as he had run the war, shunting aside his rivals in the leadership. His great adversary, General Giap, opposed the abolition of private property and the mass detention and reeducation of former South Vietnamese and ARVN officials. He was ignored and subsequently lost his post as minister of defense and his seat on the politburo. The greatest insult of all came in 1984, when the party made a documentary to celebrate the thirtieth anniversary of Dien Bien Phu, and not a word was said about Giap, who had commanded the victorious Vietnamese forces.

Le Duan now turned bitterly against China, declaring, "These Chinese hegemonists and expansionists have always been our enemies" and turning to the orthodox Soviet model to build the economy. The politburo set wildly optimistic targets, projecting 14 percent growth rates; what they achieved was closer to 2 percent. Collectivized agriculture was a disaster. If farmers produced more rice than they needed for subsistence, the surplus was sold to the state at a "negotiated price," which was often a euphemism for a loss.

Meanwhile the United States, having already devastated the country, imposed pitiless sanctions as the price it exacted for defeat. The Paris Peace Accords had committed the United States to "contribute to healing the wounds of war and to postwar reconstruction of the Democratic Republic of Viet Nam," and four days after the agreement was signed, Richard Nixon wrote a secret letter to Prime Minister Pham Van Dong promising $3 billion for reconstruction and between $1 billion and $1.5 billion for food and commodity aid. Vietnam counted on this as an integral part of its first postwar five-year plan and insisted there could be no talk of reconciliation until the promise was honored. Washington replied that nothing could happen without a full accounting of its MIAs and POWs. Not a penny materialized.

The Ford administration imposed draconian sanctions on the former South Vietnam, matching those that were already in place on the North. The Commerce Department, at the urging of Secretary of State Henry Kissinger, now froze all South Vietnamese assets held by American-owned banks and their foreign subsidiaries. And Vietnam was still obligated to repay the $150 million in loans that the Thieu government had owed—plus interest.

Two weeks after the fall of Saigon, Vietnam was subjected to the most stringent of export controls, which barred U.S. citizens from sending any form of humanitarian aid. In September, the United States vetoed Vietnam's application for membership in the United Nations. Sanctions were tightened further despite complaints from American corporations, which had lost about $100 million in assets and were lobbying hard for renewed access to the Vietnamese market.

If critics of the war hoped for a change under the Carter administration, they were disappointed. Although the new president sent an envoy, Richard Holbrooke, to talk to the Vietnamese about a possible reconciliation, there was no reframing of the basic purpose or morality of the war. "The destruction was mutual, you know," Carter said. "We went there to defend the freedom of the South Vietnamese, and I don't feel that we ought to apologize or to castigate ourselves or to assume the status of culpability."

Congress had never ratified Nixon's offer of assistance, and in June 1977 it amended the foreign aid bill to formally rescind it, with a bipartisan consensus that made for strange bedfellows: liberal Democrats eager to promote Carter's human rights policy and implacable right-wing anti-Communists. The United States even blocked all assistance from the World Bank and the Asian Development Bank, as well as loans from the International Monetary Fund. In June 1978, with its economy in desperate straits, Vietnam agreed to join the Soviet-controlled Council for Mutual Economic Assistance (COMECON), further alienating China.

Six months later, 150,000 Vietnamese troops invaded Cambodia, bent on removing Pol Pot's genocidal Khmer Rouge regime from power. The timing could not have been worse. Ten days earlier China, the main backer of the Khmer Rouge, had announced that its new leader, Deng Xiaoping, would be making a state visit to the United States the following month. When he arrived in Washington on January 29, the two countries signed an agreement to establish full diplomatic relations. Within four days, Deng was at a rodeo in Texas, decked out in a cowboy hat. Two weeks after he returned to Beijing, 200,000 Chinese troops poured across Vietnam's northern border, killing thousands as they meted out punishment for the invasion of Cambodia. The Vietnamese were "naughty children" who had to be "spanked," Deng told Carter. China began radio broadcasts urging ethnic Chinese in Vietnam to rise up against the government, and Vietnam responded by herding thousands of them onto ships and pushing them out to sea, part of the mass exodus of what the world called the "boat people."

In September 1979, the Carter administration decided that the Khmer Rouge, still headed by Pol Pot though no longer in power, would occupy the country's seat at the United Nations. Relations with Vietnam would remain frozen until it withdrew from Democratic

Kampuchea, as the Khmer Rouge called Cambodia, and that would not happen for another ten years.

By 1980, much of Vietnam was on the brink of famine. China had cut off food aid, and the Soviet Union declined to make up the gap. Visiting Russian "experts" were widely detested, boorish, humorless, shambling around the country in their cheap suits. A joke made the rounds. Moscow to Hanoi: *Tighten your belts.* Hanoi to Moscow: *Please send belts.*

William Broyles, who had been a Marine lieutenant in Quang Nam during the war and was now the editor-in-chief of *Newsweek* magazine, went back to Vietnam in 1984. In his book *Brothers in Arms,* published the following year, he wrote, "Vietnam today is a country accustomed to sacrifice, on the verge of having sacrificed enough."

After Le Duan's death in July 1986, a younger generation of leaders emerged, and the Communist Party's Sixth National Congress introduced a set of reforms known as *doi moi*—variously translated as "renewal," "innovation," or "new methods"—which set out the goal of building a "socialist-oriented market economy." In Moscow, Mikhail Gorbachev had initiated reforms of his own, which culminated in the collapse of the Soviet Union. COMECON disintegrated, and Soviet bloc aid dried up almost overnight. Vietnam accepted the terms of an IMF loan package, loosened controls on landownership, encouraged small businesses, invited foreign investors to visit, and invested heavily itself in the educational system it would need to create a skilled workforce.

In Cam Lo district, Ngo Xuan Hien and Nguyen Thanh Phu began to notice the changes in village life. With the privatization of rice production, farmers like Phu's family began to turn a profit. Oil lamps were replaced by electric light. Cassette players provided music for weddings and festivals. Women began to wear imported cosmetics. People clustered around to see the novelty of black and white television, with a single set in the village for public viewing. A lot of the programming was leaden government propaganda, with a leavening of Russian lessons. But there were also puppet and magic shows for the kids and the nightly announcement of the lottery winners. Long after midnight, men would gather round to watch live broadcasts of soccer matches on a Russian sports channel.

At the state-owned black pepper farm, Hien's father got a pay raise, and in 1988, now twelve years old, Hien was sent to spend the summer with old friends of his parents in Hanoi, his first vacation. He marveled at the city's many lakes and its green parks, though there were still few motor vehicles in the streets other than the Russian Zil limousines carrying party dignitaries and visiting VIPs, and little to eat but tofu and water spinach, a Vietnamese staple.

Hien did well in high school, and his father sent him to Dong Ha to learn English, which was now beginning to be taught in preference to Russian. Phu was also a good student and picked up a little of the language from a man in his village who had been an interpreter for the Americans and spent a year in a reeducation camp.

Both of them went off to college after graduation, Hien to Hue and Phu to Danang, part of the great migration of young people to the cities in the early reform years. They both majored in English, since it was clear by now that this was the way to get ahead in the new Vietnam. The first tourists had begun to arrive, eager for the vicarious experience of seeing a country that perhaps only existed in their minds as "the 'Nam" or Indochine. Forty thousand of them came in 1988, and despite the warnings of hard-line officials fearful of an influx of sex tourism, drugs, and other capitalist evils, 1990 was officially declared "Visit Vietnam Year." Within four years, the annual number of visitors had risen to a million.

The ancient city of Hue, though still scarred by the Tet Offensive, was one of the main attractions. Hien overcame his natural shyness and approached foreigners on the street to ask if he could talk with them in order to improve his conversational English. They'd go to parties together, enjoy a few drinks. Some of the American visitors were veterans of the war, and travel agencies in Hue had begun to offer tours of the DMZ. Khe Sanh was always the centerpiece of these visits, although the A Shau Valley to the south, being a sensitive border area, was still off-limits.

After graduating from Hue University, Hien got a job as a teacher in Khe Sanh town. Many of his students were from the Bru-Van Kieu minority, and he learned a little of their language. A natural mimic, he even spoke Bru with a local accent. Phu, meanwhile, used his English to find work as a freelance tour guide, shuttling back and forth between Hue and Danang, picking up visitors at the airports, taking them to see China Beach and the ancient trading port of Hoi An, accompanying them on boat rides down the Perfume River in Hue to see the grand tombs of the Nguyen emperors.

Phu had come to think of Americans as large, well-fed people, and for that reason he was struck by the distinctive sight of one tall, thin man in his middle years, who always seemed to be coming or going from one or other of the airports. Later, he would learn that the name of this anomalous American was Chuck Searcy.

The Smoky Landscape

THE INTELLIGENCE ANALYST and the Marine grunt: their wartime experiences could not have been more different. Yet when Searcy and Manus Campbell left Vietnam, their emotions were not dissimilar. Searcy described himself as "sad, bitter, and angry, a walking shell"; Campbell was "alive on the outside but dead on the inside." But both had enlisted for three years, and the military was not quite done with them.

Campbell put in a month at Camp Lejeune and then five more on a tank landing craft in Europe. He was in Naples, Rome, and Spain, drunk much of the time, "keeping the Free World free." In 1968, when both he and Searcy left Vietnam, 16,899 American soldiers died, by far the worst year of a lost war, and the Marines of I Corps took the brunt of it. The Summer of Love was a distant, implausible memory. At Woodstock the following August, the most enduring moment in the "three days of peace and music" was Jimi Hendrix's feedback-drenched butchery of "The Star-Spangled Banner"—"playing his guitar the way a grunt tears into pussy," as Michael Herr put it. In California, Charles Manson's Family had embarked on its murderous rampage. *Sgt. Pepper* had given way to "Helter Skelter." And the war ground on.

Campbell finally made it home to New Jersey for good on May 9, and the very next day brought yet another chapter in the ruinous saga of the A Shau. The Marines had already made one attempt to reenter the valley, two days after Nixon's inauguration in January, attacking the PAVN's Base Area 611 and authorized for the first and only time to cross briefly into Laos. Now the 101st Airborne, Westmoreland's old division, stormed an obscure mountain that the Vietnamese called Dong Ap Bia, the Mountain of the Crouching Beast. But the name the grunts gave it was written on the bottom of a case of C-rations that somebody nailed to a fire-blackened tree: Hamburger Hill.

Official reports said that sixty-three Americans died in the ten-day battle, but that was just on the hill itself; the whole operation in the valley cost 108 lives, and the after-action reports estimated one thousand North Vietnamese dead. Defoliants, B-52 strikes, and artillery shelling left Hamburger Hill naked. It was the last major battle of attrition of the war, and yet again the A Shau was the emblem of its horror and its futility. On June 8, the day after the final shot was fired, Nixon announced the withdrawal of the first 25,000 troops, the start of Vietnamization.

"For a time," said a classified report on the operation, "the enemy was cautious about re-entering the valley in strength, but it was only a matter of time before [PAVN] logistics would again move through terrain the Allies had once securely held." For another three years, the Americans continued to batter the A Shau to no discernible end. The after-action reports tried to put the best face on each new action—the brief insertions of small units, the Arc Light raids and tactical airstrikes, the ambushes and firefights, the herbicide runs, the CS gas drops, the KIAs and MIAs—but the Americans never did regain a foothold in the Valley of Death.

"We live in the smoky landscape now, as the exhausted troops seek the roads home," the journalist Pete Hamill wrote toward the end of the war, in the liner notes for Bob Dylan's album *Blood on the Tracks*. "The signposts have been smashed; the maps are blurred."

No one knew what to do with the vets when they returned home, especially those who came back as damaged as Manus Campbell. In time, PTSD acted as a kind of generic shorthand for their struggles, and for some, the acronym even became a perverse badge of honor. The term didn't even exist when the conflict ended, although two scientists who organized "rap groups" with members of Vietnam Veterans

Against the War as early as 1970—Robert Jay Lifton, a Yale psychiatrist, and Chaim Shatan, a Canadian clinician at New York University— limned its main features. Not until ten years later was PTSD included in the American Psychiatric Association's *Diagnostic and Statistical Manual of Mental Disorders*. The condition was characterized, the *DSM* said, by "re-experiencing the traumatic event"—in Campbell's case the ambush on Hill 674—and a "numbing of responsiveness to, or reduced involvement with, the external world."

PTSD typically manifested itself in substance abuse, recurrent nightmares, bad choices, bad sex, violence, alienation, and failed human relationships, and Campbell experienced all of these things. Yet each man's story varied in its particulars. You could have taken a dozen grunts from Alpha 1/4 and put them through the same fire in Quang Tri and Thua Thien, and they would have come away from it in a dozen different ways. As Jewish survivors say of the Holocaust, it was not 6 million; it was one plus one plus one.

Like so many combat Marines, Campbell had become addicted to what Herr called the "fast wash of adrenaline." One of the first things he did when he got back to New Jersey was to buy a brand-new Dodge Charger, the ultimate low-slung, streamlined, split-grille, sleek-backed muscle car. He also bought a plastic gun, which he kept beside him as he drove, sometimes reaching for it instinctively if another car cut into his lane on the Garden State Parkway. After thirteen months of living, eating, and sleeping with an M-16 at his side, he felt naked without a weapon but too spooked to touch a real one. "But then," he said, "I thought, what am I going to do with a fucking plastic gun? It was just that fear you always had, feeling unsafe all the time."

He had been a drinker as a teenager, even before enlisting, but now it got worse. Alcoholism was the classic form of self-medication among the traumatized returnees, and for most who finally kicked the habit it lasted for ten or fifteen years. In Campbell's case, it took eighteen. For almost all that time he was a New Jersey state trooper—lots of veterans went into the police—and for that he needed to carry a real gun. It was a macho world of hard-drinking Irish- and Italian- and Polish-American guys, and there was no better way to get the adrenaline pumping than to strap on a pistol and a bulletproof vest, fire up the siren and the flashers, and chase down drunks and criminals on the parkway. Perhaps, Campbell said, he was courting suicide by cop rather than suicide by military. But enlistment in the Marines had been the first time his father ever expressed pride in him; his graduation from the New Jersey State Police Academy was the second.

Thanks to the wiles of the recruiter in Georgia, Chuck Searcy still had sixteen months of his three-year enlistment to serve after leaving Saigon. He spent them in Germany. It was an opportunity to chill out, to reflect on the war, and to put the past year into perspective.

He was assigned to a comfortable office in the ancient and lovely university town of Heidelberg. It was the year of the Prague Spring, and the Soviet invasion of Czechoslovakia occurred within weeks of his arrival. It was rewarding to get a close-up understanding of these events, but Cold War military intelligence brought as many absurdities as insights. There were agents in the field to be fed and watered, like the little old lady in tennis shoes who was paid a few dollars a day to take photos of the new post office building in Vladivostok. *Is that really on the list of strategic bombing targets?*

On the day he got out of the army in October 1969, Searcy found himself in a small antiwar demonstration outside the U.S. consulate in Frankfurt, more observer than participant. The Germans he met were cautious about broaching the subject of Vietnam, but they were curious to hear about his experiences. Most of them opposed the war, but no one insulted him or called him a babykiller. He decided to stay on. He liked the people, the beer was excellent, and there was an abundance of good-looking women. The $150 a month he got as a student under the GI Bill was enough to live on, and he bought a beat-up old Volkswagen to explore the country, picking up hitchhikers along the way. It was the kind of footloose interlude that might have drifted along indefinitely, but by the spring of 1970 it began to feel like a self-indulgence, given the increasingly convulsive events at home.

Military discipline had disintegrated with Vietnamization, with racial conflict, rampant drug use, the fragging of hundreds of unpopular officers. B-52s were bombing Cambodia; campuses were in turmoil; there were four dead in Ohio, shot down by the National Guard at Kent State. It was time to go home, to pick up his studies for the third time, to reconnect with his family.

Although he had turned against the war, there was nothing ideological about Searcy's dissent. He didn't see himself as a political radical; he simply saw the war as immoral, pointless, driven by a culture of official lies. He still trusted that the checks and balances of the democratic system would eventually set things to rights.

The University of Georgia campus had been transformed in the four years he'd been away. It was all long hair and headbands and the sweet reek of marijuana. Dorm rooms rocked to the sound of the Allman Brothers Band of Macon. The Black Panthers occupied much of the campus in a protest against racism. After Kent State, thousands of students joined the biggest demonstration in Georgia's history, demanding that the college president, Fred Davidson, sign a letter to Nixon denouncing the bombing of Cambodia. They shut down the school for two days, but Davidson—speaking for the conservative majority of the faculty—refused, instead issuing a restraining order against any further show of dissent, citing the threat of "destruction of university property."

Searcy had grown a beard in Germany, although his hair was still on the short side. He kept a low profile, taking the pulse of the place, not saying much yet about the war. But that began to change in the spring of 1971, when an army buddy called to tell him about an upcoming protest.

Since Hamburger Hill, the antiwar movement had been propelled to a new level by a series of events that were invariably rooted in the horrors of I Corps and the obsession with breaking the Ho Chi Minh Trail. First came the exposure in November 1969 of the My Lai massacre in Quang Ngai, which had been covered up for more than a year and a half. After that there was the secret bombing of the PAVN's border sanctuaries in Cambodia and the ground incursions in the spring of 1970. In December, Congress passed the Cooper-Church Amendment, barring any use of American ground troops in Cambodia and Laos.

The contradictions of the war effort had become untenable. The whole point of Vietnamization was for the ARVN to take over the fighting, but its catastrophic invasion of Laos in February 1971 merely proved its limitations. The withdrawal of American troops meant an even greater reliance than before on aerial bombing of the Trail, which had never worked and led only to greater public anger at the unending destruction. When Nixon squeezed hard on one area of the problem, it only bulged out on another. Like Westmoreland, he had become the Sorcerer's Apprentice, refusing to accept the reality of failure.

Vietnam Veterans Against the War had recently staged a three-day event that it called the Winter Soldier Investigation. The reference was to Thomas Paine's contempt for the "summer soldier and the sunshine patriot," the kind who had deserted at Valley Forge. Intent on showing that My Lai, though an extreme case, was no anomaly, more than 150 vets gave accounts of rape, torture, random killing, the burning of villages, the cutting off of ears, and secret operations in Laos. One told of nineteen firewood collectors being gunned down at the garbage dump outside the Cam Lo resettlement camp in Quang Tri.

But telling stories in a banquet room at a Howard Johnson's in Detroit was no substitute for bringing them to the streets of Washington, D.C., where the ruinous decisions were being made. The two-month-long Marine operation in the A Shau Valley and Laos in 1969 had been Dewey Canyon I. The American component of the 1971 Laos invasion was Dewey Canyon II. So, someone said, let's call this one Dewey Canyon III—"a small incursion into the country of Congress." John Kerry, the former commander of a Swift Boat in the Mekong Delta, said he would take the message of Winter Soldier to the Senate Foreign Relations Committee. The atrocities were not just systematic, he said in his testimony on April 22. They were committed "with the full awareness of officers at all levels of command." The returning vets had "a sense of anger and a sense of betrayal which no one has yet grasped." More than a quarter of those in VA hospitals had attempted suicide, Kerry said.

Searcy was nervous about going to Washington, worried about his parents' reaction. But in the end he joined the crowd, 200,000 strong, that converged on the capital for the most famous antiwar protest of them all. Defying a court order, the veterans camped on the National Mall for days. Joined by Gold Star mothers, they brought their discharge papers to prove that this was not a false-flag operation. Bands played "Give Peace a Chance" and "The Age of Aquarius," "America the Beautiful," and "God Bless America." Quakers handed out free PB&J sandwiches.

On the day after Kerry's testimony, hundreds of veterans filed up to a microphone set before a security barrier at the Capitol. They made brief speeches—name, birthplace, unit, reasons for anger—then turned and threw their medals onto the Capitol steps, some with a contemptuous underhand toss and others like a pitcher winding up for a fastball. A grainy film of the event captured Searcy, handsome, bearded, and already charismatic. "Chuck Searcy, Athens, Georgia," he tells the crowd. "I'd just like to say that we're veterans of Vietnam and we're telling the American people that the war is wrong. I want to ask you, who are you going to believe, the veterans of Vietnam or Tricky Dick?" He draws back his arm and hurls something, hard.

The gesture was unplanned; it wasn't his medals he threw, just whatever was in his pocket that day, a wad of paper maybe, or a handful of change. He was still holding something in reserve, wanting to believe that the system could work in conventional ways. Searcy had left Vietnam with the Army Service Medal, the Vietnam Service Medal, the Joint Service Commendation Medal, the Good Conduct Medal—basically the standard assortment of gongs and ribbons they gave you if you did your job, kept your head down, and didn't screw up. He took them quietly to the office of the junior senator from Georgia, David Gambrell, a pleasant, middle-of-the-road Democrat. Senators had the power to stop the war, didn't they? Gambrell was out, so Searcy left the medals on the desk of a startled aide. A few weeks later they came back to him in the mail. But he felt he had made his point.

Two weeks later, on the first anniversary of Kent State, a classmate at UGA, one of the few who knew Searcy had been in Vietnam, said he was putting together a candlelight memorial service, on a grassy area in front of the main library. Would Searcy be willing to say a few words?

He'd never given a formal speech before, but he wrote one that afternoon and found that he had unsuspected gifts of eloquence. He didn't shout and pound the lectern like so many of the antiwar activists; his tone was more wistful and elegiac than angry. He recalled the shoeshine boys, the old men with their wispy Ho Chi Minh beards, the graceful young women with their *ao dais* and their parasols, the wrinkled grandmothers selling mynah birds on the street. He evoked memories of Saigon's elegant tree-lined boulevards, the statues and fountains and flower stands, the tin and tarpaper shacks of the poor, the fishing boats on the glittering river, the hole-in-the-wall restaurants pungent with fish sauce, the smell of Vietnam. He spoke about the overcrowded orphanages; the Americans staggering out of the PX under the weight of stereos, televisions, and refrigerators; the bodies left lying in the street during Tet, caked with blood and dirt; the moments when your mind would wander back to the people at home. What were they doing now? Dancing? Playing golf? Watching these same scenes on TV? He wondered what had happened to his Vietnamese friends, using the honorific pronoun for older men or those of higher status, like Ong Long, the cyclo driver.

He was mobbed, asked to speak to other groups. The speech was reprinted in *The Christian Century*. Other vets came out of the wood-work, and the next morning nine of them gathered at a coffee shop to found a college chapter of VVAW, which quickly gathered seventy or eighty supporters.

But as the war effort disintegrated, the antiwar movement was pulled in centrifugal directions. At a chaotic VVAW event in Kansas City that November, Searcy recalled, there was "a haze of marijuana smoke, a lot of emotion, a lot of FBI agents in suits and ties." Someone proposed scaling the White House fence during the lighting of the national Christmas tree and setting it alight with flamethrowers. Scott Camil, yet another Marine vet from I Corps and a well-known radical, raised the idea of assassinating politicians who were militant support-ers of the war.

John Kerry, whom Searcy had just met, had quit the organization, and Searcy thought about doing the same. But he decided there was important work to do at the state level that could keep its distance from these lunacies. His VVAW chapter kept its protests low-key and deliberately unthreatening. After all, this was still Georgia. He visited local Rotary Clubs and Kiwanis, spoke to high school classes, orga-nized voter registration drives, wrote letters to the editor, and handed out petitions at Bulldogs football games.

But the understated character of his dissent did nothing to heal the breach that had opened up with his family. Hayes Searcy demanded to know what they had done to his son over there. Had they turned him into a Communist? How could he still call himself a patriot, a true American? His parents, who by this time had moved to South Caro-lina, couldn't face their neighbors. *We don't want to see you anymore,*

*we want you out of the house. No visits, no phone calls, no contact of
any kind.*

Chuck dropped out of school again and threw himself into George
McGovern's campaign in southern Georgia, even though he knew the
senator from South Dakota had a snowball's chance in hell of winning
the state. It wasn't a matter of being liberal or conservative, he said. All
that mattered was ending the war.

Even though more and more Americans now felt that way, Nixon
duly took 75 percent of the vote in Georgia. He promised that his
second term would bring "peace with honor," but then, just before
Christmas, more bombs rained down on Hanoi. This new campaign
was designed to break a deadlock in the Paris peace talks and to pun-
ish the North for its refusal to leave the areas of Quang Tri and Thua
Thien that it had liberated during the Easter Offensive. But it shocked
the conscience of millions of Americans when an errant payload fell
on Bach Mai Hospital, one of the best in Vietnam, killing twenty-eight
of the staff.

An armistice was declared a month later, a week after Nixon's inauguration. There was a reciprocal release of prisoners, including Nguyen
Thanh Phu's father, who went home to Quang Tri, and that fall Henry
Kissinger and Vietnam's chief negotiator, Le Duc Tho, one of Le Duan's
closest hard-line allies, were jointly awarded the Nobel Peace Prize,
though Tho declined to accept it.

One day in the middle of all this, the phone rang. *Chuck, this is your
daddy. Are you busy? You got time for a cup of coffee?* Chuck said, "Yes
sir."

They went to a waffle house, beat around the bush for a while chatting about the weather and catching up on family news. Then Hayes
cleared his throat and said that he and his wife, Carolyn, had been
talking about this thing some more and decided that Chuck was right.
The war in Vietnam was a terrible business, and it was time for the
suffering to end. Both men teared up. Hayes never gave the reasons for
his change of heart. The war simply cleaved thousands of American
families in this way, and some, like the Searcys, had the good fortune
to find a path to reconciliation. Millions never did.

———

Vietnam had shredded the American story, the shared belief in the nation's nobility of purpose and the righteousness of its victories. "She goes not abroad in search of monsters to destroy," Secretary of State John Quincy Adams had written of the United States in 1821, but that precept had gone unheeded.

Breaking through what has been described as America's "self-induced national amnesia" about the war came the first wave of memoirs and novels, virtually all of them growing out of the horrors of I Corps: Caputo, Ehrhart, O'Brien, Herr; *Born on the Fourth of July,* by Ron Kovic, paralyzed from the waist down in a firefight on the DMZ near Dong Ha; *The 13th Valley,* by John Del Vecchio, an unsparing blow-by-blow account of fear and death in the unforgiving geography of the Da Krong Valley.

Nothing, however, touched the raw nerve of the postwar years more painfully than the movies. Sitting in a darkened theater was a visceral experience that allowed for little nuance, for few of what Caputo called "the moral ambiguities of a conflict in which demons and angels traded places too often to tell one from the other, even within yourself."

Hollywood had steered clear of the war until it was over, with a single notable exception. John Wayne's paean to the Special Forces, *The Green Berets,* released on the Fourth of July 1968, was a parable of good and evil based on the PAVN's attacks on the Green Beret bases at A Shau and nearby Nam Dong—"a film so unspeakable, so stupid, so rotten and false in every detail," wrote Renata Adler in *The New York Times,* "that it passes through being fun, through being funny, through being camp, through everything and becomes an invitation to grieve, not for our soldiers or for Vietnam (the film could not be more false or do a greater disservice to either of them), but for what has happened to the fantasy-making apparatus in this country."

With the synchronicity of Vietnam, Watergate, and the Church Committee hearings on the abuses of the CIA, the theaters were drenched in paranoia. *The Parallax View* and *The Conversation* told of sinister conspiracies by government and powerful private corporations. *Three Days of the Condor* was about a murderous rogue cabal within the CIA. In *All the President's Men,* Robert Redford's whispered conversation with Deep Throat in a darkened underground parking garage seemed the perfect metaphor for the mood of the times.

The earliest batch of postwar Vietnam movies offered emotional catharsis to some, but for others, especially the veterans themselves, they brought only further bitterness, grief, and confusion. *The Deer Hunter* dealt with the shock of return and the impossibility of emotional reconnection to uncomprehending friends, family, wives, and girlfriends. In *Coming Home* and *Born on the Fourth of July,* the lead characters were confined to wheelchairs, literally unmanned by the war, one wallowing in self-pity and the other screaming with primal rage.

Eventually Hollywood turned the clock back to the war itself, evoking in very different ways the realities of combat as experienced by ordinary grunts like Manus Campbell. They came back obsessively to the singular horrors of I Corps: *Hamburger Hill,* with its relentless depiction of carnage in pursuit of a lost cause, and Stanley Kubrick's *Full Metal Jacket,* with its psychopathic Marine drill sergeant and its strange, stylized reconstruction of the street fighting in Hue during Tet, re-created in a derelict industrial complex in London with palm trees imported from Spain because of Kubrick's fear of flying. And then, whether the vets loved it or hated it, which they did in roughly equal measure, there was Oliver Stone's *Platoon,* which hurled them straight back into the shadowed, jungled reality of places like Hill 674 and LZ Torch, facing an invisible enemy in the night, the green mountains of the Philippines serving as an almost seamless stand-in for Vietnam.

Above all, of course, there was Francis Ford Coppola's *Apocalypse Now,* in which the war dissolved into one long hallucination. *I love the smell of napalm in the morning.* And Brando's mad Colonel Kurtz in the flickering shadows of Cambodia: *The horror, the horror.*

Many vets did their best to return to the rhythms of normal life. A few exorcised their memories through poetry and prose. Some refought the war and screamed for public recognition. Others still, like Manus Campbell, turned in on themselves and did battle with their demons.

Listening to his reflections on his life in the postwar years, it was tempting to divide it neatly into discrete stages, like the acts of a play. But that wasn't how recovery from PTSD worked. "Healing is not a process, but happens in special moments, discontinuously, and not in a smooth flow," wrote the psychologist Arthur Egendorf, who, like Robert Jay Lifton and Chaim Shatan, organized rap sessions for traumatized veterans and wrote a classic book called *Healing from the War.* Egendorf came to the problem with unique credentials. He had studied under Kissinger at Harvard and worked in military intelligence in Vietnam, running French agents who had served in Indochina and Algeria and were now recruited by the Americans.

As the paradigm of the warrior's uneven progress to recovery, Egendorf used the story of Odysseus, whose return home took twenty years. "Before his journey was over," he wrote, "he lost all his comrades, matched wits with dangerous goddesses, battled one-eyed monsters and vengeful storm kings, and suffered a passage through hell."

Egendorf's book came out in 1986. Campbell had been a cop for sixteen years by then, but he was leading a kind of double life, or multiple lives perhaps. He wanted nothing to do with other veterans and refused to ask the VA for help. He blocked out all talk of postwar politics, of bitter issues like Agent Orange. When he ran into someone who introduced himself as a former Marine, he thought to himself, *No, you're a former human being.* Numbed by alcohol, he experienced what Lifton had called "a vast breakdown of faith in the larger human matrix supporting each individual life, and therefore a loss of faith (or trust) in the structure of existence."

He was on his second marriage after too many other women, some of them married. "Women have always played a crucial role in the drama of soldiers' homecoming," Egendorf wrote—all those "confrontations, seductions, and intricate dealings with feminine forces." More than once Campbell woke up screaming or leaped out of bed and attacked his wife, striking her in the head, thinking she was VC, a story that was not uncommon among those who had seen combat at close quarters.

At the same time, he had picked up the New Testament for the first time in years and been intrigued by an ad in the local *Asbury Park Press* about classes in Transcendental Meditation. Later, he and his second wife began to host a Friday-night TM group, early steps in a protracted spiritual journey. And he began to meet weekly with a psychotherapist in Manhattan.

Late one winter night, working the graveyard shift at the police station, he had the radio tuned to a talk show on ABC; the host was interviewing the author of a new book on veterans and PTSD. It was Egendorf. Campbell bought the book the next morning, read it cover to cover in two days, picked up the phone, and called the author. "Let's meet," Egendorf said.

They continued to do so for many years, and through their conversations, Campbell came to understand that the trauma so many Vietnam vets were experiencing was about something more than the horrors of combat. Fighting hand to hand, island to island in the South Pacific had been every bit as brutal, but World War II had been seen as righteous, and the survivors had come home as victors, greeted with civic parades, with flags and confetti. In the Good War, everyone was a hero. Homecoming from Vietnam offered none of that affirmation. It meant confronting the people they had been before they were sent to fight, with all their teenage insecurities, the need to prove their manhood as warriors, the things they had seen and the things they had done. In Campbell's case, it was obviously the desire to earn his father's approval, and then the weight of guilt when he failed him, when he turned out to be just another terrified grunt in a fighting hole, watching others scream for their mothers. *Why did I do nothing to stop it?* And everyone who came back in one piece had to face the inexplicable mystery, the gossamer line and burden of survival: *Why him and not me?*

"What do you do with an experience that touches your core?" Egendorf asked. "Bury it? Run from it? Stalk it like an enemy? Charge into it with full force? Surrender to it?"

His answer was to paraphrase Brando's Colonel Kurtz. You have to make a friend of the horror. If you run away from your trauma, you will always be its prisoner.

Benefit of the Doubt

A MONG THE SLEW of postwar movies about Vietnam, none had a deeper or more direct influence than the political outlier: Sylvester Stallone's two-part revenge fantasy, *Rambo: First Blood,* which bore not on the traumas of the past but on the polemics of the present. By the time the first part was released in 1982, the Reagan administration was embroiled in Central America, another Cold War battlefield with a similar Cold War enemy and similarly dubious Cold War allies, in a landscape of forested mountains and peasant villages that must have seemed, to the Special Forces who secretly served there, uncannily reminiscent of the Truong Son range in Vietnam and Laos. When conservatives talked about overcoming the Vietnam Syndrome in El Salvador, what they meant was, in John Rambo's famous question, *Do we get to win this time?*

It was easy to sneer at the franchise for the crudeness of its fantasies, and Rambo himself might have seemed like just another crazy vet, a stock figure of the postwar imagination. But the movies were woven around genuine grievances. For all of Reagan's talk of Vietnam as a "noble cause," he was no great friend of the Veterans Administration, slashing its budget during his second term. In the first of the two movies, what motivates Rambo is his rage at the government's callous treatment of a friend who has died of cancer, an unacknowledged victim of Agent Orange. The sequel, *First Blood II,* is about Rambo's mission to bring back Americans missing in action, supposedly still held as prisoners of war somewhere in the jungles of Vietnam or Laos, betrayed by cowardly bureaucrats, duplicitous CIA agents, and an indifferent public.

For Americans, the fights over Agent Orange and the fate of the missing were two of the most bitter legacies of the war. The Vietnamese and the Lao had to deal with these things too, and more besides, like the continued human toll from unexploded ordnance and the huge number of physical disabilities. But the process that unfolded as each side struggled to come to terms with the aftermath of the conflict was a study in the inequities of power, which is really the story of all politics. The multiple legacies of the war could not all be addressed at once, and ultimately only the U.S. government had the power to dictate the sequence in which that happened. But others would use whatever leverage and resources they had as private citizens to inflect the process, to do what their government couldn't or wouldn't do.

Where the impact of the war fell on Americans, it was the vets themselves who led the fight, though their politics were all over the map, from the farthest right-wing fringes of the Rambo crowd to the angriest of the medal-throwers on the steps of the Capitol. Where it fell on the Vietnamese, which it did much more heavily, it would take a loose community of intersecting interests to lighten the long shadow of the war. The veterans were central to this too. They had a unique kind of credibility, no matter the cause that their government had pursued. But they couldn't do it alone. They would need to join forces with others: those who were driven by religious faith and humanitarian experience, scientists with the capacity and will to unravel the mysteries of dioxin, others who could apply institutional muscle at the highest levels.

The postwar politics of Agent Orange were awash with fears of official conspiracies and cover-ups, beset by the uncertainties of scientific knowledge about the effects of dioxin on the bodies of those who had been exposed to it. Between the United States and Vietnam, the human legacy of Operation Ranch Hand was a political third rail, poisoning any hope of full reconciliation for well over twenty years. In their search for facts and in their demands for action, the former enemies moved on parallel tracks, each with its own interests and imperatives.

On the rare occasions they intersected, it was in a spirit of mutual suspicion or open antagonism. Even after U.S.-Vietnamese diplomatic relations were restored in 1995, American officials were forbidden for several years to utter the words *Agent Orange* in public, with their insinuation of war crimes, reparations, and corporate liability.

On the domestic front, facing up to the effects of the rainbow herbicides on human health meant navigating a force field that pushed and pulled people in conflicting directions. The veterans themselves were driven by anxiety, anger, and a sense of betrayal; scientists searched for verifiable data; politicians had to respond to what those data showed—and often influenced how they were collected in the first place—and were answerable, at least in theory, to those who demanded changes in public policy; lawyers and judges also looked to science but needed time to develop a body of case law; and humanitarians clamored for immediate answers that neither the scientists, the politicians, nor the courts of law were able to provide.

Each of these disciplines worked according to its own timetable. Science, by its very nature, was iterative, testing hypotheses, conducting studies, evaluating results, operating by arcane rules that few lay people, least of all angry veterans, understood. Politics moved in fits and starts according to the pressures of the moment and the constellation of forces in Congress. Lawsuits could drag on for years. The humanitarians, though, were driven by what Martin Luther King, Jr., called "the fierce urgency of now," insisting that in the absence of scientific certainty, the best available data and the most openhearted ethics had to be combined to short-circuit the delays. The nation owed its veterans the benefit of the doubt.

It was much harder to apply these arguments to Vietnam. The one exception, ironically, began in the earliest days of Operation Ranch Hand, when a group of American scientists, motivated not by its impact on those who were fighting in Vietnam, but by what was being done to the people who lived there, did everything in their power to get the herbicide campaign shut down.

Protests from the scientific community, including several Nobel Prize winners, began soon after the campaign moved into its full operational phase in March 1965. They were broadly worded at first, driven by the precautionary principle: much more was known about the power of new technologies than about their possible consequences. The loudest voices at this early stage were concerned mainly with the effects of Ranch Hand on Vietnam's natural environment. E. W. Pfeiffer was a zoologist, Gordon Orians an ornithologist, Arthur Westing an ex-Marine captain and forest ecologist who had studied the effects of 2,4-D and 2,4,5-T, the ingredients of Agent Orange, in the 1940s. In December 1966, with the defoliation approaching its peak, Pfeiffer persuaded the American Association for the Advancement of Science to set up a special committee to examine the environmental impact of the herbicides. The following September, the AAAS wrote to Robert McNamara proposing a study by the National Academy of Sciences or some other independent body. The Pentagon replied that there was no reason for concern, since one had already been commissioned, from the Midwest Research Institute (MRI) in Kansas City.

The MRI study, issued in December 1967, turned out to be little more than a literature review. The basic message was that there was no cause for alarm—with one possible exception: the arsenical Agent Blue, the main herbicide used for destroying food crops. Pfeiffer denounced the report as a "snow job," and in July 1968 the AAAS, after furious internal divisions and resignations, demanded a halt to the use of Agent Blue and a thorough field investigation, perhaps under UN auspices. Impossible under wartime conditions, the Defense Department said. Besides, the Pentagon argued, the cacodylic acid in Agent Blue was pentavalent arsenic, no more toxic than aspirin. That was true enough at the point of delivery, the AAAS scientists responded, but the chemical could be rapidly broken down by microorganisms in the soil and converted into its trivalent form, a known carcinogen. *Arsenate* could become *arsenite:* a single letter of the alphabet; a world of difference.

Pfeiffer lost patience and decided to organize his own mission, under the banner of the Society for Social Responsibility in Science. He and Orians spent two weeks in South Vietnam in March and April 1969. They were pleasantly surprised by the cooperation they received from the Military Assistance Command Vietnam, which included laying on helicopters and Swift Boats to inspect some of the sprayed areas. They were even allowed to fly on one of the bigger Ranch Hand missions, a formation of seven aircraft, each loaded with one thousand gallons of chemicals. But there wasn't much they could conclude from a distance, and they accepted MACV's argument that the herbicides were important in protecting American soldiers from ambush. If the mangrove forests lining the waterways of the Mekong Delta had not been defoliated, Pfeiffer said, he would have feared for his life.

That summer and fall, the whole debate changed. In June and July, half a dozen Saigon newspapers defied government censors and published reports from Tan Chau district in Tay Ninh province, right on the Cambodian border, with pictures of hideously deformed fetuses: one with a face like a duck, another that looked more like a sheep, another that had three legs wrapped around its head and half its face missing. Four of the papers were promptly shut down, but the word was out.

These reports caught the attention of John Constable, a surgeon and navy veteran who had volunteered in a Saigon hospital during the Tet Offensive, and Matthew Meselson of Harvard Medical School, one of the world's leading molecular geneticists. Meselson got hold of an advance copy of a report by a private company, Bionetic Research Laboratories, that had been commissioned in 1965 by the U.S. National Cancer Institute. The study had administered 2,4,5-T, one half of Agent Orange, to pregnant lab rats and mice and found that it was teratogenic. In other words, it caused birth defects in rats and might do so in humans. Pfeiffer compared 2,4,5-T to thalidomide, and Meselson sent a copy of the Bionetic report to Richard Nixon's science adviser, Dr. Lee DuBridge.

By this time, the political winds had shifted radically in the United States, after the horrors of Hamburger Hill, the revelation of the My Lai massacre, and the creation of the federal Environmental Protection Agency. In April 1970, the Department of the Interior barred many domestic uses of 2,4,5-T, although it would be another nine years before the EPA banned it altogether. In Vietnam, after much resistance from the military, the C-123s flew their last Agent Orange mission on April 16 of that year, although small amounts were still used to spray base perimeters until September.

Meselson, Constable, and the forester Art Westing spent five weeks in Vietnam that summer, accompanied by one of Meselson's graduate students, a brilliant young chemist named Robert Baughman. Westing kept a detailed daily journal of the trip, which began with a meeting in Paris with officials of the Provisional Revolutionary Government.

The scientists collected as much firsthand information as they could.

They visited the biggest pig farm in Southeast Asia, near Bien Hoa, whose owner claimed that thousands of pigs had died after a spray flight passed over. A chicken farmer in Binh Duong province, just outside Saigon, told a similar story. Fishermen said there were fewer fish than before in the rivers and they were smaller, but perhaps that was because ARVN soldiers liked to go fishing by tossing hand grenades into the water. Westing kept an open mind; there was no way to corroborate these anecdotal reports.

The Americans visited a Vietnamese hospital where large numbers of children had cleft lips, later identified as one of the most common malformations associated with Agent Orange. Examining the medical records at the Tay Ninh provincial hospital, Constable confirmed the abnormally high rate of miscarriages and deformed infants. South Vietnamese government officials spoke of a secret study of birth defects. Westing gathered data on "spray drift," the risk that people could be exposed to the volatile chemicals even if they were far from the flightpath. "Worst herbicide problem is from drift—real probs at least 5 km or more," he noted in his diary. He found that drift could occur even from military garbage dumps where the supposedly empty barrels were discarded.

Everywhere the team went, they took samples of fish and crustaceans, breast milk and human hair, jars of fish sauce bottled in different years. Later these were analyzed in a Harvard lab using an advanced form of high-resolution mass spectrometry developed by Baughman, who found very high levels of TCDD in the breast milk of nursing mothers. It was impossible, however, to correlate their findings with the location of past spray flights, since the military refused to divulge those records. Once the team flew north to I Corps, the stories became more dramatic. Local officials of CORDS, the military-civilian civic action program, told them it was too dangerous to venture into the sprayed areas. "You could go into the A Shau Valley," one said, "but you wouldn't come out." Still, Meselson and Constable were given permission to fly over a remote area of Quang Ngai, the southernmost of the five provinces in I Corps, where the rice terraces had recently been sprayed with Agent Blue. Meselson took photographs of the long, brown swaths of dead vegetation and the surrounding bomb craters, the result of "maximum suppressive fire" before the spraying. They were VC fields, the military assured them; the local Montagnards didn't grow terraced rice. But Meselson checked that with Gerald Hickey, an anthropologist with the RAND Corporation, who knew more about ethnic minority culture in Vietnam than any other American. Not true, Hickey said. The local H're people had always farmed that way.

The ethnic villagers might have endured bombing and shelling and napalm, but crop destruction was the last straw, severing them from their ancestral lands, their presiding spirits, and their livelihoods. They were left with no alternative but to flee to the resettlement camp outside Quang Ngai city, where they depended on handouts of rice from the military. "The plight of the Vietnamese peasant is similar to that of the American Indian of times past," Westing wrote in his diary. "By exterminating the bison, the American white culture brought the Indian to his knees without having to exterminate him as well. We drove the Indian into the forts begging for food. That's what we are doing in Indochina on a much vaster, more sophisticated scale."

The refugees said that at least ninety children and several old people had died in one village after their fields were sprayed. Everyone had used the same pond for their drinking water. All of them had fled from Ba To district, where Meselson had photographed the ruined fields. "Left because the valley had become evil," Westing noted, "so evil that they even killed their buffalo (very extreme measure)." The team clipped samples of the refugees' hair, looking for the presence of arsenic. The H're resisted at first, thinking it would steal part of their body and spirit. So Meselson cut off some of his own hair to show that the procedure was harmless.

After Westing flew home, Meselson stayed on for a few days in Saigon, where he asked Gen. Creighton Abrams, the commander of MACV, what he thought of Operation Ranch Hand from a military point of view. "You want to know what I think?" Abrams answered. "I think it's shit." He said his son John, who had served for two years as an army lieutenant in the heavily sprayed Central Highlands, agreed.

Later, Meselson called Brig. Gen. Douglas Kinnard, who had served two tours in Vietnam and commanded troops during the Cambodia incursion. Kinnard told him that he knew of no situation, other than providing security for base perimeters, in which the use of herbicides had been helpful to the war effort. The removal of vegetation along lines of communication to prevent ambush had actually been counter-productive: after the spraying, the number of enemy KIAs went down, while American deaths increased. The PAVN and the Viet Cong simply developed more creative ambush techniques. The defoliation of forest cover was a waste of time, Kinnard said, because it acted so slowly. "It was like sending them a greeting card: *Dear enemy, This is to let you know that we are spraying the forest where you are hiding. In four or five weeks all the leaves will fall off, so you'd better move somewhere else. If you stay where you are we will see you from the air and shoot you dead. Yours sincerely.*"

On December 26, 1970, the AAAS held its annual assembly, in Chicago. As Meselson was delivering his report on the team's mission that summer, the great anthropologist Margaret Mead, a future president of the organization, came up to the podium, gave him a warm hug, and announced that she had news: "Ambassador Bunker and General Abrams are initiating a program for an orderly, yet rapid phaseout of the herbicide operations."

American helicopters and ground crews did continue to spray smaller amounts of Agent White until the following February, and crop destruction with Agent Blue "in very remote areas" continued until December. When Ranch Hand was finally shut down altogether, what remained of these two herbicides was transferred to the ARVN as part of the Vietnamization program. There is no record of how they were used.

Despite the good news, Meselson continued to worry about the lasting effects of the arsenic in Agent Blue, which were never studied. Agent White, though it persisted for a long time in the soil, raised fewer health concerns, though it was associated with diarrhea, weight loss, and damage to the liver, kidney, spleen, and central nervous system. TCDD, however, was now recognized as a singular threat. As early as March 1965, Dow Chemical's chief toxicologist had concluded that dioxin was "exceptionally toxic" to humans. Meselson put it more strongly. It was "100 times more poisonous than the most powerful nerve gas," he said. "An evil genius could not devise a toxin with more evil properties."

When the military gathered up all the unused barrels of Agent Orange from Danang and Bien Hoa and smaller "turnaround" bases—an operation called Pacer IVY—they added up to 1.37 million gallons. Another 850,000 were still stored at Gulfport, Mississippi, awaiting shipment to Vietnam. The question now was what to do with them.

The air force considered several options: Should the defoliants be returned to their manufacturers? Used as raw material for manufacturing other chemicals? Buried deep underground? Stored indefinitely in nuclear waste bunkers? They opted in the end for incineration but decided this couldn't be done safely in the United States. So the barrels were shipped to Johnston Island, part of a remote atoll in the North Pacific, a former nuclear and biological warfare test site that was now used to store chemical weapons. In 1977 the last of the Ranch Hand chemicals were carried out to sea and burned: Operation Pacer HO.

But on the bases where the herbicides were stored and loaded onto aircraft, there had been the predictable quotient of human error and mechanical failure that tends to accompany the more deliberate cruelties of war. About one in a thousand barrels leaked, some as a result of a manufacturing defect and some from mishandling, said Alvin "Dr. Orange" Young, the air force's leading herbicide expert. Residue slopped onto the ground as the chemical agents, mixed with oil, were pumped into tanker trucks and thence to the thousand-gallon tanks aboard the C-123s. The gallon or two remaining in the bottom of a barrel might be casually disposed of by pouring it on the ground or tossing it into a general garbage dump. Local people often used the discarded barrels to store gasoline, diesel fuel, or household goods.

The worst contamination was at Bien Hoa, in the area where the chemicals had been stored, and at the Pacer IVY collection site. There were at least four spills from the bulk storage tanks, the biggest of them about 7,500 gallons of Agent Orange. The job of cleaning up the mess fell to local women, who worked in sandals with neither gloves nor other protective clothing. The only safety gear available had been designed for Western men and didn't come close to fitting.

In the immediate postwar years, Americans didn't want to think much about the aftereffects of the defoliation. The first vets to suggest that their unusual health problems might be related to Agent Orange tended to end up in VA psych wards. In Vietnam, meanwhile, doctors were seeing a high incidence of cancer in fighters returning from the southern battlefields, and large numbers of abnormal pregnancies and birth defects in their offspring.

Scientists were now fully aware of the dangers of dioxin but needed to determine who had been exposed to it, where, when, and for how long. The concentration of the chemicals in Vietnam was much greater than when they were used in the United States. It was also known that the TCDD problem had worsened after the production process was ramped up to meet Pentagon demands, when manufacturers failed to maintain proper temperature controls. TCDD levels also varied significantly in different batches of Agent Orange—Dow Chemical prided itself in keeping them lower than other companies; and the levels in Agent Purple, which had been used early on in the A Shau Valley and on the Ho Chi Minh Trail in Laos, were even higher. Could procurement data shed light on which barrels were the most heavily contaminated, and could the operational records show where these were used? Was it possible to establish a clear cause-and-effect relationship between dioxin exposure and the array of health problems that began to manifest themselves in veterans, or was it all just guesswork? Given these unresolved questions, Agent Orange proved to be a scientific, political, cultural, emotional, and ethical minefield of unique complexity, a kind of symbolic surrogate for people's feelings about the war in general.

The unease among scientists grew steadily, and not only because of Vietnam. In 1976 an industrial accident at a chemical plant in Seveso, Italy, released a gas cloud laden with dioxin, sickening hundreds of local residents and killing thousands of farm animals. Three years later Taiwan suffered a mass poisoning event, known as "Yucheng disease," from dioxin-contaminated rice oil. In 1980 scientists gathered in Rome for the first international conference on persistent organic pollutants (POPs), a family of compounds including dioxin and polychlorinated biphenyls (PCBs) that came to be known as the "forever chemicals" or the "dirty dozen."

Although the Veterans Administration continued to look the other way, public attitudes had begun to shift, thanks in large part to a 1978 CBS documentary called *Agent Orange: Vietnam's Deadly Fog* and a lawsuit filed by a vet with terminal cancer, Paul Reutershan, which by 1979 had expanded into the largest class action suit in U.S. history.

Four months after the last of the herbicides were incinerated off

Johnston Island, Bobby Muller, a Marine vet who was confined to a wheelchair after a bullet ripped through his spine at the Cam Lo bridge in Quang Tri, formed an organization that called itself the Council of Vietnam Veterans, later renamed as Vietnam Veterans of America. The group was born of anger. Thousands of vets felt disparaged, neglected, reduced in the public mind to stereotypes like the deranged Travis Bickle in *Taxi Driver,* the self-pitying Luke in *Coming Home,* or just the babbling homeless guy on the street corner.

McGeorge Bundy, formerly national security adviser to Kennedy and Johnson and later head of the Ford Foundation, told Muller why the veterans' demands were being ignored. "You have to know Vietnam makes powerful people in this country uneasy," he said. "They feel embarrassed, ashamed, guilty, various emotions, but they're all negative, and they're simply not going to deal with it. And you as the veterans are the legacy of that conflict, and you're therefore going to be shunned."

The government seemed deaf to the vets' claims that their rash of postwar illnesses, their wives' miscarriages, and their children's birth defects might be connected to their service in Vietnam. They were told that American troops were never in the area when the herbicides were sprayed, which they knew to be a lie.

This was finally confirmed in 1980, at the first of many congressional hearings on Agent Orange, by someone who spoke from personal experience. Max Cleland, the head of the VA at the time, had been left a triple amputee by a carelessly dropped grenade during the relief of Khe Sanh. He said that he'd witnessed the spraying himself over a two-week period in the spring of 1967 at LZ Sally, a landing zone in the Co Bi-Thanh Tan Valley, where Manus Campbell's company was ambushed later that year. But that left "a very difficult case of scientific linkage" to human disease, Cleland said. Injecting 2,4,5-T into lab rats under controlled conditions was not the same thing as measuring the exposure of troops more than a decade earlier. This was true, of course, but to Muller it was an infuriating equivocation. How much science was needed before compassion kicked in?

So how could Cleland's question about the linkage be answered? The first challenge was to identify a suitable group of veterans for an epidemiological study, and the choice was those who had flown the C-123s.

On the face of it, this seemed logical, since their daily exposure to the chemicals was a matter of record. But they were also a problematic group, a self-selected cohort, proud of the reputation they had cultivated as a daredevil elite, with a strong psychological stake in proving that the defoliants were harmless. It was true that their onboard herbicide tanks might have leaky valves or be hit by groundfire, and sometimes the interior of the aircraft had to be scrubbed down after a mission. But unlike grunts in the field, C-123 pilots were from the officer class, and they were in a sealed cockpit; the greater risk was to the equipment operators and the loaders and handlers on the ground. If pilots came in contact with the chemicals, they knew that when they got back to Danang or Bien Hoa, they could look forward to a cleansing shower and an immediate change of clothes.

When the study found that the Ranch Hand aircrew were in robust health, it gave the air force a cudgel to beat back the claims of other vets. Maj. Jack Spey, president of the Ranch Hand Association, who went on to become a plainclothes operative in the secret air war in Laos after the herbicide campaign ended, was especially combative. In a 1982 letter to the House Committee on Veterans Affairs, he deplored the "scientifically unsupported sensationalism and emotionalism" around the issue of Agent Orange and said that "the most exhaustive epidemiological study ever undertaken by this country's scientific community on a military population" should have put the debate to rest.

Instead, Congress mandated a more comprehensive research program under the auspices of the Centers for Disease Control. Among the many studies it produced, two stood out. One was the Vietnam Experience Study, which took a broad-brush approach to veterans' health problems, taking into account not only their exposure to Agent Orange but also diseases they might have contracted for other reasons, including the psychological stressors of combat. The other was a massive effort to assess the possible exposure of individual combat troops, based on two sets of military records: one showing the coordinates of each spray run and the other the location of units on the ground at the time. Once these two data sets were computerized, they could be combined to calculate the exposure risk. The CDC called this the "hits" method.

But because it was based on tracking the movements of entire battalions, not individual companies, it was a blunt instrument. Manus

Campbell's experience had been typical: while he was on the road to the A Shau Valley with Alpha 1/4, for example, the rest of his battalion was up on the DMZ, sixty miles away. Battalions could also be temporarily split up, and individual companies could be assigned to other commands for joint operations. And there were innumerable other variables to take into account, from the character of the local vegetation to the weather on the day the planes went over.

Meanwhile the class action suit by veterans inched its way through the legal system, and in 1984 New York District Court judge Jack Weinstein announced an out-of-court settlement, with no admission of liability from the manufacturers of the defoliants. The Agent Orange Settlement Fund grew, with interest, to $325 million, which was eventually paid out to more than fifty thousand disabled veterans or their widows. For the first time, political pragmatism, or a sense of moral obligation, took precedence over scientific certainty.

The court appointed two expert consultants to advise on the settlement: Jeanne Stellman, an occupational health specialist at Columbia University, and her husband, Steven Stellman, an epidemiologist with the American Cancer Society. In time, their work would have a major influence in reshaping the debate about Agent Orange, both at home and in Vietnam.

While the CDC studies were under way, the Stellmans had been conducting one of their own, sponsored by the American Legion. Starting with a random selection of seven thousand veterans, they found a clear correlation between exposure to Agent Orange and significant health problems. The key to assessing risk, they argued, was to combine the "hits" method with the veterans' personal accounts of their experience.

The Stellmans were scathing about the "mega-science" approach that had infected the CDC studies, which were shut down in 1989. These had cost tens of millions of taxpayer dollars, lacked independence, and produced largely worthless results. "CDC study oversight was controlled by a White House political organ," the Stellmans told Congress, and "the Ranch Hand advisory group is inbred and secretive." The methodology of the Ranch Hand study was absurd, trying to quantify the exposure risk by dividing the total volume of chemicals sprayed by the number of men in the aircrews. The CDC, meanwhile, had broken the most elemental rules of epidemiology by "attempt[ing] to investigate, shotgun-like, every conceivable question at once." Epidemiology was an inexact science, and what was needed was multiple small-scale studies that looked at particular groups and specific health problems. Looking at the movement of whole battalions defied common sense, since many if not most of the troops would never have been anywhere near a spray run. Others had been at much higher risk from prolonged exposure—nurses at field hospitals, engineering units, crews involved in perimeter spraying, and scout dog handlers, whose animals were known to suffer from high levels of testicular cancer.

The information necessary to feed studies like these, the Stellmans went on, "seems to have been a well-kept secret, and would have been buried after the CDC abandoned its Agent Orange studies had the federal court not obtained them through Freedom of Information Act requests." By using the military's declassified after-action reports and command chronologies, the flight records—known as the HERBS (Herbicide Reporting System) tapes—and the Daily Air Activity Reports, as well as the Army Chemical Corps records of operations that were not part of Ranch Hand, it should be possible to get both a fine-grained sense of which American troops had been most at risk and what the consequences of the herbicides were for the Vietnamese.

Jeanne Stellman would end up spending more than thirty years making sense of all these data. As digital technologies evolved, and with funding from the National Academy of Sciences and the National Institutes of Health, she put together a state-of-the-art database. This tabulated almost twenty thousand Ranch Hand sorties, though she estimated that about one-seventh of the records were missing. For each mission, there were details of the herbicide used, the amount sprayed, and the precise location. Using these geographical coordinates, a veteran could see his "exposure opportunity" within five kilometers of a spray run, calculated on a logarithmic scale.

The Stellmans combined the Ranch Hand records with wartime demographic data, a list, compiled by the U.S. military, of every hamlet in South Vietnam. The magnitude of the herbicide campaign was now both clear and startling. Between 1961 and 1971, more than 20 million gallons of herbicides were sprayed, covering as much as one-sixth of the surface area of South Vietnam, an area almost the size of Massachusetts. Agent Orange accounted for more than 60 percent of this amount, followed in order by White, Blue, and Purple. More than three thousand rural villages had come under the spray. That translated into at least 2.1 million people, and perhaps as many as 4.8 million—a figure that included only residents, not combatants or transients. In 2003 the Stellmans published the results of their groundbreaking research in *Nature* magazine. For anyone seeking to understand the magnitude of the defoliation campaign, their work became the gold standard.

In 1991, exactly twenty years after the last spray planes took off, the veterans finally got what they had been clamoring for, or at least a measure of it. But when the breakthrough came, they felt as much bitterness as relief: their suspicion that the government's inaction was the result of something more sinister than indifference or incompetence was confirmed.

The Veterans Administration had consistently rejected any claim that postwar health problems might be related to Agent Orange. By 1984, the same year Judge Weinstein settled the vets' class action suit, Congress had run out of patience and passed the Dioxin Standards Act, which forced the VA to set up an expert advisory committee to study the evidence. If this was found to be ambiguous, the veterans should be granted the benefit of the doubt. But the brick wall at the VA remained, and by the time Reagan left office in 1989, 31,000 Vietnam veterans had seen their claims for compensation dismissed.

With new leadership and a new name for the VA, which now became the Department of Veterans Affairs and was elevated by George H. W. Bush to cabinet level, the debate was transformed. An independent expert, retired Adm. Elmo R. Zumwalt, Jr., was asked to review the entire body of research and come up with recommendations. No one expected him to reach hard and fast conclusions; he was simply asked to determine "whether it is at least as likely as not that there is a statistical association between exposure to Agent Orange and a specific adverse health effect."

Zumwalt's credentials were impeccable, based not only on his military seniority but on a compelling personal story. As commander of naval operations in Vietnam, he had ordered the defoliation of river-banks in the Mekong Delta, where his son, Lt. Elmo R. Zumwalt III, commanded a patrol boat. In 1988 the younger Zumwalt died of Hodg-kin's disease and non-Hodgkin's lymphoma. His infant son had already been born with sensory integration dysfunction, a brain disorder.

Admiral Zumwalt's report, completed in May 1990 and initially clas-sified, included a list of diseases, including twenty kinds of cancer, that met the criterion of "at least as likely as not." He highlighted the special risks to the Marines in I Corps. "Army personnel generally engaged the enemy and returned to base," he noted, "whereas Marines consistently remained in areas presumably sprayed by Agent Orange."

He readily acknowledged that the science of immunotoxicology was still in its infancy, but that wasn't the point. The weight of moral obliga-tion was so strong that the veterans shouldn't have to wait any longer. It was time to put an end to the "embarrassingly prolonged Agent Orange controversy" and "finally to right a significant national wrong commit-ted against our Vietnam Veterans."

The most shocking part of Zumwalt's report was his blistering cri-tique of official deception, echoed in the title of a report from the House Veterans Affairs Committee later that year: "The Agent Orange Cover-up: A Case of Flawed Science and Political Manipulation."

Zumwalt held nothing back. Among the sources he drew on were three Vietnamese studies of birth defects, published in 1989—probably the first time the work of Vietnamese scientists had been officially recognized. Like Judge Weinstein, Zumwalt brought in the Stellmans as expert consultants, citing their "stunning indictment of the [VA] Advisory Committee's scientific interpretation and policy judgments," excoriating the committee's "blatant lack of impartiality."

The bias was not accidental. "Political interference in government-sponsored studies associated with Agent Orange has been the norm, not the exception," he wrote. "In fact, there appears to have been a sys-tematic effort to suppress critical data or alter results to meet precon-ceived notions of what alleged scientific studies were meant to find." He found the same pattern of "deception, fraud and political interfer-ence" in the studies commissioned by Monsanto and other chemical companies. To scientists and public health specialists, the scandal was inseparable from the Reagan administration's broader effort to limit regulations on hazardous chemicals and shield industry from claims of liability.

For the vets, the clinching proof of an official conspiracy was a letter Zumwalt included in his report from a chemical weapons expert, James Clary, who had written the air force's classified evaluation of Operation Ranch Hand in 1971. Addressed to Sen. Tom Daschle (D-SD), himself a former captain in Air Force intelligence, the letter said that from the very start of the program, military scientists were "aware of the potential for damage due to dioxin contamination in the herbicide," but were not overly concerned "because the material was to be used on the 'enemy.'" No one had thought much about the risk to American troops, but Clary now singled out their exposure in three heavily sprayed areas as especially worrisome: War Zones C and D, close to Saigon, and I Corps, which he noted was "garrisoned mostly by Marines." Clary's assertions have never been corroborated, but as far as the veterans were concerned, the burden of proof had been met.

After the Zumwalt report, the Agent Orange Act of February 1991, which passed in both houses of Congress with unanimous consent, seemed almost a formality. It established a "presumptive service association" between a veteran's presence in South Vietnam and a list of specified diseases. Anyone who had served in the country between January 1962 and May 1975 and suffered from any of these conditions would be eligible for compensation, and further studies by the National Academy of Sciences and the Institute of Medicine led to a steady expansion of the "presumptive" list to include common diseases like prostate cancer and type-2 diabetes. Eventually, benefits were even extended to veterans of the Blue Water Navy, even if they had never set foot on the Vietnamese mainland and even to those who had served on air bases in Thailand.

In a narrow sense, Maj. Jack Spey had not been wrong. The subject was indeed clouded with emotion, and the evidence was limited and contradictory. But the Agent Orange Act was not dependent on hard scientific fact; it embodied the formula Bobby Muller had demanded for years, combining the best available data with basic human decency—with a good admixture of political pragmatism and guilt.

What thousands of veterans took away from the painful saga was a belief in official betrayal. In the case of Agent Orange, it was grounded in solid evidence and shared by veterans from all across the political spectrum. But a second conspiracy theory also took root, one that was more pernicious because it lacked any foundation in fact. It was fomented by the most extreme conservative voices, the true believers in the stab-in-the-back theory—that the troops had been betrayed by traitorous civilians. Their lightning-rod issue was the supposed abandonment of surviving prisoners of war in Southeast Asia. Although the facts were against them, these conspiracy theorists did not lack for political influence, which peaked at much the same time as the release of Admiral Zumwalt's report on Agent Orange and went on to change the course of Chuck Searcy's life.

Untangling the Tangle

RECONCILED WITH HIS FAMILY, and in the first of two marriages, Chuck Searcy had become something of a man about town in Athens, Georgia, dividing his time between Democratic Party politics and a new vocation as a newspaperman. The plan to start a paper grew out of his involvement with a local church group that published an amateurish biweekly news sheet. The city deserved something better, he thought, and he hashed out the idea with a member of the UGA faculty, Pete McCommons, one of the leaders of the Kent State protests on campus with a reputation, another Georgia paper wrote, as "an all-around rabble-rouser." They launched their new venture in 1974, calling it the *Athens Observer,* and it became a city institution.

At the same time, Searcy was striking up what would become an enduring friendship with State Sen. Max Cleland, the triplegic veteran of Khe Sanh who went on to become head of the VA under Jimmy Carter and then served for six years as a U.S. senator before falling to a particularly nasty smear campaign by his Republican opponent, Saxby Chambliss, in the hyperpatriotic months after 9/11.

Searcy had first worked with Cleland to push through a state senate bill to waive tuition fees for returning veterans who couldn't afford college. Now he hoped to dip a toe deeper into electoral politics by managing Cleland's 1974 campaign for lieutenant governor. A more parochial form of politics intervened, however. Two years earlier Searcy and McCommons had managed to get themselves arrested with six others during a peaceful sit-in to protest UGA's campus housing policy; they were fined $500 each and given a year's probation. In the overheated spirit of the times, they were dubbed the Athens Eight—"which was far in excess of our importance by any stretch of the imagination," Searcy said dryly. "But it was a convenient way to put us in a box as obnoxious Communists and radicals and perverts."

"As much as anyone I've known," McCommons wrote in *Flagpole,* another local magazine that he started after the *Observer* folded, run into the ground by new owners, "Chuck has a Zelig-like ability to be where the action is." Incorrigibly social, he moved easily among worlds: gadfly activism, mainstream politics, and the emerging rock and roll scene that was turning Athens, a town more familiar with country-western shows at the Holiday Inn lounge, into an unlikely center of the 1970s counterculture. The band that made the biggest stir was the B-52s, who took its name from the beehive hairstyles of their female singers, which were said to resemble the nose cone of the giant bomber that had flattened Vietnam. To mark the first anniversary of the *Observer,* Searcy and McCommons laid on a celebration at the Taylor-Grady House, an antebellum Greek Revival mansion that epitomized old Georgia. There were crystal champagne glasses and canapés. The B-52s turned up uninvited, bent on mayhem. When time came for the guests to leave, they couldn't find their hats; eventually these were spotted, nestled among the chandeliers.

But just as he had chosen not to hurl his medals onto the Capitol steps, Searcy was not temperamentally inclined to toss hats onto light fixtures. He went back to school one last time and finally graduated in 1979. It had taken fifteen years. He was in his mid-thirties now, and it was time to buckle down to a real career. Armed with his newspaper experience, he went to Washington. Cleland offered him a job at the VA, but he ended up instead in a midlevel position in communications at the Small Business Administration that gave him a crash course in the arcane workings of the federal government. After Carter lost the presidency to Ronald Reagan in November 1980, however, Searcy had no interest in serving under a new president who spoke of Vietnam as a noble cause. Better to dedicate himself to local politics in Georgia. His wife decided to stay put in the capital, and that led to the end of his first marriage. But he never lost touch with Cleland. Every time they met, whether it was in Washington or at a meeting of veterans with PTSD at a strip mall in Atlanta, the greeting was the same: a cry of "Hey, brother!" and a one-armed bear bug, powerful enough to tumble Searcy into the wheelchair.

By 1985 Searcy was married again, to a creative, independent-minded elementary school teacher. Cleland turned up at the wedding, an unexpected guest. His new wife was "a wonderfully engaging party animal," Searcy said, who hung out with members of R.E.M., the best-known band to emerge from the blossoming Athens music scene. The following year he threw himself into a rambunctious, shoestring campaign for the U.S. Senate by Congressman Wyche Fowler, a fellow veteran of military intelligence, though he hadn't served in Vietnam.

They crisscrossed every one of Georgia's 159 counties. They did coffee shop breakfasts, fundraising dinners, the Rattlesnake Roundup. One obstacle Fowler faced was the pronunciation of his first name. *Which? Wish?* In fact it was *Whysh,* and what better medium to put that across to people than radio? So the campaign bought spots on scores of local stations for $50 or $75 a pop. On the Wyche and Chuck Show, they told stories, sang gospel songs, and traded folksy anecdotes.

So what's all this fuss about social security, Wyche?

Well, Chuck, I saw that too and I was just talking about it with Miss Melba Jones down there in Valdosta.

And the phone would start ringing.

Beyond his unpronounceable name, Fowler had other problems with historically conservative Georgia voters. First, he represented a heavily African-American district that was later held by the civil rights icon John Lewis. Second, he was divorced and thus open to attack by his opponent, Mack Mattingly, the Republican incumbent, for a supposed lack of family values.

"You need to tell voters about your mom," Chuck said. So they made a TV commercial.

This guy Mattingly says so many bad things about me that if they were true, my momma wouldn't invite me home for Sunday dinner. Cut to the sweet-faced old lady and a puppy dog that jumps up on Fowler's lap and starts licking his face.

He won the Senate seat by 22,000 votes, perhaps the most sensational upset in that year's midterm elections.

It was almost twelve years now since the war had ended, but when Searcy went back to Washington as an aide to Fowler, the wounds were still raw. Maya Lin's Vietnam Veterans Memorial had been inaugurated in 1982, close to the Lincoln Memorial. The idea for the Wall, as it came to be known, had come from a former army infantryman, Jan Scruggs, who had the notion after watching *The Deer Hunter* and fighting his own battles with PTSD. Hailed on one end of the political spectrum as a symbol of peace and healing, it was denounced on the other as "a black gash of shame," with Lin's Asian ancestry adding to the rancor. Not every antiwar activist loved it either. If the names of the Vietnamese dead had been included, they argued, the Wall would have been nine miles long.

Tens of thousands had assembled at the Wall, on a cold, blustery day in November 1982, for the first Vietnam veterans parade since the war, also organized by Scruggs, many of them in wheelchairs or hobbling on canes or tapping their way with white sticks, dressed in ragged combat fatigues or full-dress uniform and led by their former commander, William Westmoreland. But political leaders were still wrestling with their discomfort, and the only current senior official in attendance was the newly appointed chairman of the Joint Chiefs of Staff, Gen. John W. Vessey, Jr., who had served as an artillery commander in Vietnam and later oversaw the final stages of the secret war in Laos.

Searcy made the ten-hour drive from Georgia for the event. At dawn the next day, he went back to the Wall before heading home. A handful of solitary figures stood on the muddy walkway, and he fell into conversation with one of them, John Kerry, the newly elected lieutenant governor of Massachusetts, who was standing alone in silent introspection.

Searcy returned to Washington in January 1987 as Wyche Fowler's press secretary, though that title didn't do justice to his expansive responsibilities. By that time, millions were making their way to the Wall to meditate, to weep quietly, to leave flowers and keepsakes, to touch the incised names of those they had known and loved and lost. A generation of veterans had ascended to high office, each with his own distinct piece of the Vietnam story. Kerry entered the Senate in 1985. John McCain, the emblematic POW, shot down in a bombing run over Hanoi, held and tortured for six years in Hoa Lo, the old French colonial jail known as the Hanoi Hilton, took his seat in 1987, part of the same class as Wyche Fowler.

But despite being close to the pulse of national politics, Searcy never felt fully at ease in Washington, and after a brief spell on Capitol Hill, he left once more, this time to take up a position as executive director of the Georgia Trial Lawyers Association.

For Manus Campbell, the postwar politics of Vietnam—the veterans' ascent to elected office, the polemics over the Wall, the Rambo fantasies of surviving POWs, the bitter fights over Agent Orange—might have existed in a parallel universe to which he had no connection. Other than in his nightmares and flashbacks, Vietnam remained locked in a strongbox that he refused to open.

There's something you might want to try, his therapist suggested one day in 1986, a year that brought several of the "special moments" that Arthur Egendorf had written about. It was to spend a few days at the Insight Meditation Society, a retreat center in a lovely old mansion in the peaceful woods of central Massachusetts. The society had been established ten years earlier on the principles of Theravada Buddhism, the form of the religion that had taken root in Southeast Asia. One of the society's founders, Jack Kornfield, a clinical psychologist who had trained as a monk in Thailand, Burma, and India, said that its purpose could be encapsulated in two lines from an ancient Buddhist text: "The world is entangled in a knot. Who can untangle the tangle?"

The first step toward achieving insight, *vipassanā,* was to accept the five precepts of moral conduct: to refrain from killing, from stealing, from lying and false speech, from sexual misconduct, from alcohol and drugs. After spending ten days at the center that summer, Campbell never touched another drink. He grew more and more disenchanted with life as a state trooper, and his colleagues didn't fully trust a man who had lost his taste for knocking back a beer and a shot. It was now just a matter of hanging on until he could retire with a pension.

Just before Christmas that year, *Platoon* hit movie screens, the first in Oliver Stone's Vietnam trilogy. "It was the first time anyone had shown the blood and guts of our experience," Campbell said. This was what his worst combat experiences had been like, the terror of the sudden staccato spit of an AK-47, the taunting calls from the blackness of the jungle: *Tonight you die, Marine.* But it was the movie's soundtrack that transported Campbell to a different place. The time he spent listening to it, as he did repeatedly, became what he called his "grief hour." For years he'd been unable to shed tears over Vietnam, but Samuel Barber's *Adagio for Strings*, already a kind of unofficial national anthem of grieving that had helped carry Americans through the funerals of FDR and JFK, allowed them to break through. "I started sobbing," Campbell said, "and then I filled fifty-five-gallon barrels with my tears."

This didn't mean his problems were solved; in many ways, the tangle only grew more tangled. As Egendorf said, the flow of recovery was discontinuous, and the ambush on Hill 674 continued to plague Campbell's dreams. "The stream had the power of a tsunami," he said once. "I was in a canoe that had overturned. I was upside-down in the water with the weight of ten canoes on top of me, filled with dead and wounded Marines. The water was bloodred and filled with ghosts, and the soldiers were on my shoulders, pushing me deeper."

He drove sometimes to a small state park near his home where there were hiking trails and cranberry bogs and meandering brackish streams where he had canoed with his family as a child. He sat quietly there and watched the clouds of dragonflies, their wings beating the summer air in a shimmer of gold. In these better moments in his fitful process of healing, the dream took other forms. "Now the stream is decorated with monuments to the living and the dead," he said. "I can see fish and colorful rocks, trees, birds, and reptiles. There's a tree swing. My canoe is full of friends and family, enjoying nature. I'm wearing a bathing suit, or I'm naked, carrying a paddle instead of a gun."

His search for understanding spiraled in many directions, buffeted by events both external and internal. He explored new forms of therapy, like a retreat in the high desert of New Mexico with a teacher named Steve Gallegos, who was part American Indian and promoted a therapeutic method called the Personal Totem Pole Process, which purported to put people in touch with their inner "feeling animal." Campbell's proved to be a dolphin, and on the last day of the retreat, he dived into the bracing cold of a pond to swim with it. He broke down when he recounted the experience to Gallegos, and the two men wept together.

Venturing further down the path of Native American spirituality, he went on a vision quest in the Absaroka Mountains of Wyoming led by a man who had been trained by the Lakota Sioux and was assisted by Ann Rockefeller Roberts, daughter of the former vice president. "I was out of my mind for five days in the wilderness," he said. On the last night, after his fire burned out, "I had a dream where all these people were sitting on a log shaking rolls of toilet paper at me and saying, 'Blame Manus, blame Manus.' It was all about my shame. When I woke up, my whole body was shaking. I couldn't talk about it for days."

And so the turbulent rhythms of recovery went on. There was a hundred-mile-an-hour car chase on the parkway. The nineteen-year-old driver was drunk. She resisted arrest; they grappled on the ground as she screamed insults and obscenities. He hit her with a dozen criminal charges and moving violations, and she responded with a false accusation of rape. "I decided that was the universe tapping at my window," he said. After an internal affairs investigation exonerated him, he quit the police and applied to the VA for 50 percent disability. His stepdaughter asked him why he still carried a gun, and he had no answer. The cops told him he could trade it in for a $100 gift certificate at ShopRite.

By this time he had lost his father. The old man had always been ruled by insecurity, seeing his son's fears as a reflection of his own. But the relationship began to change after Campbell's revelatory experience of connection to the dolphin in New Mexico. An intense dream came to him that night, of an insistent voice that said, *Call your father, call your father.* Their conversation the next morning was the first breach in the wall that had kept them apart. By the time Manus Senior died, the reconciliation was complete; he had even listened to his son's descriptions of meditation and experimented with it himself.

Admitting to fear, and no longer condemning himself for feeling it, defined more and more of Campbell's journey. In 1991 he and his second wife went to Tibet. Under the guidance of Lama Tsultrim Allione, one of the first American women to be ordained in the Tibetan Buddhist tradition, they traveled for a month through rugged and forbidding landscapes where they lived on a diet of boiled eggs and canned mandarin oranges and learned the practice of *chöd*, whose followers confronted their fears by meditation in terrifying places—cemeteries at night, or charnel houses, offering up their bodies to their inner demons and turning them into allies.

For a spell Campbell counseled at-risk kids on the dangers of alcohol and drug abuse, but his jobs never lasted long, and he spent long periods out of work. He had two bad car crashes in a matter of months, rear-ended both times. His second wife threw him out. He tried his hand at poetry and sculpture. A girlfriend gave him a month of sculpture lessons; he carved the face of a woman on one side of a sixty-five-pound block of alabaster and the face of a lion on the other. He liked to paint; there was a freedom in it, the liberating feeling that you couldn't make a mistake. He painted a fist with a child's face in it, all in black. *Manus,* he knew, meant "hand" in Latin. The enclosing fist was the relationship he'd had for too long with his father. He painted the head of a Marine, a swirl of contradictory colors. The helmet was pale blue, not olive green, an aspiration to tranquility. The nose was black, the serpentine form of Vietnam an ugly slash in the center of the face.

In 1997 a bullying supervisor fired Campbell from the last of his jobs, as a night security guard at a warehouse owned by an electronics store, Nobody Beats the Wiz, and he returned to the Insight Meditation Society. He'd been going there regularly since his first short retreat in 1986, and this time he stayed for six months, spending much of that time in complete solitude. "It was intense, it was heaven and it was hell," he said. "I'd hear footsteps coming down the hallway and I'd think, *They're coming to get me.*" The ambush on Hill 674 played over and over in his head. He thought of the motto that so many of the grunts had scrawled on their helmets and flak jackets: *You haven't lived until you've almost died.* But gradually the flashbacks began to ease.

He began meeting regularly with a teacher he met there, a veteran named Joseph Kappel, who had been a combat helicopter pilot in Vietnam before spending twenty years as a Buddhist monk in Thailand, haunted by thoughts of all the people he had killed. This had been his own way of dealing with PTSD, and eventually he'd gone to the VA and been granted 100 percent disability. *Don't you think,* he suggested to Campbell, *that it might be time for you to do the same?*

While Campbell walled off all thoughts of politics, Chuck Searcy waded in deeper. On the face of it, given his liberal opinions, his new job in Atlanta might have seemed an odd choice, working for what people tended to think of, he said, as "a bunch of greasy lawyers trying to get money out of rich corporations." But he saw the justice in their underlying purpose and worked hard to focus the group on issues like consumer safety and public health. As the 1992 election approached, the Republican Party reserved a special corner of hell for trial lawyers— "sharks in tasseled loafers" was a favorite epithet—and seized on tort reform as a potent campaign issue. "Lawyers have become the new 'Willie Horton' of this election cycle," Searcy wrote in an op-ed in *The Atlanta Journal-Constitution*. But the real targets, he said, were not the lawyers themselves but "consumers, victims, average Americans whose lives can be shattered by asbestos exposure, the Dalkon Shield, or silicon breast implants, or toxic pollutants in their communities."

In one sense, all this was a long way from Washington, yet it gave him further insights into how the levers of power worked. He had seen the political process from inside the executive branch, from the perspective of a grassroots election campaign, from the legislative side, and now he saw how outside interests could influence policy decisions. It all added up to a set of valuable lessons that he banked for future reference.

In the wider world, many things had changed. Vietnam had finally withdrawn its last combat troops from Cambodia. The vets had their Agent Orange Act. Corporations were clamoring for access to the Vietnamese market. George H. W. Bush had laid out a four-step road map for normalized relations, though no matter how great their political differences, the most powerful veterans in Washington all agreed—or in Kerry's case *accepted* might have been a better word—that as far as the multiple legacies of the war were concerned, the Vietnamese could expect nothing until they met the United States' first demand, for "the fullest possible accounting" of the Americans who had been left behind.

Yet in the new era of economic reforms and foreign tourism in Vietnam, the logic of normalization was creeping forward in informal ways over which the government had little control. Searcy had been putting in long hours at work and had stacked up a lot of unused vacation time. In 1991 he allowed himself a fishing trip to the Amazon, where news reached him that his father had died; while Chuck grieved, he could at least take comfort in the knowledge that after the bitter divisions of the past, he and Hayes had been fully reconciled. After that trip, as he thought about other destinations, chance took a hand, as it often will. One day an old friend named Forrest Dale, a fellow product of the military intelligence school at Fort Holabird, called him. He was living now in Seattle, where he'd gone into the travel business, but he happened to be in Atlanta for a convention. Maybe they could get together for dinner? By the time dessert came, they'd decided to go back to Vietnam. Dale knew how to get cheap tickets. Searcy took a month's leave.

The first vets to return after the war had been a group from Vietnam Veterans of America who traveled to Hanoi in December 1981, headed by Bobby Muller and with one member from each of the four services. They were not naïve; they realized that their trip might be manipulated for propaganda purposes. They had to agree, reluctantly, to lay a memorial wreath at the Ho Chi Minh Mausoleum, and their hosts took full advantage of their presence to denounce the evils of the defoliation campaign, the issue on which their resentments ran deepest. But what struck the vets most, as they wandered the spartan streets of Hanoi, was the attitude of ordinary Vietnamese, especially since their visit coincided with the anniversary of the 1972 Christmas bombing, and one of the party was a pilot who had flown forty-seven missions over North Vietnam.

"It was an emotional roller coaster, it rocked us," said John Terzano, who had served in the navy. "People asked who we were. 'Are you Americans? Welcome.' We had these images of Vietnam frozen in our minds, and now we could replace them with images of a real country. It turned out that it was our American hearts and minds that were still captive to the war, not the Vietnamese."

By the time Searcy and Dale left home in September 1992, a good number of veterans were returning for short trips, taking the first organized tours of the DMZ, searching for old landmarks, making the pilgrimage to Khe Sanh, walking the battlefields where comrades had fallen.

As the plane came in to land in Ho Chi Minh City, both men suffered a full-blown panic attack. "What were we thinking?" Searcy wondered, looking back on it. "We'd both been GIs, the country had been devastated, the U.S. embargo was still in place, and we were coming back for a holiday, for God's sake."

They went looking for the old blanket factory barracks in Binh Loi district, but it was long gone; people in the neighborhood had only hazy memories of the place. Next door was the former headquarters of the ARVN's Joint General Staff; that was still there, but painted now in revolutionary red and gold. Searcy found a nearby riverside restaurant he remembered, and they had lunch there. A former ARVN sergeant who spoke good English gave them a tour of the Mekong Delta. Every step of their journey had to be approved in advance by the police, but they traveled without incident, all the way north to Hanoi and the port of Haiphong and back again by bus, train, car, boat, and rickety Russian airplane. They stopped off in several places along the way, including Hue and the port of Vinh, once the assembly point for supplies headed down the Ho Chi Minh Trail. Nothing was left of the city after Operation Rolling Thunder. In its place were dismal, dimly lit rows of identical cement apartment blocks, a little piece of East Berlin ten miles from the birthplace of Ho Chi Minh.

Like Muller's group, and like virtually all the vets who had returned since, Searcy and Dale were stunned by the absence of animosity. At worst, people seemed a little withdrawn, but more often it was, *Who are you? Were you in the war? So was my father, my brother, my cousin. Where did you serve? Why have you come back? Welcome.* The only thing that seemed to puzzle the Vietnamese was why the United States refused to allow normal relations without a full accounting of its POWs and MIAs. Weren't the Vietnamese already helping with that, opening their archives to inspection, allowing spot visits of their prisons?

Searcy went back again a year later, this time with the wife of a Marine vet who didn't feel ready himself to confront the past. The roads were a little better, and talk of full diplomatic relations was now in the air. Cooperation on the POW/MIA issue was much improved, and foreign visitors no longer had to register their travel plans with the police. "Where would you like to go?" a cyclo driver asked. "I can take you anywhere you like."

Back in the United States, Searcy managed to wangle an appointment with William Westmoreland, joined by his friend and her Marine husband. Would the general be interested in taking part in a film that would include a meeting with his former adversary, Vo Nguyen Giap? "Don't they have some pretty nice golf courses over there now?" Westmoreland asked. But not even the prospect of playing eighteen holes on the green turf of Vietnam was enough to lure him back.

On Christmas Day 1993, Oliver Stone released *Heaven and Earth,* the last of his Vietnam trilogy. It was based on *When Heaven and Earth Changed Places,* the autobiographical novel-cum-memoir by the Vietnamese writer Phung Thi Le Ly—now known as Le Ly Hayslip after her American ex-husband, Dennis. It was one of the most powerful books to come out of the war, yet another product of the particular horrors of I Corps.

Hayslip told the unflinching story of a peasant girl from a village outside Danang, of ancestors and ghosts, of a family torn asunder by war. In her account, no nationality or faction had a monopoly on evil: the French, the Moroccan *goumiers* allied with them, the ARVN, the NLF, and the Americans all brought their own serial forms of cruelty. Colonial troops brutalized Le Ly's neighbors, and South Vietnamese soldiers did the same; she herself was tortured as a teenager, was raped by "liberation" fighters, and serviced the Americans in Danang as a prostitute. But the deeper theme of the book was endurance, transcendence, and reconciliation, and it was not hard to see that as the message that postwar Vietnam conveyed to the veterans who returned.

Hayslip was one of the first to suggest explicitly that they do so. Her East Meets West Foundation, which she had set up in 1988, urged veterans to return and "re-enlist." One reason the Vietnamese had dealt better with the aftermath of the war, she argued, was that they had been able to revisit the scenes of the violence. Americans should do the same: "No doctor, no hospital, no psychologist," she said, could do a better job of healing what the psychiatrist Robert Jay Lifton called their "unconsummated grief."

Searcy had read Hayslip's book and now went to see the movie, at a screening in Atlanta where the author was making a personal appearance. Afterward they chatted, and he told her he'd never stopped thinking about Vietnam. Perhaps the time had come to go back there for good and do something useful. "Wonderful," she said. "Go."

By this time Searcy had gotten to know Bobby Muller, who had created a charitable arm for his new organization, the VVA Foundation.

In 1988 he'd begun to explore with Vietnamese officials what a private vets' group might accomplish, the kind of modest humanitarian step that could start to build mutual trust, something less controversial than Agent Orange that USAID might get behind. He proposed an assistance program for Vietnamese who, like him, had been disabled by their wartime injuries. How about going to Hanoi to run the program? he suggested to Searcy.

Searcy was conflicted. He'd made other well-connected contacts in Democratic Party circles, like Hershel Gober—"Hersh" to his friends—a former secretary of veterans affairs in Arkansas who had now been appointed by Bill Clinton as deputy secretary of the federal VA. Gober had served two tours in Vietnam with the Marines and the army, earning a Purple Heart. He'd also been part of a joint American-Vietnamese musical group, the Black Patches, that was the brainchild of retired Maj. Gen. Edward Lansdale, the fabled pioneer of clandestine operations and psychological warfare. They had toured military bases and composed songs designed to rally local public opinion behind the U.S. war effort, and Gober had even released three albums of his own, which he performed in full dress uniform, standing under the Stars and Stripes, with more than a passing resemblance to Staff Sgt. Barry Sadler delivering "The Ballad of the Green Berets."

"I have a job for you," Gober said to Searcy one day. Searcy was more than ready to move on from the Trial Lawyers Association, and now he had two competing offers to weigh. While Muller's would take him back to Vietnam, Hersh Gober's would thrust him into the worst postwar fever dreams of the far right.

"Bring Our Daddy Home"

E very conflict has its prisoners of war, and in every war some of the dead are left behind. After World War II, almost 80,000 Americans were missing in action; in Korea there were about 8,000. The MIA count in Southeast Asia was surprisingly small, 2,646, about 80 percent of whom were airmen who went down where the bombing was heaviest and the PAVN's defenses were strongest.

Like Agent Orange, the fate of the MIAs and the putative POWs became a surrogate for emotions about the war itself. For the families of the missing, it meant an agonizing struggle between clinging to the possibility of life and accepting the probability of death. For conservative veterans and politicians, every body left unrecovered was grit ground into the open wounds of defeat. Vietnam's economic reforms in the late 1980s inflamed their fear that the mantra of "No Man Left Behind" would be trampled in the rush to normalize relations with the Communist enemy for the benefit of faithless politicians and venal corporations, and above all the treasonous veterans who had galvanized the antiwar movement—John Kerry being the worst of them.

Right-wing conspiracy theories and the politics of grievance have been a recurrent feature of American history, and they crystallized into a coherent worldview with the trauma of Vietnam, which bred the belief that a malignant global elite was bent on the destruction of the United States and the creation of a New World Order. Its most vocal advocates vowed that they would continue to be guided by the oath they had sworn on enlistment: "to defend the Constitution against all enemies, foreign and domestic." They had fought the foreign enemy with courage and skill and with God on their side; from now on, the key adjective was *domestic*. They pointed to the Tet Offensive as the moment when the rot had set in, thanks to the unholy alliance between what they would come in time to call the Deep State and Fake News.

At the sharp edge of the conspiracy theory was the belief that American prisoners had been abandoned after the war and that politicians had covered up the inconvenient truth of their survival. The truest of true believers was a handsome, square-jawed Green Beret, Maj. James "Bo" Gritz, aka Swamp Fox, the reputed model for both Rambo and Brando's Colonel Kurtz. Gritz had commanded a twelve-man team on the Cambodian border with a force of 150 local irregulars he called his 'Bodes. "The job of the Special Forces can be summed up in one word," he told an interviewer. "Kill, kill, kill"—a directive he boasted of personally following more than four hundred times.

The core of the grievance went back, as so many problems did, to Richard Nixon. The Pentagon had always treated POWs and MIAs as two separate categories, but Nixon blurred the distinction. If you couldn't prove a man was dead, how could you prove he was *not* dead? The impossibility of proving a negative was the fertile soil in which conspiracy theories germinated.

The combined POW/MIA concept had immediate populist appeal. In November 1969, Nixon signed a bill declaring a National Day of Prayer for U.S. Prisoners of War in Vietnam, and a billionaire Texas businessman named Ross Perot paid for full-page national newspaper ads that showed two children at prayer, with the caption: "Bring our daddy home safe, sound, and soon." Two young women came up with the idea of a nickel-plated POW/MIA bracelet, and by 1972, about 4 million Americans were wearing one.

Nixon's public rationale had been that America was obliged to go on fighting in order to bring home the hundreds of men being held in North Vietnamese jails. His true goal, Neil Sheehan argued, was "to buy time and divert attention from the fact that instead of ending the war he was trying to win it." But by 1972, Nixon was looking for the exit ramp, and the POW/MIA issue took on a different coloration. No longer a pretext for prolonging the conflict, accounting for all the prisoners and bringing them home was the key to his promise of "Peace with Honor." The somber black POW/MIA flag was created in January 1972 by a group calling itself the National League of Families of American Prisoners and Missing in Southeast Asia. In the decades that followed, it would be flown over the White House and displayed at post offices, in kids' playgrounds and city parks, and on the floor of the New York Stock Exchange. But its stark image of the bowed head of an American soldier flanked by a guard tower and a strand of barbed wire made no visual reference to MIAs. The flag subsumed them into the single symbolic figure of the prisoner.

The politics of the league were a tangled web of race, class, and gender. The idea for an organization of families came from the wife of a navy pilot, James Stockdale, who was being held in the Hanoi Hilton along with John McCain. Those who coalesced around Sibyl Stockdale embodied, in the words of the historian Michael J. Allen, "the high Cold War feminine ideal," a telegenic vision of a wholesome middle-class America under siege. They wore A-line dresses and used lots of hairspray and had Beaver-Cleaver kids and lived in immaculate homes with manicured lawns on navy, air force, and Marine bases, mostly in southern California. Stockdale herself had a master's degree from Stanford and fiercely conservative views. "We should land U.S. Marines on North Vietnam and claim it as U.S. territory," she said. The women who gathered around her were all white, like almost all the pilots, who were generally from the officer ranks—a starkly different demographic from the working-class grunts fighting on the ground, where African-Americans and Latinos accounted for more than one in six of the dead.

After the 1973 Paris Peace Accords, Operation Homecoming brought back 591 prisoners known to be in North Vietnamese jails. But a small number of others, perhaps one hundred, mainly airmen who might have survived their shootdown, failed to reappear. These "discrepancy cases" left a loophole through which Henry Kissinger drove a train. With every missing man a potential living prisoner, the demand for "the fullest possible accounting" of their fate became his main justification for an economic embargo on Vietnam that lasted for two decades. Absent that accounting, there would be no trade, no aid, no access to international finance, no discussion of Agent Orange, let alone of the 300,000 Vietnamese MIAs, the souls condemned to wander. To stand

Clausewitz's dictum on its head, POW/MIA politics were, from Vietnam's perspective, war by other means.

Not that this won Kissinger any fans among the most hard-line conspiracy theorists. Gritz called for him to be tried for treason, "as an accessory to the murder of our POWs who died in Cambodia and Laos after he turned his back on them."

But the fixation on living prisoners had no basis in fact. There were "live-sighting" reports, but they almost invariably referred to people who were already accounted for, or they couldn't be corroborated, or they were simply hoaxes. A House Committee on Missing Persons in Southeast Asia reported in 1976, "No Americans are still being held as prisoners in Indochina," and a presidential commission two years later came to a similar conclusion. But for the most hardline POW/MIA advocates, this was not closure but rather the start of a decades-long cover-up. Rambo was its cultural touchstone, and Bo Gritz was the point of intersection where reality and fantasy merged.

The "Rambo faction" spun theories that the POWs had been murdered by the Communists in captivity, that their remains were stored in a warehouse in the jungle to be used as bargaining chips, that they had been shipped off alive to Moscow, even assassinated by the CIA to conceal the secret of their survival. But the most persistent myth was that the prisoners were still being held in secret camps in Laos. "They're still there to this day, locked in bamboo cages or caves in the mountains . . . used as slaves, forced to drag plows in rice paddies," declared Charlton Heston, one of many right-wing celebrities who joined the crusade. There was always "evidence" for these delusions: the letters usa carved into a rice field; a large letter к, said to be a pilot's distress call, formed from rice stalks; satellite images showing the shadows of men that "looked too long for Asians." A local cottage industry sprang up in fake dog tags and animal bones, with organized networks of "remains traders."

Funded by Ross Perot, Gritz rented a house in Thailand and recruited a team of mercenaries—veterans of the Special Forces and Navy SEALs and anti-Communist Lao rebels who had previously worked for the CIA—for what he called Operation Lazarus. Gritz led his team on four abortive missions to Laos and another four to the "Golden Triangle" on the borders of Laos, Thailand, and Myanmar. Hollywood got in on the act with movies like *Uncommon Valor* and the *Missing in Action* franchise, in which Gene Hackman and Chuck Norris led intrepid raids in Laos, mowing down faceless Communist prison guards, bringing the gaunt survivors home to a heroes' welcome, and redeeming American honor in the face of gutless bureaucrats and traitorous CIA agents.

While the Rambo faction took up much of the oxygen in the room, the symbolic meaning of the POW/MIA flag became steadily unmoored from its origins. For most Americans, by the late 1980s, Vietnam had receded into the rearview mirror. After cheap military victories in Grenada and Panama, America was becoming a nation where people were learning to say "Thank you for your service" as routinely as they said "Have a nice day." The flag morphed into an easy shorthand expression of bipartisan support for all veterans, past and present.

For thousands of Vietnam vets, reverence for the POW/MIA flag fused with their love of motorbikes. Riding a big Harley was a powerful bonding experience. The vets wore leather jackets emblazoned with patriotic symbols and the insignia of their units—eagles, flags, M-16s, grinning skulls, and lightning bolts. Even as their paunches swelled and their beards turned gray, biking re-created the rush of adrenaline they had experienced in Vietnam and the camaraderie of the foxhole. For many, it was just a good excuse for drinking and partying.

In 1987 half a dozen veteran bikers gathered in New Jersey for a vigil in honor of POW/MIAs. One of them, Ray Manzo, a decorated Marine who had fought in I Corps, suggested the idea of an annual ride to the Vietnam Wall in Washington. Someone else suggested that they call their group Rolling Thunder. This would evoke the roar of massed motorbikes as they crossed the Arlington Memorial Bridge, but of course it was also the name of the four-year bombing campaign over North Vietnam. The first Rolling Thunder ride attracted just 2,500 riders, but the snowball effect was extraordinary. Eventually it would bring half a million to Washington each year on Memorial Day weekend, thousands of them flying the POW/MIA flag.

The Rolling Thunder event continued for thirty-two years until it was dissolved in 2019, with thousands of its more militant participants peeling off to join the recently formed Bikers for Trump. But the annual ritual had accomplished much more than Gritz and Rambo to keep the POW/MIA mythology alive. The black flag was installed in the Capitol Rotunda in 1989, recognized by Congress as "the symbol of our Nation's concern and commitment in resolving as fully as possible the fates of Americans still prisoner, missing, and unaccounted for in Southeast Asia." No other war was mentioned, and the image of the prisoner said nothing about MIAs. "These men are all dead, and I'm not interested in dead men," Perot said.

There was satisfaction in this for the POW/MIA lobby, but there was also anxiety. Ronald Reagan had worked hard to reclaim the war in Vietnam as a righteous cause, but as his second term wound down, the activists concluded that he had gone soft on Communism. Just as the symbolism of the flag had become unmoored from reality, it also diverged from the slow evolution of U.S. policy. In August 1987, Reagan appointed General Vessey as a special envoy to Hanoi to discuss the POW/MIA problem, which the Rambo faction saw, not without reason, as a first small step toward normalizing relations. Even Reagan and his top military officers were now suspected by the conspiracy theorists of giving aid and comfort to the enemy.

The shift in policy was simple pragmatism: if the goal was to bring home those who had been left behind, the deep freeze in relations had done little to advance it. Since 1985, tentative efforts to excavate airplane crash sites, beset with mutual suspicion, had recovered few human remains. Now, however, both sides had a powerful interest in developing a more civilized relationship. Vietnam, embarking on its economic reforms, was desperate for Western aid. Not understanding why the Americans seemed so obsessed with what seemed like a tiny number of missing men in comparison with their own losses, the Vietnamese saw that a more cooperative approach could work to their benefit. American corporations, meanwhile, were clamoring for a piece of the economic pie before their foreign competitors sliced it up.

The reaction to Reagan's heresy was nothing, however, compared to the furor that greeted George H. W. Bush in 1991. "By God, we've kicked the Vietnam Syndrome once and for all," Bush announced when the troops came home from Desert Storm to a heroes' welcome. If only things had been that simple. For many Vietnam vets, Desert Storm was just more salt in the wounds. They derided those who had driven

Saddam Hussein out of Kuwait as "30-hour warriors" and asked where their own parades had been. There was further fury in April, when Bush announced his road map for normalized relations with Vietnam, even though he still made progress on the POW/MIA issue its first precondition.

A month later Vietnam granted permission for the United States to open a POW/MIA office in Hanoi, which became known as "The Ranch," the first official American representation since the war. The head of the office, Garnett "Bill" Bell, was a former army infantryman who had fought in the defense of the Bien Hoa air base during the Tet Offensive. He was a staunch anti-Communist, wary of his Vietnamese counterparts, and suspicious of the information they gave him, but he spoke the language fluently, and veterans always tended to trust each other more than they did civilians.

By the end of that year, there had been fifteen joint search missions, ferried to suspected crash sites in Soviet-made helicopters. As a reciprocal gesture of good faith, the United States agreed to provide a token amount of aid, $1 million, for prosthetic devices for war amputees. The vehicle was a new fund for war victims, established by Sen. Patrick Leahy (D-VT), that would eventually be expanded to more than fifty countries. The only condition was that the money had to be channeled through private humanitarian groups, not the Vietnamese government.

Since 1980, Ann Mills Griffiths, the president of the League of Families, had been a member of an interagency policy group on the POW/MIA issue, with access to classified documents—unheard of for a civilian. To the "nut fringe," as she called them, this tagged her as just one more conspirator, complicit with two governments that lied as easily as they breathed, and in 1990 a more militant group of families broke with the league and set up a rival organization. Then, just as the Hanoi office was getting started, the real counterattack began, with the publication of new "evidence" of surviving prisoners, including a blurry photograph of three men in a prison camp. It turned out to be yet another hoax, a doctored image originally published in a Soviet magazine in 1923, but by that time, urged on by Sen. Bob Smith (R-NH), the Senate had appointed a select committee to carry out a fresh investigation. It would be chaired by John Kerry, with Smith as the minority vice-chair, and John McCain and three other Vietnam veterans among its twelve members.

Lt. Gen. George Christmas, a Marine who had been wounded in the 1968 battle of Hue, suggested that the solution to the problem was "a Desert Storm style roll across Vietnam." *The Wall Street Journal* ran an editorial headlined "Bring on Rambo" and commissioned a survey that showed that 69 percent of Americans believed that live prisoners still languished in Southeast Asia, though for what reason other than inscrutable Oriental sadism no one could say.

McCain was now added to the enemies list. Never one to bite his tongue, he responded in kind, decrying the live-POW activists as "some of the most craven, most cynical, and most despicable human beings to ever run a scam." More treacherous still were the corporations pushing for an end to the embargo, whose enthusiasm provoked dismay even at the Ranch. Bill Bell, a button-down Texan who usually chose his words with care, wrote later that with wages capped at thirty dollars a month for a six-day, ten-hour-a-day work week, "American businessmen were not about to rock the boat, not for Old Glory, Apple Pie, Mom, or the POW/MIAs." It became an article of faith for the activists that the Senate committee was a Trojan Horse whose true purpose was to end the embargo.

Nineteen ninety-two was an election year, and Bo Gritz decided to run for president under the slogan of "God, Guns, and Gritz." After taking one-tenth of 1 percent of the vote, he wandered off into the netherworld of antigovernment militias and the Christian Identity movement, setting up a survivalist community in Idaho called Almost Heaven, promoting his martial skills through a training program called SPIKE (Specially Prepared Individuals for Key Events), selling nutritional supplements, and ranting on his radio talk show about Jews and feminists and faggots and the New World Order, in which Americans would be forced to learn Esperanto and stamped with a universal bar code—"the mark of the beast discussed in Biblical prophecy."

Ross Perot, however, was a genuine threat to Bush's reelection, and the POW/MIA crusade was the heartbeat of his campaign. As his running mate, he chose James Stockdale, whose wife, Sibyl, had set the ball rolling for what became the League of Families. Perot insisted that there was "overwhelming" evidence of surviving prisoners in Laos, and Bush was shouted down at a meeting of the families with cries of "No more lies! Tell the truth!"

Perot offered only the most nebulous of policy ideas, a populist mish-mash of economic nationalism, grievances against elites, and unhinged accusations that took him deep into Bo Gritz territory. "Mr. Perot has shown a great appetite for conspiracy theories," *The New York Times* wrote, "lending an open ear to theories of secret global cabals, to Byzantine tales of vast criminal enterprises undertaken with secret Government approval."

He held raucous mass gatherings in major cities, with flashing electronic signs that said "Take Our Country Back." Years later the veteran Democratic strategist James Carville made the obvious comparison: "If Donald Trump is the kind of Jesus of the disenchanted, displaced non-college white voter, then Perot was the John the Baptist of that sort of movement." In the end, the Texas billionaire took 19 percent of the vote, enough to cost Bush reelection and—in one of those be-careful-what-you-wish-for moments—hand the presidency to Bill Clinton.

The Vietnam revanchists hated Clinton, who had taken refuge from the draft as a Rhodes scholar among the dreaming spires of Oxford. With this history, there was no way he could get out ahead on the matter of normalization. He needed the veterans in Congress as a shield to cover his advance.

On January 3, 1993, just before his inauguration, the Senate select committee finally delivered its report, after listening to two hundred hours of testimony and examining millions of pages of declassified material. It said that both Vietnam and Laos were now actively cooperating in the search for the missing—General Vessey said the Vietnamese were "bending over backward" to be helpful. It found no credible evidence of surviving prisoners, and it laid to rest once and for all the canard that POWs had been knowingly abandoned.

Yet the report conceded that anyone who couldn't be proved dead might theoretically still be alive, which gratuitously revived the old proving-a-negative problem. The conspiracy theorists were given more fresh ammunition when the Senate followed up with a resolution to end the embargo, passed over the fierce objections of Bob Smith and other conservative Republicans. Those who believed the commit-tee was a Trojan Horse rested their case when they learned that its staff director, Frances Zwenig, a friend of Chuck Searcy's who had run Wyche Fowler's Atlanta office before moving to Kerry's staff, had joined the new U.S.-Vietnam Trade Council.

Clinton marked his first Memorial Day as president by visiting the Vietnam Wall, where he was introduced by the chairman of the Joint Chiefs of Staff, Colin Powell, who had come a long way since his days of burning villages and spraying crop fields in the A Shau Valley. Clinton's call for an end to the divisions of the past was greeted with boos and cries of "Traitor!" and "Coward!" from vets wearing com-bat fatigues emblazoned with POW/MIA patches. Yet even as he was speaking, McCain and Pete Peterson, another former inmate of Hoa Lo prison and later the first U.S. ambassador to Hanoi, were on their way to Vietnam for another round of talks on the issue.

With the Senate investigation wrapped up, the POW/MIA office in Hanoi was placed under the control of the regular military, and priori-ties changed. Doubtless there would be more live-sighting reports to check out, but almost all the energy now went into searching airplane crash sites for human remains—digging up "a lot of ash and trash," as Ann Mills Griffiths put it. Though the term was rarely used, in part because it forced the families to accept the bitter reality of loss, the acronym that most accurately described the missing men was no lon-ger POW or MIA but KIA/BNR. Killed in Action, Body Not Recovered.

The following February, Clinton lifted the embargo, opening the path to full diplomatic relations. Mills Griffiths did not attend the ceremony.

As the war itself had shown, defeat tended only to inflame grievances, and the POW/MIA militants, having lost their main battle, saw no rea-son to abandon rearguard actions. They found an appealing target in Chuck Searcy.

Searcy and Zwenig had been friends since working together on Fowler's Senate campaign, but Searcy didn't claim to be any kind of expert on the controversy. During his two trips back to Vietnam, how-ever, he'd heard complaints that the government's cooperation was not getting the response it deserved. Hersh Gober was equally frustrated that the end of the embargo hadn't put the issue to rest, and as he cast around for someone with the political smarts and diplomatic deftness to lower the temperature of the debate, his friend Searcy seemed to fit the bill.

Searcy was still mulling over Bobby Muller's idea of moving to Hanoi to run the VVAF's prosthetics program. It was a tough decision. His second marriage was over, and there was a new woman in his life. She felt like a keeper, a dynamic advocate for women's rights who was rising to national prominence—one of the "New Women of the New South," according to the purple prose of *The Atlanta Journal-Constitution:* "In the Old Spice–scented halls of the Capitol, Stephanie Davis might seem as out of step as a Rockette at a tent revival ... a Jewish intellectual in a home of Baptists and Buddhas." She lived by her family's credo: "To do justice and have a helluva time doing it." She had a cat called Emily's List.

Though separation would be difficult, Muller's offer was only for two years, which wasn't a lifetime. At the same time, Searcy was pushing fifty, and the job that Gober had in mind was a big one—to be head of the POW/MIA office at the Department of Defense. It carried a handsome six-figure salary, a promise of long-term financial security, and it would reconnect him to the legacies of the war, with more travel to Vietnam.

But as a journalist for the *Journal-Constitution* wrote later, "the Clintonistas might as well have tossed him a live hand-grenade." The attacks came at him from all sides, starting with the usual suspects on the far right, including Sen. Strom Thurmond (R-SC), and Bob Smith and Jesse Helms from the POW/MIA select committee, who denounced the nomination as "an unconscionable insult to the families of those still missing from the Vietnam conflict." Exhibit A was Searcy's misdemeanor conviction as one of the "Athens Eight." They also painted his appointment as payoff for his role as an advocate for trial lawyers, those sharks in tasseled loafers, and the Clinton-Gore campaign.

The mainstream vets' groups were split over the lifting of the embargo, although the biggest of them, the Veterans of Foreign Wars, eventually accepted that it was the best way to make more progress on the POW/MIA question. But putting a former antiwar activist into the top job at the Pentagon was an intolerable insult, said George R.

Kramer, the VFW's commander in chief, since "[the protesters'] actions had played into the hands of their Communist captors."

The League of Families found itself in an awkward position. Searcy went to see Ann Mills Griffiths, following up with a letter that said he hoped he could play a constructive role "as an outsider with a fresh view and a willing ear," suggesting that "the Vietnamese have been more forthcoming than you are willing to admit." But while Mills Griffiths had distanced herself from the Rambo faction, Searcy was just too hot a potato.

A week later the league issued a statement saying that his nomination "defies logic." His worst offense was not even his past antiwar activism but his "active involvement with American business corporations interested in lifting the U.S. embargo"—even though this had been the official policy of two administrations for more than three years. It was ironic, because Vietnam had done virtually all that had been demanded of it, there was bipartisan agreement that the "fullest possible accounting" of MIAs and nonexistent POWs would remain the centerpiece of U.S. policy after full diplomatic relations were finally restored, and Ann Mills Griffiths had done more than anyone to make that happen.

Hersh Gober, not a man easily deterred, suggested an alternative job for Searcy, a senior but less sensitive position as congressional liaison to the VA. *Everything's set up, I've got your office ready,* he told Searcy. *We're going to be a great team.*

But Bobby Muller was still pushing Searcy hard to take the job in Hanoi. Searcy went to see him one day to talk through his dilemma, and Muller, a loud, charismatic, and profane Long Islander, exploded. *The VA? Are you serious? Are you fucking serious? Take that job, and you're dead. Dead, dead, dead.*

Chuck, you're too young to die was the way Muller remembered the conversation. *I mean, the VA is such a fossilized bureaucracy.*

The salary the VVAF was offering was a third of what Searcy would have made in Washington, but the ex-Marine was famously persuasive.

Searcy expected another eruption when he broke the news to Gober. *I'll be goddamned,* Gober said. *But here's another proposition, one you can't refuse. I'll take Muller's job in Vietnam, and you can have mine.*

Joke or not, Searcy's mind was made up. The VVAF job promised to deliver practical results rather than bureaucratic frustrations. And while Stephanie Davis proved to be the great love of his life and their friendship endured, she had no interest in marriage.

Well, okay, Gober said. *I guess you gotta do what you gotta do. And I'll support you all the way.*

Ross Perot may have had no interest in dead men, but dead men were now the Pentagon's clear priority, at a cost of tens of millions of dollars a year. Most of the crash sites, at least in principle, were now accessible; in their travels to Hanoi, the members of the Senate select committee had persuaded Vietnam to drop its last restrictions on sending American search teams into the sensitive border areas where most of the MIAs had died. The Pathet Lao government had given similar assurances.

Where there was bombing, there were shootdowns, and where there were shootdowns, there were MIAs. Everything was interconnected, and the worst of it invariably went back to the same geography. About four hundred airmen had been shot down in the reconnaissance flights and bombing sorties over the Ho Chi Minh Trail in the remote borderlands of Laos. The five-man crew of a Ranch Hand C-123 was also lost there in 1967, crashing with its full load of chemicals into a mountainside in Savannakhet province, twenty miles from its border with Quang Tri. But the F-4 Phantom fighter-bomber accounted for the majority of the losses over Laos, its twin engines leaving a distinctive smoke trail that was easily visible to antiaircraft gunners at night.

Of those who went down on the Vietnamese mainland, 80 percent were in the three provinces that sandwiched the DMZ. In Quang Binh, to the north, it was mainly F-4s again, but south of the seventeenth parallel, it included every conceivable variety of flying machine. Quang Tri and its southern neighbor, Thua Thien, were littered with the wreckage of one-man spotter planes, lumbering transports, big gunships, Phantoms and Intruders, Skyraiders and Super Sabers, Starfighters and Thunderchiefs brought down while supporting combat operations with rockets, napalm, and cluster bombs. But the most vulnerable of all were the helicopters, every kind from the tiny two-man Cayuse, to the ubiquitous Huey, the workhorse and symbol of the war, to the massive Chinook, which could sling-load a two-and-a-half-ton artillery piece and set it down on a hilltop firebase. Twelve thousand choppers saw service in Vietnam, and almost half were lost, along with almost five thousand of those aboard.

The A Shau and Da Krong valleys saw the worst of the carnage, together accounting for more MIAs than any other place in Vietnam. The first of the scores of choppers lost in the A Shau was one of the big CH-46 Sea Knights shot down when the Special Forces base was overrun in March 1966. On April 19, 1968, the first day of the 101st Airborne's assault on the valley, thirty-five helicopters went down, the worst single-day loss of aircraft in the war.

The shootdowns went on long after Nixon had Vietnamized the conflict. The last of them was in June 1972, when a big AC-130 gunship—the "Angel of Death"—was brought down by a SAM missile at the foot of Hamburger Hill. Twelve Americans died, and none of the bodies was ever recovered. Wartime rescue missions were next to impossible in the valley, with its potent antiaircraft batteries and the most forbidding terrain in Vietnam.

The first American search teams to visit the A Shau operated under tight restrictions and were dogged by bad weather, just as military operations had been during wartime. They found the wreckage of one helicopter and the rotted remains of a cargo net with some burned boots and scraps of fabric, a helmet riddled with shrapnel holes, an entrenching tool, and some empty C-rat cans, but no human remains. They went on from there to a crash site in Quang Tri's Cam Lo district, but found only a pile of miscellaneous scrap that a local farmer added to each time his hoe struck metal.

Now, with the new priorities in place and easier access, officials at the Ranch had a detailed list of known and suspected crash sites to work from, selecting the most promising leads for "active pursuit." In Quang Tri and Thua Thien, there were 185 of these cases to resolve, with 336 men presumed dead. There were 88 cases across the DMZ in Quang Binh, another 145 men. By far the largest single concentration was in the A Shau, where 34 sites with 82 unrecovered bodies made the list.

By 1993, Vietnam had agreed to open its military archives to aid in the searches, including the records of its antiaircraft units. Ted

Schweitzer, a maverick entrepreneur working under contract for the Defense Intelligence Agency, argued, however, that this wasn't necessarily the best place to look for clues. A more reliable source, he told a Senate hearing, was the local people who had scavenged the crash sites for scrap.

However, Schweitzer added, "It has to be something that the Vietnamese, the common Vietnamese person, feels in his heart he wants to do for America. If he has a souvenir, war memorabilia, something he picked up from a crash or a war site in the Highlands in 1967 or from a crash up in the mountains someplace."

Gaining their trust meant extending reciprocity, he went on: "The more steps the United States takes to ease the hardships on Vietnam, the more warmth the common Vietnamese citizens will feel toward us and will come forward with materials."

But trust was especially hard to come by in the A Shau. These were the first Americans local people had seen since the war. Although Kinh Vietnamese from the lowlands had moved into the valley after 1975, the core of the population was still the Katu and the Pacoh and the Ta Oi, long-term allies of the PAVN, and more than a few of them had had a hand in shooting down the planes in the first place.

One of the first of the new wave of joint U.S.-Vietnamese missions was the search for the remains of Party Line One, the helicopter that went down in August 1967 while scouting the operation that would have sent Manus Campbell's battalion into the A Shau Valley. In July 1993 a twenty-man search team came looking for the downed chopper, which had crashed on a steep, thickly forested hillside a couple of miles east of the old A Shau base, where the cement foundations and some shattered remnants of the buildings were still visible.

The Americans ran into what the official report called "a high degree of animosity." Two witnesses agreed to talk—but only to the team's Vietnamese members. The village headman remembered the crash; in fact, he said, it was a friend of his who had climbed a tree and shot the helicopter down. Another man had gone up to the site later, looking for valuable scrap metal. The villagers presented two pieces of evidence: a data plate, whose serial number confirmed that this was indeed the lost helicopter, and an eight-inch fragment of bone. The search team wasn't allowed to keep the bone, and without scientific analysis, who could even say if it was human? The remains traders were well supplied with animal bones.

Near a small stream, the searchers came upon more evidence: parts of the helicopter's twin rotor shafts and blades, though most of the metal had been hacked off and carried away. They found a small electronic gizmo of uncertain purpose, also with a serial number, and a scrap of fabric backed with Velcro that might have come from a flying suit. After a quarter-century of monsoon rains and animal predation, there was no other trace of the missing crew.

A second team returned five months later, making a closer examination of the crash site and mapping its precise GIS coordinates, though it was impossible to do much more because of the usual atrocious weather. A third and final mission was put off until the following April, after the winter rains had abated. Conditions were now at the opposite extreme, with hundred-degree temperatures, suffocating humidity, and hourly water breaks. It was a cross between an archaeological dig and the forensic investigation of a cold case. The team spent ten days on the site, crawling around on hands and knees, raking the soil, collecting it in buckets, and sifting it through screens. They turned up bullets of various calibers, both American and Vietnamese, three zipper pull tabs, three metal buckles, various pieces of belting, a scrap of fabric— the remnant of a sock? They rappelled down the sheer drop-off into a nearby ravine and found the armored pilot seat in the streambed. But the most important discovery was the shattered shaft of a human tibia, two molars, and several other teeth.

These small tokens of death were packed up and sent off to the central laboratory of the Defense POW/MIA Accounting Agency, where DNA analysis eventually confirmed that they were the remains of Marines from Party Line One: Cpl. Thomas A. Gopp, the helicopter crew chief, a fresh-faced twenty-year-old from New London, Ohio; Lance Cpl. John B. Nahan III, twenty-one, of Allegan, Michigan, one of thirteen children; Lance Cpl. Jack Wolpe, twenty-five, of Newburgh, New York, a varsity letterman in football, baseball, and basketball, born in Lithuania of Jewish parents who had survived the Nazi death camps; and navy Corpsman James P. McGrath, just eighteen, of Chicago. POW/MIA case 0784 was closed.

Other searches took much longer, with multiple missions spread out over many years, even decades, and excavations that could last for weeks at a time, interspersed with diligent efforts by the Vietnamese military to track down and interview more witnesses. Many of the searches brought no results. But by early 2022, more than thirty years after the effort began, of the 2,646 men missing in action at the end of the war, the remains of 1,082 had been recovered. All over the United States, from the White House to the playgrounds, the stark black image of the abandoned prisoner continued to fly, though not a single report of a living POW was ever confirmed. "You Are Not Forgotten," the legend said. It would have been unthinkable, though more accurate, to say, "You Do Not Exist."

15

The Third Rail

WHEN VIETNAM and the United States held their first talks about normalizing postwar relations, in 1977, Jimmy Carter's negotiator, Richard Holbrooke, laid out two preconditions. First, account for our POWs and MIAs. Second, no more demands for money, starting with the billions promised by Richard Nixon. Not a word was said about Agent Orange, and the issue would remain taboo for years.

By 1994, the door had been unlatched on the first two problems, but the third remained stubbornly locked. What the Vietnamese found especially galling was the gulf between their experience and that of the American veterans. The Agent Orange Act was born of a strange mix of guilt, compassion, and political pragmatism. Where Vietnam was concerned, none of these things seemed to apply. The treatment it received was born instead of the punitive rancor of defeat, the refusal to acknowledge the human consequences of the war, an ingrained mistrust of Communist deceit and propaganda, and above all the fear that *dioxin* was a codeword for reparations. Vietnam was expected to meet an impossible burden of proof that had not been asked of American veterans—to show a cause-and-effect relationship between dioxin and disease in individual cases, which no Vietnamese scientist, and for that matter no American scientist, could ever hope to do.

In this impasse, the United States had virtually unlimited power and Vietnam almost none. The only way to redress this imbalance was for private citizens to leverage whatever influence and resources they had.

On one hand, this was a political problem, of stressing the unfairness, the glaring double standard. On the other, it meant giving Vietnamese scientists the recognition and credibility they deserved, collaborating with them on new studies that could help both sides get a better handle on the problem. All that work would take serious money, which wasn't going to come from Washington.

The dismissal of Vietnamese scientists as crude propagandists is extraordinary in hindsight; *shameless* is not too strong a word. Their early findings were dismissed as if they were term papers produced by tenth-grade chemistry students. In fact, the first important Vietnamese research had been done by a physician of global renown, Dr. Ton That Tung.

Tung was born into the rarified elite of Hue, where his family lived in a mansion on the Perfume River that had once been home to a princess of the royal court. As a child, he was often taken to visit the Purple Forbidden City, where he formed a dim view of his cousin Bao Dai, the last of the Nguyen emperors, "a fool given to a life of pleasures," who spent most of his time hunting and chasing women.

Tung studied at the well-known École de Médecine de Hanoi, and after the 1945 revolution, he founded the Vietnamese Red Cross, became personal physician to Ho Chi Minh, and was later a renowned battlefield surgeon at Dien Bien Phu. His specialty was diseases of the liver, and in the course of the American War, he published two papers in *The Lancet*, one of the world's most prestigious medical journals, the first on a revolutionary technique for liver surgery and the second on liver cancer. Ho Chi Minh had now assigned him to find out more about the health effects of the American defoliation campaign.

One of Tung's former students was Nguyen Thi Ngoc Toan, a fellow member of the Hue elite, daughter to one of the emperor's six most senior mandarins, and the wife of a general who had commanded PAVN forces during the siege of Khe Sanh. Now, at forty, she was Hanoi's leading ob-gyn, treating other military wives, including General Giap's. Toan was startled at the number of birth defects she was seeing in the offspring of veterans and took her findings to her old teacher and mentor, who was also hearing of a rash of stillbirths, miscarriages, and "monster fetuses" in both women and farm animals in the heavily sprayed province of Vung Tau, near Saigon.

In 1970 Tung published the first of three studies of the possible health effects of Agent Orange. The first, based on the experience of 179 refugees from the South, summarized the immediate physical effects of the spray as well as the subsequent incidence of miscarriages, and it added three detailed descriptions of birth defects in infants—one each from the three northernmost provinces of I Corps, Quang Tri, Thua Thien, and Quang Nam.

His second study documented the incidence of liver cancer in four Hanoi hospitals, comparing prewar statistics with those from 1962–68, when many war veterans were being treated. The increase was more than threefold. Tung's next study was the most detailed of the three, a survey of birth defects in the offspring of almost one thousand veterans who had served in the South for periods of three to four years. It contained some tantalizing details. A summary of the rate of birth defects in thirteen locations in the former South Vietnam showed that the highest figure was in the city of Hue—higher even than the Tu Du Maternity Hospital in Saigon, the country's leading ob-gyn center, which had collected many of the most grotesquely deformed fetuses as well as documenting a high incidence of uterine cancer in young women. This was startling, but another of the appendices hinted at the reason: this was a detailed chronology of many herbicide flights on the outskirts of Hue that did not appear in the declassified air force records, the so-called HERBS tapes.

In 1979 Tung went on a lecture tour of the United States and met with scientists at the Veterans Administration. But beyond the small concession of being granted a U.S. visa, none of his work had any impact on the American government.

When Bobby Muller led his delegation of veterans to Hanoi in 1981, Foreign Minister Nguyen Co Thach—who was recognized across the political spectrum as a brilliant and creative diplomat, even by POW/MIA hard-liners like Sen. Bob Smith—told the group about a new scientific body Vietnam had just set up under its Ministry of Health, which was keen to enlist the help of foreign scientists. Its official name was the Committee to Study the Consequences of Chemicals Used in Wartime, but everyone called it the 10-80 Committee, for the month and year of its creation.

Its chairman, Hoang Dinh Cau, had also been a student of

Dr. Tung's. He was a specialist in lung cancer, dean of the Hanoi Medical School, and vice-minister of health. Like Tung, he had received an elite French education, and it showed in his urbane manners and his invariable beret. If foreign researchers wanted someone to open official doors, Cau was the man who could make it happen. He seemed to know everyone, from Giap down to the ethnic minority villagers of the A Shau Valley, where he had spent time during the war, sent there by Ho Chi Minh himself.

Cau's deputy, Dr. Le Cao Dai, was a hepatologist, like Tung. A celebrated war hero, he too had served at Dien Bien Phu and had firsthand experience of the defoliants while traveling down the Ho Chi Minh Trail in the early months of 1966, when the secret spraying of Laos was at its most intense. After crossing the Lao border, he headed south on the newly constructed Road 20, accompanying military units carrying medical supplies and equipment to the forward headquarters of the Trail at La Hap, bound for the A Shau.

The English-language version of Dai's journal, translated by Lady Borton, was published after his death in 2002. In the entry for April 6, 1966, when he would have been somewhere in Savannakhet province, he wrote: "As we crossed over a hill with dwarf trees, we heard the sudden sound of planes. We hunkered down, hiding behind the tree trunks. One, two, three C-123s buzzed over the treetops in the valley below us and to our left. As they zipped by, the airplanes spread a mist as fine as fog over the jungle." He realized that it must be a chemical of some kind, but he had no idea what it was, or what its consequences might be.

When Dai eventually reached the Central Highlands, he set up a four-hundred-bed field hospital, which he ran for the next five years. "The United States launched innumerable chemical spraying operations to defoliate the jungle," he wrote, and he constantly had to find new locations, spacing out the wards, each a complex of bamboo-thatched bunkers and each in a different valley, to minimize the threat from the herbicides and the incessant bombing. "I was director of the largest hospital in the world," he joked to Borton. He conducted complex battlefield surgeries while an assistant pedaled a bicycle to provide him with electric light. His scalpels were fashioned from salvaged American aircraft parts; stethoscopes were made from the remnants of flare tubes; the rubber casing from the planes' electrical wiring systems was repurposed as IV tubing. He was struck by the number of cases of liver cancer he was seeing.

In 1983, the 10-80 Committee convened an international symposium in Ho Chi Minh City, the first of its kind, where scientists from twenty countries assembled to discuss the consequences of what the committee insisted on calling "chemical warfare." Vietnamese researchers presented papers on birth defects, infant mortality, and liver cancer. Cau's report focused on the environment of the A Luoi Valley, as the A Shau was now known. Its pristine rain forests had degenerated into arid scrubland, he said. Scores of bird and animal species, many of them rare, had vanished. The tigers and elephants and clouded leopards were gone, many doubtless eaten by starving fighters and local residents. Cau estimated that sixteen hundred people had died in the valley since the war, whether from the effects of the herbicides or from starvation, and many others struggled with congenital disabilities.

After the conference, Arnold Schecter, a dioxin expert from the State University of New York at Binghamton, took active steps to coordinate the efforts of Vietnamese and American scientists. Working closely with Le Cao Dai, whom he called "the Albert Einstein of Agent Orange and dioxin research," he embarked on annual trips to Vietnam, analyzing soil samples from sprayed areas; examining dioxin levels in the fatty tissue of women at the Tu Du Maternity Hospital; and sampling blood, breast milk, fish, and sediments from the Saigon River. He and Dai were able to take samples at the Danang and Bien Hoa air bases. In Danang, they found the highest levels of dioxin ever found in human blood in Vietnam, in residents who ate fish from a lake next to the base. At Bien Hoa there were jaw-dropping levels of TCDD in the soil in areas where the chemicals had been stored and spilled. There were also disturbing amounts in some of the food Schecter bought from nearby city markets.

Schecter accompanied the Vietnamese scientists to international meetings, like the conference on persistent organic pollutants, which had become a regular event, now renamed the International Dioxin Symposium. In 1987 Dai flew to Las Vegas for the annual meeting, where he presented a paper on TCDD in human adipose tissue, showing the dramatic differences between samples taken in sprayed locations in the former South Vietnam and unsprayed control areas in the North. Schecter helped the Vietnamese researchers get their work published in reputable academic journals, including the three studies that were cited in Admiral Zumwalt's 1990 report. After the Agent Orange Act was passed the following year, the Institute of Medicine of the National Academy of Sciences was charged with carrying out more research, and Schecter pressed it to take the work of the 10-80 Committee seriously. They were eager to collaborate with American scientists, he said, and his own fieldwork generally corroborated their findings. But how could a desperately poor country emerging from decades of war be expected to meet Western peer-review standards, when testing a single sample for dioxin could cost over $1,000, and only a handful of highly specialized labs in the world had the necessary equipment to do it?

As he traveled around the country, Schecter's research filled in some pieces of the puzzle, though it had something of a scattershot quality. There might be high levels of dioxin in the fish from a street market in Bien Hoa, for example, but where had the fish come from? Schecter couldn't say. It was also necessary to screen out what scientists call "confounding variables." There were many possible sources of dioxin, such as paper mills, municipal incinerators, and cement factories. If you found it in an industrialized urban area, there was no way to be sure it came from Agent Orange.

Schecter agreed with Jeanne and Steven Stellman that the costly studies of American veterans hadn't accomplished much. If scientists wanted to do a convincing epidemiological study, he said, Vietnam was the ideal laboratory. American soldiers had been in and out of the country for a year or thirteen months and most never went near a Ranch Hand run; the Vietnamese lived there permanently, eating what they grew on the contaminated land, not C-rations. They drank from the ponds and streams that had been sprayed and ate the fish that swam in them. The message of double standards did not need to be spelled out.

Although politicians in Washington weren't listening, the ground had begun to shift under their feet once Vietnam opened its doors to foreign visitors. The speed of change was astonishing to Vietnamese themselves. In 1994 eighteen-year-old Ngo Xuan Hien, one of the first to be born in the postwar baby boom in Quang Tri, made his second trip to Hanoi. He found the city transformed. There were more cars on the streets, food was more plentiful, and there was so much new construction that he lost his way while trying to find the house of the family friends with whom he'd spent the summer six years earlier. He lost count of the foreigners he saw strolling around the lovely Hoan Kiem Lake, the spiritual heart of the city, exploring the narrow streets of the Old Quarter, sampling the unfamiliar cuisine. The government had begun to keep statistics on tourist arrivals, and in that year, for the first time, the figure hit one million.

With the passage of the Agent Orange Act, Americans had become painfully aware of how the defoliant had blighted the lives of their veterans. Now at least some of them were beginning to understand that the Vietnamese were suffering too, and in much greater numbers. The evidence was there in plain sight for anyone who cared to look.

The Tu Du Maternity Hospital had collected specimens of hideously deformed fetuses and stillbirths—Siamese twins, Cyclops eyes, shrunken limbs emerging from shapeless blobs of flesh. Stored in jars of formaldehyde, they made a gruesome addition to the Exhibition House for American and Puppet Crimes, although this name had been toned down by 1990, when it became the Exhibition House for Crimes of War and Aggression. Doctors at Tu Du lobbied both the Vietnamese government and prospective foreign donors to create residential centers for children whose disabilities might be ascribed to Agent Orange, and in 1992 a "Friendship Village" for presumed dioxin victims was established outside Hanoi by an army veteran named George Mizo, who had been court-martialed and dishonorably discharged for protesting the war after his platoon was decimated during the Tet Offensive.

The following year Susan Berresford, a senior official and future president of the Ford Foundation, paid a visit to Hanoi. Ford, the largest private philanthropy in the United States at the time, had a checkered history in Vietnam. McGeorge Bundy, the former national security adviser and one of the main advocates of escalating the war, had gone on to serve as president of the foundation from 1966 to 1979.

After the Paris Peace Accords in 1973, Ford had opened an office in Saigon, but as soon as the city fell, it was closed down, and all the Vietnamese staff were arrested. Even so, Ford had maintained an interest in the legacies of the war through its Bangkok office. In 1975 it gave a grant to the Harvard geneticist Matthew Meselson to compile aerial photographs of defoliated areas. Another grant helped Bobby Muller's Vietnam Veterans of America Foundation get off the ground. In 1990, though still hazy about the concept of private philanthropy and whether it was truly independent of the American government, Vietnam made overtures to Ford as it groped toward better relations with the non-Communist world.

Berresford agreed to launch some modest cultural and academic programs through the Bangkok office, but she was interested in doing more. Before she left Hanoi, her hosts took her to a hospital to see children suffering from physical and mental disabilities they ascribed to Agent Orange. She was shaken when they showed her a room with shelves lined with deformed fetuses in glass jars. Would Ford be able to help? Berresford told them she was sympathetic, although birth defects and disabilities weren't one of the foundation's traditional areas of grantmaking.

In the fraught atmosphere of Clinton's first term, with conservatives still fuming over the end of the embargo, the topic of Agent Orange in Vietnam was just too inflammatory for most Americans to touch. But Americans were not the only ones showing up in Hanoi looking for ways to get involved.

In October 1994 two Canadian scientists, Chris Hatfield and Wayne Dwernychuk, arrived in the Vietnamese capital. They were the founders of a small company in Vancouver called Hatfield Consultants, which had almost twenty years of experience working on dioxin. Dwernychuk was an obsessively data-driven scientist with a sideline as a rock guitarist. Hatfield was a big, imposing man with a strong entrepreneurial drive and a personality that filled the room. He'd had a fascination with Southeast Asia ever since he traveled around Thailand, Indonesia, and Malaysia on the cheap in 1965 as a footloose twenty-year-old, picking up most of what he knew about the war in Vietnam by hanging out in Bangkok bars where American soldiers came for R&R.

The two men had made the company's reputation by analyzing how dioxin accumulated in the effluent from most of the two dozen or so paper and pulp mills in British Columbia. They found high concentrations in fish, shellfish, crabs, and downstream sediments, leading the government to issue health advisories, ban the consumption of crabs, and order the mills to switch to a nonchlorine bleaching method that eliminated the toxin, which they did at their own cost of hundreds of millions of dollars.

Chris Hatfield saw Asia as a promising new area for his company, and he opened small offices in Bangkok and Bogor, Indonesia, looking for environmental review projects, though not thinking much at this point about dioxin specifically. A younger scientist, Thomas Boivin, came on board in 1992 to run the Bogor office, having spent several years living with Inuit hunters and fishermen in the far north of Quebec. Like Dwernychuk, who was almost a generation older, he had a passion for rock and roll, and like Hatfield he was a fish man. "I knew everything you'd ever want to know about Artic char, and more," he said. But none of them knew much about Agent Orange, even Dwernychuk, who was the main dioxin expert on the team.

In the early nineties, Chris Hatfield said, investing in Vietnam was the "flavor of the month" in Canada. He signed up to join a trade delegation for small businesses, but there didn't seem to be much on offer. Who in Vietnam would have the money to hire his firm? He wrote to the Canadian Trade Commission. Perhaps doing something on dioxin would be the answer, he suggested. The commission got right back to him. *In that case, there are some people you should probably meet, from a government body called the 10-80 Committee.*

When Hatfield and Dwernychuk met with the committee, they suggested that they might train its scientists in field research techniques, using TCDD as a test case, and Hoang Dinh Cau was interested. But the larger aspiration was to do a soup-to-nuts analysis of a single location that had been heavily sprayed during the war, something more systematic than Arnie Schecter's earlier work, to see if this might lead to any larger conclusions. Hatfield got some initial funding from CIDA, the Canadian International Development Agency, and soon he was back in Hanoi.

At Noi Bai airport, he climbed into a beat-up Russian Lada taxi. As it crossed the Thang Long bridge on the way into the city, he looked down at the Red River, running broad and sluggish, the current broken by sandbanks. It was intimidating. Vietnam was a big country, and down in the Mekong Delta, it was nothing but rivers; how could they identify the right place for a survey? "It felt like looking for a grain of sand in a boxcar," Hatfield said.

The 10-80 Committee had some maps of the areas that had been sprayed, but Hatfield Consultants wanted more precise data, which only the U.S. military could provide. So the next step was a trip to Washington, where they tracked down an officer who had maps that marked the spray lines. The air force wouldn't release these, but it was willing to share a copy of the same raw data file that Jeanne Stellman was analyzing in New York to assess the exposure risk for American troops—the HERBS tapes. These came in the form of an indigestible stack of dot matrix printouts, compiled from original computer punch cards, that put Hatfield in mind of the New York City phone book. But they had the geographical coordinates of the flights, and together the Hatfield team and the 10-80 Committee set about turning them into detailed maps.

The committee pinpointed a handful of possible locations for a study, and Le Cao Dai took Tom Boivin around to look at some of them. They went to the Ma Da forest near Bien Hoa, the one-time NLF stronghold known as War Zone D; the mangrove forests of the Ca Mau peninsula at the southernmost tip of the country; and Ben Tre in the Mekong Delta, a name that had entered the collective memory of the war during the Tet Offensive, when an American officer was reported—perhaps apocryphally—to have said that "it became necessary to destroy the town in order to save it."

But none of these places seemed right. Much of the Ma Da forest had been flooded by a Soviet-built hydropower plant or turned into forestry plantations. Ben Tre had been heavily developed, the natural terrain altered beyond recognition. Some of the Ca Mau mangroves had been replanted and others replaced by farmland.

But there was another place that might work, Dai told Boivin, a remote mountain valley near the border with Laos. Both Dai and Hoang Dinh Cau knew it well. It was an old stronghold of the PAVN, critical to Vietnam's struggle in the American War. The local ethnic minority people had been loyal to the revolution since the days of the anti-French resistance and the building of the Ho Chi Minh Trail. Dai studied the data from the HERBS tapes and did some math. He counted 224 Ranch Hand missions over this valley, and a colleague calculated that this added up to 549,274 gallons of herbicides.

The valley was hard to get to, a three- or four-hour drive west from the city of Hue over a terrible road that had seen bitter fighting during the war. And it was a politically sensitive area, being right next to the border. The first American search teams had only recently been authorized to work there, looking for airmen missing in action. But if Hatfield got permission—and with the backing of the 10-80 Committee that was likely—it would make an unparalleled site for a long-term study. It was entirely rural, populated by poor farmers. There was no industry, none of the "confounding variables" Schecter had worried about. If you found TCDD there, it had only one possible source: the herbicides. The name of the valley had changed since the war, the Canadians learned. These days it was known as A Luoi, because that was the name of its largest town. But back then the Americans had called it the A Shau. Having been the key to the war, the valley was now, improbably, about to become the key to unlocking the peace.

The Things They Carried Back

CHUCK SEARCY left Atlanta on the day before the 1994 midterm elections. The plan, once he arrived in Hanoi, was to stay for six weeks, laying the groundwork for Bobby Muller's new prosthetics program, before flying home for a break over Christmas. He would return for good in early January, in time to meet a visiting delegation from the U.S. Information Agency.

He broke the journey in Bangkok. When he awoke jet-lagged in his hotel room on the morning of November 9, it was still the previous evening in Atlanta, and he switched on CNN to watch the returns coming in. "After an hour," he wrote in a fax to Stephanie, "I almost wished we didn't have global communications."

The midterms were a Republican landslide, the first time the party had controlled both houses of Congress since 1952. Adding to the sting, the new House speaker was from Searcy's home state of Georgia: Newt Gingrich, armed with his Contract for America. The Senate majority leader would be Bob Dole, one of the fiercest critics of normalization with Vietnam. The embargo might be over, but clearly there was still a treacherous road to navigate before full diplomatic relations could be restored.

As soon as Searcy got back to Hanoi in January, the United States and Vietnam signed an agreement on postwar property claims, its terms dictated by the stark imbalance of power. Vietnam would pay more than $200 million to companies and individuals who had lost their assets after the fall of Saigon. Searcy found some of the small-print items startling. IBM would be reimbursed $5 million for computers left behind and now worthless. A USAID official got $25,000 in compensation for the high-end power boat he'd abandoned at his house in the beach resort of Vung Tau.

Searcy set up temporary shop in a modest hotel room close to Hoan Kiem Lake. He fell for the city's magical blend of elegance and decrepitude, the sense of its stirring to life after years trapped in a cocoon of time. A new four-lane highway to Noi Bai airport had just been completed, the last of the big Soviet-built infrastructure projects. Vietnam Airlines was replacing its worn-out Russian Ilyushins and Tupolevs, which had an alarming habit of falling out of the sky, with a spanking-new fleet of Western airliners. As Ngo Xuan Hien had found, visiting from Quang Tri in 1994, there was new construction everywhere. Sometimes the symbolic quality of the changes was inescapable, a tangible passage from the past to the future. Workers had begun to demolish most of the old Hoa Lo prison, where John McCain, Pete Peterson, James Stockdale, and other American airmen had been confined and tortured, preserving only a remnant of the building as a tourist attraction.

There were still no reliable taxi services; you went everywhere by *xich lo*—cyclo. If you needed a car and driver, you had to make a reservation twenty-four hours in advance at the front desk of the hotel. Searcy opted for a bicycle and learned how to slalom through the crowded streets.

In the evenings the city was dark apart from the fitful oil lamps illuminating shadowy groups of people huddled together to eat on three-legged stools or the dim glow of a black and white TV set perched on a high stand for public viewing. Across the street from his hotel, the grand old Metropole offered fine dining for foreign visitors at correspondingly high prices, payable in dollars. Otherwise there was no shortage of street food, and Searcy found a little Italian place that turned out a decent pizza and served wine that was better than the usual Vietnamese imports from Bulgaria.

He found a place to print up VVAF letterhead and relied on the fax machine for most of his communications, since phone calls tended to cut out every few seconds. One day he bumped into a young French-

Canadian computer whiz who was helping to set up Vietnam's first internet service. He gave Searcy the address of the office where this was getting organized, and one chilly winter's evening Searcy got on his bike and pedaled through the darkened streets until he found the place, an ugly Soviet-style building on the outskirts of the city. There was a sliver of light under a door on the fifth floor, and inside he found a dozen young people working amid a clutter of keyboards, cables, and hard drives. There was a big green ledger, like something out of an old-fashioned grocery store in a Norman Rockwell painting, where you could put your name down for e-mail service. There were just a handful of names, addresses, and passport numbers on the first page. One of the techies told Searcy that this was the list of subscribers for the whole country; he was number seventeen.

It seemed as if everyone wanted to learn English. The director of Hanoi TV was hoping to set up an English-language teaching program, and they discussed the possibility of striking deals with Nickelodeon and *Sesame Street*. Perhaps, Searcy wrote to Stephanie, "Ted and Jane" in Atlanta would be interested in TBS helping. The Vietnam-USA Society invited him to a concert at a cultural center near the Ho Chi Minh Mausoleum, where the kids lined up in their smartest clothes and read poems in English and sang "Edelweiss" and "Quack Quack Went the Duck." The local TV cameras sought him out, his first step in becoming a local celebrity.

Meanwhile, like most foreigners, he struggled with the intricacies of learning a tonal language. *Ma,* ghost; *má,* mother; *mà,* but; *mã,* horse; *mả,* tomb; *mạ,* rice seedling, and also metal plating. He suffered the usual share of beginner's blunders and blushes. He was lucky to have a good language teacher, he told a group of doctors; they explained that his choice of tones made it sound as if he were describing the healthy state of his genitals. The comedy of language persisted when he was introduced in meetings as Mr. Sexy, which was how Vietnamese sometimes pronounced his name.

On July 11, 1995, Bill Clinton at last announced the resumption of full diplomatic relations. With McCain running interference against recalcitrant Republicans, he finessed the decision as the best way of pressing for the fullest possible accounting of POWs and MIAs. There still weren't many places to go for celebratory drinks in Hanoi, but Searcy joined a crowd that gathered at a new place called the Polite Pub, on a narrow, winding street close to Hoan Kiem Lake. The owner switched on CNN, and sometime after midnight Hanoi time, Clinton appeared in the Rose Garden to make the official announcement. Ann Mills Griffiths again declined to attend the ceremony. There were whoops and cheers and whistles and beer-soaked toasts, the pop of camera flashes and the glare of TV klieg lights. It was the start of a flourishing business for the pub, which was still there a quarter-century later, transformed into Polite & Co., an upscale cocktail bar.

Searcy rolled up his sleeves and got to work—beginning to build, as he put it, on the ashes and bones of war. His days were a blur of meetings: State Department officials at the newly opened U.S. Liaison Office; representatives of the Ministry of Health and the Foreign Ministry; doctors at the Olof Palme Institute, the best pediatric hospital in the country, named for the assassinated prime minister of Sweden, where Searcy's prosthetics program would be based, and at Bach Mai Hospital, which had been severely damaged during Nixon's 1972 Christmas bombing campaign.

Of all the initiatives to lessen the suffering of victims of the war, aid to the disabled might have seemed to be the least contentious. But even this had been a struggle at the beginning, a laborious step in the political process of unpicking the Gordian knot of war legacies, one by one, in a delicate sequence.

The first to make the public case for a disabilities program had been Fred Downs, the director of the VA's prosthetics office. Downs had fought as an infantryman in Quang Ngai province in 1967–68, yet another veteran of the worst period of the war in I Corps, and lost an arm in combat. He went home with four Purple Hearts, a Bronze Star with Valor, a Silver Star, and what he thought was an enduring hatred for Vietnam and all things Vietnamese. But he worked closely with General Vessey, Reagan's special envoy, and on Christmas Day in 1988 he tested the waters with an op-ed in *The Washington Post*.

"The families of our men still missing in action as well as the disabled child in Hanoi," he wrote, "can benefit from the private generosity for which our country is so well-known." The phrasing was deft, with its subtle emphasis on the words *as well as* (the MIAs came first), *child* (an easier path to the heartstrings than adults), and *private* (the channel the U.S. government would use when it finally granted its first $1 million aid package). Even so, Downs said many years later, "it was as if a bomb had gone off. Many veterans were still angry, they didn't want any talk of relations with Vietnam. Everything was wrapped up in the POW/MIA issue, and they didn't believe a word Vietnam was saying." But he was resolute. "I'd put blood in the soil of Vietnam," he said. "I felt like I was a part of it, and it was part of me."

By 1993, humanitarian aid had inched up to $3.5 million, and USAID gave Bobby Muller's VVAF the million-dollar grant he needed to modernize the rehab department at the Olof Palme Institute. Once Searcy fitted it out with ovens and workbenches, routers and band saws, the second part of the program kicked in. Vietnamese technicians were already making prosthetic limbs for amputees. The task now was to train them to use the new equipment to produce high-quality lightweight, custom-fitted orthopedic braces, starting with kids crippled by polio, cerebral palsy, or clubfoot who were hobbling around on crude contraptions made of wood, metal, leather, and bamboo.

Searcy wondered why so many kids suffered from the same disabilities. If they were the children of veterans, or families who had moved from the South after 1975, might it have something to do with Agent Orange? His Vietnamese colleagues were circumspect. Who could say? Vietnam had neither the money nor the technical capacity to seek an answer to the question. And with the emphasis on improving trade relations, the government—or at least its emerging civilian leadership—was reluctant to touch the raw nerve.

Soon after arriving in Hanoi, Searcy had dinner with Chris Hatfield at the Army Hotel. "He and the other Hatfield guys, whom I met later, were so low-key and humble," he said. "They were pure scientists. They knew exactly what they were doing, and when they offered their help to the Vietnamese they promised to share everything, to be completely transparent. Hatfield was a commercial company, but there was nothing in it for them financially." In fact, Chris Hatfield said, he'd been prepared to invest $200,000 of the company's own money. In the end, they would sink twice that amount into their work in Vietnam.

"I thought, these guys are angels sent from heaven," Searcy said. "They're dealing with a taboo issue, and everyone will benefit from having the hard science they can provide. I thought they were wonderful people, and I've never changed my opinion."

Within a year the orthotics clinic was in full swing, treating thirty or forty kids a month, and it became a fixture on the itinerary of visiting VIPs. Mother Teresa came to see it, and Searcy offered to help her find a location for a new center where her nuns could care for sick and dying children and orphans, although that plan was eventually abandoned. George H. W. Bush and his wife, Barbara, stopped by during a trip sponsored by Citibank, and Searcy took the opportunity to praise the former president's role in loosening the embargo, which, he told a reporter, "is largely responsible for the fact that we are here today."

He pushed other doors open. Big companies like Coca-Cola and Nike had arrived within days of the resumption of diplomatic relations, seeing the potential of Vietnam to become the next Asian Tiger. He got himself elected to the board of directors of the newly established American Chamber of Commerce in Vietnam, serving for the next eight years. He persuaded Motorola to equip every ambulance in Hanoi with a radio. The Ford Motor Company agreed to outfit two trucks so that VVAF could provide prosthetics to kids in rural areas. The relationships he cultivated with these giant multinationals raised eyebrows, or worse, among the more radical vets who looked on the corporations as vultures who had come to feed on whatever scraps of meat might be left on the bones of war.

For a decade after Bobby Muller led his first delegation to Hanoi, it was next to impossible for veterans to engage with the Vietnamese. They were threatened with violations of the 1799 Logan Act and the 1917 Trading with the Enemy Act. "Twenty years ago you wanted to arrest us for *not* going to Vietnam," said John Terzano, who had accompanied Muller on that trip. "Now you want to arrest us for going there."

But by the early 1990s, a good number of vets were returning, joining organized tours or traveling solo. Some came for a week or two, others for longer, and a handful began, like Searcy, to have thoughts of staying on. Sometimes people accused them of being anti-American, but Searcy batted away the charge. "In my opinion, criticism is the highest form of citizenship," he said. He dismissed the idea that his return was motivated by guilt. "The answer to that was always no. I don't find guilt a useful emotion."

The vets came back for many reasons. For many, it was a way of facing down their demons; for others, it was simple curiosity. They carried many things, each reflecting a man's own particular history. They carried their memories and their nightmares, of burning hooches and tactical airstrikes and the scarlet-orange fire and black smoke of napalm and the throb of a Huey overhead, of flooded fields and leeches and the brown mush of C-rations, of the reckless bravery of the enemy, of spider holes and claustrophobic tunnels and shit-smeared punji sticks, of the camaraderie of the bunker and the mess hall and the death of the guy next to you, of surfboards and mamasans and number-one-short-time-*boom-boom* during in-country R&R at China Beach, of the USO shows with Bob Hope and Ann-Margret and Raquel Welch, of the allure of Vietnamese women and the generous spirit of so many of the people they had, for reasons now unfathomable, been taught to think of as *gooks* and *dinks*.

Some carried the echo of predeparture barroom arguments with fellow vets who stared at them and said, *Better you than me, pal,* or as often as not, *What, are you out of your fucking mind?* Many carried their physical wounds or the mental scars of PTSD and often a drive to free themselves from the snares of drugs and alcohol. Some carried a mess of moral injury and a passionate desire to make amends. A few still carried the rage against their government that had consumed them for years, and even when talk of reconciliation began, they refused to believe any of the fine words that came out of Washington. Like Searcy, they carried the memory of too many official lies.

The politics of those who went back to Vietnam ran the gamut from far left to far right. Some carried a fistful of money to give to George Mizo's Friendship Village and the disabled children who were presumed to be victims of Agent Orange, filling the gap in small ways where their government pinched pennies or gave nothing at all. Manus Campbell would be one of these. Others revived the old missionary desire to bring the Montagnards to Jesus, like retired Marine Lt. Col. Oliver North, who had fought on the DMZ. Honoring those who had "died face down in the mud," his famous words at the Iran-Contra hearings, he hooked up with a South Carolina–based group called Vets with a Mission, which eventually set its sights on the A Shau Valley and established a clinic in memory of a comrade whose Huey had been shot down there.

In those early days in Hanoi, Searcy liked to hang out with Joe Bangert, a former Marine from Philadelphia, whose story embodied the sometimes surreal contradictions between Vietnam and Viet Nam, the war and the country, the war and the peace and the process of personal redemption. Bangert had been a helicopter door-gunner in Quang Tri in 1967. He was a long-time friend of John Kerry's, though they made an odd couple: Kerry, the Boston Brahmin, and Bangert, a self-described Yippie and certified wild man. They'd met during the Winter Soldier investigation in Detroit at the end of 1970, where Bangert gave some of the most harrowing testimony, of atrocities he'd witnessed in Quang Tri: half a dozen kids shot dead on a whim, a young woman killed and her body skinned. After that he became one of the leaders of the Dewey Canyon III protests in Washington. A cover of *The Economist* showed him on the steps of the Supreme Court, a wild mass of black hair and a ferocious beard, teeth bared, brandishing a plastic machine-gun in the air.

Now, a quarter-century later, Bangert was a successful entrepreneur, granted the concession to handle arrangements for all private flights into Vietnam, taking care of everything from landing rights, customs clearance, and security to hotels, limos, and concierges. With foreign investors pouring into the country, it was a lucrative business, and he was generous in sharing the wealth among his Vietnamese employees.

One night, as the bars were closing, he and Searcy picked up a couple of bottles of wine and made their way to the Long Bien bridge. Nothing embodied the wartime mythology of the city more than the bridge, the only connection at that time between Hanoi and the port of Haiphong, repeatedly bombed and just as repeatedly rebuilt. A Vietnamese man trailed them until they found a place to settle on the center span, high above the Red River. They sat there drinking and smoking local cigarettes, trading war stories in the moonlight as the old French steel structure shuddered under the weight of a passing freight train. The man joined them. Homeless, he lived under the bridge. He wore a steel helmet fashioned from an old shell casing. He said his parents had been killed in one of the bombing raids; he stood vigil on the bridge every night, honoring their spirits.

During Searcy's first couple of years in Hanoi, tensions between Vietnam and the United States gradually eased, with the notable exception of the continuing taboo on any talk of Agent Orange. Clinton chose Pete Peterson as the first U.S. ambassador to Hanoi. As a former fighter-bomber pilot and inmate of Hoa Lo and a three-term congressman, he was as bulletproof against right-wing attacks as any nominee could have been.

Peterson liked to stroll the streets of the city, getting to know ordinary people. Only recently widowed, he charmed everyone by marrying a Vietnamese-Australian woman he met at a diplomatic reception within a couple weeks of arriving. His ability to transcend his own bitterness disarmed critics on all sides. Ted Osius, the embassy's first political-military officer, who became ambassador himself seventeen years later, recalled Peterson saying, "I had six and a half years to build up my animosities; then I left my hate at the gate."

Searcy nudged along the process of reconciliation in ways both large and small. Just about every American visiting Hanoi seemed to pick up his business card, and every Vietnamese woman in the city seemed to want to marry him, and every man, to introduce him to his sister. He eventually rented an upstairs apartment in the French Quarter in the old residence of Le Duc Tho, Vietnam's hard-line chief negotiator at the Paris peace talks. But before that he lived for a while on the edge of Truc Bach Lake, north of the Old Quarter, where John McCain had been shot down by a SAM missile in October 1967, on his twenty-third bombing raid over the North. There was a memorial at the spot, and until at least the late 1980s, it was blackened by the cigarette butts ground into McCain's sculpted face as a mark of contempt, his name misspelled.

Searcy learned that one of his neighbors was an old man named Mai Van On, who had come running from a nearby air raid shelter, plunged into the deep water, and saved McCain, who was entangled in his parachute cords, from drowning. He had then tried, less successfully, to rescue him from a furious mob converging on the scene with rifle butts and bayonets. When McCain came for a visit toward the end of 1996, one of at least twenty trips he made to Vietnam before his death, Searcy set up a reunion. The senator gave Mr. On a fifty-cent souvenir key ring from the Senate in a small plastic box; the old man, now pushing eighty, told a reporter that while he didn't agree with many of McCain's views on Vietnam, he wished him a long life and prosperity, which was somehow very Vietnamese.

Searcy also urged his old friend Max Cleland to visit. Cleland had made a speech at the Wall where he talked about the "hole in the soul" of those who had fought in Vietnam. He had confronted every imaginable adversity since Khe Sanh, yet the prospect of going back to heal the hole in his own soul proved too big a hurdle. "Just stop asking," he told Searcy finally. "It's not going to happen."

But countless other veterans did come looking to heal, and they quickly learned that Searcy was the man to check in with. One typical visitor had struggled through three shattered marriages, as well as years of drug and alcohol addiction, ending in a violent altercation in which he'd almost killed another man, before a sympathetic judge remanded him for psychiatric care. Searcy took him to dinner with the celebrated author Bao Ninh, who had fought with the PAVN's Glorious 27th Youth Brigade on the Ho Chi Minh Trail and seen most of his comrades killed. In his searing autobiographical novel, *The Sorrow of War,* the narrator's girlfriend is gang-raped by soldiers, and slogan-spouting political commissars send countless young recruits to needless deaths. Since its publication, Bao Ninh had become a virtual recluse, drinking too much himself. Although Vietnam had never recognized PTSD as a medical condition, any American veteran would have diagnosed it from passages like this:

> Often in the middle of a busy street, in broad daylight, I've suddenly become lost in a daydream. On smelling the stink of rotten meat I've suddenly imagined I was back crossing Hamburger Hill in 1972, walking over strewn corpses.... In my bedroom, on many nights the helicopters attack overhead, the dreaded whump-whump-whump of their rotor blades bringing horror for those of us in the field.... But the whump-whump-whump continues without the attack, and the helicopter image dissolves, and I see in its place a ceiling fan. Whump-whump-whump.

Americans were not the only ones haunted by the famous opening sequence from *Apocalypse Now.*

A Vietnamese in Disguise

SEARCY WAS THE FIRST VETERAN to settle permanently in Hanoi, and thoughts of returning to Georgia steadily receded as the charms of the city took hold of him. He found himself part of a small group of Americans who were beginning to converge on Vietnam. There were other vets, a handful of private philanthropists, humanitarian aid workers, business people interested in doing good as well as making money, and scientists looking to connect with the 10-80 Committee.

Other than the vets, the most important seeds of reconciliation had been planted by groups who were in Vietnam during the war and opposed it for reasons of faith. There were Mennonite relief workers and Protestants of Church World Service, but above all there was the American Friends Service Committee, a group founded by Quakers. AFSC's field director in Vietnam was the first name on the Rolodex of visitors and returning veterans. People called her "the oracle." During the war, she'd spent two years in Quang Ngai province, and she was in Hanoi in the weeks preceding the final drive on Saigon in 1975. In the 1980s she was the first American allowed to live in a village, to harvest rice, to ride a bicycle. Her name was Lady Borton, which sometimes led people to believe that she must be an eccentric English aristocrat; in fact she was American, and Lady was short for Adelaide.

You could see the shape of this loose emerging community as a kind of Venn diagram of separate but overlapping interests, each taking on a different slice of the multiple legacies of the war. Some focused on humanitarian aid, especially to the disabled, others on Agent Orange; some came to heal PTSD or remove unexploded wartime ordnance. Searcy and Borton formed the point where all these circles intersected, and as the community coalesced, they became its twin pivots.

One thing that drew Borton to Searcy, she said, was that "he was a southerner through and through," as she was herself. True, she came from a different part of the South—suburban Alexandria, Virginia, a bedroom community for Washington, D.C.—but there were plenty of commonalities in the social rigidity, the unforgiving segregation.

She was a government brat. Her father's side of the family were devout Quakers who had risen high in official circles, and as a child, her idea of fun was skidding around with friends in the polished hallways of the Pentagon. Her father had worked for AFSC in Europe after World War I, feeding refugees. During Lady's childhood, he was a senior official in the Commerce Department. She learned to specify this, since simply saying that he "worked for the government" was understood in the 1950s to be an evasive euphemism for the CIA. He was a specialist in enforcing Cold War embargoes, but what she filed away in her memory bank was his stories about the creative ways people got around them.

Her uncle, Hugh Borton, had served for three years with AFSC in Japan in the 1920s and went on to become one of the country's leading scholars on Japan and president of the Quaker Haverford College. A conscientious objector, he worked with the State Department during World War II. One of the government's few fluent Japanese speakers, he was a principal architect of the postwar reforms that disbanded the Japanese army, drafting the peace plank of the new constitution. "It's because of him that Japan still has an emperor," Borton said. In 1947 AFSC and the British Friends Service Council were joint recipients of the Nobel Peace Prize for "their pioneering work in the international peace movement and compassionate effort to relieve human suffering."

After American combat troops arrived in Vietnam, AFSC, in line with Quaker philosophy, was equally obligated to aid civilians on both sides of the conflict and in both halves of the divided country. It proposed a program that would combine humanitarian aid shipments to the North with hands-on relief work in the South, in both government- and NLF-controlled areas. But evenhandedness sits uneasily with the realities of war. Hanoi rejected AFSC's offer to send in resident staff, in the belief that working in the South meant collaborating with the Americans and their "puppet" regime. The United States, for its part, said that sending medicines to the North or to areas of the South under enemy control could result in fines, jail time, and the loss of AFSC's nonprofit status.

When the group tried to do an end-run around these restrictions by having supporters send money to purchase and ship supplies from Canada, the government ordered banks to refuse to honor any checks made out to the Canadian AFSC. The dispute opened fissures within the organization, and a newly formed group, Quaker Action, resorted to civil disobedience, shipping a boatload of supplies to Haiphong in defiance of the government. Some individuals were more radical still, the most extreme case being Norman Morrison, a young Quaker from Baltimore, who burned himself to death in November 1965 below Robert McNamara's office window at the Pentagon, after handing off his infant daughter, Emily. To many Americans, it was an incomprehensible act; how could this be reconciled with pacifism? To the Vietnamese revolutionaries, Mo Ri Xon was a hero.

The Quang Ngai program began operations the following September, with a childcare center for refugee orphans. A quarter of the population of the province were refugees by this point, and within a year 70 percent of the villages were destroyed. The town hospital was overwhelmed with the dead and wounded, the windows turned into sandbagged firing slits. Adding a clinic for prosthetics, AFSC was soon turning out two hundred artificial limbs a month, many of them destined for children who had stepped on unexploded cluster bombs.

From the start, the program was pulled in contrary directions. Quang Ngai had been an insurgent stronghold since the days of the Viet Minh, home to Col. Vo Bam and many other revolutionary luminaries, like Prime Minister Pham Van Dong—"independent by tradition, hardened by poverty and rural isolation," wrote Tim O'Brien, who served there with a battalion of the 198th Infantry Brigade. But in a war without fronts, there was no way to determine the loyalties of an individual, a neighborhood, or a village, and AFSC never asked.

This was enough for many people to tar the organization, and Quakers as a whole, as anti-American, even Communist. At the same time, it was impossible to work in Quang Ngai without maintaining good relations with the American military authorities, and that led to further internal polemics. Quakerism was about bearing witness, so was that best accomplished by leaving Vietnam or remaining in place? AFSC's New England office complained that staying in Quang Ngai amounted to "an unacceptable degree of complicity in the Vietnam War" and argued that leaving the country "might start a chain reaction among other American relief agencies to get out of Vietnam." The national leadership pushed back: this was an *American* war; surely then, the *American* Friends Service Committee had a special obligation to mitigate its horrors. They stayed.

The province was hit hard by the 1968 Tet Offensive, which began with coordinated attacks on Quang Ngai town at four a.m. on January 31. The AFSC doctor Marjorie Nelson had just left for Hue to join a friend to celebrate the Lunar New Year holiday. After hiding for four days in a bomb shelter as fighting raged in the streets, the two women were captured by the NLF and taken to a camp in the A Shau Valley, where they were held for six weeks together with a group of American POWs.

Artillery shells blew holes in the walls of AFSC's rehab center, and the staff watched as entire neighborhoods were flattened by airstrikes. "It makes you ashamed of being American," wrote the program's field director, Dick Johnson, in a letter home. "We've killed more of our friends and allies than the VC could ever kill." What angered him most was Westmoreland's announcement on the radio that the Viet Cong had seized control of the Quang Ngai hospital, using civilians as human shields. It had never happened; the hospital was untouched. "I have now seen this line of guff and humbug with my own eyes," Johnson wrote, "and I think it stinks."

On March 16, Charlie Company of the Eleventh Infantry Brigade of the Americal Division swept into a hamlet on the coast five miles east of Quang Ngai city. It was Son My, part of the village of My Lai, and birthplace of Col. Vo Bam, the first architect of the Ho Chi Minh Trail. Marjorie Nelson was released two weeks later. Before they let her go, her captors gave her a souvenir, a comb made out of aluminum from a napalm canister and engraved with the image of two doves.

Lady Borton joined the oversight committee of the Quang Ngai program in 1967 and was sent there two years later as the team's assistant director. She stayed for two years, doing the paperwork and the accounting, picking up mail and supplies from the U.S. military base, taking refugee children to the daycare center. When kids finished their treatment at the prosthetics clinic, she drove them back to their homes in remote villages the rest of the team never visited. She cut an imposing though unthreatening figure, twenty-seven years old with a mass of auburn curls, and apparently fearless. She took a *Newsweek* reporter to My Lai, the first journalist to go there since the massacre, knowing that it was just one of many mass killings. It simply happened to be the biggest, and the only one Americans had heard about.

She enjoyed hanging out with the Vietnamese staff and patients at the rehab center, learning the language and the etiquette, how to use the right honorific, when to address someone deferentially as "older sister" or "senior aunt." When she picked up the mail at the local American base she wondered at the naïveté of the MPs who searched the maids' baskets for weapons and contraband, knowing as she did that the women, even as they flirted with the Americans, were acting as the eyes and ears of the Viet Cong, scoping out the dimensions of the buildings they cleaned, memorizing details of the shipments they helped to unload, passing along the chatter they overheard from ARVN soldiers.

After she came home, she and a fellow veteran of the Quang Ngai program, a Quaker conscientious objector named Eric Wright, set up house on a farm deep in the Appalachian hollows of southern Ohio. She got a job driving a school bus for mentally disabled kids. In her downtime, she wrote magazine articles for *Harper's* and *Ms.* and played with ideas for a novel about Vietnam. She and Eric organized antiwar activities through AFSC. They listened to the Watergate hearings on the radio. They baked bread and raised goats they called Goodness and Mercy.

AFSC, meanwhile, kept up its running skirmishes with the authorities, with struggles over the embargo that illuminated many of its absurdities. After the 1973 Paris Peace Accords, the organization was granted a license to send fishing nets and farming tools to communities in the liberated zone of northern Quang Tri. In June 1975, after the fall of Saigon, it sent a shipment of sweaters and knitting yarn. The State Department ruled that the sweaters were okay, but not the yarn to make them; one was humanitarian aid, but the other qualified as economic assistance, because of the value added. AFSC went ahead anyway, and dozens of other groups of "co-conspirators," including a fund to support the Bach Mai Hospital in Hanoi, joined them to form a new consortium they called Friendshipment. The Ford administration backed down, and after Jimmy Carter took office, the restrictions on humanitarian aid were gradually relaxed.

Life as a bus driver suited Borton nicely. The kids were often hard to handle, but she kept them in line with tough love, and they seemed to love her back. The job gave her a steady income and time to write, and the school district was relaxed about granting her leaves of absence. She used them to travel back and forth to Asia during what she called the "years of silence" between the end of the war and the *doi moi* reforms, when relations between the United States and Vietnam were frozen in mutual antagonism.

She found herself in Hanoi in March 1975, leading a small delegation of educators. To be her travel companion-cum-minder, the Vietnamese government assigned a woman named Le Hoai Phuong, one of its few English speakers, who would become a lifelong friend. People called her the Elephant, because she was a hard worker who never forgot anything. Writing about her later, Borton called her Flower.

Borton went to see the director of the East German–funded Viet Duc Hospital, Ton That Tung, who had done the earliest Vietnamese studies of Agent Orange. He was eager to see any scholarly materials on dioxin, but it was impossible for him to subscribe to Western scientific publications. Perhaps she could help? There wasn't much to offer at the time other than the wartime AAAS studies, but over the years that followed she made a regular habit of bringing armloads of journals and books to Viet Duc and other hospitals, not just academic studies but English dictionaries, and popular texts on women's health like *Our Bodies, Ourselves.*

The politburo had laid out a plan to take Saigon in two years, beginning in the spring of 1975, never imagining that the regime in the South would unravel as quickly as it did. By the end of March that year, the strategic city of Buon Ma Thuot, two hundred miles north of Saigon, had fallen. The defense of Hue and Danang quickly crumbled. On the roads to Saigon, ARVN soldiers stripped off their uniforms, threw down their weapons, and fled. In Hanoi, people gathered in the street in front of a huge map on which workers colored the liberated provinces in red as they fell, adding new ones before the paint had time to dry on the last. All that remained was the final drive on the South Vietnamese capital, the Ho Chi Minh Campaign.

The early 1980s brought the deepest freeze of the years of silence, with the economy in ruins, Vietnamese troops in Cambodia, and hundreds of thousands of refugees streaming out of the South in fragile, overcrowded boats.

In February 1980, on the eve of another Tet holiday, Borton boarded a trawler called *Red Crescent 2* at the Malaysian port of Kuala Terengganu for the twenty-mile crossing to the island of Pulao Bidong. The captain pointed to the wreckage of a fishing boat. "Vietnam!" he yelled over the noise of the engine. A child's rubber sandal was still bobbing in the remains of the engine room. He scrawled a number on the steamed-up window glass: "150." A tiny fraction of those who became food for the sharks in their attempt to escape.

The rat-infested camp on Pulao Bidong housed thirteen thousand boat people, and it occurred to Borton that she had a kind of ancestral affinity to them: her Quaker forebears, three hundred years earlier, had been poor laborers who sailed to America to escape from poverty, and the sloop her family owned had once carried Estonian refugees across the Atlantic, fleeing from the Russians during World War II. She spent six months in the camp as a health administrator and wrote a book, *Sensing the Enemy*, about her experiences there, interspersed with memories of wartime Quang Ngai and the riotous kids on her school bus.

"Are you a Buddhist?" a man asked her one day.

"Maybe a little," she answered, and told him about the Quaker belief that the Holy Spirit is equally present in every person regardless of sex, race, color, religion, or political beliefs. So killing another person was the same as extinguishing the Spirit.

"Maybe is like our Buddhist a little," the man replied.

Returning to Vietnam, she was surprised by the reception her book got when she circulated drafts to friends in Hanoi. There were stories in these pages of former ARVN soldiers, people who had spent time in reeducation camps, but she heard few objections. These were just stories about people, free from ideological commentary.

In 1983 she visited the Tu Du Maternity Hospital in Ho Chi Minh City. She'd been haunted by thoughts of Agent Orange since her first meeting with Dr. Ton That Tung in Hanoi, but Tu Du was something different. It was a shattering experience. Doctors took her into a darkened room. When they opened the shades, the room was flooded with light that bounced off long rows of glass jars. It was Borton's first sight of the fetuses they had collected, and as she looked at them she saw her own face reflected in the glass. For years she avoided mirrors.

Contact between foreigners and Vietnamese was rigidly controlled at this time, but she went ahead and asked for permission to live for a while among ordinary villagers, as she had with the boat people. In December 1986, her request was granted, the first time since the war that such a thing had been allowed. The result was a second book, *After Sorrow*, which told the stories of the people she got to know in a village in the Mekong Delta, another in the Red River Delta, and in Hanoi, "the biggest village in Vietnam."

By this time she was a writer of some repute. When she was nominated for a prestigious MacArthur Fellowship, the so-called "Genius Award," the administrators asked the historian Douglas Pike, a veteran State Department expert on Vietnam, for a confidential opinion. "Chiefly she seems to be a special kind of religious figure," he wrote, "—that is a propagandist (employing the correct, original definition of that term: <u>one that propagates the faith</u>)." This may not have been meant as a compliment, though she would no doubt have taken it as one.

For as long as Vietnamese troops remained in Cambodia, no American organization could establish a fixed presence in Vietnam, even one with AFSC's unique credentials. Instead, it ran its aid program out of Laos, a country otherwise so closed to visitors from the West that people compared it to Albania or North Korea.

The Vientiane office was run by a young American couple: Jacqui Chagnon, who had been in Saigon during the war, and her husband, Roger Rumpf. In 1968 Chagnon was two courses short of graduation from George Washington University, but an indulgent adviser granted her time off to do volunteer work overseas, and an offer came from Catholic Relief Services in Saigon. She moved into a compound a few hundred yards from the Tan Son Nhut air base, which also housed USAID staff and some enigmatic military types who were rumored to be with the covert Studies and Observations Group (SOG). She had just turned twenty-two, and even though public opinion had turned sharply against the war by the time she arrived in Saigon that October, she was still a political naïf. "I honestly didn't know much about Vietnam," she said. "I wasn't an antiwar activist. I was uninformed, illiterate, I'd never been to a demonstration. My parents were furious at me for going into a war zone. But I'm a very spur-of-the-moment person; I just wanted the experience."

Foreign aid workers in Saigon didn't keep their innocence for long, and the first jolt to Chagnon's came when the local papers ran their gruesome photographs of deformed babies and fetuses in Tay Ninh province. The nuns she worked with told her that huge quantities of herbicides were also being sprayed in the Central Highlands and in the mountains around Khe Sanh. "The sisters were my touchstone," she said. "Until that moment I had no sense that my government was doing anything wrong." She was introduced to Buddhist monks and nuns who had been jailed for taking part in protests, and found that many of the French-trained priests she met were equally disillusioned. This startled her, since President Thieu was a Catholic and the church was supposed to be a mainstay of his regime.

She soon grew disenchanted with the work, which was entirely dependent on support from USAID, and fired off an angry eight-page letter of resignation. She spent the next two and a half years managing a team of fieldworkers for another private American organization, International Voluntary Services (IVS), which had worked in Indochina since 1957 and was regarded as a template for the creation of the Peace Corps. This brought her closer to the realities of the conflict outside Saigon. The group worked in both South Vietnam and Laos, and in the course of the war, eleven of its roughly four hundred volunteers were killed; another three were captured and imprisoned by PAVN forces. One of the mysterious SOG men warned Chagnon that the two IVS staffers in Tay Ninh were at risk, so she drove out there and threatened to have them put on the first plane home if they refused to leave the area.

It was not ideology that turned Chagnon against the war, but the empathy she felt for Vietnamese civilians: fifteen-year-olds forced into prostitution, children in the burn wards after a napalm attack. Back in the United States, she finally graduated from college and went on the road for four years with the church-backed Indochina Mobile Education Project, which paid her $150 a month to travel around giving talks about the war to anyone who would listen.

"A pretty, sturdy young woman with very long dark-brown hair," wrote the *New York Times* reporter Gloria Emerson, who encountered Chagnon in Iowa City in 1972. She carried a wok wherever she went, cooking Vietnamese food for events organized by the Mobile Education Project. Like Chuck Searcy in Georgia, she spoke to Rotary Clubs and Kiwanis, keeping her distance from the radical currents in the antiwar movement. She wondered why students at Berkeley spent hours debating whether to carry the NLF flag in protests. It wasn't their flag to wave. She preferred to visit small towns and rural communities, where she talked about the effects of the herbicides on farmland, the strength of Vietnamese families, their reverence for ancestors and elders. She asked farmers to imagine what it was like to fill in a thirty-foot bomb crater when you had neither a tractor nor farm tools.

In Missouri, she met Rumpf, a charismatic young farm boy and conscientious objector who had just been ordained as a theologian in the United Church of Christ. From that moment, their lives, both personal and professional, were yoked together. She was voluble, and he was taciturn, but it takes two to make a marriage. If proof were needed that they were kindred spirits, they had only to point to the fact that each of them drove a buttercup-yellow VW Beetle.

In Washington, Chagnon and Rumpf spent two years with an organization that had been formed in April 1965 by one hundred clergy opposed to the war. After broadening the membership, they called their group Clergy and Laity Concerned About Vietnam, and in 1967 they organized the historic antiwar speech given by the Rev. Martin

Luther King, Jr., at Riverside Church in New York. "The war in Viet-nam is but a symptom of a much deeper malady within the American spirit," King said. "If we ignore this sobering reality, we will find our-selves organizing 'clergy and laymen concerned' committees for the next generation." And indeed, after the war was over, and others broke out in Central America, the group found a need to continue its work, dropping the "About Vietnam" from its name.

One day in 1978, word came that AFSC was looking for someone to run its postwar reconstruction projects in Laos and Vietnam, based in Vientiane. The Pathet Lao government had kicked out every foreign NGO but two: AFSC and the Mennonite Central Committee. AFSC's first husband-and-wife team was leaving; would Chagnon and Rumpf be interested in replacing them? Of course.

Laos is a country that people tend to fall in love with, and even after a new generation of backpackers arrived there many years later, armed with their copies of the Lonely Planet guide, it continued to invite clichés—*off the beaten track, gentle charm, remote and undis-covered.* Even amid the devastation of the postwar years, Rumpf and Chagnon fell under its spell. They served two long stints with AFSC, with interludes in Washington and Hanoi, before making their home in a wooden house on the banks of the Mekong in 1994.

Their predecessors had not been allowed to leave the Lao capital, and Chagnon and Rumpf together with the Mennonites—another husband-and-wife team—were the first Americans to set foot in the ethnic villages of Laos's southern panhandle since the Hatchet forces and Spike teams and captured pilots of the war years. Having grown up on a farm, Rumpf was a Mr. Fixit, which was useful in a country almost entirely lacking technical skills and equipment. Irrigation pumps were assembled to run backward; tractors sat idle in the fields because the drivers didn't realize they had to change the oil.

For anyone seeking to know what was happening in Laos in the 1980s, the couple became a kind of one-stop information shop. When a "yellow rain" fell on the villages of the Hmong, former allies of the CIA in its secret war in the North, it was Rumpf and Chagnon who traveled there to investigate. The Reagan administration claimed that the mys-terious substance was produced by Soviet-supplied chemical weapons, but that theory was largely debunked when Matthew Meselson, the

Harvard scientist who had done so much to get the defoliation campaign shut down in Vietnam, concluded that the "yellow rain" resulted from the defecation of swarms of honeybees. When the Rambo faction of the POW-MIA movement was at its most belligerent, it was Rumpf and Chagnon who were asked to check out the mysterious letters and symbols carved into rice fields and the live-sighting reports. Some of these described a tall, gaunt, bearded foreigner in the company of armed guards; the "prisoner" turned out to be Roger Rumpf.

Postwar life in the rural hinterland was much as it was across the border in Quang Tri and the A Shau Valley, but if anything the hardships were on a more drastic scale, and they were certainly less visible, less of a concern for the government. When harvests failed, parents stopped sending their children to school so that the whole family could scour the forests for crashed American airplanes and wrecked Soviet trucks, looking to sell enough scrap metal to buy rice. Rumpf and Chagnon were the first to bring Laos's crisis of unexploded ordnance to public attention. Children were picking up cluster bomblets and treating them as toys. Farmers were being blown to pieces as they hoed their fields, so Rumpf and Chagnon came up with an ingenious solution: to send thousands of shovels to the rural areas, which were less likely to set off an explosion.

They lobbied for American aid to remove the unexploded ordnance (UXO), but while embassy officials were sympathetic, Congress wasn't, and the Lao government wasn't much interested in asking for help from those who had dropped the bombs. It took the Europeans to step in first, a former U.S. embassy official said, recalling that at one diplomatic luncheon, the German ambassador, after one too many glasses of wine, exploded at his American counterpart: "Why is it that we fuckers have to be the ones to clean up what you fuckers did?"

As in Vietnam, where there were unexploded *bom bi*—cluster munitions, literally "steel-bearing bombs"—there was the possibility of dioxin. On one of their first trips outside Vientiane, Rumpf and Chagnon went to Xepon, the small town across the border from Khe Sanh that had been obliterated during the ARVN invasion in 1971. They heard strange and unsettling stories. Local people remembered airplanes trailing a fine white spray. Doctors reported a rash of mysterious birth defects. Veterinarians told of farm animals born with extra limbs. No one knew the reason, and it was hard to find out more. "In those days there were no roads into the mountains," Chagnon said. "You had to walk, sometimes for days." They went to see the prime minister, Souvanna Phouma, but he told them he knew nothing about the spraying. Rumpf took Arnold Schecter to Xepon, where the toxicologist took some samples, but the results didn't reveal much.

Chagnon began to wonder if she might have been at risk of exposure herself, having lived so close to Tan Son Nhut, the first headquarters of Operation Ranch Hand. "Roger and I had long, heavy conversations before I got pregnant," she said. "And then, in 1983, our daughter, Miranda, was born." The child had multiple congenital defects: a dysfunction of the urinary tract, an almost nonexistent thyroid—fortunately both treatable by surgery and medication—and cognitive disabilities. Chagnon had no idea whether these conditions might be linked to dioxin, but the doubt always preyed on her.

On a visit to her husband's family farm in Missouri, she told her brother-in-law, Ed, about the rumors they'd heard of defoliation in Laos. "Let's go to the hay barn and feed the horses," he said. Breaking out a stash of beer, he told her war stories he'd been ordered never to divulge. He'd been an aircraft mechanic, seconded from the air force to work with the Special Forces and "sheep-dipped" in Thailand, supplied with false papers, and stripped of his military ID. Given a high security clearance, he said he'd even flown on *Air Force One* and played midair poker with Lyndon Johnson. He'd been shot down three times on secret rescue missions—twice over Laos, he thought, and once in Vietnam. He'd fixed mechanical problems on the C-123s and wrestled with the problem of equipping smaller T-28 aircraft for spraying. He said he'd been exposed to Agent Orange when a barrel ruptured, and blamed this for his postwar health problems. He swore Chagnon to secrecy; she could say nothing about their conversations until after his death, which came in 2014.

Chagnon and Rumpf continued to run AFSC's Vietnam programs out of Laos until 1990. But after the withdrawal of the last of its troops from Cambodia, Vietnam was at peace for the first time in half a century. The ice in Hanoi broke, the first foreign NGOs were allowed to operate, starting with religious groups who had been in Vietnam during the war, and Lady Borton came to stay. She found a room to rent on Hang Chao, a street where medieval scholars, too poor to afford the real thing, had gathered to eat rice soup, which gave the street its name. From her window, she could see the ornate rooftops of the eleventh-century Temple of Literature, the loveliest of the city's ancient monuments. But it was a challenging place to work: there was still only one international flight a week; communications with AFSC's headquarters in the United States had to be routed by fax through Australia; and faxes cost twenty-five dollars a page.

As normalization approached, a tiny community of resident Americans took shape—English teachers, UN volunteers, a handful of other faith-based groups. None of them had Borton's experience or her language skills, and if they'd worked in Vietnam during the war, it had been in the South, where all the rules were different. There were strict conditions for operating in Hanoi: each group was assigned a representative from the Union of Friendship Organizations, who was your partner, interpreter, facilitator, minder, and if you were lucky, your friend. Borton was lucky; the union paired her with Le Hoai Phuong, the Elephant, whom she hadn't seen since 1975.

When Chuck Searcy arrived at the end of 1994, Borton was one of the first people he met. By that time she'd returned from a spell back home to take care of her aging father, and she'd moved into the party-owned La Thanh Hotel, an old French seminary that had once been used as a prison. She lived there for the next fifteen years, sleeping in an ancient ebony bed that had once been occupied by one of the nuns, shielded from the rats and roaches by a mosquito net, warned of ghosts that roamed the former cells. There were two rooms, one of them an office that she shared with Phuong, and a narrow hallway, where they installed a table for meals. They hired a cook, Chau. The only thing Chau knew how to make was rice, but before long, her old two-burner Russian stove was turning out some of the best food in Hanoi, and the table at the La Thanh became the go-to place for impromptu lunches, for trading stories, for making connections.

Borton picked up where she had left off during the war, shipping prosthetics to Quy Nhon, the coastal town to which the government had moved AFSC's old Quang Ngai prosthetics clinic. At first the work wasn't easy, given the shaky telephone system. At the same time, these limitations played to Borton's strengths: she had a gift for what she called "Respect and Right Relationships," and every contact, every negotiation, had to be done in person. That meant weaving her way from meeting to meeting through the narrow, crowded streets of the city on her bicycle.

She saw more than her share of the first generation of returning veterans as they experienced what she called "the great shuddering," engaging with what they had done to Vietnam and what Vietnam had done to them. One day a rare international call came over the crackling phone line. It was from someone she knew well, Tim O'Brien, a fellow writer she regarded as a mentor. They had taught workshops together at the Joiner Center at the University of Massachusetts, whose director at the time was a veteran of the First Air Cav in Quang Tri.

At a Bread Loaf writers' conference in Vermont, they'd needled each other about their shared wartime experience in Quang Ngai. *We shot 'em up and we sent 'em over to Lady to patch 'em up*, he said.

Yeah, she shot back, *We patched 'em up and sent 'em back to you and you shot 'em up again.*

By the time O'Brien called her in Hanoi, he had become famous, thanks to the book he'd published in 1990, *The Things They Carried*. Now *The New York Times Magazine* wanted to send him back to Quang Ngai to revisit the places where he'd fought. He was terrified, struggling with depression, calling his shrink several times a day. As he and Borton talked, Phuong was carrying on an animated conversation in the background, and hearing the sound of Vietnamese triggered a panic attack in him. The line went dead.

She found his number in Boston and called him back. *Come. I'll take care of you, I'm known here, it'll be fine, I'll pick you up at the airport.*

She gave Phuong a copy of the book. *This is by my friend Tim O'Brien. It's the best thing ever written about the war by an American. Take a look at it, and tell me who should take him back to Quang Ngai.*

Phuong read the book overnight and said she would do it.

They picked him up at Noi Bai airport, where he was still agitated, having lost his stamped entry form. Phuong talked him through immigration, and they squeezed him into the back seat of the car, sandwiched between Borton and his girlfriend, Kate, to prevent him from jumping out.

On arrival in Quang Ngai, O'Brien and Phuong had to check in with the provincial people's committee, and found them hard and suspicious. "Like a different country," Phuong told him. "These people I don't like much, very crude, very difficult. I think you had horrible bad luck to fight them."

An American MIA search team was working out of the government guesthouse. "Which is splendid," O'Brien wrote. "And which is also utterly one-sided. A perverse and outrageous double standard. . . . Even in the abstract, I get angry at the stunning, almost cartoonish narcissism of American policy on this issue."

He went back to the landing zone where he'd been posted, LZ Gator, south of Chu Lai—"thirty or forty acres of almost-America." There had been outdoor movie shows, two volleyball courts, and floor shows by Korean dancing girls in spangled miniskirts. Now it had been "utterly and forever erased from the earth. Nothing here but ghosts and wind."

They drove to My Lai. "Evil has no place, it seems, in our national mythology," he wrote. "We erase it. We use ellipses."

One day he was greeted by two middle-aged Vietnamese women. "Me Wendy," one said, a name the GIs had given her during the war.

"Dear God," he wrote, "we should have bombed these people with love."

By this time, Borton was a well-known figure in Hanoi. Since her return in 1990, she had been able to speak freely with people, without asking official permission, and she had fallen in with a coterie of well-connected women. Of these, none was more important than the elegant and sophisticated Madame Nguyen Thi Binh, the former foreign minister of the Provisional Revolutionary Government and now Vietnam's vice president, and the gynecologist Nguyen Thi Ngoc Toan, who had raised some of the earliest alarms about birth defects in the offspring of veterans.

"Hanoi was really a very small town," Borton said. "All the wives and widows of the military elite from the French and American wars knew each other, and they allowed me into their inner circle. They were like sisters to me. They'd invite me out for lunch at Thanksgiving because they knew it was an important holiday for Americans and I had no family. They told me stories no other foreigners knew. They'd find musty trunks that hadn't been opened for years and pull out the love letters that husbands and wives had exchanged from the front during the French War."

It was about more than personal friendship. These women also had serious political clout, although they wielded it quietly. As the Vietnamese saying has it, the men run the village, but the women run the men. With Agent Orange still a political third rail, Toan saw a niche that Borton could fill, complementing the work the Vietnamese themselves were doing to advocate for the victims. She had deeper experience with wartime and postwar Vietnam than any other American, she was trusted, and she had the full backing of the organization she worked for, AFSC.

Toan went to Giap himself to press the case for Borton. Until his eightieth birthday in 1991, the general had lived under virtual house arrest, and former fighters had not been permitted to form a veterans' association, the hard-liners fearing that it would become a base of support for him in the ongoing intraparty conflicts. But he still carried huge moral authority as Ho Chi Minh's most loyal ally, and he gave his blessing to the idea. His wife was already part of Borton's circle of friends, and now she was able to visit him at his residence and eventually translated and annotated his memoir of Dien Bien Phu and another of his childhood and youth. Her reputation as a writer grew steadily, with her translation of Le Cao Dai's wartime journal and a biography of Ho Chi Minh that included one of the finest collections of archival images of Vietnam ever published. After she was featured in a popular TV show along the lines of *This Is Your Life,* everyone seemed to know her. People joked that she was really a Vietnamese disguised as an American, which was something Bobby Muller was also heard to say about Chuck Searcy.

PART III

REDEMPTION

When we recognize our capacity to do harm,
we can reconcile with others who we feel have hurt us.
This ethics of recognition might be more of an antidote
to war and conflict than remembering others,
for if we recognize that we can do damage,
then perhaps we would go to war less readily
and be more open to reconciliation in its aftermath.

—VIET THANH NGUYEN, *Nothing Ever Dies*

18

Policing the Brass

IT SEEMED FOREORDAINED that Searcy and Borton would join forces, but they had to choose their priorities with care. He'd arrived in Hanoi at a fraught moment, midway between the end of the embargo and the resumption of diplomatic relations, and hard-liners on both sides were alert to any possibility of breaking up the delicate minuet of normalization. Searcy had experienced this personally in the rear-guard fight by the POW/MIA lobby; Borton worried about missteps by Americans figuring out how to conduct themselves in Vietnam. Searcy's VVAF was granted a license to operate within a year, which was unheard of: veterans got special treatment. But the other groups now working in Vietnam—and by 1995 there were several dozen—were still waiting for legal registration. Tourists, meanwhile, were running around offering English lessons without a license. These were accidents waiting to happen, and plenty of people in the security forces would have been happy to manufacture a diplomatic incident out of some petty infraction.

One particular episode crystallized Borton's anxieties. Visiting a new dam project with a group of irrigation experts from the Cambodia office of AFSC, she noticed a lot of bubbles rising to the surface. "Must be one damn big fish," she muttered. But it was water seeping from the base of the dam. With the pace of new construction, Vietnam was in the grip of "cement fever," and the concrete had been adulterated because someone had made off with part of the shipment. "Corruption had been rampant in the South, and it was rampant in the North too," Borton said. "And it still is." Vietnamese tradition dictated the offer of small gifts to people you worked with, which all too often meant an envelope stuffed with cash. AFSC had a strict policy against "envelopes," but it compromised by accepting small gifts of local produce, reciprocating with bags of malodorous dried squid, a Vietnamese favorite, that Borton and Phuong carried under the hood of their Land Rover.

These problems prompted them to write a little handbook based on Borton's principles of Respect and Right Relationships. It was a catalog of do's and don'ts. Start by understanding that Vietnamese has twenty different ways of expressing the pronoun *you*, according to a person's age, social standing, and place in a family or institution. Don't lead with your checkbook; that sets up an unequal power relationship, and the Vietnamese have had enough of being made to feel like beggars. Don't give unsolicited advice; they've had enough of that too, and they often know better. Always remember the Vietnamese adage: "When entering a family, follow its practices; when entering a river, follow its flow." The booklet was published by the U.S.-Indochina Reconciliation Project, an organization that grew out of AFSC's peace division and that had begun to organize annual conferences that brought Vietnamese, Lao, and Cambodians—academics, scientists, government officials—to the United States to explore areas of cooperation. The booklet was translated into many languages, circulated at the U.S. embassy, and was reprinted in Vietnam's English-language newspaper; the only thing that was cut was the section on corruption.

The flow of the river was especially choppy in the final months before normalization, and the waters surrounding the topic of Agent Orange were the roughest of all. The Americans refused to talk about it, and their obduracy enraged the Vietnamese security establishment, for whom it was the most bitter of all grievances.

This didn't mean nothing could be done, and Searcy and Borton made natural allies, the first resident Americans to take on the issue in Vietnam. "An American would probably call it 'lobbying,'" Borton said, though she preferred the Vietnamese idiom: "Being active around the village well." Their efforts had to be unobtrusive, and at this stage Borton enjoyed more latitude than Searcy did. While she had AFSC's enthusiastic backing, Searcy had to go out on a limb with his boss, Bobby Muller, who was wary of getting involved in the issue that more than any other risked derailing the process of reconciliation. Even so, Searcy said, "while Bobby was reluctant and criticized what I was doing, he didn't seriously try to stop me."

Searcy and Borton traveled to a military base near the coastal city of Quy Nhon, where the U.S. military had stored CS antiriot gas, part of the enormous chemical footprint it had left on Vietnam. Perhaps one day, they thought, it might serve as a training venue for the cleanup of sites contaminated by dioxin. Meanwhile they had begun to work closely with Le Cao Dai, and Borton helped him figure out the rules for citations so his work could be published in Western scholarly journals.

Her contacts in high places proved a priceless asset. "In those early days of good-cop, bad-cop diplomacy, when we were trying to shame the U.S. into taking action on UXO and Agent Orange, Lady did so much of the legwork," Searcy said, "a lot of behind-the-scenes conversations and unofficial communications before things finally broke in the right direction—and all without any fanfare."

One day he brought Chris Hatfield to the round table at the La Thanh, the first time Borton had met the Canadian and the beginning of what evolved into a long-lasting partnership. She introduced Arnold Schecter to two of her women friends, farmers from the Mekong Delta whom she'd written about in *After Sorrow*. It was the first time he'd met people whose lives had been directly touched by the defoliants. The legs of one were disfigured by chloracne, the chronic skin condition that was the only disease ever acknowledged by Dow Chemical to be directly associated with exposure to dioxin. After the C-123s passed over, soaking them with the spray, people had washed their faces with urine; it never occurred to farmers that the water in the rice fields might be contaminated. The other woman had delivered grossly deformed babies. Of course, Borton acknowledged, the connection could never be proved. Schecter closed his eyes, she remembered, and said, "True, but sometimes I need to put aside being a scientist and listen as a human being."

It was harder, however, to put aside being a scientist and be attuned instead to the delicate rhythms of diplomacy. In June 1995, Schecter was back in town, his twelfth visit in fourteen years. He'd collected new blood and tissue samples and medical records from Le Cao Dai, and Borton and Searcy met with him at Dai's office before he left for the United States. All three of them pleaded with him not to take this material out of the country. It was terrible timing, with official diplomatic recognition of Vietnam hanging in the balance. But Schecter protested that his work was mandated by Congress, and he wouldn't be dissuaded. On July 1, ten days before President Clinton announced normalization, customs agents at Noi Bai airport refused to allow him to take his samples out of the country, but he insisted. Borton was infuriated—and she was not known as a person quick to anger.

Schecter took the story to a reporter at *The New York Times*. "Nothing like this had ever happened to me before," he complained. "It's astonishing that such a thing could happen on the eve of United States diplomatic recognition of Vietnam." Fortunately, the paper had held the story until two days after Clinton's announcement.

By 1996 the Ford Foundation was ready to act on the request that had been made to Susan Berresford three years earlier, and it opened an office in Hanoi. Its first director stayed for a little over a year before being replaced in 1997 by a soft-spoken agricultural development specialist named Charles Bailey. He had a professorial manner and a natural gravitas, and just as important, he was backed by the foundation's influence and a sizable checkbook.

Bailey's journey to Hanoi had begun thirty years earlier and two thousand miles away, high in the Himalayas. He'd grown up in an adventurous family with a love of travel. As an undergraduate at Swarthmore, he absorbed much of the nonviolent philosophy of the Quakers, who had founded the college in the nineteenth century. The campus was alive with antiwar activity, and Bailey joined the April 1965 March on Washington, organized by Students for a Democratic Society. His views on Vietnam deepened thanks to a seminar with Kenneth Waltz, an early critic of the war, who had his students read the manuscript of his book *Man, the State and War*, a seminal work on international relations. Bailey thought about declaring himself a conscientious objector but opted instead for the Peace Corps. That gave him an extended deferment from the draft, and later, when it was replaced by a lottery, he lucked out with a high number.

He graduated in 1967. "Play hell with your brains, and speak truth to power," one of his professors said at the ceremony. The Peace Corps assigned him to a remote village in Nepal, near the Tibetan border, a three-day uphill hike from the nearest road. He learned Nepali, lived in a mud and stone house with no glass in the windows and no running water. Sometimes the volunteers were invited to the embassy in Kathmandu. The U.S. ambassador, Carol Laise, happened to be married to Ellsworth Bunker, ambassador to Saigon at the time. She told her young audience to be patient, quoting Rudyard Kipling: "You can't hurry the East." It was Bailey's first encounter with an American diplomat, and he never forgot it.

The villagers turned out to be well aware of what was happening in Vietnam, and they were initially suspicious of the Peace Corps—the word *Corps* had a military ring to it, they told him. He hastened to assure them that while he might be American, he was not "one of those guys." The important part of the organization's name was *Peace*. One day the new tomato fields he'd helped his middle-schoolers plant were infested by swarms of grasshoppers, and he and the students went after them with a hand-held insecticide sprayer, smaller but similar to the ones Colin Powell's ARVN troops had used in the hills above A Shau. "This is what the Americans are doing to kill the forests in Vietnam," a tenth-grader from the village school told him. How on earth did the boy know about that, up here in the trackless mountains of Nepal? *Oh, we listen to Radio Peking.*

Bailey joined the Ford Foundation in New Delhi in 1972, and during his time in India, he went on a retreat to learn the principles of *vipassanā* meditation, as Manus Campbell did during his struggles with PTSD. Bailey then took a break to get a Ph.D. in agricultural economics from Cornell and rejoined Ford in 1982, with postings in Egypt, Sudan, Bangladesh, and East Africa. Berresford was known for hiring smart people and giving them free rein. In Vietnam, she gave Bailey an initial annual budget of $3 million. "I asked Susan what kind of program she had in mind," he said. "Her answer was, just go there, you'll figure it out, which was a very nice mandate." There was no talk of

Agent Orange or the horror she'd felt on seeing all the deformed fetuses on her earlier visit to Hanoi. It would be more than a year before Bailey gave any thought to the problem—and even then it was only by chance.

As the turn of the century approached, the demand for orthotics and prosthetics was so enormous that Searcy's project at the Olof Palme Children's Hospital couldn't keep pace. In 1999 he expanded the program to Bach Mai. This time he did so without government funding, raising $200,000 with a sponsored bike ride from Hanoi to Saigon, twelve hundred miles in eighteen days. Many of the eighty or so riders were disabled veterans, half a dozen of them on handbikes. Two or three were blind and rode on the back seat of a tandem. There were celebrities too, like Greg LeMond, three-time winner of the Tour de France, and Diana Nyad, who had swum from Havana to Key West without the aid of a shark cage at the age of sixty-four.

There was one hitch, and it came, as hitches often did, from the authorities in Hue. How would disabled riders cope with the tortuous switchbacks of the Hai Van Pass? It was too dangerous. Searcy took a deep breath: *We are moved by your concern for our safety. We are inspired by the way you rose to meet even harder physical challenges during the war. Crossing the pass on the excellent road you have built will be a symbol of our friendship.* The next morning they rode on, pausing for celebratory drinks in Danang.

John Kerry, who was on one of his frequent visits to check on the progress of the MIA searches, joined the final sixty-mile leg of the trip at the coastal resort town of Vung Tau, along with Ambassador Pete Peterson. "You have been riding across a huge bridge all the way from Hanoi," Peterson told the riders. "This is a bridge of healing, a bridge of compassion, a bridge of forgiveness, and a bridge to the future."

Along the way, they had stopped at hospitals and orphanages and met Vietnamese amputees. South of the DMZ, these were not just civilian victims of the bombing but former ARVN soldiers. A North Vietnamese fighter who was seriously wounded, unless he was fortunate enough to have access to a field hospital with a skilled surgeon like Le Cao Dai, was very likely to die. The survival rate for an ARVN infantryman, who could be whisked away from the battlefield in a medevac helicopter, often within minutes, was exponentially greater, even if it left him without all four limbs.

The politics of UXO-related disabilities were much less complicated than those of Agent Orange. If someone's leg was blown off by a cluster bomb, a *bom bi,* you didn't need to waste time and energy arguing about cause and effect. Heading off the next generation of accidents was the obvious next step. " 'Policing our brass,' as one former Marine general put it, seemed like a no-brainer," Searcy said. And Quang Tri was the obvious place to start.

By this time, American vets were taking regular tours of the Quang Tri battlefields, and Searcy or one of his Vietnamese friends in Dong Ha, the nondescript town that had anchored the southeastern corner of Leatherneck Square, would sometimes go with them. Often they started on the coast at Vinh Moc, just above the point where the DMZ had sliced the province in two. During Operation Rolling Thunder, sixty families had survived here in a complex of tunnels hacked out of the limestone rock. It was a quiet and somber place, unlike the famous Cu Chi tunnels outside Saigon, which were mobbed by tourists. There was a small monument with a dozen rusting bomb casings of various sizes at Vinh Moc, some still with their yellow-stamped serial numbers and date of manufacture. On one typical day, a group of kids had climbed over the chain-link fence around the bombs to be photographed, holding up two fingers in the peace sign that all Vietnamese seem to learn at birth. A wizened old woman was squatting on a stool puffing on a fat cigar; a small group of French backpackers was clustered around the soft drinks stand; and a middle-aged Vietnamese man, badly disabled, was sprawled on a nearby bench.

Seeing visitors, the man got to his feet, dragging one leg behind him, stabbing a finger in the direction of one of the numbered tunnel openings and making small grunting sounds. As he descended deeper into the underground labyrinth, he pointed out small illuminated niches where sculpted figures depicted scenes of the villagers' lives during wartime. In one of them, a doctor was delivering a baby, one of at least seventeen born down here during the bombing.

The self-appointed guide emerged at last into blinding sunlight and a narrow walkway that backed onto the booming surf of the East Sea. There was a small museum there, with a collection of photographs and flags and a tripod-mounted antiaircraft gun. One of the grainy photos showed a small boy holding a rifle. The English-language caption said, "My childhood, what have I got? It is the ground that I lie on and the tunnel that I walk in." The man gestured toward the image, jabbed again at his chest, and grunted some more. *That's me. I was born in the tunnels.* He held up four fingers and pointed again. *Four years old.*

It was a short drive on country roads flanking the Ben Hai River, the centerline of the old DMZ, to the huge Truong Son National Martyrs Cemetery, which honors those who died on the Ho Chi Minh Trail. Quiet and tree-shaded, its neat symmetrical rows of simple headstones are divided into sections by the province of birth, and Searcy always joined the other visitors in burning an offering of incense.

Beyond the cemetery was Con Thien, and then Route 9, and the parade of names that still haunted the memory of those who had served in Quang Tri. Cam Lo, where the refugees had built Tin City out of scraps from the Marine base, was now a thriving little town. In the hills above the highway was Camp Carroll, but the only sign that the huge artillery base had ever existed is an ugly cement monument in a clearing. Farther west were battlefields whose names were indelibly imprinted on the memory of Marines who served here—the Rockpile, the Razorback, Mutter's Ridge—and the string of firebases and landing zones that had been engulfed again by the forests.

Nearby was the site of the Vandegrift Combat Base, where the troops had assembled in April 1968 for another massed assault on the A Shau Valley and Manus Campbell had spent the final weeks of his tour. Another five or six miles brought you to Da Krong, where Route 9 intersected with the Ho Chi Minh Trail. Now a paved road leading south to the A Shau, this was part of the western section of the new Ho Chi Minh Highway. Begun in the year 2000, it was the biggest infrastructure project in Vietnam's postwar history, tracing the course of the original Trail and promoted as a memorial to those who fought and died there.

The highway had many practical and strategic purposes. It was an alternative to the traffic-clogged Route 1 along the coast, it was a border security corridor, and it was designed to lift the ethnic minority

being dismissed by the U.S. government as baseless propaganda, the work of Vietnamese doctors was vital in gathering the first evidence of the impacts of Agent Orange on human health. The most important of them, from top to bottom, were Ton That Tung of Hanoi's Viet Duc Hospital; his student Nguyen Thi Ngoc Toan, shown here with her husband, Lt. Gen. Cao Van Khanh, who commanded North Vietnamese forces at the siege of Khe Sanh; Hoang Dinh Cau, head of the government's 10-80 Committee, which studied the effects of dioxin; and his deputy Le Cao Dai, here with his wife, the artist Vu Giang Huong.

In 1968, Charles Bailey, future head of the Ford Foundation's Hanoi office, was a Peace Corps volunteer in the remote village of Sankranti in eastern Nepal, where he helped villagers cultivate new varieties of fruit and vegetables and high-yield wheat seeds.

In 2013, in the town of Dong Ha, Quang Tri province, Charles Bailey chats with Le Thi Hoa, whose birth defects were likely the result of exposure to dioxin. She was now hoping to start her own small business, a coffee shop.

RIGHT Phuong An 2 is known in Quang Tri as "the Agent Orange village" because of the high incidence of birth defects. Nguyen Van Loc and his wife, Le Thi Mit, are shown here with their son, Truong, soon after the death of his brother, Lanh.

BELOW In Quang Tri's Tan Hiep village, Nguyen Van Bong and his wife, Tran Thi Gai, had four children with birth defects. Gai is seen here with her daughter, Tai, whose sister Tuyet had recently died, and an infant granddaughter.

BELOW In 2001, Lady Borton and her colleague Le Hoai Phuong, center, with Chuck Searcy, second from right, and Grant Bruce of Hatfield Consultants, far left, visited an army base in the city of Quy Nhon where soldiers had found corroded barrels of wartime CS antiriot gas.

At an abandoned scrap-metal yard near the Rockpile, a former Marine outpost, a team from Project RENEW, the organization started 2001 by Chuck Sear and his Vietnamese partners in Quang Tri, collects a cache unexploded armor-piercing 37-mm projectiles.

Retired PAVN Lt. Col. Bui Trong Hong, left, is Project RENEW's chief technical officer. Ngo Xuan Hien is the group's communications and development manager.

Nguyen Thanh Phu visits a scrapyard on Route 9 near Khe Sanh. Phu manages Project RENEW's Mine Action Visitor Center in Dong Ha and is in charge of mine risk education program, giving instructional lessons to groups of local schoolchildren.

In 2018, Project RENEW created Vietnam's first all-female explosive ordnance disposal team, whose members had to overcome resistance from husbands and family members who saw their work as too dangerous for women.

Le Minh Chau was born in a village in the PAVN's War Zone D, a heavily defoliated area near the city of Bien Hoa. Despite his severe birth defects, he went on to become an accomplished mouth painter, seen here in his studio in Ho Chi Minh City.

Visiting the Truong Son National Martyrs Cemetery in 2019, U.S. ambassador Daniel Kritenbrink joined Quang Nam, center, vice-chairman of the Quang Tri provincial people's committee, in burning incense to honor the estimated 20,000 fighters who died on the Ho Chi Minh Trail.

ne scholar has described the booming
Vietnamese tourist industry as promoting
"Memory with the Pain Removed."
lockwise from above: Nostalgic images
f French colonial "Indochine" are part
f how Vietnam is marketed to foreign
isitors; Bach Ma National Park, a former
rench hill station in Thua Thien province,
as become a mecca for well-heeled
irdwatchers; and a visit to Hamburger Hill
now a highlight of organized tours to the
Luoi Valley as an "ecotourist" destination.

Susan Hammond,
pictured here in her
office in Bartonsville
Vermont, created
the War Legacies
Project in 2008 with
a gift from a Vietnar
veteran dying of an
Agent Orange–relate
disease. The group
runs humanitarian
aid programs for
presumed victims o
dioxin in Vietnam a
Laos.

theologian Roger umpf, the late usband of War egacies Project chair cqui Chagnon, at eir home in the Lao pital, Vientiane. On e table are once-thal "pineapple" uster bombs, used rural areas as oil mps once they have en defused.

Artificial limbs are produced in the workshop of the Cooperative Orthotic and Prosthetic Enterprise (COPE), in Vientiane, many of them destined for people disabled by cluster bombs dropped by American aircraft during the war.

n Ly Vongkansa, severely disabled with hrogryposis, was born in a village in avan province, Laos, that was heavily ayed with defoliants. Her people, the Oi, believe that birth defects are the rk of angry spirits.

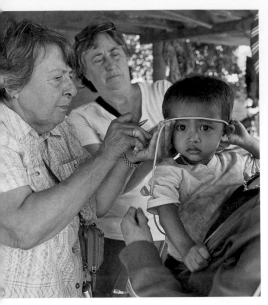

Suspecting a case of hydrocephalus, one form of which is related to dioxin exposure, Jacqui Chagnon, left, and Susan Hammond examine two-year-old Sodsai, in the heavily sprayed border village of Lahang on the Ho Chi Minh Trail in Laos.

Visiting the Ho Chi Minh Trail Museum in Hanoi in 2019, Chuck Searcy encountered former PAVN Lt. Tran Tuyet Mai, one of the young volunteers who helped build Road 20, a critical section of the Ho Chi Minh Trail connecting Vietnam and Laos.

In October 2019, Manus Campbell finally revisited the scene of the traumatic ambush of his company on Hill 674 in Thua Thien-Hue province fifty-two years earlier. Nine young Marines died that day in what he would always remember as "the stream fight."

people out of poverty and "backwardness" and integrate them into the national mainstream. It would open up access to natural resources, create new urban centers and job opportunities, although the main benefits flowed to the lowland Kinh who moved into the mountain valleys under a policy of planned migration.

Many of the hillsides were a monotonous quiltwork of new plantations. "This land was all covered by forests before it was defoliated," Searcy said. "There were bears and monkeys and big cats. Now it's just acacia, acacia, acacia"—a fast-growing crop that could be harvested after only five years. A smallholding might bring a poor farmer as much as 50 million *dong*, more than $2,000, as much as he otherwise earned in a year. Turned into woodchips in a nearby factory, his new crop might end up as cheap furniture from IKEA.

On both sides of the DMZ, in the unsprayed rain forests of Quang Binh and the murderous battlefields of the Da Krong and A Shau valleys, the government had created nature reserves to protect whatever wildlife was left. When the wars were over, and Vietnam opened its doors to the world, conservationists spotlighted these remote forests as the home of rare species, including the semimythical saola, which people called the Asian unicorn. But in one of the darker ironies of peace, this celebration of the natural world was like a flashing neon sign for anyone looking to eradicate it. Le Quy Minh, a naturalist from Thua Thien, lamented that the new highway had sliced up the forests like a pizza cutter, leaving them almost devoid of wildlife. Some of those responsible were just poor villagers looking to toss more protein into the family cookpot, but the bigger problem was the illicit wildlife trade. With much of Asia awash with new money, anything that was thought to have medicinal or aphrodisiac properties or could be nailed to your wall as a status symbol—which basically meant anything with horns, scales, or a penis—was fair game.

Pangolins, once ubiquitous in the hills around Minh's village, had almost vanished. Chinese buyers cooked their scales in oil, vinegar, and boys' urine, or roasted them with earth and oyster shells and ground them into powder. Although the animal's scales are made of keratin, which gives them essentially the same curative power as toenail clippings, Chinese medicine ascribed to them almost miraculous qualities. They could stimulate lactation in nursing mothers, it was said, soothe a hysterical infant, cure skin diseases, arthritis, malaria, deafness, even cancer. Traditional texts said they could help women possessed by devils and ogres. Men believed that the animal's blood, like the penis and eyes of a tiger, could boost virility. A kilo of pangolin scales could fetch $600 on the black market. Most people disliked the Chinese, Vietnam's ancient enemy, but everyone wanted their money.

Khe Sanh, ten miles short of the Lao border, was always the highlight of the veterans' tours, whether or not they were former Marines. Searcy had gone there on one of his earliest trips to Vietnam, and it gave him a first inkling of the particular niche he might eventually occupy in the country's healing process, and his own, although it would take him several more years to put it to practical effect.

Once a remote Bru-Van Kieu village, Khe Sanh town was now a bustling place with budget hotels and computer stores and karaoke parlors and a steady stream of cross-border truck traffic. The base itself was ringed with coffee plantations, as it had been in the days of the French, and the mountains were deceptively lush, because areas that had been carpet-bombed or napalmed or defoliated had been replanted. The small river that rose in the hills above the town had been dammed, transforming the wartime landscape, although you could still pick out the green peaks that had been notorious to the Marines from the hill fights in the spring of 1967.

Like most old battlefields, Khe Sanh was a haunted and melancholy place. When the former Marine William Broyles visited in 1984, there was "all this *stuff*—old guns, tanks, barbed wire—just rusting away." Now the scrap was gone, and the base was part historical monument, part shrine. Some of the trenches and bunkers had been reconstructed, and there were various pieces of military hardware dotted around: a tank, an armored personnel carrier, a twin-rotor Chinook, the wreckage of a smaller helicopter positioned in a nosedive into the ground, an intact C-130 transport on a section of the old planked-steel runway, one of the planes that had ferried supplies in and out of the base during the siege.

There was a small museum in an A-frame building and a coffee shop run by Nguyen Viet Minh, a good-natured man who joked with visitors about his name: "Viet Minh, Viet Cong, now Viet Nam!" He had learned a little English in college. "Some people have many emotion when they come here," he said. "They witness by their own eye some bad things happen. Everything very bloody, everything shock them, life, death, and they cannot forget it." One time, he remembered, he'd heard the repeated slamming of a car door in the parking lot and a woman's screams. He took her in, fixed her a cup of local coffee, tried to comfort her. After half an hour she was calm enough to tell her story. She was the widow of a Marine who had died at Khe Sanh during the siege, on the day their first child was born. The news hadn't reached her until the baby was five days old.

In the visitors book, many of the messages paid homage to the memory of fallen comrades, appending the Marines' motto, "Semper Fi." Some said things like "Never Forget" or "Never Again" and were scrawled with peace signs. Others cursed out the American government for its war crimes. A few snarled at the treasonous liberal media and cowardly politicians who had stabbed the troops in the back. One of the messages in this vein was signed by a Marine major, a woman who had seen action in Afghanistan and Iraq.

On the red-dirt remains of the airstrip, an old man invariably trailed behind visitors, trying to sell them a trayload of spent bullets and fake American dog tags. Nearby, other men burned stubble to make room for more coffee bushes, and when smoke drifted over the base, it was like an elusive ghost-memory of the battle. Searcy pointed to a line of trees at the perimeter. When he came here for the first time, he said, he'd come across two small boys herding cows there. There was an artillery shell lying on the ground, intact and unexploded. The boys told him that such things were everywhere, and Searcy asked if anyone ever came around to clean them up. The boys shook their heads, and the younger one, who was no more than eight or nine, reached out a foot to poke at the shell, just out of curiosity. "I yelled at him, *No! No!*," Searcy said. "And that was my first real awareness of the problem." As time went on, he decided that he would do something about it.

In the years of normalization, Searcy was not the only private citizen looking at what might be done in Quang Tri. In 1995 an American woman named Jerilyn Brusseau, whose brother had been shot down in a Cobra helicopter near Saigon, had come to visit. On her parents' dairy farm in Washington State, Brusseau had mastered a recipe for cinnamon rolls that were later marketed as Cinnabon, an American fast-food icon. Now she and her husband were devoting much of their time to an organization called PeaceTrees.

Searcy went with them to Quang Tri, where they wanted to plant one thousand trees, symbolizing the spirit of reconciliation and rebirth. The people's committee listened politely but said there was just one problem. It wouldn't be safe to plant the trees, because most of the province was still riddled with UXO. At least once or twice a week, the newspapers published reports of local people killed and maimed while tilling their fields, cutting firewood, or collecting scrap metal.

Any initiative by foreign groups in Vietnam depended on the attitude of the relevant provincial people's committee, and this varied widely. Quang Tri's neighbor, Thua Thien-Hue, was a notoriously tough nut to crack, and the city of Hue still had some of the haughty sense of its own superiority and a wariness of outsiders, although by this time the citadel and imperial tombs, which had been designated a UNESCO World Heritage Site, were attracting a steady flow of tourist cash. Quang Tri officials were more open-minded. The province had few sources of outside income, and Searcy had commissioned a small study showing the threat UXO posed to its economic development.

His main ally was Hoang Nam, a handsome and personable young man in his late twenties who was a rising star in the Quang Tri Communist Party, on his way to becoming chairman of the people's committee in Da Krong district, one of the poorest in the province, and clearly fast-tracked for bigger things. Most of the population of Da Krong were Bru-Van Kieu, and they suffered a disproportionately high level of casualties from UXO. Though Nam was born in the North, his father—the only one of three siblings to survive the war—was from Cam Lo district.

Despite Nam's enthusiasm, the old guard of the Vietnamese military were skeptical. Searcy, unencumbered as a veteran by diplomatic niceties, went to see a general at the Ministry of Defense, Le Tan, only to be subjected to a finger-wagging, forty-five-minute-long lecture about Vietnam's long history of resisting foreign occupation and the perfidy of American imperialists. When the United States allocated an initial $3 million for UXO removal, Le Tan retorted that no offer from Washington would come without strings attached. It was just one more excuse for the Pentagon to insinuate itself into Vietnam's domestic affairs.

Searcy got in touch with a retired army colonel he knew in the State Department. There was no question of sending in American personnel, the colonel said. All the Vietnamese needed to do was draw up a list of the demining equipment they needed, and it was theirs. He wrote up a memo to that effect, and Searcy agreed to act as a back channel. He delivered the note to the Defense Ministry with his assurance that the proposal was sincere. Within two weeks they had an agreement.

The people's committee agreed to clear part of the site of the old Marine base in Dong Ha. It removed three hundred unexploded items, and Brusseau's group planted its first trees. Over the next few years, Col. Chuck Meadows, a Marine who had earned a Silver Star for conspicuous gallantry during the battle of Hue, became the group's director, and several professional demining groups arrived, notably a German organization, SODI/Gerbera, which was already working in Laos. In early 1999 it began mapping Cam Lo district, one of the worst-affected areas in the province. Next came the Mines Advisory Group, MAG, newly formed in Manchester, England, and two smaller American organizations.

Since his Vietnamese colleagues in Hanoi had the prosthetics program running on cruise control, Searcy felt by the end of the decade that the time had come to focus single-mindedly on the UXO problem. Nam became his closest ally. Despite the generational age difference, Searcy teased him, "You were always the boss." That was the way it had to be, he believed. Americans might have something useful to offer, but that was not the same thing as having control. Lady Borton's philosophy of Respect and Right Relationships echoed something his mother had taught him as a child: *Listen to people, and always show respect.*

Launching a new organization depended as much on money as it did on political support, and Searcy estimated that he needed at least half a million dollars to kick-start the program. In the year 2000, the pieces fell into place. A delegation from the Vietnam Veterans Memorial Fund came to visit, led by its president, Jan Scruggs, who had first proposed the idea for the Vietnam Wall in Washington. With him was Christos Cotsakos, a decorated fire-team leader with the 101st Airborne who had been wounded in Quang Tri. Since the war, Cotsakos had made a pile of money as founder of the electronic trading platform E-Trade. He contributed $250,000, matching a grant Searcy had received from the Freeman Foundation of Vermont, which had a longstanding interest in Asia.

Bill Clinton came to Vietnam in November of that same year. It was during his lame-duck period, when outgoing presidents have the freedom to speak without fear of electoral retribution. Yet it was no time for major new policy initiatives; those would have to wait for his successor, whoever that might be. Clinton spent much of his two days in Vietnam fretting about the recount that was under way in Florida, and the threat of a stolen election. After eight years in office, he was still dogged by his image as a draft-dodger, and he took pains, like all his predecessors, to put the POW/MIA issue front and center. The most memorable part of his trip, he said, was a visit to an F-105 crash site outside Hanoi, where he lavished praise on the villagers who had volunteered to join the team searching for the pilot's remains. Some angry American vets condemned him for this, but Searcy's friend Hersh Gober, who was now secretary of veterans affairs, told them it was long past time to get over their bitterness. "Some will never be satisfied," he said, "but I suggest they be like these Vietnamese and put the past behind them."

It was Searcy and Borton who had first suggested that Clinton should come to Vietnam, and always working behind the scenes, they took the lead in shaping the message he delivered. "We made an interesting pair," Borton said. "I could do the Vietnam part. Chuck knew more than anyone about the politics of Washington, since he'd worked on the Hill. He knew everyone—John Kerry, Max Cleland, Hershel Gober."

They made the rounds of everyone they knew in Hanoi, and all of them said sure, why not have Clinton come? After that they flew to Washington, on their own dime, and did the same thing there. "What's interesting about Chuck," Borton said, "is that he went about it in a very Vietnamese way. He's circuitous. So around and around and around we went, as they do." This approach worked, and now the trip was on Clinton's schedule.

Borton drafted some suggestions for what he should say in his main address. "He couldn't just list the problems—UXO, Agent Orange, MIAs," she said. "The moment you do that, one thing has to come first and another thing has to come last, and something will always be left out. It becomes a political morass. He can't apologize, and he won't, much though you might want that," she told the Vietnamese. Instead, she thought, Clinton's key message should be "shared pain."

Having no taste for high-profile public events, Borton left town during the president's visit. But in his historic speech at Hanoi National University, he used the language she had suggested, singling out the healing work of the veterans who had returned to Vietnam and touching briefly on unexploded ordnance, now a relatively safe topic. He said not a word about Agent Orange.

The demining groups working in Quang Tri made sure that there was a side event on UXO, with an exhibit of posters, photographs, and artwork, and an assortment of bombs and mines. Three teenage boys traveled to Hanoi for the occasion, all of whom had lost arms or legs or been blinded or badly burned in explosions. As usual, Clinton arrived late and unsettled his aides by wandering off-script. He promised $700,000 for hospital supplies for UXO victims in Quang Tri and vowed that the United States "will work with Vietnam until every bomb and mine is cleaned up, no matter how long it takes." He lauded the courage of the three boys, the inspiration they provided. Searcy nudged them to stand up and be recognized.

By the following summer, the time had come for him to set up his new organization, which would be based in Dong Ha. The name he and Hoang Nam eventually settled on was Restoring the Environment and Neutralizing the Effects of War. The purist might have said that the full name was a bit clunky, but the acronym, Project RENEW, worked just fine.

Milk That Glowed in the Dark

E VEN THOUGH Bill Clinton made no public statements about Agent Orange, undercurrents of pressure bubbled beneath the surface of his speech. By the time the president arrived in Hanoi, Chris Hatfield's team of Canadian scientists had presented new facts that made it impossible for the United States to go on avoiding responsibility for the disaster that Operation Ranch Hand had inflicted on Vietnam. What brought this about was their investigation of the legacy of dioxin in the A Luoi Valley.

It wasn't easy to get permission to work in such a sensitive location, even for the 10-80 Committee. The valley still saw almost no foreigners other than the MIA search teams and Japanese dealers buying up scrap metal. But Searcy joined the Hatfield team on one of their trips there, sat in on a meeting with the provincial authorities in Hue, and came away impressed by the Canadians' ability to win over officials who were so often wary of outsiders. There was a transparency about them that inspired trust.

Hatfield and the 10-80 Committee put together a joint survey team, and the Canadians read everything they could get hold of about the valley and its wartime history. Wayne Dwernychuk in particular was steeped in the literature on dioxin, and by the time they got there in 1996, they had a pretty good idea of what was known and what wasn't.

The chemistry of the herbicides was well understood. The growth of plant cells is regulated by hormones, and the defoliants that combined 2,4-D and 2,4,5-T, Agents Purple and Orange, mimicked this hormonal action, accelerating the process to abnormal levels. In effect, they forced the plant to grow itself to death.

Many of the details of the spraying were also known. Le Cao Dai's colleague Dr. Tran Manh Hung, the committee's leading technical expert, had calculated with some precision the volume of chemicals that had been sprayed on the valley. Hatfield had maps of the flight paths and could figure out the areas where their search for dioxin should be concentrated.

The extreme toxicity of dioxin was also clearly established, and there was plenty of evidence of its persistence in the environment as one of the dozen "forever chemicals." Hatfield had a good idea of the average concentration of TCDD in Agent Orange, and knew that accelerating the production process had increased the amount of dioxin as much as three-thousand-fold.

In heavily forested areas, Agent Orange volatilized rapidly on the foliage, and through photolysis—degradation by sunlight—it was gone in a matter of days, weeks at most, lingering longest where the dense vegetation grew back quickly or because a first application reached only the top layer of the dense forest. One flight path in the valley was repeated eleven times. When the defoliant reached the ground, it lingered much longer. The half-life of dioxin in surface soil was known to be between nine and fifteen years. Buried deeper in the subsoil, it might be anything from twenty to one hundred years. In pond, lake, and river sediment, it was about one hundred. In the human body, it was estimated at eleven to fifteen years.

The presence of dioxin was measured in parts per trillion, or ppt, and the maximum safe levels had been set in most Western nations as well as Vietnam. The Vietnamese standard for cropland was 40 ppt. For forests it was 100, for rural residential land 120, for urban residential areas 300, for recreational land 600, and for commercial and industrial areas 1,200. So Hatfield had several valuable benchmarks for judging the degree of contamination, although Western notions of "safe" were much too generous for the A Luoi Valley, where living conditions bore no resemblance to those in rural areas of the United States or Canada. The ethnic minority people lived intimately with the land, farming without machinery and eating only locally produced food. Kids went

barefoot, playing on the earth floor beneath their stilt houses, and toddlers everywhere have a habit of eating dirt.

"You don't have to be a rocket scientist to know that if you spray
dioxin on people there are going to be health effects," said Grant Bruce,
a member of the Hatfield team. But beyond that generality, pretty much
everything else remained uncertain, other than it was a known human
carcinogen and definitely caused chloracne. Published epidemiological
studies in Vietnam were almost nonexistent, other than the early work
of Ton That Tung and Le Cao Dai and a Ph.D. thesis on birth defects
in Quang Tri's Cam Lo district by Dr. Nguyen Viet Nhan, head of the
genetics department at the Hue University of Medicine and Pharmacy.
By the mid-1990s, the 10-80 Committee had a dioxin lab in Hanoi, but
its test results were not very enlightening. High-resolution mass spectrometry was only just coming into common use in the United States
and hadn't yet reached Vietnam. The existing technology in Vietnamese labs could show if a sample exceeded one thousand parts per trillion, but Boivin said that was about as much use as a doctor telling you
that you had a temperature over one hundred.

A good amount was known about the high concentrations of dioxin
in breast milk, mainly through the work of Arnold Schecter. "Credit
where credit is due," said Dwernychuk. Both Schecter and Le Cao Dai
had published studies of dioxin levels in blood. Dai was able to demonstrate a higher incidence of mortality and abnormal pregnancies in
villages that had been sprayed and of birth defects in the families of
veterans, and in 1995 a Russian scientist had detected signs of alteration in genetic material. The following year, around the same time Hatfield arrived in the A Luoi Valley, the Vietnamese government began
an investigation of birth defects in neighborhoods around the big air
bases at Bien Hoa, Danang, and Phu Cat.

But the only way to pull the whole puzzle together was a comprehensive survey of the sort Hatfield now undertook, a kind of life-cycle
study that would track the path of dioxin transmission from the spray
tanks on the C-123s through the soil and water, into the food chain,
and finally into the human body, in a single confined location where
there was no other possible source of contamination with TCDD. The
A Luoi Valley also happened to have been the place that more than
any other had shaped the course and outcome of the war. With the

first eighteen months devoted to ironing out the political sensitivities, the project from start to finish took them the better part of five years.

The valley was still badly disfigured by the herbicides, and as yet there were no acacia plantations to hide the scars. The forty-mile drive from Hue took them more than three hours, maneuvering around mudslides caused by the erosion of the defoliated hillsides. Outside every hut in the valley there were stacks of scrap metal and unexploded munitions, waiting for buyers. No demining teams had yet come to the area, and the local authorities gave them statistics on postwar casualties: 274 dead and another 224 injured by UXO. The victims had little prospect of getting immediate medical attention, since there was only one health center in the valley, in A Luoi town, and rudimentary clinics in a couple of other communes.

It was hard to keep a low profile. Curious crowds gathered wherever they went, and gaggles of kids trailed them around. Yet suspicion of foreigners had abated somewhat since the first MIA search teams arrived in the valley three or four years earlier, and the Hatfield team got a surprisingly warm welcome. "There were big parties," Dwernychuk said. "They would fill a bamboo tube with rice wine and give us straws and keep an eye on us to make sure we were drinking enough. And the military and police were very cooperative."

At A Shau, the runway and the foundations of the old Green Beret base were still visible, pitted with fish ponds in old bomb craters. "I got goosebumps being there," Dwernychuk said. "All the ghosts of history."

They sampled up and down the valley, tracking the documented flight paths, following the Yellow Brick Road. They took samples from sixteen sites altogether, sticking their stainless-steel probes into forest soils and farm fields, scooping out sediment from fish ponds, cutting up bottom-feeding grass carp, buying pork and beef from local markets and chickens and ducks from individual households, sampling manioc, sweet potatoes, leafy vegetables, rice, and vegetable oils. The samples from fish were especially important, both because of the inherent chemical properties of dioxin and the character of the local diet. Dioxin is hydrophobic and lipophilic: in lay terms, it dislikes water and loves fat, attaching itself to organic particles in sediment and seeking out adipose tissue. In fish, it builds up in fat and in the liver. Fish made up the bulk of the local protein diet. Moreover, Dwernychuk remembered, "People were so poor that they ate the whole fish, they didn't throw out the organs, they ate the liver, which is where the dioxin concentrates." As dioxin moved up the food chain, it concentrated further in a process called biomagnification. By the time the toxin reached humans, it had increased twelvefold.

The contamination at the old Ta Bat and A Luoi military bases, abandoned three months before the fall of the A Shau Special Forces camp, was somewhat higher than in the surrounding farmland but still within tolerable limits. In the fields, the amount of dioxin was negligible, degraded by the forces of nature. "The background level was about the same as my garden," Boivin said.

The old A Shau base was a different matter. It was apparent right away that the contamination of the soil, sediments, fish, and ducks was orders of magnitude worse. "We knew that the C-123s definitely used the airstrip, that they sprayed the base perimeter, that they washed out the spray tanks with water from the A Sap River, and that there had been spillage, like there was at Bien Hoa and Danang," Dwernychuk said. More than likely, the barrels of herbicide stored at A Shau had been smashed to pieces, like the rest of the base, when it was overrun by the PAVN in March 1966.

There was a sting in the tail of the first survey, however. The plan had been to send the samples to Canada for analysis. By a happy coincidence, Vancouver was home not only to Hatfield but to AXYS, certified by the World Health Organization as one of the best dioxin labs in the world. But even with the political clout of the 10-80 Committee, it took six months to get permission for the shipment before the Canadian embassy finally weighed in. Had the samples been properly preserved and refrigerated for all that time? Hatfield couldn't be sure. If not, the lab results couldn't be trusted. As in a criminal investigation, the integrity of evidence and the chain of custody was critical. Since this couldn't be guaranteed, there was only one option: come back and repeat the survey the following year. This time Hatfield would narrow the focus to the A Shau base and the adjacent A So commune, concentrating on the food chain and the dioxin that ended up in blood and breast milk.

The members of the Hatfield/10-80 team varied each time. Le Cao Dai had now moved over to the Vietnamese Red Cross, and most often it was Tran Manh Hung who accompanied them. A former PAVN fighter, "He was brash, tough as nails, and he didn't exactly have a great bedside manner when it came to taking blood samples," Boivin said. "But he knew how to get things done." He always carried a camera and recorded everything the Canadians did, so they nicknamed him "Dr. Video."

The only accommodations in the valley were at the government guesthouse in A Luoi town, but on their return in November 1997 they found all the rooms taken by an MIA search team and had to sleep in the schoolhouse. Boivin wondered if the Pentagon might be taking advantage of the opportunity to do its own dioxin sampling, but never got a chance to ask. "They would just go off into the jungle without talking to us or even acknowledging our presence," he said, "until the last night, when everyone went out and got drunk."

Hatfield had told the U.S. embassy about their project, and the Americans seemed wary. What would the study involve? Who was funding it? Who were they working with? What were their motives? Could the embassy attach someone to their team? One American did show up during the survey. He knew a lot about remote sensing technology, but generally kept his distance and was altogether a puzzle. The Canadians joked that they'd seen him talking into his shoe like Maxwell Smart, the comic spy in the old *Get Smart* TV show.

By the time of their second trip, remote sensing technology had become an important element of their work. A Canadian satellite, RADARSAT, which was launched at the end of 1995, gave them a much sharper sense than earlier satellite imaging of the topography of the sprayed areas and wartime environmental damage. They used this imagery not only to map the A Luoi Valley more accurately but to do the same for other areas—the Ma Da forest and the Ca Mau peninsula, which they'd rejected earlier as test sites; Vung Tau, near the mouth of the Saigon River; Quang Tri and the DMZ.

This second stage of the study was harder than the first, because the ethnic people were so resistant to giving blood. "For them it was like giving their spirit," Boivin said. "They were known to be fierce people, and the Katu could be nasty buggers." One woman told them with pride that she'd helped to shoot down American helicopters. Eventually some of the villagers agreed to cooperate, although they were willing to give only a tiny amount of blood, three milliliters each, which meant that the samples for analysis had to be pooled composites of blood taken from twenty people. Filling out questionnaires was an added headache, because everyone seemed to be named Ho, in honor of Ho Chi Minh. Two women had exactly the same three names, except that the tonal accent on one of the vowels was different. Vietnamese was always a tough language for foreigners.

It was clear from local health workers that there were many more birth defects in A So commune than elsewhere in the valley, especially in those under twenty-five—born, in other words, after the spraying ended. Again there was no conclusive proof that Agent Orange was responsible, and since this was the poorest part of the valley, malnutrition might have been a contributing factor, especially if the fetus hadn't received enough vitamins during the first trimester. Even so, the evidence kept accumulating that the uptake of dioxin was still happening long after the war.

This time Hatfield took no chances with the samples. Instead of seeking permission from the authorities in Hanoi, the team simply took their coolers to Ho Chi Minh City, where a contact in the 10-80 Committee's local office got them to Tan Son Nhat airport and had the samples loaded straight onto the plane. The lab analysis in Vancouver yielded some striking results: the highest concentrations of dioxin were in older men, which made sense because of its long half-life in the body and because they'd been eating the fish and other local foods for longer. Men also ate more in relation to their body weight. On top of that, women expelled a lot of their dioxin load through their breast milk—the only way it can be excreted from the human body—which was an important if chilling insight.

The third and final part of the study, which Hatfield conducted in 1999, was the clincher. By now the media had gotten wind of the fact that something newsworthy was happening in the A Luoi Valley, and a camera crew from CBS's *60 Minutes* showed up, interviewing Tom Boivin, still in his mid-thirties and baby-faced, and Tran Manh Hung, "Dr. Video." As usual, it was raining when they arrived, the mountains half-hidden under a sullen sky. Oddly, the report made no mention of the connection to the old Green Beret base or Hamburger Hill or anything else that might have sparked associations for American viewers. It was just a remote, anonymous valley, somewhere in deepest Vietnam. The reporter, Christiane Amanpour, also went to the Tu Du Maternity Hospital, interviewed Arnold Schecter about his research in Danang, and met an American vet and his daughter, who suffered from spina bifida—a birth defect that the VA had put on its list of presumptively dioxin-related conditions in the offspring of veterans.

The emotional power of Amanpour's report was undeniable. Here was an American child with spina bifida, and here was a Vietnamese child with the same condition. It was an overt statement of moral equivalence, creating the first widespread public awareness that the curse of Agent Orange had fallen on the Vietnamese as well as on American veterans.

Before this final part of their survey began, Hatfield had gotten hold of declassified military maps and other records showing the detailed layout of the A Shau base. This allowed them to pinpoint sections where the contamination was likely to be worst—the perimeter, which had been sprayed to create a clear line of fire, the airstrip, and the storage and loading area. This time they brought along a demining expert from Gerbera, the German company that had just begun work in Quang Tri. It was impossible to go far without his metal detector squawking its warning. They also took soil samples at the foot of Hamburger Hill, where a lot of people had been killed and maimed by UXO, although all they ever turned up there was bottle caps. Hatfield's final report made a point of stressing that any future work on Agent Orange in the valley had to be accompanied by a serious effort to clean up the UXO, although this didn't happen until 2004, more than thirty years after the last bombs had fallen, when the PAVN at last began a systematic clearance operation.

In every respect—ground contamination, food, blood, and milk— the findings of the third survey were worse than those from their earlier visits. One day Boivin, who had an impulsive streak, ventured out onto the base alone, sticking his steel probe into the ground to pull up soil samples. He got a slap on the wrist from the 10-80 Committee for such risky behavior, but he also got a sample with about nine hundred parts per trillion of dioxin, more than twenty times higher than the prescribed safe level for farmland. This was nothing compared to the concentrations Hatfield would later find at the storage and spill areas at Bien Hoa and Danang, but the contrast with other parts of the valley, plus the dramatic evidence of how the dioxin had migrated up the food chain and into the human body, were the last pieces in the jigsaw puzzle they had set out to assemble.

The Canadians took blood samples from well over five hundred people this time, equal numbers of males and females, and sampled breast milk in four communes, focusing on primiparous mothers—women who had given birth only once. Again the dioxin levels were much higher at A So than anywhere else. In Boivin's words, "they glowed in the dark." Infants in the valley were often breastfed until the age of three, and some mothers also worked as wet nurses. The dioxin level in their milk decreased substantially as they expressed it. In other words, the most life-giving substance in the world was passing on the worst man-made toxin in the world to their babies, whose daily intake of dioxin was as much as twenty times higher than the maximum safe level set by the World Health Organization.

From the start, both Hatfield and the 10-80 Committee insisted that the whole exercise was ultimately about people and how to protect them from harm. "The human dimension cannot be divorced from the scientific endeavor," Dwernychuk wrote in their final report. "On moral and humanitarian grounds, sincere efforts are required to help those least able to help themselves." This was the fusion of science and compassion for which American vets had clamored for years, finally supported by hard scientific data.

Hatfield recommended a modest plan to improve the bare-bones health system in the valley and a program to educate residents on the risks of dioxin and how to reduce them by minimizing contact with the soil and not eating fish from the crater ponds. There was no realistic prospect of cleaning up the A Shau base. Remediating a site of comparable size in Canada had cost $170 million. No foreign donor would ever commit that kind of money, and Vietnam was still clawing its way out of postwar poverty.

"If you sealed off the site with a chain-link fence, like you would in Canada or the U.S., people would just take it down and use it for other purposes," Dwernychuk said. In the end, in 2006, the botanist and forestry expert Phung Tuu Boi, who was reforesting thousands of acres in the valley with acacia, got modest funding from the World Bank to plant a ring of honey locust trees with long, sharp thorns to deter people and farm animals from wandering onto the base. The idea came from Lady Borton, who had the same trees on her farm in Ohio and knew from her days in Quang Ngai that the Vietnamese used their beans to make shampoo. And, Boi added, his trees might restore to the Katu and the Pacoh some of the spirits that had been driven from the valley by the evils of war.

The study by Hatfield and the 10-80 Committee transformed the debate on Agent Orange in Vietnam. "We theorize that the pattern of TCDD contamination recorded in the Aluoi [*sic*] Valley serves as a model for the contamination throughout Southern Vietnam," Dwernychuk wrote. "Human exposure, and subsequent contamination through the food chain transfer of TCDD, would be highest in areas of former military installations." He called this the "hot spot" theory. One reason the discussion of Agent Orange had always been paralyzed was that so much of the country had been sprayed that it was impossible to know how and where you could start to deal with the consequences. Hatfield cut through that particular dimension of the fog of war. Other than transmission through the food chain, which could be reduced by smart public health policies, the fields and forests that had been sprayed were no longer likely to present any immediate danger. Where there had been a pervasive fear of the unknown, there was now a problem that was manageable—if the political will was there.

Hatfield and the 10-80 Committee had come up with solid, irrefutable scientific data, and it pointed the finger of responsibility straight at the past actions, and present inaction, of the U.S. government. So how would the United States react, given that it still refused even to talk about the problem almost five years into the new era of normalized relations?

The Hatfield team prepared to present their findings to the U.S. embassy in Hanoi. "Choose your language very carefully," the Canadian ambassador advised.

"It was the most bizarre meeting I've ever been to in my life," Boivin said. Showing up promptly at ten a.m., they found themselves facing a battery of two dozen Americans. No introductions, no exchange of business cards, no offer of coffee, not even a glass of water. The Canadians were used to the informality of their own diplomats, but American protocol was something new to them. When Ambassador Peterson entered the room, everyone snapped to attention like soldiers on inspection parade.

He listened to the presentation in silence, expressionless. When they finished, he got up to leave, without a word. Chris Hatfield caught up with him and said he had some questions. First off, would the U.S. support an independent study, maybe paid for by UNDP [the United Nations Development Programme], which had already expressed interest? Peterson said no, he didn't want the UN involved. He was a well-liked man, known for his warm human touch, but as he turned to go, all he said to Hatfield was, "You have given me a big political problem."

However, that didn't mean for a moment that the U.S. government was in any hurry to solve it. Peterson did begin to speak in general terms about encouraging cooperation between American and Vietnamese scientists, but for anything more significant to happen on the ground, there had to be a new constellation of forces, one that would build on the data gathered in the A Luoi Valley, the nascent alliance between Lady Borton and Chris Hatfield's team, and the awakening interest of Charles Bailey of the Ford Foundation, who was now entering his fourth year in Hanoi.

The End of Our Exploring

VETERANS, SCIENTISTS, pacifists driven by faith, politicians more interested in looking forward than looking back: all of them chipped away at the painful obstacles to normal relations with Vietnam—first POWs and MIAs, then prosthetics for the disabled, then the removal of unexploded ordnance, and now at last the legacy of Agent Orange. But the vets who were most damaged by the war fought a concurrent battle of their own, and they largely fought it alone.

The things that Manus Campbell carried back to Vietnam were heavier than most, and he followed a long and circuitous path to get there. He had some inkling now of why men went to war, of what he had taken to Vietnam and what Vietnam had taken from him. His thoughts began to echo those of Charlie Sheen, Private Chris Taylor, as he is choppered away from the battlefield at the end of *Platoon*: "The war was over for me now, but it will always be there for the rest of my days. Those of us who did make it have an obligation to build again and to teach to others what we know and to try with what's left of our lives to find a goodness and meaning to this life."

Still unanchored, Campbell craved a life freed from restraints and conventions, and he was never going to find it sculpting alabaster in his apartment or working night security for Nobody Beats the Wiz. He'd looked to Asia for spiritual insights, but apart from his trip to Tibet in 1991, he'd never really gone to the source. Now his disability pension from the VA gave him the means to do so. "When you travel somewhere new outside, you also travel somewhere new inside," he said, quoting the Buddhist monk Matthieu Ricard.

In 2006 he went to India for the first time, beginning a full-immersion course in the myths and mysteries of Hinduism. He marveled at the sublime symmetries of the Taj Mahal in Agra and the erotic temple carvings of Khajuraho. He threw himself into the chaos of Varanasi, holiest of all Hindu cities, and went on a retreat in Sarnath, where the Buddha had preached his first sermon and the two great religions parted ways. On a later trip he made a longer retreat in Bodh Gaya, where he saw worshippers scramble to catch one of the heart-shaped leaves as it fell from the ancient fig tree where the Buddha was said to have attained enlightenment.

When he got home, he found his thoughts turning more and more to Vietnam and the possibility of return. He began to read about the country it had become, not the war that had scarred him. He came across an article one day in which a veteran who had already gone back encouraged others to do the same. The man's name was Chuck Searcy.

Campbell's first time back was in January 2007. It was just a ten-day trip, a toe in the water. He spent a day or two in Saigon, which he'd never seen in wartime, and made the pilgrimage to My Lai, where American troops had slaughtered more than five hundred unarmed men, women, and children while he was pinned down under mortar fire at Con Thien. He wandered around outside the small museum in a daze of grief and nausea. Two dogs circled; he was sure that they sensed the dark energy in him and were going to attack. It was his blackest moment in a long time.

He headed north to the ancient Chinese trading port of Hoi An, near Danang, which was fast becoming a magnet for foreign visitors, and ended up with a couple of days in Hue, where an ambitious effort was under way, under the auspices of UNESCO, to restore the walled imperial citadel, much of which had been reduced to rubble during the Tet Offensive. He was drawn to the city, which most visitors consider the most beautiful in Vietnam. He visited the secluded Tu Hieu monastery, the "root temple" of the spiritual leader Thich Nhat Hanh.

He saw a map of the DMZ one day on the wall of an internet café, and the owner offered to arrange a tour. He laughed. "No, I've been there already. I'm more interested in peace now."

"In that case," the woman said, "you should meet my teacher." It was a Buddhist nun, Sister Minh Thanh, who was a devotee of Thich Nhat Hanh's principles of "engaged Buddhism" and taught at Tu Hieu. She told Campbell that American soldiers had come there once and interrogated one of the monks. Speaking no English, he couldn't understand their questions, but they'd decided he was VC and shot him dead.

Now the sister had opened a center for disabled children and orphans called the Beloved School. Campbell saw the ostracism the kids suffered, the stigma that attached to those who looked and acted different and too often were hidden away by their parents out of shame. He gave the sister a little money, the first of many years of monthly checks.

He found intervals of tranquility in the temples and gardens of Kyoto and the Shinto shrines of Kobe, in the ornate gold and white *wats* of Thailand and Laos. Buddhism was becoming the main spiritual force in his life, although he found inspiration in Hinduism, too, seeing the common roots from which the wisdom of both religions sprang. In the end, all religions were human constructs, no less fallible than the Catholicism of his childhood. His father had been an ardent believer, but it had done nothing to silence his inner anxieties. Tibetan teachers said the demons were inside us and that the unmastered ego was capable of wreaking destruction. That hinted at the singular virtue that Campbell found in Buddhism: its insights into the workings of the human mind. Perhaps it was no coincidence that many of those who shaped his process of recovery, like Arthur Egendorf and Jack Kornfield, melded Buddhist teachings with Western psychology.

But his search for spiritual equilibrium was far from over, and he went back to India, settling for a while this time in the southern state of Kerala, in the huge oceanside ashram that had grown up around the humble birthplace of Mata Amritanandamayi Devi, better known as Amma, or the "hugging saint," who traveled the world packing hotel ballrooms and sports arenas and offering embraces to anyone willing to stand in line with a "hugging token." By the time he met Amma, she had bestowed *darshan*—the blessing received when one views a deity, a holy person, or a sacred image—on tens of millions of people.

After that, Campbell said, his life "went a little sideways," not for the first time. His girlfriend had thrown him out of their New Jersey apartment, and he met a Swedish woman at the ashram and moved to

Sweden with her for six months as she battled a diagnosis of ALS, Lou Gehrig's disease. Back in New Jersey, he found himself homeless at sixty. He rented a room in a motel, crashed with his family, went back to Amma's ashram.

In Bangalore, a master of kriya yoga asked him how he had come by the name of Manus.

"Irish," he answered. "There are lots of Manuses in County Donegal. My father was a Manus too. In Gaelic, it means great."

In Sanskrit, the teacher told him, it had multiple meanings. As in Latin, it meant "hand" but also "mind" and "man born of woman." In the Vishnu Purana, *manusya* alludes to the wise man who overcomes pain and attains true wisdom.

With a small group of other devotees, Campbell went on tour with the hugging saint, stopping at Hyatts and Hiltons and Marriotts and Best Westerns in a dozen cities in Canada and the United States. They traveled to Japan and to Sri Lanka, where the president asked Amma for "divine intervention and merciful blessings" to end his country's civil war.

In Los Angeles, Campbell fell into conversation with another Sri Lankan, a man named Jake. The idea of returning to Vietnam for good was clearer in his mind now, but finding his own spiritual anchorage was only one part of the equation. There were bigger questions of purpose to answer. Thich Nhat Hanh counseled engagement, but what did that mean? Most of the returning vets wanted to give something back, to make amends in their own small way for what their country had done. But what was that something, and who should benefit? Like many others, Campbell decided it would be the children.

He and Jake threw themselves into the planning, and after three weeks they had photos, video, a full analysis of what the Beloved School needed, and a website. Campbell registered a small not-for-profit in New Jersey that he called Helping the Invisible Victims of War. He put in some of his own money, and others chipped in. It added up to $30,000, and in Vietnam that kind of money could go a long way.

In January 2010, retracing his first steps in wartime, Campbell flew into the old Marine-army base at Phu Bai, now transformed into the civilian airport for the city of Hue. He rented a small apartment near the Beloved School, on a leafy block close to the Perfume River. Looking for a speech therapist for the kids, he was introduced to the famous geneticist Dr. Nguyen Viet Nhan. The new life he had chosen was hard at first, with the language barrier and his unfamiliarity with everyday customs and etiquette. He was always conscious of the jarring contrasts with the past. For a soldier who had fought in Vietnam, it was disorienting not to be shunted hither and yon at someone else's command but to move around as you pleased, free to act on your own initiative. "As a vet with PTSD, you always struggled with the problem of isolation," he said. Early in his stay, he learned the words for "being alone": *mot minh.* But he found comfort in working at the Beloved School every day, kicking a ball around with the kids on weekends, treating them to ice cream, taking them to bathe in the hot springs at the foot of a saddleback mountain near the city, small things that were gifts to himself as much as to them.

If you were interested in healing the wounds of war, and particularly the legacy of Agent Orange, Hue was the ideal place to start. The university was a renowned center of scholarship and research, and outside of Hanoi and Saigon, the city had the best hospitals in Vietnam. If they had the means, families from the surrounding provinces brought their children to the city for diagnosis and treatment of their birth defects. The man to whom they came seeking answers was Dr. Nhan, who had conducted one of the few small-scale epidemiological studies of a heavily defoliated area. His field research, done under the auspices of the 10-80 Committee, had focused on a commune in Quang Tri's Cam Lo district, where his mother-in-law had grown up. He had found a startling number of households there with two or more disabled children, and some with as many as five.

Campbell found that the kind of engagement preached by Thich Nhat Hanh was anything but straightforward: Buddhist principles and Buddhist practice were not always in alignment. He went back to Con Thien and the DMZ with a monk who had a taste for beer with a shot of Red Bull. He took small gifts of cash, rice, blankets, and school supplies to the villages of the Bru-Van Kieu in the mountains around Khe Sanh and found that the monks he traveled with expected a commission for their services. Often the monks in Hue and Danang seemed more interested in material show than in charity. Who could harvest the biggest donations to build the most ostentatious pagodas? Worst of all, thousands of dollars he donated to the Beloved School went astray, and Sister Minh Thanh asked for more. Buddhist institutions, it turned out, could be just as prone to corruption, vanity, petty jealousies, and office politics as any other.

It became a cliché to say that for the veterans—and indeed for most foreign visitors—"Vietnam" was a war, and it was a country. It was "Indochine"; it was "The 'Nam." It was a state of mind, a brand name, a shorthand for trauma. For Campbell, and for all those who returned, the heart of the matter was to find a way to reconcile the boys they had been in wartime with the men they had become in its aftermath.

It wasn't always easy to make sense of the country they went back to, especially in an area imprinted as deeply by war as the northern provinces of I Corps. Vietnam had become a complicated and mesmerizing place, riddled with paradoxes, a demographically young country where most people had no active memory of the conflict and little apparent interest in it. It was a tightly controlled and often corrupt one-party state, yet there were few signs of that in the energetic rhythms and traditional rituals of daily life. By the time Campbell came back, Vietnam was a fully paid-up member of the World Trade Organization, on course to becoming one of the great economic success stories of the developing world. Freewheeling boom towns, UNESCO World Heritage Sites, ravishing landscapes, and miles of golden beaches—all this existed side by side with rural backwaters where stooped figures in conical hats labored beside their water buffalo in the complex green geometry of the rice fields, as if nothing had changed in half a century. As Campbell's fellow ex-Marine Suel Jones liked to ask, had the United States bombed Vietnam back into the Stone Age or forward into the twenty-first century? Here in I Corps it could often feel like both.

Invariably the vets encountered the same open welcome that Vietnamese extended to almost all visiting Americans, whatever their age or purpose. This often startled them, and it moved them to find ways of reciprocating. "In so many ways the Vietnamese hold us in high esteem," Searcy said one day. "They assume that we are decent and honorable people, and in a lot of ways it makes those of us who live here want to be as good as we can be as Americans." It was about making yourself worthy of the forgiveness that the Vietnamese seemed so ready to offer.

It was rare for a veteran to travel to Hanoi without crossing paths with Searcy, and Campbell met him there soon after he arrived in Vietnam, introduced by mutual friends who had adopted a Vietnamese child. Dissimilar as the two men were in many ways, they quickly warmed to each other, and Campbell joined the new chapter of Veterans for Peace that Searcy and others had just founded, an organization started in the early 1980s by a group of vets who saw U.S. involvement in Central America as the slippery slope to a new Vietnam. Searcy began to put together an annual veterans' tour, which included a stop at George Mizo's Friendship Village outside Hanoi, a visit to Project RENEW in Dong Ha, a whistlestop circuit of the DMZ, a loop around the A Luoi Valley. In later years he added a side trip to My Lai. Sometimes just a handful of vets came; other times it might be an unwieldy party of forty.

They could be a fractious bunch, organizing material support for victims of the war but sometimes squabbling over the best way to use it. Some excoriated any hint of cooperation with USAID—which these days was the main channel for humanitarian aid—given the agency's role in the war, when it provided support for the strategic hamlet program and had a seat on the 203 Committee, which identified targets for Operation Ranch Hand. Searcy found these criticisms ironic and exasperating. If the purpose of the exercise was redemption, that surely had to apply to institutions as well as individuals. He and others had been pounding on the door of the government for years to do the right thing, and now, when they'd forced that door open, it made no sense to slam it shut again.

Vietnamese bureaucracy could also sometimes stymie the vets' best intentions. Many of them wanted to bring aid to the A Luoi Valley, but Thua Thien-Hue was still a tough place to work, with something of the stiff-necked hauteur of a city whose culture had been shaped by royalty, colonial officialdom, Catholic priests, monks, and mandarins.

They demanded to know why Campbell's business card said he was there to help the Invisible Victims of War. How did he know that's what the children were? But in a place like the Beloved School, if a child was disabled, blind, or mentally impaired, how were you supposed to prove that those conditions were a consequence of dioxin exposure?

It was impossible; that was the whole point. More broadly, how could you separate the legacies of the war from the hardships of life in the places where the destruction had been greatest? In the villages of Thua Thien-Hue and Quang Tri, the scars reached deeper into the present than anywhere else in Vietnam, and there were fewer signs of the new prosperity. Many women saw no economic option but to abandon their babies on the steps of an orphanage or a pagoda. So were these infants the victims of war? And in the end, why did the specific cause of their hardships even matter?

When Campbell eventually decided to leave Hue after three years, it had nothing to do with the city's tangled politics. The decision was made for him by the *crachin*, the long dreary months of overcast skies and constant drizzle, which twice laid him low with pneumonia. But where would he go next?

Former Marines invariably gravitated toward I Corps, with all its lacerating memories. "It was like a buried piece of shrapnel, working its way to the surface," William Broyles wrote. No one kept count of the number of resident veterans in the country, though the rough estimate was about forty, and the largest cluster had congregated in Danang. The city had given them their first taste of Vietnam, and now in peacetime, it offered them sunshine, beaches, cafés, and bars, a relaxed pace of life.

Suel Jones had been one of the first to settle in for a long stay. He was the son of a Southern Baptist deacon and a Sunday school teacher from East Texas—"recruited as a Marine from birth," he said. On Memorial Day in 1967, he had gone after an antiwar demonstrator with his bare fists. But when he came back to The World, he found that the acceptance of Jesus Christ as his personal savior did not sit well with the Sixth Commandment, "Thou shalt not kill." He spent time in a VA psych ward in Seattle, took to the road, did too many drugs, hung out in hippie communes, lived for years in a remote cabin in the Alaskan wilderness while working the oil fields, went to India and found a guru, and was transformed from Bubba Jones into Abhiraj, Fearless King.

Jones had been a fire team leader in Delta Company of the First Battalion of the Third Marines at Con Thien and the Rockpile, and in the A Shau Valley, earning two Purple Hearts. Bill Ervin of Boulder, Colorado, had been a machine-gunner in the same company at the same time, though they didn't know each other until 2008, when they met in Danang. Ervin had been returning regularly for close to fifteen years by that point, leading tours of the old battlefields; when his wife died, he decided to move back for good.

David Clark of Albion, Illinois, had signed up for the Marines on his seventeenth birthday, and as soon as he arrived in Danang two years later, he decided that the key to survival was to cultivate a harsh, macho persona, brandishing the M-16 he carried everywhere to intimidate any Vietnamese he encountered. Now, he said, "I decided that if I was destined to die in Vietnam, I planned to do so on my own terms."

Larry Vetter, another Texan, returned in 2012, initially with the idea of staying only a couple of months, just long enough to help a family with two disabled kids, presumed to be victims of dioxin. But he stayed on. Captain Larry, as everyone called him, had been a patrol leader in the Third Marine Reconnaissance Battalion, a swashbuckling outfit whose crest was a skull and crossbones and whose Latin motto was *Celer, Silens et Mortalis*—"Fast, Silent, and Deadly." His vivid and detailed account of his experiences was commercially published, as was his Vietnam novel, *Blood on the Lotus*.

Jones and Ervin had put pen to paper, too, Jones with a self-published memoir and Ervin with a slim volume of photographs and poetry. For its epigraph, he chose the famous line from T. S. Eliot:

And the end of our exploring
Will be to arrive where we started
And know the place for the first time.

Several of these men had found love in Danang. Ervin started a small travel business, and he and his Vietnamese wife continued his battlefield tours. Captain Larry married his own tour guide from an earlier visit. Clark's wife was a devout Catholic, a high-spirited woman named Nguyen Thi Thanh Huong, though everyone called her Ushi, a nickname she acquired because of her supposed resemblance to a character in a Dutch TV comedy show. Ushi was also the name of the restaurant she owned on the main tourist drag in Hue, another stop on

Searcy's annual tour. All three men dressed for their weddings in traditional costume, looking like sexagenarian mandarins from the court of the Nguyen emperors.

Their personal politics, oddly, didn't seem to get in the way of their friendships. Clark worked closely with a regular visitor from Sioux Falls, South Dakota, a gentle, soft-spoken man with a white goatee named Mark O'Connor, who had served with the army's 123rd Aviation Battalion. Clark's politics were firmly to the left; O'Connor's were far to the right. In later years he liked to wear a red MAGA hat. But his humanitarian impulses were constant; each spring he ran a program to take bicycles to the A Luoi Valley so the ethnic minority children could get to school. He bought the bikes in lots of dozens at a time at knock-down prices through Ushi Clark's local connections.

The Danang vets liked to hang out at bars on China Beach, guzzling Hue's famous Huda beer and Jack Daniel's on the rocks with former Viet Cong fighters who were now their drinking buddies—a mutual un-Othering of the Other, you might say. Both sides had suffered similar privations, and the Americans had not chosen the fight, their Vietnamese friends told them; their government had. Often they were joined by another ex-Marine who told graphic tales of being parachuted into the mountains on the Lao border on black ops and sprayed with Agent Orange from helicopters. His stories turned out to be pure fabrications—he'd never set foot in Vietnam during the war—though no one could say whether this was the product of a disordered psyche or whether he was just an inventive con man. Eventually he vanished and was never heard from again.

At the end of the evening, with a few Hudas under their belts, the Marines would climb onto their big Harleys and Yamahas and roar off into the sultry night like aging Hells Angels. Sometimes they organized small groups to zip around the old Marine battlefields on Dangerous Dave's Daredevil Tours (motto: "We'll get you there but not always in one piece") or Bill's Long and Winding Road Trip ("We'll get you there but we don't always know when or how"). The new road from Da Krong to the A Luoi Valley, passing close to the section of the old Trail that Manus Campbell had once fought to destroy, drew them back like a magnetic field.

Campbell was no aging Hell's Angel, and he hadn't touched a drink in more than twenty-five years. He moved to Hoi An, twenty miles down the coast from Danang. He made a point of finding an apartment in a quiet corner of town, because by the time he arrived the old Chinese trading port, now a UNESCO World Heritage Center, was fast becoming the face of Vietnam's tourist boom on steroids.

Relics of French colonial rule, old battlefields, ancient monuments: all of these were being folded into a great economic bonanza based on what some scholars call "the manufacture of nostalgia," though another prefers "memory with the pain removed."

In the past, Hoi An must have been a jewel box. It had largely escaped wartime destruction, and the narrow, grid-pattern streets were still lined with ornate homes, temples, colonial mansions, and assembly halls built by merchant guilds from the southern provinces of China. But to accommodate the flood of tourists, the shophouses, some dating back to the 1500s, were being transformed into boutique hotels, restaurants, coffee shops, smoothie bars, wine bars, souvenir stands, and tailor shops offering same-day suits, shirts, and silk dresses at a fraction of the price you'd pay at home. Beyond the small pedestrian zone of the "Ancient Town," the streets were gridlocked by tour buses. The miles of pristine sand that stretched all the way north to China Beach were being steadily walled off from the public by luxury resorts and condotels, many of them owned by East Asian investors, though Vietnamese military officers were also said to have cornered a good share of the lucrative business.

In Hue, package-tour groups were trooping around the Citadel behind guides holding up colored umbrellas with corporate logos, and taking dragon boat cruises down the Perfume River to visit the tombs of the Nguyen emperors, stopping off at the seven-story Thien Mu pagoda to see the rusted blue Austin Westminster that had driven the monk Thich Quang Duc to his self-immolation in Saigon during the Buddhist protests of 1963.

Western visitors to Hue could soak up the ubiquitous legacy of the French era, with a good measure of colonial kitsch thrown in. They could pamper themselves at La Résidence, the gleaming-white five-star Art Deco hotel that had been built as an addition to the mansion of the *résident supérieur* of Annam. They could savor the tasting menu at its restaurant, Le Parfum, or sample gourmet French-Vietnamese fusion cuisine in impeccably restored green-and-yellow-painted mansions where musicians slipped on the costumes of the imperial court over their blue jeans and sneakers and serenaded them with Vietnamese classical music, played on traditional stringed instruments, adding little party tricks for the foreigners, like a sly segue from these ancient melodies into the theme from *The Godfather*.

From Hoi An or Danang, the tourists could book the popular half-day tour to My Son, a complex of crumbling redbrick temples from the vanished empire of Champa, dedicated to the worship of Shiva, though many of the ruins are the result of B-52 strikes in 1969. On the outskirts of Danang there were the caves and grottoes of the Marble Mountains, where the Americans had a helicopter base and the Viet Cong operated a clandestine hospital. Out beyond the tip of China Beach, tourists with a green bent could go in search of endangered langurs on the Son Tra peninsula, which the Americans called Monkey Mountain. Sybarites could splash out $400 a night at the oceanfront Intercontinental Resort Danang Sun, on a horseshoe beach at the foot of the mountain.

"The Puritan belief that Satan dwelt in nature could have been born here," Michael Herr had written of the terrifying mountains of I Corps. But now the Truong Son range, with its stunning natural beauty and its echoes of wartime, was also ripe to be monetized.

There were especially lucrative opportunities in the colonial hill stations built by the French elites as a refuge from the summer heat. Manufactured memories were in full flower at Sun World Ba Na Hills, twenty-five miles west of Danang. The French had built an idyllic retreat on Ba Na Mountain in the 1920s, with elegant villas, guesthouses, restaurants, and tennis courts. The original buildings were long gone, abandoned during the war against the Viet Minh, scavenged by local people for construction materials, and then flattened by American bombs. Ba Na had overlooked the PAVN's most important stronghold in Quang Nam, and fighting raged for months in 1968 in the flatland at the foot of the mountain, which the Marines called Happy Valley. The lower slopes had been blanketed by at least two dozen Ranch Hand missions.

The Danang People's Committee had discussed the potential of Ba Na as an ecotourism reserve, but after the site was sold in 2007 to the Sun Group, one of Vietnam's biggest real estate companies, any resemblance to ecotourism was purely incidental. Now visitors were whisked to the summit by a cable car that dropped them off at the Gare de l'Indochine, where they could stroll around a Disneyfied replica of a French provincial town, complete with the Café Postal, the Buffet La Lavande, a brasserie, a cathedral modeled on Notre Dame, and a turreted medieval chateau, as well as a wax museum with figures of Queen Elizabeth II, Mr. Bean, and Johnny Depp as Captain Jack in *Pirates of the Caribbean.* All this was the work of Falcon's Creative Group of Orlando, Florida, building on its earlier successes like the Charlie and the Chocolate Factory Experience at a theme park in England and The Curse of Darkastle at Busch Gardens in Williamsburg.

Twenty miles to the north, the ideals of ecotourism were still alive on Bach Ma Mountain. Home to one of Vietnam's first national parks, it rose vertiginously to five thousand feet from the edge of a coastal lagoon, where fishermen bobbed about in coracles and women harvested shellfish that they cultivated on the rims of submerged bicycle tires. The residents of Hue had built their hill station at Bach Ma in 1931, just as crowds of Parisians were flocking to the great Exposition Coloniale to marvel at the successes of France's *mission civilisatrice* and the strange and exotic habits of the inferior races.

To the south of Bach Ma was what the Americans called Elephant Valley, a transit route where the insurgents used the animals to transport weapons and supplies. The A Shau Valley was due west, and in the summer of 1969, as part of an operation that was a sequel to the Hamburger Hill campaign, the Americans had built a firebase at the summit. The scars of war were everywhere, in the ruins of Monsieur Bony's hotel, dark green with moss and engulfed in vines; in the Swiss cheese walls of the Chapelle des Soeurs de Jeanne d'Arc; in the bomb craters; and in the fighting holes and tunnels dug by North Vietnamese sappers.

Yet the entrancing beauty of the mountain was still largely intact. Ancient rotting steps led downhill to gin-clear rivers that tumbled over rocks and waterfalls. Patches of dappled sunlight in the dark stands of evergreens were alive with butterflies, canary yellow, orange and white, electric blue, translucent wings patterned with brown veins like airborne X-rays. There were more than 330 species of birds, and Bach

Ma was on the bucket list of birdwatchers from all over the world, who paid a premium for expert guided tours. Sometimes they might hear a bird call that sounded like derisive laughter, the cry of the Red-headed Trogon. If the Katu people heard it, they would rush straight home, thinking the bird was mocking them. They lived in a world of such omens: a fallen tree or a peacock egg lying on a forest path spelled out warnings.

Even after Manus Campbell moved to Hoi An, he never stayed in one place for long. He joked that he was a Sagittarius, and Sagittarians were known for their itchy feet, but it was always about more than that, a deeper questing restlessness.

He often took off in search of quietude: another trip to Kyoto, a solo retreat at a Krishnamurti center in Thailand. He fell into the habit of escaping each year from the commotion of Tet, when there was little to do but close your ears to the cacophony of car horns and firecrackers before the streets emptied out for the duration of the holiday. Though he could sometimes seem diffident, even tinged by melancholy, he had a gift for human connections, and if he wanted a travel companion, it was rarely hard to find one. Chuck Searcy joined him one year on a trip to Sri Lanka, where they wandered among the tea plantations. In Danang, Campbell befriended the writer Le Ly Hayslip, who frequented the orphanage at a pagoda that housed more of his invisible victims of war, and they traveled together to Myanmar.

The country captivated him. Its people were the kindest he'd ever met, he said, with the exception of Americans. But the new dimensions of Buddhism he encountered there only complicated the questions he had struggled with, the riddle of what drove men to war. He traveled upcountry to Rakhine state, on the border with Bangladesh, the land of the Muslim Rohingya, who were now being slaughtered, raped, and burned out of their homes by soldiers and religious militants. Buddhists, it seemed, were as capable of bigotry and violence as the fanatics of any other faith.

He took a ferry upriver to the ancient temple town of Mrauk-U, heading deeper into the mountains in a dugout canoe until he reached a village where the women of the Chin minority had their faces tattooed as children. He was startled from his room one morning by the clamor of people running through the streets and loud noise that sounded like the barking rattle of machine guns. In an instant he was back on Hill 674. But all he had heard was a house on fire.

The ties of friendship pulled him back to the United States for a spell to care for a dying army veteran, Mike Cull, a fellow Irish storyteller who had been one of the best known and best liked of the returning vets, running an educational program with his Vietnamese wife in the coastal city of Nha Trang. After laying his friend to rest, Campbell went back to Vietnam, a return that now felt like a homecoming. He settled in Hanoi this time, renting a small apartment close to lovely Hoan Kiem Lake, a block away from the Polite Pub, where Chuck Searcy had toasted the resumption of diplomatic relations.

He often went to Hoan Kiem in the cool of the early morning, always with his camera slung around his neck, photographing the tai chi ladies, the young lovers, the girls in their *ao dais* and wedding dresses, the flautists and the drummers, the badminton players, the old men dreaming the day away on park benches by the water's edge. Sometimes the old men turned out to be veterans themselves, and Campbell would take a seat next to them and trade war stories.

It's not uncommon for a foreigner sitting by the lake to be approached by a student with a shy request for help to improve his or her English. If the request comes from a young woman, it may take a second to decipher any possible subtext. But more often than not the overture is made in all innocence, and one day Campbell fell into conversation with a studious young woman named Nguyen Thu. In time, she took to calling him "Father," and he called her "Daughter." When her mother learned of this, she told Thu that she should love and honor Manus without reservation, just as she loved and honored her birth parents.

He joined Thu for a trip to the family's home province of Ha Tinh, midway between Hanoi and the former DMZ. She showed him glimpses of the dark side of modern Vietnam—the prostitutes trolling the beaches, young women from the Tai Dam ethnic minority, the "Black Tai," driven by poverty into the sex trade and drug abuse and now suffering the scourge of HIV-AIDS. Her ancestral village was close to the port city of Vinh, where war matériel had once been offloaded from ships at the start of the Ho Chi Minh Trail. Obliterated by more than five thousand wartime airstrikes, the "Red City" was now postwar Vietnam at its ugliest, rebuilt with dreary apartment blocks as East Germany's contribution to Le Duan's vision of a socialist utopia.

Thu introduced Campbell to her real father, who had fought on the opposing side in Quang Tri and risen high in the ranks of the PAVN, retiring as a major general. During the war he had spent a year storing munitions bound for the Trail in the limestone caves of Phong Nha in Quang Binh province, safe from the bombs.

Now the caves were the heart of another of Vietnam's national parks and a mecca for backpackers, one more face of the tourist boom. There were eco-homestays and spelunking adventures, and a company called Jungle Boss that offered trekking tours, often stopping to burn incense at a small temple whose bell was made from an old bomb casing. This marked the site of Hang Tam Co, Eight Ladies Cave, named for a group of young women volunteers who had been entombed there by a rock-slide from a B-52 strike. Like the women Campbell and Searcy had met at the Ho Chi Minh Trail Museum in Hanoi, they had been teenagers working on the famous Road 20 to the Lao border.

The highlight of a trip to Phong Nha was an excursion to what American bomber pilots called the Disappearing River Cave. Young men in PAVN-style pith helmets met the tourists at a landing stage that had once been the Xuan Son ferry crossing, a key transit point on the Trail, a prime target for Operation Rolling Thunder, and a graveyard for F-4 Phantoms, many of whose crewmen were still "active pursuit" cases, out there somewhere in the limestone karst. A mile or two up the Con River, the tourist boats turned into a small side channel that branched off to the left until it vanished beneath a great rock overhang like a half-drawn curtain. Inside, the backpackers filed along wooden walkways that led past stalactites and stalagmites and dripping flow-stone, floodlit in pale and subtle colors and further illuminated by the pop of camera flashes from selfie sticks, like a cloud of fireflies.

Campbell spent a week in Thu's ancestral village, hanging out with her father though politely declining to share his breakfast, which con-sisted of several glasses of rice wine. They shared memories of their time in combat in Quang Tri, and the old man told Campbell stories of the Phong Nha caves. He enjoyed teasing him with the singsong call "Tonight you die, Marine," because he'd been one of those singing it in the darkness of the jungle. But now, half a century later, it was some-thing they could both laugh about.

The Road to Damascus

I F THE STORY OF Agent Orange was a study in the imbalance of power, the work of Hatfield Consultants and the 10-80 Committee in the A Luoi Valley had opened a new and defining chapter. For most of the veterans who returned to Vietnam, like Manus Campbell, the legacy of the defoliant was the worst of all the wrongs they wanted to set right. What they could bring to bear on the problem was their moral authority, their usually modest checkbooks, and their sweat equity. The scientists had their own kind of credibility, assembling the data, pushing the boundaries of what was known. Lady Borton and Chuck Searcy, who moved with ease in these overlapping circles, both knew a good deal about how to work the levers of influence in both governments, though it was mainly behind the scenes. But Ambassador Peterson's terse response to Hatfield's A Luoi report showed where the limits lay. There were still higher rungs of the ladder of power and influence to be climbed if his "big political problem" was to be solved. The Venn diagram, with Searcy and Borton at its hub, had to be enlarged.

When Charles Bailey arrived in Hanoi to run the Ford Foundation's Vietnam program, Agent Orange was the furthest thing from his mind. His specialty was agriculture, and he started by looking for ways to support struggling farmers, which naturally took him to the poorest rural areas. Toward the end of 1998, he traveled with a group of Vietnamese agricultural scientists to Lam Dong province in the Central Highlands—present-day Dak Lak. He saw hillsides patchworked with new plantations of pine. "Agent Orange," a member of the local people's committee explained. "All the forests that were here before were destroyed; there was just eroded soil and landslides." Bailey remembered his middle-schoolers in Nepal, spraying their tomato plants to get rid of grasshoppers, telling him how the Americans were killing forests in Vietnam. *Damn, that kid was right,* he thought to himself. *So why is nobody doing anything about it?*

Perhaps this was something Ford could help with, he suggested to his Vietnamese colleague Ngo Thi Le Mai, a politically astute young woman who administered the foundation's grants. She arched an eyebrow. *Charles, are you really sure?*

He met Chuck Searcy soon after the Dak Lak trip. Bailey had read about him in an article in the *South China Morning Post,* in which Searcy complained that while the United States seemed ready to go on devoting unlimited resources to the search for its MIAs—on which the Vietnamese were being more than helpful—his prosthetics program, now almost four years old, still had to operate on a shoestring.

The two men met for a long lunch. "Maybe it wasn't memorable for Charles, but it was for me," Searcy said. He did most of the talking while Bailey listened, sphinxlike. Searcy laid out what he thought American veterans could do about the various legacies of the war, stressing both the virtues of their independence and their moral authority and the limits of their resources and political clout. He told Bailey that while they had been able to make some progress on disabilities, the impasse over Agent Orange was their greatest frustration: no one in the American government would even talk about it, and there wasn't much the vets could do but offer small-scale, piecemeal support for some of its presumed victims. An institution like Ford could make a real difference; the foundation's size and reputation would make it hard for the government to ignore them.

"Charles was noncommittal," Searcy said, "but he's a smart guy, and I could see a spark in his eye."

That spark, Searcy came to understand, had been lit by what Bailey had seen in Dak Lak. That trip, he concluded, had been "Charles's Paul-on-the-Road-to-Damascus moment."

Bailey smiled at the description. "I suppose you could say that was when I began to move from being a conventional funder to an advocate looking to deal with the legacy of the war," he said. "Obviously I would have to get my ducks lined up in a row, so I went out looking for ducks."

Later that year Bailey made his first trip to A Luoi district, still unaware of its wartime history or the work Hatfield and the 10-80 Committee were doing there. He went with Le Van An, a lecturer at the Hue University of Agriculture and Technology, who wanted to show him what the university was doing with Katu farmers in the commune of Hong Ha. Bailey liked what he saw and made a grant to the university that allowed it to expand its work with the Katu, helping them to improve their farming techniques, access more land, and market their produce. It was the first of several trips to the valley. On one, Bailey met a Ta Oi woman with eight children, seven of them disabled. Later he got funding for a project to pipe clean water into Dong Son village, where people living close to the A Shau base had been moved for their safety.

As Searcy had anticipated, Bailey's decision to focus on Agent Orange added an entirely new element to the equation. Endowed with vast resources, the Ford Foundation's name alone opened doors at the highest levels. If Lady Borton convened a conversation, it was clustered around the table in the lobby of the La Thanh, lunching on whatever her cook produced that day from her two-burner Russian stove. Ford meetings were more likely to be conversations over dinner at Bailey's elegant Hanoi home. Yet despite these differences of style and means, Borton, Bailey, Searcy, and the Hatfield scientists all shared the same priority: to get material support to those who were already suffering the consequences of Agent Orange and to protect those who might still be exposed to dioxin from the hot spots. Thirty years had passed since Operation Ranch Hand. How much longer was Vietnam supposed to wait?

Their efforts gathered momentum in the months after Chris Hatfield presented the report on the A Luoi Valley to the U.S. embassy. One thing Searcy and Borton appreciated about Pete Peterson was that he laid on monthly breakfasts at his residence for the American NGOs in Hanoi. Toward the end of March 2000, they and Bailey, together with Chris Gilson, the Hanoi representative of Catholic Relief Services, went there to hear a presentation on dioxin by the embassy's health attaché, Dr. Michael Linnan, a former Marine sergeant in Saigon who had gone on to become an epidemiologist with the Centers for Disease Control and Prevention. It started promisingly enough. "Agent Orange and dioxin is an issue of great interest to Vietnamese and Americans," Peterson said. "We want to move forward with the Vietnamese, not against them."

However, Linnan began by regaling them with droll anecdotes about the macho culture of the Ranch Hand crews and went on to recycle all the arguments American veterans had heard a decade earlier, reciting the inconclusive results of the CDC and Ranch Hand studies and insisting that "there are no proven risks associated with dioxin." Which was technically true, but with the Agent Orange Act, the word *proven* had been taken off the table; American veterans had been given the benefit of the doubt. But Vietnamese claims were still dismissed as unfounded propaganda. If there was a lack of cooperation, Peterson said, it was the fault of the Vietnamese. Linnan obfuscated the specific problem of Agent Orange by suggesting that the United States was prepared to spend $38 million on a national program to test the blood of those who had been exposed to dioxin. But this seemed like flagrant misdirection: dioxin came in many forms and from many industrial sources. TCDD, the unique fingerprint of Agents Orange and Purple, was the only one for which the United States bore responsibility.

Linnan also took some calculated jabs at Hatfield's A Luoi report, emphasizing the low levels of dioxin they had found in most places. Yes, there may have been "small hot spots," but at most there might be "four or five or six airfields" in "extremely rural areas where people are poor"; so any birth defects were more likely the result of malnutrition. Bailey asked for a copy of Linnan's PowerPoint presentation; the embassy refused.

Infuriated by what they had heard, Searcy, Borton, Bailey, and Gilson repaired to the nearby Au Lac Café. Borton typed up her detailed notes of the meeting and sent them to Wayne Dwernychuk, who was now back in Vancouver. He fired back a list of what he considered to be Linnan's factual errors and distortions, finding the attempt to minimize Hatfield's hot-spot theory especially galling. There were not "four or five or six" but hundreds of potential sites, and the biggest—Bien

Hoa, Danang, and Tan Son Nhut—were not in rural areas but in three of Vietnam's most densely populated urban centers.

The following month Susan Berresford, now head of the Ford Foundation, spent a week in Hanoi with a group of trustees. Their schedule included a meeting with the deputy prime minister, Nguyen Manh Cam. Bailey's colleague Ngo Thi Le Mai told him that Cam was likely to ask for a donation to the Vietnamese Red Cross Agent Orange Victims Fund, which was now run by Dr. Le Cao Dai. Bailey told Berresford that he thought this was a good idea. *How much did you have in mind?* she asked. *How about $150,000? That's about the average of our grants here,* he replied. *Fine,* Berresford said. Seven years after her first visit to Hanoi, Ford could finally embark on the kind of program Vietnamese officials had asked for—a serious effort to aid the victims of dioxin.

The Red Cross showed him a list of all the donations they'd received up to that point, a thick concertina of old-style computer printout on perforated paper. They were all small gifts from Vietnamese individuals and local businesses. Finally Bailey found a record of $25,000 from an American private company, the only one they had ever received from a foreign source. "So I think our $150,000 kind of got their attention," he said with the flicker of a smile. "Though in a way I think it helped us even more than it helped them, because it gave me a clear view for the first time of the enormity and scope of the problem."

The Red Cross appealed to President Clinton for help on the eve of his visit that November. Dai said a million Vietnamese had been sickened by TCDD, and anything from 100,000 to 150,000 suffered from birth defects. Quang Tri was rife with cerebral palsy. The United States should clean up the big wartime spill at Bien Hoa, where as many as twenty thousand residents were at risk from dioxin-laden runoff from the air base. "It's a question of moral responsibility," Dai said. "I would like to see [Clinton] collaborate on research, offer financial help to victims and clean up the former air bases, which are still contaminated. It might be expensive, but America is a rich country."

Clinton had sidestepped the question, even when President Tran Duc Luong raised it in their one-on-one meeting. But by tradition, the U.S. president is also the ex officio head of the American Red

Cross, and that was enough to justify a meeting; Clinton simply had to put on a different hat—and he did so, writing later to Nguyen Trong Nhan, head of the Vietnamese Red Cross, that "I share many of your concerns."

Dai's reference to the former air bases echoed what Wayne Dwernychuk had said—there were countless potential dioxin hot spots in Vietnam. It would be a monumental undertaking, however, to identify the worst of them. This was the next challenge.

A month after Berresford's visit, the Hatfield team was back in town, and Bailey got himself invited to a meeting at their hotel in the Old Quarter—"one of those places where the rooms were too small and the furniture was too big." Dai and several other Vietnamese scientists were also there; Bailey was the only other foreigner.

"Charles, being a very polite guy, let the Vietnamese go first when the discussion began," Boivin said. "Afterward, he stuck around and asked some sharp questions. We started exchanging e-mails, and he said he'd really like to keep in touch."

"That meeting was the moment when I saw how we could do this," Bailey said, "use science to shed light on the problem. But we had to be careful and rigorous about it." It would take several more years to lay the groundwork, with a clear understanding of what was required to overcome the stubborn skepticism of U.S. officials.

The tentative conversation bumped along, more fits than starts. It was true that political dynamics on the Vietnamese side didn't help. Vietnam had split its work on dioxin into two parts. The 10-80 Committee remained at the Ministry of Health, while a new body—the National Steering Committee on Overcoming Consequences of Agent Orange/Dioxin in Vietnam, or Office 33 for short—was housed in the Ministry of Natural Resources and Environment. Hoang Dinh Cau was now in his eighties and ailing, and Le Cao Dai had left the 10-80 Committee to run the Agent Orange Victims Fund at the Vietnamese Red Cross.

On the U.S. side, resistance from Linnan and others like him was only one of the many obstacles. Ironically, the degree to which Americans were now sensitized to the legacy of Agent Orange worked in some ways to Vietnam's detriment. Since fish were now known to be the most important transmission route for dioxin in the food chain, the debate got dragged into what came to be known as the Catfish Wars.

Aquaculture had become an important growth industry in Vietnam, but when a new trade agreement was signed at the end of 2001, angry American catfish farmers, based in conservative southern states and with powerful backers in Washington, set about lobbying against cheap Vietnamese imports as a threat to their business. The Mekong Delta had been heavily sprayed with Agent Orange. What if these fish were contaminated with the toxic chemical that seemed to have done such terrible things to our veterans?

The scientific dialogue stalled too. At an international conference at the Daewoo Hotel in Hanoi in March 2002, the two countries signed a memorandum of understanding on future scientific cooperation to study the effects of Agent Orange. The particulars were spelled out a year later. The National Institute for Environmental Health Sciences (NIEHS) and Vietnamese scientists would jointly conduct a three-year, million-dollar study, analyzing dioxin levels in three hundred mothers with children suffering from birth defects, and in a healthy control group of the same size.

It turned out to be a false dawn. After two years of postponements and finger-pointing, the plan was shelved. The study's lead investigator, David Carpenter, said diplomatically that the problem was one of "two different cultures coming together and not communicating well," although in an interview some years later he was more candid: "I thought at the time and still think that it really was that our government did not want to know the long-term effects of Agent Orange exposure."

A leaked embassy memo, signed by Ambassador Raymond Burghardt, gave credence to this. It said that the priority was "to counter the Vietnamese propaganda campaign that hinges on non-scientific but visually effective and emotionally charged methodology"— presumably a reference to the images of terribly deformed children in foreign media reports. "Allegations of adverse impact of Agent Orange/dioxin are grossly exaggerated and unsupported by any objective measure," the memo concluded.

It was now fourteen years since the Agent Orange Act, and Vietnam was still being held to egregious double standards. "It was an insult, and we jumped on it like a chicken on a June bug," Searcy said, his Georgia accent sounding a little more pronounced than usual.

But who exactly was a "victim of Agent Orange," and how many were there? The numbers had always been soft, which inevitably threw the uncertainties of science back into the overheated realm of politics and perception. Le Cao Dai had estimated that there were a million victims, perhaps 150,000 of them children with birth defects. MOLISA, the Vietnamese Ministry of Labor, Invalids, and Social Affairs, came up with a figure of half a million with disabilities, though some officials said this was an undercount, since so many people were afraid to come forward because of the stigma. The Vietnamese Red Cross said 3 million people had suffered adverse health effects. No one would ever know how many had died of cancer.

It offered no explanation of how it arrived at the figure of 3 million, but it was the kind of big round number that worked its way easily into the journalistic bloodstream, to the point of becoming received wisdom, endlessly repeated down the years, morphing even into assertions that more than 3 million Vietnamese were still "suffering from deadly diseases." The Vietnamese Ministry of Health had opened an additional can of worms in 1998 by expanding the VA's list of diseases presumptively associated with dioxin exposure to include three vague catchall terms—"unusual births, deformities and birth defects, and mental disorders." The orphanages and care centers that became a regular stop for foreign reporters, filmmakers, and activists housed children with all kinds of disabilities, presenting the inevitable risk of confirmation bias. Readers and viewers could be innocently misled into thinking, for example, that a child with Down syndrome was an "Agent Orange victim," although the condition was unrelated to dioxin.

The analysis of Operation Ranch Hand by Jeanne and Steven Stellman, published in 2003, supercharged a debate that already generated more heat than light. The Stellmans had never set out to estimate the number of Vietnamese victims. What they produced were the first authoritative statistics on the sheer magnitude of Ranch Hand: more than 20 million gallons of herbicides deployed; one-sixth of the land area of South Vietnam sprayed; anything from 2.1 million to 4.8 million people exposed. These were shocking numbers, but for angry veterans and activists, 4.8 million *exposed* translated easily into 4.8 million *affected*. The political boulder of Agent Orange kept rolling back down the hill. The more the Americans dragged their feet, the more the Vietnamese resented the double standards. The angrier they became, the easier it was to dismiss their claims as baseless propaganda.

Ever since the first steps were taken toward normalization, the Vietnamese had struggled with their own internal divisions. Economic reformers were reluctant to derail the diplomatic process or the associated trade benefits by mentioning the darkest of all the legacies of the war; military leaders, doctors, lawyers, and veterans demanded that the United States accept moral responsibility for its actions, especially now that these had been so vividly illustrated by the work of Hatfield and the 10-80 Committee in the A Luoi Valley and the Stellmans' report. A few months after it was published, a group of them formed the Vietnam Association for Victims of Agent Orange/Dioxin (VAVA) and announced that they were filing a lawsuit against the manufacturers of the herbicides in the U.S. courts, using the 1789 Alien Tort Claims Act.

VAVA hoped that the American NGOs in Hanoi would rally behind their case, but Lady Borton cautioned them that this would be counterproductive. The essence of NGOs was their independence; there could be no question of them acting at a government's behest. The blowback would hurt everyone. Having spent two days doing back-channel research with a federal judge she knew, it was clear to her that the lawsuit was destined to fail, and she told her Vietnamese contacts as much. Bailey had VAVA's American lawyers to dinner at his home in Hanoi, but otherwise he too kept his distance from the lawsuit; it was not something in which Ford could get involved.

The case went before the same New York judge, Jack Weinstein, who had settled the class action suit by American veterans in 1984. Though clearly sympathetic at a human level, he was boxed in by the law. The companies had acted under contract for the government, which enjoyed sovereign immunity, and that exempted them from liability.

Weinstein's judgment came just three weeks after the NIEHS study fell apart, and it might have seemed that all doors had slammed shut. But that wasn't entirely true. For one thing, the U.S. government was not a monolith.

There was now a new U.S. ambassador in Hanoi, Michael Marine. Less constrained than his predecessors in approaching the third rail of Agent Orange, he arranged for an energetic young EPA scientist, Vance Fong, to spend a year at the embassy and collaborate with Office 33. Fong's major accomplishment was to get the Vietnam Academy of Sciences the high-resolution gas chromatography mass spectrometry system it needed to replace the cruder method it had been using for dioxin analysis.

Another small but ultimately more significant development passed almost unnoticed. The United States had fought a war here to prevent China from toppling Asian dominoes; then it had supported the Chinese when Deng Xiaoping delivered his spanking to the "naughty children" of Vietnam. Now, however, it began to take notice of China's new muscle-flexing in the South China Sea and found reason to make common cause with Vietnam against its perennial enemy. The Pentagon and the Vietnamese Ministry of Defense held their first high-level talks, at a conference funded by Bailey, and in 2004 the guided-missile destroyer USS *Curtis Wilbur* dropped anchor in Danang. A year later Defense Secretary Donald Rumsfeld agreed to give Vietnam technical material on Agent Orange, including details about the Danang air base. This had nothing to do with acknowledging responsibility, but it was a baby step in the right direction. Call it enlightened self-interest, a new twist in the eternal shape-shifting of geopolitics.

The A Luoi study had dispelled the idea that every square inch of South Vietnam that had been sprayed might still be poisoned; everybody's secret fear, Bailey said, had been that the problem was just too overwhelming to deal with. But the hot spot theory said that it was manageable. The danger could be isolated; it would be on and around the former military bases like A Shau where the chemicals had been stored, loaded, and spilled. Once these bases were identified, they could be cleaned up.

The most urgent thing, from Bailey's point of view, was to pinpoint the areas that were still contaminated to show who was still at risk and where the incidence of disabilities and birth defects was most likely to be related to exposure to dioxin. Just as not every area that was sprayed was still contaminated, not every disabled person in Vietnam was a victim of Agent Orange. In principle, this should allow humanitarian support to be steered toward those for whom the United States bore the greatest moral responsibility.

"So I wondered," Bailey said, "how about doing a kind of chemical history of the war?" What he meant by this was a systematic study of U.S. military facilities to figure out where the herbicides were likeliest to have left their toxic footprint. This brought another of Hatfield's insights into play: since the bigger bases were located in urban areas, any samples taken there were likely to contain other dioxin congeners—related members of the same chemical family—from industrial sources. Wayne Dwernychuk proposed a solution: if more than 75 percent of the dioxin in a sample was TCDD, it could have only one source: the herbicides. "That would be the smoking gun," Bailey said. "It would be like looking at the sample through a microscope and seeing a tiny stamp that said 'Made in USA.' It's ours; we own it."

But even if you knew where all the former installations were, how could you test all of them for contamination? Many had been dismantled for construction materials; some were active Vietnamese military bases, off limits to foreigners; others had been paved over for development; and innumerable smaller facilities like firebases and landing zones had long since been swallowed up by the forests. As they were trying to figure out how to proceed, by good fortune, the basic information they needed was suddenly at hand.

It was the result of a prodigious piece of research by a former infantryman named Michael Kelley. After years of poring over military maps and records and interviewing other veterans, he produced a book called *Where We Were in Vietnam*, a doorstop volume of well over eight hundred pages, with type that required a magnifying glass. It listed every base, every LZ, every firebase, every airstrip and heliport, every quarry and field hospital and engineer camp, every docking facility—2,735 installations in all, each with its precise geographical coordinates, its date of construction, and which military units had served there. "Kelley deserves a medal," Bailey said.

Lady Borton learned about the book from friends at Vietnam Veterans of America, and she gave a copy to Tran Manh Hung, "Dr. Video," who took it upon himself to go through it line by line. With input from Andrew Allan, one of Hatfield's technical experts, he winnowed the list down to twenty-eight facilities that seemed most likely to be contaminated. Borton, who had a degree in math and chemistry, and Dwernychuk, the Canadians' main dioxin expert, drew up a proposal, and Bailey made a grant of almost $300,000 to the 10-80 Committee— like all of his grants for dioxin analysis it went to the Vietnamese, who then conducted the fieldwork with Hatfield, with the 10-80 team always headed by Dr. Hung.

The key was to use the same uniform methodology everywhere, the same comprehensive approach Hatfield had taken at the A Shau base. Dwernychuk did the technical analysis and wrote up the reports; Hung and Borton, the only westerner to accompany the team at every stage of the hot spot survey, made sure the samples were scrupulously logged, labeled, and cross-checked. Borton insisted on including samples from the base perimeters. She was the only one who had actually been on an American base during the war, not only in Quang Ngai but at Danang and Tan Son Nhut, and she'd observed the routine use of defoliants to keep down vegetation. The main risk to U.S. veterans, she was convinced, came not from spraying in the combat zones "but from the dousing between the two concentric coils of barbed wire used on base perimeters, to eradicate cover for Viet Cong sappers, and on any swatch of green, to eradicate cover for rats and vermin." Depending on the season, these perimeter areas were either dioxin-laden dust or dioxin-laden mud that could be breathed in, ingested, or absorbed through the skin. Perhaps, she thought, this explained the rash of unusual birth defects among female veterans who had been stationed on the bases.

"There's no way we could have done the survey without Lady," said Tom Boivin, who by now had taken over as president of Hatfield Consultants. "She covered our asses, never took any credit, never asked to be paid. Ninety percent of the time we had no idea what she was doing. She was our technical assistant, our bodyguard, our translator and interpreter. She could do anything from taking liver samples from a tilapia to getting the ear of the prime minister, and everything in between. I think of her as a kind of Mother Teresa, who also happened to like knocking back tequila shots in the evening."

But identifying twenty-eight bases didn't mean they were able to sample all of them. Several were in active use by the Vietnamese military, off limits for security reasons. But the worst of the hot spots emerged clearly, and not surprisingly they were the main hubs of Operation Ranch Hand, Danang and Bien Hoa, as well as Phu Cat, between the coast and the Central Highlands.

"Ford was the best bloody client I've ever worked for," Boivin said, though he still worried many years later that they might not have caught all the hot spots. "I still believe there are others that haven't been adequately addressed, and that there's still potential contamination out there."

Borton shared his concern, especially about four huge American bases: Nha Trang, on the southern coast; Can Tho, in the Mekong Delta; Pleiku, in the Central Highlands, where Chuck Searcy had first set foot in Vietnam and where spray planes from Danang reloaded; and Tan Son Nhut, on the outskirts of Saigon. This one worried her most. It had been heavily used by the C-123s early in the war, when the primary rainbow chemical was Agent Purple, the most heavily contaminated of the major herbicides, and now it was Ho Chi Minh City's international civilian airport, renamed Tan Son Nhat. There was no way the government would grant permission to take samples in such a sensitive location. Borton at least had a good idea where to look, knowing that the spray planes had always parked next to Air Marshal Ky's private hangar, and she'd found out through discreet questioning where that was. Logically this area, which the Americans called Charlie Sector, must have been the location of the chemical storage tanks.

She and Tran Manh Hung decided to take a flight together out of Tan Son Nhat, sitting separately, pretending they didn't know each other, while he took photos of the suspect area out of the window. He used these to make a quick, surreptitious visit one night in April 2005, just long enough to collect two samples of soil and three of sediments from a fishpond and a drainage ditch that flowed into a densely populated neighborhood. Analysis showed high levels of TCDD in one of the samples from Charlie Sector, but while the data were included in the final Hatfield/10-80 Committee report, it was never possible to do any further research.

Frustrated that the full nationwide survey she'd hoped for did not come to fruition, Borton embarked on smaller initiatives of her own. She continued to work with Hatfield, taking a group of Vietnamese officials to Canada, with support from AFSC, to look at a dioxin cleanup project that might offer a low-cost model for containing the contamination at the Danang air base. She was constantly hatching new ideas: health programs for toddlers and adults, an Adopt a Hot Spot program with Unitarian churches, a joint project with American and Vietnamese doctors to test Vietnamese veterans for diabetes, which the VA recognized as a dioxin-related condition. But after parting ways with Ford, it was always a challenge to keep such initiatives going without the kind of financial backing the foundation could provide.

In January 2006, Hatfield presented the hot spot study to the Vietnamese government, and Bailey gave it to Ambassador Marine. Now that everyone knew where the worst hot spots were, the priority was to isolate the active threat to those who lived on and around the bases. Phu Cat was the smallest of the three, and the Vietnamese took care of that one themselves, capping the contaminated soil in a landfill with help from the Czech government, the Global Environment Facility, and UNDP, which also chipped in funding for some of Hatfield's research at Bien Hoa. "We all knew that Bien Hoa was the Holy Grail," Boivin said, but if the goal was to tighten the screws on the U.S. government, Bien Hoa was too big a hurdle—in large part because it was still an active air force base and more politically sensitive. Danang would have to come first.

Wartime maps of the Danang base showed the likeliest areas of contamination. The worst was at the northeastern corner of the main runway, where the spray planes had been loaded. One soil sample there contained 365,000 parts per trillion of dioxin, more than three hundred times the level considered safe for industrial land in most Western countries. There was another bad spot at the south end of the base, where the herbicides had been stored and redrummed during the Pacer IVY operation in 1971.

The next step was to wall off these areas to remove the ongoing risk. "You have to remember that the airport was nothing like it is today," Boivin said. "It was still half-military and half-civilian, but even though the Vietnamese Air Force used it there was no perimeter fence. People could come and go as they pleased." A few hundred yards away from the loading area was a small lake, Ho Sen, that collected runoff from the base. Men fished there. Kids used it as a swimming pool. There were no restrictions.

Hatfield tested the blood of the fishermen and sampled the fish they ate, which turned out to have dioxin levels up to one hundred times higher than the safe consumption limit set by Health Canada. They tested residents of the surrounding neighborhoods, as well as airport workers, who showed the highest levels of TCDD in blood and breast milk ever recorded in Vietnam.

The purpose of Bailey's next tranche of funding—$1.3 million this time—was to block any further spread of the dioxin. "They built a high brick wall with guard towers, put a temporary six-inch-thick cap on the worst area, lined the drainage ditch, and put in a carbon filter to capture and clean runoff from the former storage area," he said. "The Ford Foundation had never spent so much money on cement!"

Once the barriers were in place, Hatfield did a further round of tests to be sure the dioxin was truly locked down. By January 2008, it was clear that the threat had been contained. "Before and after testing was the key," Bailey said. "Do the intervention, circle back, see if you've moved the needle—and we found that, yes, we'd moved it almost to zero."

This bought the time necessary for the U.S. government to take the next step, to figure out the best way of destroying the dioxin once and for all. As Le Cao Dai had said, such a project would not come cheap, but the United States was a rich country.

Bailey would eventually invest $17 million in programs related to Agent Orange, and over the next decade, he raised another $30 million from private sources, including the Rockefeller Foundation, HSBC Bank, and Hyatt Hotels, for social services to disabled children living around the Danang airport, and the Bill and Melinda Gates Foundation and Atlantic Philanthropies, which funded Vietnam's new dioxin lab in Hanoi.

More than $7 million of the Ford money went to educating Americans about Agent Orange, and there was certainly the need for that, even though it called for a certain amount of black humor. By the mid-2000s, Danang had become a hub of Vietnam's tourist boom, a jumping-off point for Hue and Hoi An and miles of unspoiled golden beaches, and word of the dioxin hot spot had gone viral. Message boards on sites like TripAdvisor began to fill up with skittish messages about the city's sinister reputation.

"I have read about the continuous effects of this awful chemical. Does anyone know what the risks are for tourists?"

"What chance is there of contracting the disease if traveling to Vietnam? I am thinking of canceling my trip."

Someone else asked whether the Hyatt and Intercontinental hotels would be safe for her children.

Looking back, Bailey saw 2006 as the end of what he called "the frozen period," finally jolting loose a more enlightened U.S. attitude. After the string of earlier setbacks, that year brought a cascade of positive developments, and it's fair to say that Bailey had a hand in most of them. Or as Tom Boivin put it, "If it wasn't for Charles Bailey, none of this good shit would ever have happened."

Ford paid for a dozen Vietnamese scientists to attend the annual international symposium on persistent organic pollutants, or POPS—the "forever chemicals"—which was held that August in Oslo. Bailey forged an especially close friendship with the physician and toxicologist Le Ke Son, the head of Office 33, who had earlier succeeded Le Cao Dai as director of the Agent Orange Victims Fund at the Vietnamese Red Cross. Later he and Bailey would co-author a book on Agent Orange. They dedicated it to Vo Quy, whom Ho Chi Minh had personally assigned to investigate the ecological impact of the herbicide campaign. During the war, improbable as it sounded, he had been in the A Shau Valley, doing research for his monumental two-volume study, *The Birds of Vietnam*. Revered as the founding father of Vietnamese environmental conservation, he became a household name thanks to his popular TV show. Children called him Professor Bird.

Bailey was also savvy about the role of the media. When *The Washington Post*'s Tokyo correspondent, Anthony Faiola, came to town, Bailey introduced him to all the right people, resulting in a long front-page article on the eve of President George W. Bush's November 2006 visit to Hanoi. Faiola's story checked all the boxes: the Danang cleanup, the potential health problems of those who lived around the base, the stricken children in the orphanages and peace villages, the work of Vietnamese scientists, the moral responsibility of the United States, Vietnam's desire for better relations, and its increasingly market-driven economy. To coincide with the release of Faiola's story, Bailey called a press conference to announce a new round of Ford Foundation grants on Agent Orange, which gave the local media a further news peg and got full coverage on TV.

Five days later Bush and Vietnamese president Nguyen Minh Triet issued a transformative joint communiqué that touched on the U.S. obligation to help Vietnam overcome all the worst legacies of the war: disabilities, UXO, dioxin contamination, and the search for both countries' MIAs. All this was set in the context of a new era in relations that would encompass trade, investment, and regional security.

After Bush left, Ambassador Marine invited Bailey to meet two visitors from Washington—Bobby Muller and Tim Rieser, a veteran Senate aide who had worked closely for years with Sen. Patrick Leahy (D-VT). Since 1989, the Leahy War Victims Fund had provided prosthetics, orthotics, and rehab services in dozens of countries, starting with Vietnam. They met at Noi Bai airport as the Americans were arriving and Bailey, his German wife, Ingrid Foik, and their two daughters, Eliza and Sabine, were heading off to Europe for the Christmas holidays.

Before their flight took off, Bailey called a reporter friend at Vietnam Television to alert her that Rieser planned to give a press conference, and that she should ask him about Agent Orange. When the family touched down in Munich, a message on Bailey's cell phone told him that Rieser had announced U.S. government funding to deal with the legacy of Agent Orange. Three months later Leahy earmarked $3 million in the 2007 budget. Even so, Ambassador Marine made it clear that "I do not accept the term 'victims of Agent Orange.'" There would be no explicit mention of the herbicides—the aid would be for disabilities "regardless of cause"—and $3 million wasn't a lot of money. But it was a start.

"You've been in Hanoi for ten years now," Susan Berresford told Bailey—much longer than a Ford Foundation representative usually stayed in country. "Maybe it's time for you to come back to New York and work on Agent Orange full time. The door has been unlatched, so why don't you see if you can push it gently open all the way?"

Great Loss and Confusion

I N QUANG TRI, Chuck Searcy and his Vietnamese colleagues had pushed other doors wide open. It was impossible to travel far in the province without thinking of the three-quarters of a million gallons of chemicals that were sprayed here, the tons of bombs that were dropped—more than on Germany in World War II, and Germany was seventy-five times larger. Bombing had been the bluntest of all the technologies unleashed in the war, the greatest of the fallacies about how it could be won, the source of so many of its memorable one-liners. Air Force Chief of Staff Gen. Curtis LeMay with his threat to bomb the country back into the Stone Age; and Nixon's vow, in response to the 1972 Easter Offensive in Quang Tri, that "the bastards have never been bombed like they're going to be bombed now." "Anything that flies on anything that moves"—that was Kissinger, relaying to the Pentagon his boss's instructions on bombing Cambodia. "Vietnam was a country where America was trying to make people stop being communists by dropping things on them from airplanes," wrote Kurt Vonnegut in his novel *Breakfast of Champions*.

In Quang Tri, the greatest tonnage fell on the narrow coastal strip along Highway 1, on Leatherneck Square, and on the mountains to the west, between Khe Sanh and the A Shau Valley. "Never were we out of sight of an endless panorama of crater fields," wrote the forest ecologist Art Westing in *The New York Times*, after flying over the province in 1973. "As far as we could determine, not a single permanent building, urban or rural, remained intact: no private dwellings, no schools, no libraries, no churches or pagodas, and no hospitals. Moreover, every last bridge and even culvert had been bombed to bits."

The best estimate was that 600,000 tons of the bombs dropped on Vietnam failed to detonate, about 10 percent of the total by the air force's count, and that didn't count the other explosive paraphernalia left over from ground combat. By 2014, the Vietnamese government estimated that 40,000 people had died from unexploded ordnance since the end of the war, with another 60,000 injured. Quang Tri, with a population of 650,000, had recorded 3,419 deaths and 5,095 injuries. More than half the accidents were from cluster bombs and M-79 shoulder-fired grenades, nicknamed "Thumpers," which the PAVN found fearsome for their range and accuracy.

After the army cleared the known minefields in the early postwar years, each province was on its own. There was no national program to deal with the larger UXO problem. So could it ever be entirely eradicated in Quang Tri? Whenever Searcy was asked that question, he said no, it was impossible to get rid of every bomb. The realistic goal was to reduce the risk to the point where the province would be safe enough for people to go about their daily business without fear of being killed or blinded or joining the ranks of the amputees.

There were clear patterns among the victims. Poor farmers returning to rebuild their villages were walking into a death trap. The majority of those who died were young men and children, planting or harvesting rice or tending their water buffalo or playing with the munitions they found, the *bom bi* that were the tempting size of a baseball. One-third of the casualties were children under sixteen. The Bru-Van Kieu of the western mountains, by far the poorest people in Quang Tri, accounted for a disproportionate share.

The highest total numbers were in districts on the heavily populated coastal plain, and that area would be Project RENEW's earliest priority. But on a per capita basis, the worst affected was Cam Lo, the home district of Ngo Xuan Hien and Nguyen Thanh Phu, the two postwar baby boomers whose lives had now intersected with Searcy's.

The deaths and injuries had become less frequent over the years—not because all the bombs were gone but because people had learned more about the risks: a study that Hoang Nam published in 2011 put the average number of accidents each year over the previous decade, since the foreign demining groups had arrived, at thirty-eight. Since then they'd come down further. Most of the victims now were the scrap metal scavengers, though the statistics were probably incomplete since it was illegal for civilians to possess explosives, and there were no doubt accidents that went unreported. "What they're mainly looking for is the bigger bombs or artillery shells, because those have the greatest value," Searcy said. Some of the methods they used to defuse them were spine-chilling, sawing or hammering away at the seam that separates the body of the bomb from its explosive charge to extract the fuse. "They know the risks, but they calculate them because of economic necessity," he said. "But the one thing they know to stay away from is cluster bombs, because they're so unstable."

In former times there were more than two dozen scrap metal dealers in the province, but these days only a few remained. One of them was on the highway near Khe Sanh town, with a yard full of metal of every kind, most of it speckled with rust. There were even a couple of colossal 2,700-pound naval shells—the navy liked to say they were the size of Volkswagens—standing on end against one wall.

Did the dealer worry about the risks? He shrugged. "I've been doing this for years and I've never had an accident. If someone brings in a bomb that looks dangerous, I just tell them to take it away again."

Searcy gave him a patient lecture. That just made it somebody else's problem. Had he heard about the collecting bins that others were using? You dug a hole, lined it with cement, put on a secure lid, locked it, and called for someone at Project RENEW or one of the other groups to pick up the bomb and dispose of it safely.

A young man pulled up on a motorbike and unloaded a clanking bag of metal. The dealer took a look inside, squatting on his haunches, and placed the bag on an old-fashioned scale. After some perfunctory haggling, he handed over the equivalent of a dollar or two.

There was a shed next to the yard, where the dealer had set up a shelf and a sheet of pegboard on the wall that gave it the look of a small museum. There was war detritus of every conceivable kind on display, from aluminum mess tins and water canteens to entrenching tools, pieces of shrapnel that might have passed for abstract sculptures, spent cluster bombs and rocket-propelled grenades. There was even one of

McNamara's rocket-shaped Air-Delivered Seismic Intrusion Detectors, an ADSID, that had been dropped on the Ho Chi Minh Trail.

Sitting there on the shelf, an inert, useless chunk of metal, it called to mind a comment by an American official about McNamara's electronic battlefield. "It was very technically successful," he said, "but when you stop to think about it, you have a $30 million orbiting reconnaissance aircraft to transmit signals, and a $20 million command post, and you call in four $10 million fighters to assault a convoy of five $5,000 trucks carrying $2,000 worth of rice. It's easy to see that it's not cost-effective." The dealer wanted a million *dong* for the ADSID, a little under fifty dollars.

There was an American helmet with a ragged hole in it that didn't bear thinking about. He was asking 100,000 for that, less than five dollars. Searcy handed him a couple of small bills for the casing of a *bom bi,* to take back to Project RENEW's visitor center in Dong Ha.

In the beginning, it was just Chuck and Nam and a skeleton staff of five. They concentrated on risk education at first, determining how much people knew about UXO, how often they encountered them personally, and how to avoid them. They trained local health workers and first responders in dealing with blast injuries, developing prosthetics programs that drew on Searcy's experience in Hanoi. But in a sense, they were the victims of their own success. They were doing a fine job of raising awareness, but when people called in reports of a grenade in a ditch, or a *bom bi* in a schoolyard, they had no capacity to respond.

That began to change in 2008, when a new group, Norwegian People's Aid, arrived in Quang Tri. A humanitarian initiative of its country's labor unions, NPA already had a stellar reputation from its work in Laos and Cambodia. Now it proposed a partnership with Project RENEW. The timing was good, since the VVMF's ten-year commitment to the project would soon be ending. The new arrangement allowed Searcy and Nam to get into the business of active clearance and to make sure all the demining groups working in the province were on the same page.

The demands for clearance operations "still varied considerably in their merit," Searcy said, with wry diplomatic understatement. "Sometimes a local person of influence or a political official would own a piece of land for development, and he'd think that it would be worth more if it was cleared of UXO. It wasn't always clearly in the public interest." Despite the goodwill of the people's committee, the work of the various groups in Quang Tri was frustrated by their lack of coordination, each having its own preferred methods and technologies. What they needed was someone with the organizational and diplomatic skills to iron out the wrinkles, and that pointed to Searcy.

By this time, serious money was flowing into Quang Tri from the United States, more or less evenly divided between the State Department and USAID, which acted as the conduit for the Leahy War Victims Fund. The Pentagon also offered to help, translating its records into a digital format with the coordinates of all its wartime bombing runs, and sharing those data with all the private groups working in Quang Tri as well as with the Vietnamese government. Matching these records with information gleaned from local villagers, Project RENEW and NPA decided to focus their efforts on known cluster bomb strikes, casting a net around them that would sweep up any other UXO in the same area. It was possible now for all the organizations to work from a single database, the only one of its kind in the world, and using it became the precondition for further aid from the U.S. government. RENEW agreed to manage the database, continuously updating it and making it available in real time to anyone with a computer. While other groups had now begun work in Quang Tri's heavily bombed neighbors, Quang Binh and Thua Thien-Hue, no other province had anything similar.

Project RENEW now had the funds, as well as the need, to enlarge its operation, and it went looking for a new home in Dong Ha. The town sits at the intersection of Highway 1 and Route 9, three or four miles from the coast. Rebuilt from the ground up since it was obliterated in the 1972 Easter Offensive, it's a nondescript place of about eighteen thousand people that gets few foreign visitors other than returning veterans and a few adventurous backpackers on their way to Khe Sanh and the tunnels of Vinh Moc.

For many years, visitors had to make do with a cheap, dingy hotel with a dodgy massage parlor. But by the second decade of the new century, there were perceptible changes: more shop signs and billboards in English and gaudy neon-lit karaoke joints like the Nonstop Club, where men liked to go in the evenings to sit with pretty hostesses, and sometimes more than that. Smarter hotels and chic coffee shops began to sprout along the main drag, Le Duan Street—named, ironically, for the local boy whose reckless military offensives and ruinous postwar five-year plans had brought so much misery to his home province. When ground was broken for the Muong Thanh Grand Hotel, part of an upscale nationwide chain, workers digging the foundations unearthed an eight-inch naval shell and a five-hundred-pound bomb.

Another American veteran who came to Dong Ha in the late 1990s was John Ward, who had fought in the A Shau Valley with the 101st Airborne. He worked with a number of humanitarian groups, including Le Ly Hayslip's East Meets West Foundation, and then started one of his own, together with a couple of lieutenants from his old company and the medic who had evacuated him when he was wounded, and together they helped to build kindergartens in three communes in the valley. With the exception of the MIA search teams, Ward said, it was the first time since the war that the people's committee in Thua Thien-Hue allowed American vets to put boots on the ground in the A Shau.

Ward installed himself in a small complex of new buildings in a park at the edge of Dong Ha. Known as Kids First Vietnam Village, it was designed as a vocational training center for disabled children, with the town's first wheelchair-accessible school. But his project ran out of steam, the buildings stood empty, and Project RENEW moved in. The centerpiece of the complex now was its Mine Action Visitor Center.

The word *mine* was really a misnomer, Searcy said. All the known minefields in Quang Tri had been cleared decades earlier, whereas UXO embraced everything from fragmentation grenades to giant naval shells fired from a battlewagon fifteen miles offshore. The word *mine* resonated more with people, however, than the technical-sounding acronym. Britain's Princess Diana had made demining her personal crusade, and in 1997 the International Campaign to Ban Landmines, the brainchild of Bobby Muller, was awarded the Nobel Peace Prize.

A collection of bombs of different sizes, tawny with rust, had been planted in the lawn in front of the visitor center, and ornamental plants were growing out of the mother pod of a cluster bomb. Inside the center were exhibits of more bombs, a variety of antique artificial limbs, primitive early wheelchairs, faded historical photographs, wall maps of the bombing and spraying in Quang Tri, and a diorama of two uniformed men at work on an unexploded bomb in what looked like a Bru-Van Kieu village in the mountains.

At the small front desk, a fat binder displayed pictures and specifications of the hundreds of different kinds of munitions that had rained down on Quang Tri, and you could buy T-shirts and small souvenirs like sticks of incense from a workshop that Project RENEW had set up in nearby Hai Lang for people blinded by explosions. A visitor was chatting with a cheerful young man in his mid-twenties who was manning the desk. His name was Ho Van Lai. In 2002, at the age of ten, Lai had been playing with his brother and a neighbor on the beach near his home when a *bom bi* exploded. The other two boys were killed; Lai lost both legs, one arm, and part of his remaining hand, and was blinded in one eye.

Another man, perhaps eight or ten years older, was leading a group of children in school uniforms in an energetic role-playing game, showing them what to do if they found a bomb. They were from a village in Cam Lo district, and their teacher had called Project RENEW's hotline number to report the discovery, in a patch of vegetation at the edge of the schoolyard, of a 37-mm antitank round and three M-79 grenades. The safety instructor had also grown up in Cam Lo, and he was now in charge of the visitor center and its educational programs. He introduced himself as Nguyen Thanh Phu. Another staff member walked over to greet Searcy. This was Ngo Xuan Hien, Phu's fellow Cam Lo native, and he was in charge of communications and development.

Later the two of them told stories of how their parents had fought for the NLF and been jailed and tortured, how they'd gone out collecting scrap metal as kids in the hard years of postwar austerity, how they'd first crossed paths with Searcy—Phu when he was working as a tour guide and saw the tall, thin American at the airports in Hue and Danang, Hien at a conference where Searcy had made the case for returning veterans as an engine of Quang Tri's virtually nonexistent tourist industry. Later they met again at a mutual friend's wedding, where Searcy sang "You Are My Sunshine."

Both Hien and Phu spoke near-fluent English, and they'd chosen to flip the order of their names, in the same manner as Viet Kieu—

"overseas Vietnamese"—in the United States. So now they went by Phu Nguyen and Hien Ngo and had a habit of calling each other "bro." They were passionate soccer fans and avid users of social media, like most Vietnamese of their generation. They liked to take long-distance bike rides around the province, clad in Spandex and hip mirrored shades, posting their route maps and smartphone photos online. Often they were joined on these outings by another Quang Tri native, Project RENEW's coordination manager, in effect its CEO, Nguyen Hieu Trung—or as he was now after his own name-flip, Trung Nguyen.

Yet while they had one foot planted firmly in the new, cosmopolitan Vietnam, Phu and Hien had never lost their emotional attachment to the villages where they'd grown up, their reverence for family and ancestors and their traditional sense of filial duty. Hien had been teaching English as a foreign language in a high school in Khe Sanh, when his brother and sister both left Quang Tri for jobs in Danang. "It was a big burden for my parents, who were retired by that time, so I really wanted to come home and find work near them," he said. He spent eight years as a "public cadre" with the provincial government in Dong Ha, which was how he met Searcy.

After that, one thing led to another. Hien saw an ad for Project RENEW, and Searcy and Nam hired him on the spot. He learned everything there was to know about UXO, worked for six months on a Pentagon-funded R&D project, and was then promoted to his present job in 2009. Phu arrived a year later, following a not-dissimilar path. While he was working in Danang as a tour guide, his mother died in a road accident, and his two sisters moved to Hue. Again, he had obligations to fulfill. "Family is a big deal, and in my area, according to custom, the man should be the successor who takes responsibility for the family," he said, "so I had to come back to the homeland and settle down." He'd also married in Hue, a young woman from the same commune in Cam Lo; their families had known each other when Phu and his wife were children. "UXO had always been part of our personal history," he said, recalling his childhood scavenging expeditions along the McNamara Line, so RENEW felt like the right challenge.

Searcy, Hien, and Phu spent a year meeting with tourism specialists, military officials, and a museum expert from Hanoi, comparing notes with a similar visitor center in Laos, figuring out how to put together a coherent picture of Quang Tri's wartime history and its continuing legacy. In 2011, on Project RENEW's tenth anniversary, they inaugurated the Mine Action Visitor Center, and Manus Campbell, halfway into his second year in Hue, traveled up to Dong Ha for the ceremony.

Project RENEW and NPA found their work in the field running on several different tracks: what they called the "nontechnical survey," which continued to pinpoint the danger areas through house-to-house interviews; the cluster bomb survey; and the rapid-response teams who followed up on reports like the one from the Cam Lo schoolyard. These still came in several times a day, usually with a call on the hotline, and the Mobile Unexploded Ordnance Teams graded them on a scale of urgency. *Bom bi* were the highest priority, because they were so unstable; while their iron casing rusted away, the aluminum trigger remained intact, and the slightest contact could set them off. First the teams inspected the site and prepared the ground to detonate the UXO in place, then they swept the surrounding area. Bigger bombs would be taken to a secure location near Dong Ha for disposal. It might take four men to load a 500- or 750-pounder carefully into a sling and carry it to the truck.

On one typical November morning, team number four was called out to a field just off Route 1, where kids played soccer and villagers tended their water buffalo. The incident had been called in by an elderly cassava farmer, an ARVN veteran. Construction workers had been improving a bridge and clearing ground to plant more of the ubiquitous acacia when a five-inch white phosphorus bomb exploded, throwing off brilliant white light. A few yards away, the advance team had found an Mk2 fragmentation grenade, and their sweep of the field also revealed three rifle-fired M203s.

It had rained hard earlier, and everyone squelched their way across the muddy field to take a look. Searcy, who always seemed nicely dressed, was wearing improbable black dress shoes. An advance team had dug shallow holes to expose the munitions, ringing them with sandbags, canary yellow and candy-cane pink. The team leader picked up a bullhorn to clear the area, and everyone retreated the mandatory hundred meters. On the count of three, another operative pressed the button. There was a dull boom, and an inverted cone of mud, smoke, and shrapnel shot thirty or forty feet into the air.

Afterward, Searcy fell into conversation with the project's chief technical officer, retired PAVN Lt. Col. Bui Trong Hong. It seemed there had been no minimum height requirement for joining the PAVN, for he was a tiny man who barely came up to Searcy's shoulder, and he seemed to have been born with a permanent smile on his face.

He was from a peasant family in Nghe An province. "I was born in 1954, the year of Dien Bien Phu," he said, "and my village was near the birthplace of Ho Chi Minh. So I'm the son of Uncle Ho." He laughed, as if this were the best joke in the world. No one in his village had learned to read and write; under French rule in the protectorate of Annam, education was a restricted privilege. Nghe An had suffered grievously during the Japanese occupation, when Indochina served as a springboard for their attacks on Malaya, Burma, and Singapore. After a series of failed harvests, maladministration by the French—still Vietnam's nominal rulers—and the appropriation of rice by the Japanese to feed their troops, more than a million Vietnamese had died in the great famine of 1944–45. Nghe An was one of the worst-affected provinces.

In March 1965, when Hong was ten, his parents told him that American Marines had landed at Danang. Operation Rolling Thunder came to Nghe An at around the same time. At first it targeted the port of Vinh, but in 1967 it progressed to the surrounding countryside. "My childhood was mixed up with a lot of airplanes and a lot of bombs," he said. "First it was the F-4s, and then the B-52s." Like all the other kids, he went out and collected the miniature parachutes on which the flares floated down at night, turning them into scarves or sewing them together to make bedsheets. In the evenings, they dispersed into improvised classrooms in the forest, where they studied under a concealed oil lamp, invisible to the bomber pilots. He saw villagers shooting at the aircraft with rifles that dated back to the First World War. He chuckled. The man seemed to regard life as an inexhaustible source of humor.

In 1968, at thirteen, he learned about the Tet Offensive and heard that American airplanes were dropping poison on the forests in the South, though no one knew what it was. He learned a song called "*Tieng dan ta lu,*" sung by a Bru-Van Kieu girl who transported munitions on the Ho Chi Minh Trail. The song is still popular today, and people like to sing it in the karaoke parlors. Later, back in Dong Ha, Phu Nguyen found a recording.

The lovely srao bird is tweeting merrily,
Praising the national liberation fighter,
Victorious at the battle west of Khe Sanh.
See the Ta Con fort in flames
And Dong Chi hill with piles of slain Americans.

The B-52 raids on Nghe An began in 1972. They were the worst, the colonel said, the planes flying so high that no one could see them or even know they were there until the ground rocked under their impact. As Frances Fitzgerald wrote in *Fire in the Lake*, the bombs were "released by an invisible pilot with incomprehensible intentions."

He joined the PAVN in that year, fighting in the liberation of Quang Tri. "It was the bloodiest time of all," he said. "I still ask myself, how did I survive?" When the war was over, he was set to work clearing the minefields. "We didn't have any proper equipment or mine detectors, we just poked at the ground with sticks," he said.

In 1998 he was assigned as military liaison to the German demining team in Quang Tri. Four years later he retired as a lieutenant colonel and joined the newly formed Project RENEW. His entire life had been defined by American bombs, but he showed no trace of acrimony. Admittedly, he had felt hatred for the Americans as a child, witnessing so much death, seeing the bombed-out schools. But as he reflected on the longer course of history, the decade-long American War seemed a passing thing, a story commonly voiced among Vietnamese of his generation. The French had occupied Vietnam for a century. The country had been repeatedly attacked by China for the better part of two thousand years. And perhaps the experience of the North had been different from that of the South. "After all," he said, "northerners never actually saw any Americans. They were an enemy without a face."

These were the stories all American veterans had heard since they began returning in the 1990s, and every tourist would hear if they cared to ask. *We won the war. It's ancient history. We don't like to look back on unpleasant things. This is a young country, and we need to put the past behind us. We need the friendship of America to achieve prosperity, and as a buffer against our ancient enemy, China. We like hamburgers and Kentucky Fried Chicken and hip-hop music and Facebook and TikTok. War is part of the natural cycle of life. Perhaps it was punishment for some wrong done in the past. We are by nature a forgiving people. Confucius said that to show anger is to sink to the level of the barbarians.*

"Or maybe it's just because you're from the West that you find it hard to understand our Eastern culture," the colonel said at last. It was the oldest cliché in the colonial book: the Inscrutable Orient. And this made him laugh louder than ever.

Every kind of bomb killed. Many were crude in conception, just big, heavy iron objects packed with high explosives, dropped from a great height and dependent for their effect on nothing more sophisticated than the elemental laws of physics. But other weapons used in Vietnam had been invented with a kind of fiendish ingenuity.

White phosphorus, employed as a target marker or an incendiary, self-ignited when exposed to air and burned at five thousand degrees Fahrenheit; you couldn't find relief by jumping into the nearest pond because it burned underwater too. Napalm, a mixture of gasoline or diesel fuel and a jelling agent that made it stick to human flesh, glowing an eerie green as it ate its way through to the bone, was cooked up in a secret laboratory at Harvard by a chemist who was otherwise well-regarded for his work on blood-clotting agents and antimalarial medications.

And then there were cluster munitions, which worked on a principle first outlined by Leonardo da Vinci. In his notebooks, along with drawings of other inventions like the helicopter and the parachute, Leonardo left a sketch of a potbellied cannon that could spew out dozens of projectiles at the same time. This weapon would "hurl small stones in the manner almost of hail," he wrote, "causing great terror to the enemy from their smoke, and great loss and confusion."

The United States had developed almost fifty different types of cluster bomb, many of them nicknamed for their appearance—guavas and pineapples and butterflies. As indiscriminate antipersonnel weapons, they were banned by an international treaty in 2008, but neither the

United States nor Vietnam had signed it. The United States continued to use them in its foreign wars, while Vietnam made the disputed argument that the treaty called for each signatory to clean up unexploded cluster bombs in its own territory. Why should Vietnam do that, since it hadn't put them there in the first place?

Hien Ngo explained how cluster munitions worked. As many as six hundred bomblets, each with its own explosive charge, were packed into an elongated canister, a mother pod. This opened a few hundred feet above the ground, spraying the submunitions in all directions, blanketing an area as big as two football fields with high-velocity steel pellets or flanged arrows that shredded anything in their path. As many as 30 percent failed to detonate.

The cluster bomb survey of Cam Lo district was well advanced, and joined again by the unfailingly cheerful Colonel Hong, a team went out one day to a country road off Route 9, close to the Rockpile. The team leader was a quiet, personable man in his early forties with a faint mustache and crinkly smile lines, a twelve-year veteran of Project RENEW. Like all the field staff, he wore military-style khakis with his name—Ngo Thien Khiet—stitched in red above the breast pocket. Visitors were required to sign a liability waiver and write down their blood group, with a guarantee that if anything happened, they'd be whisked off to the hospital in Dong Ha in the blink of an eye. Colonel Hong laughed. "Don't worry," he said, "we haven't had a single accident in fifteen years."

Khiet was tracking the progress of the survey on a color-coded chart of the district that was divided into one-kilometer grid squares, each subdivided into fifty-meter-square boxes. Red for cluster bombs, blue for other munitions, dark green for all clear, light green for forest land, white meaning not yet surveyed, and grayed-out boxes that for one reason or another were unsurveyable—water, a swamp, a rockface. Within the current square, the team had already combed the footprint of eight separate cluster bomb strikes and safely disposed of more than 150 unexploded *bom bi*. The field they were surveying now had been under cultivation with cassava and sweet potatoes, but the farmer had abandoned it. Khiet's team had already found two *bom bi* and a mortar round.

Five men walked across the field, sweeping their mine detectors slowly from left to right, while a young medic stood off at a distance. "Keep as far away from them as she is," Khiet said. "Turn off your cell phone so it doesn't interfere with their signal, and follow exactly in the footsteps of the man in front of you. *Exactly.*" As they crisscrossed the field, the detectors made a high-pitched chatter, like a flock of angry geese. Breaking the rhythm abruptly, one of them gave a loud squawk. Maybe it was another bomb or maybe just a piece of shrapnel or a bottle cap, Colonel Hong said. The spot was flagged for later inspection.

A few months later Khiet received a call to report an unexploded *bom bi* in a rice field in the village of Hai Ba, a mile from the coast. Following his usual protocol, he drove out to the scene to figure out the best way of dealing with it. There was a sudden explosion, and though Khiet was rushed to a nearby hospital, he could not be saved. He left a wife and two small children. The team member accompanying him was wounded by shrapnel but survived.

They buried Khiet two days later, on a Saturday in May 2016. By coincidence, it was the day President Obama arrived in Hanoi, a trip immortalized by his lunch with the celebrity chef Anthony Bourdain. The two of them squatted on blue plastic stools in one of the narrow streets of the Old Quarter to devour bowls of *bun cha,* the famous Hanoi dish of grilled pork meatballs.

It is unlikely that Obama heard of the incident, which was after all just the death of one more person in an obscure place as a consequence of a long-ago war. The president was in Vietnam to talk about his "pivot to Asia," discuss trade deals, and advance cooperation against threatening moves by China on the disputed Spratly and Paracel Islands. As part of this arrangement, the U.S. Navy was requesting access for its warships to dock once again at Cam Ranh Bay, the finest deepwater harbor in Southeast Asia and a vital base for the Seventh Fleet during the war. The arms embargo would finally be lifted, and there was speculation about what kind of American weapons might arrive as a result—although Khiet's death made it feel as if they'd never left.

As time went on, it became clear that the accident had been a cruel anomaly. In 2017 there were just three injuries from UXO in Quang Tri. In each of the next four years, there was not a single casualty, something unprecedented. Searcy knew that Quang Tri would never be entirely free of the menace. After all, a thousand-pound British bomb had recently been found under a runway at the Hamburg international airport, and there were still no-go areas in France contaminated by munitions and chemicals left behind from the trench warfare of World War I. The long shadow of war never disappeared, but it could be lightened, and perhaps Quang Tri was now as safe as one could reasonably hope.

By this time the United States had given more than $150 million for UXO clearance. More than forty thousand schoolchildren had gone through Phu Nguyen's educational program at the Mine Action Visitor Center. Project RENEW's workshops had fitted more than two thousand amputees with new limbs. Only two or three scrap metal dealers remained in the province, although there was still a small clandestine trade in the more lucrative munitions: Colonel Hong had been called to the police station one night after a truck driver was arrested for transporting three 750-pounders.

Quang Tri had become a model for all of Vietnam. NPA interviewers were close to completing the nontechnical survey, having visited almost eight hundred villages. A new American ambassador, Daniel Kritenbrink, had come to Dong Ha in the summer of 2019 for a workshop on cluster munitions and visited the Truong Son National Martyrs Cemetery, where he burned incense in memory of those who had fallen on the Ho Chi Minh Trail, a previously unthinkable gesture of reconciliation. The Pentagon, meanwhile, was supplying Quang Tri with advanced bomb-detection technology that used a sophisticated differential GPS system to locate UXO, accurate to one centimeter. Fifty years on, the latest-generation high-tech gizmos were here to make amends for those that had been used to identify targets for the bombs in the first place.

Vietnam still had no uniform national program for ridding the country of UXO, but one or two other provinces were at last showing interest in emulating Quang Tri's success. Work had begun in Quang Binh, immediately north of the DMZ, the second most heavily bombed province. In the A Luoi Valley, NPA teams were clearing safe paths to the summit of Hamburger Hill, where there was now a memorial marker to the battle, with an inscription in English and Vietnamese.

Hien and Phu and Trung Nguyen had reached out to officials in two other provinces: Kon Tum, in the Central Highlands, where Le Cao

Dai had operated his field hospital, and its neighbor Quang Ngai, scene of the My Lai massacre, where Lady Borton had worked for two years during the war and Tim O'Brien had returned to confront his demons.

"We have to be realistic," Phu said. "You can't make change happen overnight. You have to take very careful steps. It takes a long time for people to get to know you and find out what you do. You have to build trust. That's what we've learned over the past twenty years."

In terms of public awareness, Quang Ngai was where Quang Tri had been fifteen or twenty years ago, he said. When people found a piece of unexploded ordnance, they still tended to dump salt on it, bury it in the ground, and hope it would rust away. But the provincial people's committee was open to cooperation, and the Vietnamese Red Cross was a willing partner. Project RENEW was looking first at a district called Ba To, where the majority of the population were from the H're ethnic minority. Ten miles from the Lao border, this was where back in 1970 the Harvard geneticist Matthew Meselson had taken his photographs of the terraced rice fields left barren by Agent Blue. These days one of the most influential local figures in the district was a retired commander of PAVN forces in the Central Highlands, and he was sympathetic to Project RENEW's overtures. A lot always depended on that kind of local connection, and Phu was optimistic that the Quang Ngai initiative would take hold.

The Cam Lo cluster bomb survey had been wrapped up by this time, and other teams were at work between Highway 1 and the East Sea, on a stretch of low white dunes and scrubby salt flats that had seen bitter fighting in both the French and the American wars. The current focus was on a village in Hai An commune, a mile or two from where Khiet had been killed and close to the site of Wunder Beach, a supply base for the 1st Cav and the 101st Airborne during the Tet Offensive. In the fierce heat of late morning, everyone gathered under a tent for a briefing by Project RENEW's operations manager. She—and that was the remarkable thing: she was a *she*—was a slightly built, sweet-faced woman in her mid-thirties from neighboring Trieu Phong district. Her name was Dieu Linh, and she had come to Project RENEW in 2009, around the same time as Hien Ngo.

Linh swept her pointer across the map of the survey area, which was divided on the same grid pattern that Khiet's team had used in Cam Lo. In the field behind her, which was backed by a small Buddhist temple with ornate dragon carvings, members of the team were at work with two-person mine detectors. Their work here was being funded by the British government, and they had Union Jack patches sewn to their sleeves. They were Vietnam's first ever all-female bomb disposal team.

"There was a lot of resistance at first," Linh said. "Our husbands and families worried about us"—she herself was the mother of two small children—"and the government said this work was too hard for women. But things have changed."

The team was about to finish work for the day. It was a Friday, and they were leaving for Hue after lunch for the annual Vietnamese Women's Day outing, planning to make a weekend of it. Linh grinned. "We like to go to bars and do karaoke. Sometimes we have a massage. Last year, one of our team said, 'Now I understand why men like massages so much!'" From Hue they would head for the beautiful Bach Ma National Park, where the French had built their summer retreat. "We'll do some hiking, some sightseeing, take lots of photographs," Linh said. "And after that we'll have a big party."

She introduced the team leader, Nguyen Thi Thuy, the youngest of eight children from a family in Gio Linh district, up on the northeastern corner of the old Leatherneck Square. Thuy said that this grid square, number 97, was a confirmed hazardous area. It was a complicated place to work, because there had been such intense infantry combat here, so it had more than the usual number of mortar rounds and grenades in proportion to cluster bombs from airstrikes. So far the field had yielded up five UXO of various kinds.

Thuy issued the usual instructions. *Stay well back, and switch off your phones.* A hole had been marked off with a triangle of red and white tape. One of the women ran a line back to the steps of the temple. A foreign visitor, an army veteran who had served in the area, was given the honor of pushing the button. There was a muffled explosion. Thuy waited for a few minutes until the smoke cleared, then came back beaming, holding out a shovelful of hot shrapnel from a grenade. It was one more item to add to the inventory of UXO that the demining groups in Quang Tri had disposed of since the late 1990s. Soon, Searcy said, they would pass the half-million mark.

Angry Ghosts

A s project RENEW reached its twentieth anniversary, it had swelled from its core group of five to a staff of 280, all Vietnamese and most of them natives of Quang Tri. Since 2013 the project had also expanded in other ways: out in the backcountry, if you went looking for bombs, you also found birth defects, and if you were dealing with one, you had a moral obligation to deal with the other.

Three-quarters of a million gallons of herbicides had been sprayed on Quang Tri. In terms of volume, this ranked it ninth among the forty-four provinces in the former South Vietnam. But a more meaningful yardstick would be the intensity. Relative to its surface area, Quang Tri rose to fifth. Also, about 80 percent of the chemicals used in the province were Agent Orange, much higher than the overall average.

The maps that Hatfield constructed from the HERBS tapes revealed the geographical and military logic of the spraying, how the flight lines overlapped with the bombing runs, which places were targeted and when, and which populated areas would have been worst affected. In critical areas like Leatherneck Square, the C-123s might repeat the same run as many as six times to prevent the exuberant vegetation from growing back. Although the flights went on year-round, the optimum time for defoliation was between September and December. The timing of crop destruction missions was pegged to the agricultural cycle, targeting the harvest of corn and sweet potatoes in May and June, for example, or the planting of sticky rice in July.

As for the human consequences, in 1999 the Vietnamese government published the results of a national health survey. The population of Quang Tri at that time was a little over half a million. The survey found that the health of 15,000 was impaired by Agent Orange, including more than 5,000 who suffered from birth defects. Le Van Dang, the provincial head of VAVA, was still using those statistics more than fifteen years later, although according to his own records about 2,500 of those disabled people had since died. Almost 2,000 of the survivors were receiving a modest government stipend, normally just a few dollars a month, barely enough to cover their medical costs.

Cam Lo, the home district of Phu Nguyen and Hien Ngo, was a perfect microcosm of the dilemma faced by Vietnamese doctors and scientists. No one knew its villages better than Dr. Nguyen Viet Nhan, who had done his Ph.D. research here. With support from the 10-80 Committee, he documented birth defects in children under sixteen, comparing the numbers with those he found in Hue city. He taught local health workers how to conduct house-to-house surveys, how to recognize some common congenital disabilities, how to elicit information from families about when they might have been exposed to the defoliants. He found that roughly one in twenty households in Cam Lo had a disabled child. Almost fifty families had two or more, and some as many as five. Once these kids were identified, many of them were brought to Hue for examination by specialists, and Nhan got to know many of the families personally.

He counted 468 children in all and divided them into two groups. The first included physical defects that were easy to identify without expert diagnosis: cleft lip; cleft palate; clubfoot; polydactyly—too many fingers or toes; oscheocele, a swelling or tumor of the scrotum; hypospadias, a congenital deformity of the urethra and penis; hemangiomas, a spongy red clump of blood cells on the face or upper body, disfiguring though nonmalignant. Nhan found striking differences between Cam Lo and Hue. There were twice as many cases of cleft lip and cleft palate, three times as many clubfeet, three times the incidence of polydactyly; hypospadias was four times as common, and oscheocele and hemangiomas occurred six times as frequently.

Nhan's second category included mental retardation and cerebral palsy. He found significant levels of both in Cam Lo, and although he hesitated to ascribe a cause to them, his spot diagnosis was sometimes enough to put them in the book at VAVA—though cerebral palsy is not on the VA list of diseases associated with dioxin.

Nhan had done research in the A Luoi Valley too. In the years after the war, innumerable newborns had died there, he said over coffee one day in Hanoi. "The treatment of children by the ethnic minority people is very different than it is among the Kinh [ethnic Vietnamese]. They don't know how to take care of them. That's why today you may find proportionately fewer disabled children in A Luoi than you do in Hue. Many of them just pass away too soon."

Although the Hatfield survey of the valley had collected some local data about birth defects, Nhan seemed to have been the first to look for a correlation between Agent Orange and specific medical conditions. A modest man, he was the first to admit the limitations of his work in Cam Lo—some of his sample sizes were too small to be meaningful. Although Hue had some of the best medical facilities in Vietnam, it still lacked paraclinical testing and sophisticated diagnostic equipment. As in any impoverished rural area, many other possible factors had to be taken into account. In general, people there were smaller, poorer, sicker, and more malnourished than city dwellers, and they had much less access to healthcare. The men were likely to have more of a taste for the potent local rice wine and its supposedly medicinal version, which can be infused with anything from scorpions and cobras to whole deer heads.

Nhan pressed for more thorough epidemiological studies, but they never materialized, for the usual reason: a lack of funding. Even so, in the early 2000s, Cam Lo got more attention than most places from researchers. Small-scale Vietnamese and Japanese studies showed high levels of dioxin in blood, fat, and breast milk. An Australian economist found that families with disabled members earned less than half as much on average as healthy ones. The Asian Development Bank focused on two communes in the district, Cam Thanh and Cam Nghia, looking to boost local incomes by planting hundreds of acres of acacia in areas that had been defoliated. The researchers took samples of well water and found traces of dioxin, which they ascribed to erosion and runoff from nearby hillsides that had been sprayed. But after forty years the levels were not high enough to raise a red flag.

The last of the work during this period was done by the government's Office 33, which looked at Cam Chinh commune, next door to Cam Nghia. Like the earlier studies, it found some disturbing evidence of the correlation between contamination levels in the soil and sediments and the concentration of dioxin in breast milk. But again the samples were too small to support firm conclusions. The end result of all this work was more questions than answers, as was usually the case with Agent Orange.

The most striking part of Nhan's research was his focus on families with multiple disabled children, and that was where the story came back to the moral imperatives that guided Project RENEW. "We call them Agent Orange families, though you can never be sure that's the case," Searcy said. "So we operate on a kind of triage principle, helping out where we think the need is greatest."

Phu Nguyen's birthplace, Cam Tuyen commune, stretches from Leatherneck Square to the Rockpile. His colleague Dang Quang Toan often visited a family there who had five sons, four of whom had been born mute and unable to walk. Toan, a native of Dong Ha, joined Project RENEW in its early days and now ran its victims assistance program. With a little money, he said, no more than $1,000, you could do something concrete to change the lives of a single household. In this case, it had paid for an outside toilet that the four men, now approaching middle age, could reach with the help of a handrail. Their elderly father padded around the yard in bare feet and powder-blue pajamas. Which was worse, he asked: for a child to die before his parents, or for aging parents to leave their children alone and destitute, with no one to take care of them? It was a question you heard often in Cam Lo district.

The nearby hamlet of Tan Hiep was about a mile north of the Cam Lo River and close to Phu's childhood home. A steep staircase led down from a small shop to an enclosed yard with the usual household shrine, where there was an incense burner and a small bottle of Hanoi vodka, placed as an offering to the family's ancestors. From the top of the steps you could hear the guttural moans and keening howls of pain from Nguyen Van Bong's daughter Tai. She and her younger sister, Tuyet, were sprawled diagonally across a bare wooden bed frame, swaddled in a thick, floral-patterned blanket. Their mother sat at the end of the bed, stroking their short-cropped hair and making small comforting sounds. Tai writhed and thrashed and clutched at her legs; Tuyet lay rigid, staring at the ceiling.

Dr. Nhan's primary diagnosis was cerebral palsy, though clearly there was more to it than that. He had told the family that the girls were unlikely to survive beyond the age of fifteen, but they were now both in their twenties, although they looked much younger.

Bong said that thirty families in the village had disabled children. He and his wife, who was in precarious health herself, had four. Tai rarely slept; she screamed and groaned all night, so they had to trade round-the-clock shifts, which made it difficult for him to work.

Their other children had birth defects too. Their son had abnormal bone growths on his knees and suffered great pain during the cold, rainy months. But at least he was able to live independently in Danang, where he was training to be a motorbike mechanic. Another grown daughter was stunted: she weighed no more than thirty kilos, her arms splayed out at unnatural angles, and her hands bent outward. It sounded like a congenital contracture, akin to a clubfoot. Nonetheless, though she was often sickly, she'd learned to ride a motorbike, and now she was attending college in Dong Ha. As a child she'd spent a lot of time with Dr. Nhan, going into rehab in Hue, where he fitted her with braces. After that he'd come to the house often. Everyone in Tan Hiep knew the famous Dr. Nhan.

A couple of years later, Project RENEW had installed a new roof on Nguyen Van Bong's house, which prevented the rain coming in. But by that time the yard was silent. Tai's sufferings had ended, at the age of twenty-seven.

Hatfield's maps of the Ranch Hand flights made it possible to piece together exactly when the planes had passed over Tan Hiep and which chemicals they had dropped, suggesting when Bong and his wife might have been exposed to dioxin.

He was born in 1958, so he was only a boy of nine when the worst of the fighting came to the village. His father had been an ARVN soldier who fought at Khe Sanh and in Laos during Lam Son 719, the 1971 South Vietnamese invasion. During the early years of the war, the ARVN controlled Tan Hiep by day, and the insurgents moved in at night. "Our village was the home of Nguyen Minh Ky, the famous sniper we called Hum Xam, the Gray Tiger of Route 9," Bong said. "He shot lots of Americans. We'd stand on the riverbank and watch the bombing and the ground fighting, and we would see the corpses. But I was only a kid, so I wasn't scared."

Everything north of the Cam Lo River had eventually been turned into a free-fire zone, and Tan Hiep was evacuated, its twenty families forced to move at gunpoint by ARVN soldiers into the squalid resettlement camp in Cam Lo town, Tin City, where they were penned in with barbed wire under a dusk-to-dawn curfew. "I knew all the guys on the tanks," Bong said. "They loved children and they used to play with us and share their C-rations. Once they asked me to help them carry two dead Americans across the river." One had been white and the other black.

Between April 1967 and January 1968, three Agent Orange flights had passed right over Tan Hiep, and two more had come within a mile or two of the village. "Three aircraft would fly over together early in the morning and make a white spray," he said. "All the fish in the Cam Lo River died, and we'd wade into the water and take them home to eat."

The air force records always went out of their way to say that only uninhabited areas were targeted. True enough up to a point, Bong said with a half-smile, but not the whole story. "Even though we'd been moved to Cam Lo, people still grew maize and peas, peanuts and rice back on the other side of the river, by Tan Hiep. In the morning, once the planes had gone, my wife and her parents would go across the bridge to the fields as usual." The trees and crops would still be wet from the spray.

Jeanne Stellman's database showed the risk of exposure for American soldiers on a logarithmic scale, like the Richter scale for earthquakes. The highest recorded risk anywhere in Vietnam was 6.95; Tan Hiep rated 5.98, which was very substantial. So did the birth defects in Bong's family come from his wife's trek to the fields? Or from the dead fish they ate as children? Who could say? The best you could hope for was educated guesswork.

South of the river, in Cam Nghia commune, a particular curse had fallen on the village of Phuong An 2, close to Camp Carroll. Twenty families there had two or more disabled children; people called it the Agent Orange Village. A short way up a dirt road was the house of a woman named Le Thi Mit and her husband, Nguyen Van Loc. Of all the Agent Orange families, they were one of the best known, since the Magnum photographer Philip Jones-Griffiths had published powerful black and white photographs of them back in 1998. So they were not unaccustomed to visiting foreigners.

Mit, a small, haggard woman in her late sixties, did most of the talking. Her husband, a tiny, jug-eared man four years older, chatted with Searcy about the brood cow they'd been given by Project RENEW, to boost the family income by selling its calves at the local market.

Cam Nghia commune had been an NLF stronghold, and Mit and Loc had joined the village militia in 1966, when the serious fighting began. They married in October 1968, shortly after two battalions of the 101st Airborne installed themselves at the former Special Forces base at Mai Loc, a mile or so from their home. No trace remained of the base today; the land had been given over to rubber and pepper plantations.

Phuong An 2 had been napalmed and flattened by B-52 strikes. "Lots of villagers died, and you would see their corpses, all burned and blackened," Mit said. "Some people fled to Danang, but most of us stayed and lived in the forest or in caves." These were set into a nearby ridgeline, a couple of miles south of the village, and provided shelter for the NLF fighters.

The couple had their first child in 1971, a healthy boy. A second son followed in 1978. He had six fingers on one hand and was mentally disabled. He lay motionless in his bed, staring at the ceiling, oblivious to the world, never recognizing his parents. At four, he died. Two other boys survived. Lanh, who was born in 1982, lay on a thin mattress in a darkened room. He had shaggy black hair and an enlarged skull, which a doctor at the hospital in Dong Ha diagnosed as hydrocephalus, one type of which is on the VA's list of recognized birth defects in the offspring of women who served in Vietnam. Lanh suffered from excruciating headaches. There was a bottle of phenobarbital by the bedside to control his seizures. Several toes on one foot appeared to be webbed together, and his mother had to chew his food before feeding it to him because he had no teeth. She wondered if perhaps a worm had eaten them.

His brother Truong, who was six years younger, sat outside on the tiled floor, his shrunken matchstick legs splayed out at a thirty-degree angle. He stared into the distance with a blank expression, then came suddenly to life, letting out sharp little barks of laughter as he tried to wrap the family's six-week-old kitten in a plastic bag. Like Nguyen Van Bong's daughters in Tan Hiep, the primary diagnosis was cerebral palsy, although it was clear that not all his disabilities were physical.

Mit and Loc had sold all their possessions, even the jackfruit trees they marketed for timber, to raise the $140 they needed for Truong's medical expenses. They had taken him to Hue, where he spent six months in rehab, free of charge. The physiotherapists taught him to walk with the help of a handrail, but when he came home, his infirmities returned full force, and since then he'd spent all his time lying in bed or sprawled on the floor.

Two years later Truong was able to use the family's new indoor toilet, built by Project RENEW, the first time they had had such a luxury. But Lanh had died, putting an end to thirty-four years of misery.

The inevitable question hung in the air: did Le Thi Mit blame the Americans for the torments that had been visited on her family? She looked at the ground. No, she said, she thought it was the work of angry ghosts.

As in Tan Hiep, it was possible to make an informed guess about when Mit had been exposed to the defoliants. The flight paths traced a rough parallelogram around the village. Most of what the planes had sprayed was Agent Orange, with a couple of Agent White missions, and two of Agent Blue that destroyed crop fields about three miles to the west. She would likely have seen the first of the spray runs on September 19, 1966, when Ranch Hand mission 1087 made a low west-to-east pass along the high ridgeline south of the village, where the fighters sheltered in the caves, before kicking a right-angled dogleg to the north. Nothing had grown back on those hills since the war other than coarse invasive grasses, she said. There were two planes on that first occasion, loaded with 1,800 gallons of Agent Orange. Eleven days later, two more flights came even closer to Phuong An 2, dropping another 4,800 gallons.

One of these flights was probably the one that drenched the eighteen-year-old Mit while she was out in the fields. She remembered that the spray caused her whole body to itch furiously. When she got home, she boiled some wild leaves and rubbed the liquid on her skin, a common local remedy, but that didn't help. All her cassava died, and all the vegetables, but the family had no alternative but to eat them, since they had no other food.

But there were other possible explanations, too, for the family's troubles—what Donald Rumsfeld might have called the unknown unknowns of the herbicide campaign. The huge artillery base at Camp Carroll, three miles from Phuong An 2, was repeatedly sprayed by the Army Chemical Corps. The Mai Loc base got the same treatment. "We were constantly soaked with the stuff," said Louis Andre, who served there with the Special Forces. But those records didn't exist. The findings of the Asian Development Bank (ADB) also raised suspicions. From the six-hundred-foot ridgeline south of the village, several streams trickled down into the bowl of the valley. Could these have carried the dioxin toward Phuong An 2, as the ADB surmised?

For Jeanne Stellman, the startling clusters of birth defects in Cam Tuyen and Cam Nghia raised more questions than answers. She had the natural skepticism of any good scientist, and this often put her in an ironic position. She'd done more than anyone to document the massive scale of the herbicide campaign, calculate the risks to American veterans, and make the case for their right to benefits from the VA. In cataloguing the multiple horrors that peasant families like Mit's had endured—which included the possibility that the arsenical Agent Blue might also be a cause of transgenerational genetic damage—she was actually more sweeping than most in her moral condemnation of the war. Yet for a large and vocal segment of the veterans' community, her insistence on the scientific uncertainties was infuriating. Agent Orange had to be a black and white moral parable, stripped of nuance.

The herbicides were just one of the innumerable wartime stressors to which these people had been subjected, Stellman argued. They had also been carpet-bombed, rocketed, napalmed, and machine-gunned; starved, burned out of their homes, and forced to live in caves or moved into squalid refugee camps. Was it any wonder they had suffered a rash of birth defects? She cited the well-documented history of the Dutch

"Hunger Winter" at the end of World War II. "After they were starved and blockaded by the Nazis," she said, "there were extensive studies showing all sorts of second- and third-generational health effects."

If a family had five children suffering from different congenital disabilities, she went on, "that in itself would tend to point away from environmental exposure as a cause. Look at the Minamata disaster, for example"—the discharge of methylmercury from a Japanese chemical factory in the 1950s. "It always had the same consistent effect on the victims."

TCDD was not mercury, of course, and the only thing that might one day help to unravel these mysteries was the new science of epigenetics. Enough research had been done by the second decade of the twenty-first century to establish how dioxin causes gene methylation—something quite different from the more familiar concept of genetic mutation. Vietnamese scientists had already identified dozens of dioxin-related mutations in four different genes, likely pathways to cancer. But while mutation means a change in the underlying gene sequence, methylation is the alteration of gene *expression*.

There appeared to be only one study of the subject that related to Vietnamese affected by dioxin, and it came as no surprise that it went back, as did so many of the war's horror stories, to the A Shau Valley and the neighboring Nam Dong district. Published in 2018, it was the work of a team of Italian geneticists and an American expert on the history of the war in Thua Thien, David Biggs, to which Dr. Nguyen Viet Nhan added his imprimatur.

The geneticists took blood samples from almost almost one hundred people. Some were the offspring of parents who had lived in the two valleys during the war; others had moved to the area later. A control group of the same size was chosen from several unsprayed locations north of the DMZ, and all the samples were sent to Hue for analysis.

The results were intriguing. The children of those who had been present during the spraying showed evidence of changes in the expression of the CYP1A1 gene, which affects the placenta and sperm cells, and the IGF2 gene, which plays an essential role in fetal development. Those whose parents had arrived after the war showed no measurable change.

It was a tiny step forward, although vast uncertainties remained.

"We're at the very, very tip of the iceberg," Stellman said. "With so many transgenerational shared exposures, it's going to take a lot of work to pick apart the data—with approximately zero resources being devoted to the question. We are so far from telling the whole story."

Dr. Nhan was always a good-humored man, with a ready smile, but he seemed weary. Science was such a long, slow, painstaking business, and more likely than not, we would never have all the answers. Life was too short, he'd come to believe, and the lives of those who needed help were usually even shorter.

He'd moved from Hue to a hospital in Hanoi—"a new opportunity for me to test myself," he said. His old team was still at work, but these days they devoted themselves mainly to healing and caring for disabled kids, not to figuring out how they got to be that way. Nhan himself was now intent on doing whatever he could to forestall birth defects from occurring in the first place. He was working with young women to make sure they had all their vaccinations, that they were getting enough folic acid and vitamin B9, and educating them about infectious diseases and air and water pollution, any of which might endanger the health of their child. "You don't even need to talk about dioxin," he said. "Just focus on the mother and the baby. If you only run after the disease, you will never solve the problem."

Nhan had worked for decades to solve the riddles that bedeviled the politics of Agent Orange. On one side were the temptations of scientific research, and on the other the moral and humanitarian imperatives, and now, a quarter-century after his first work in Cam Lo, he had no doubt which of them had to take priority.

The Worst Thing, the Best Thing

O N   A   B R I S K , sunny morning in March 2019, a group of several dozen Americans and Vietnamese gathered at the U.S. Institute of Peace in Washington, D.C., two blocks from the Vietnam Wall, to reflect on the legacies of the war and how the long process of facing up to them had transformed enemies into allies. There were high-ranking government officials from both sides, past and present, military and civilian. Many of the architects of the new relationship were present, and all were given their due: Charles Bailey, Patrick Leahy, and his longtime aide Tim Rieser. Bobby Muller's wheelchair was drawn up at one end of the front row.

The idea for the meeting came from Vietnam's vice-minister of defense, Senior Lt. Gen. Nguyen Chi Vinh. He was military aristocracy, though with an ironic twist: he was the son of Gen. Nguyen Chi Thanh, commander of PAVN forces in the South, Le Duan's closest hard-line ally, Vo Nguyen Giap's great rival, father of the strategy of "grabbing the enemy by the belt," and principal military planner, until his untimely death, of the Tet Offensive. Vinh had risen steadily through the ranks, becoming chief of military intelligence and a member of the Central Committee of the Communist Party. Now he was deputy chair of the government's new Committee 701, which for the first time put Agent Orange and unexploded ordnance under a single umbrella, with both issues under military control.

The new relationship was "shaped by history but not held hostage by history," one State Department official said, and all those present hewed to a common narrative that smoothed over the many deep pot-holes of that history. The purpose was to show how the wounds of war had been healed, not to point fingers at those who had opened them in the first place. Everyone agreed on how the sequence had unfolded. The first step had been Vietnam's willingness to account for American MIAs—and no one was much inclined at this late date to point out that until this unilateral demand was met, no other dialogue was possible. Once the joint searches began, there was room for reciprocity, with government support for humanitarian projects, notably the prosthetics program that Muller had created and Chuck Searcy had run during his first five years in Hanoi. Next, the United States had taken responsibility for UXO removal, and tiny Quang Tri was the heart of that effort, a model, Vinh said, not just for Vietnam but for the world. What remained was the most intractable problem of all: Agent Orange, and by 2007 there was finally the political will in Congress, with bipartisan support, to deal with its legacy in a serious way.

There was a lot of gray hair in the room that day, and a good number of people whose lives formed unbroken strands in the half-century-long skein of this history. Muller was the best-known of them. It was fifty years, almost to the day, since he had been shot and paralyzed near Con Thien. He had been the unquestioned leader of the campaign for fair treatment for American veterans, the earliest advocate for extending equal generosity to Vietnamese victims of the war, and at the age of seventy-three his fire seemed to burn undimmed.

Ann Mills Griffiths was there too, after more than forty years still the chair of the National League of Families of American Prisoners and Missing in Southeast Asia, though her staff had dwindled to one. Her brother Jimmy, the radar intercept officer on an F-4 Phantom, had gone down in September 1966 in shallow waters off the coast of Nghe An province.

The search for Jimmy Mills epitomized the no-matter-how-long-it-takes philosophy of the MIA searches. Joint U.S.-Vietnamese teams began looking for his remains in 1993 but found no trace of the aircraft until thirteen years later, when a fisherman snagged a piece of wreckage in his net. Scuba divers returned repeatedly to scour the ocean floor, and in 2017 they found the first bone fragments, which DNA analysis identified as those of the pilot, Capt. James Bauder. By that time, there had been well over twenty missions to the site, and when the Pentagon scheduled one more for June 2018, Mills Griffiths said it should be the last; what had been done already had brought her family a measure of peace. But this time the team returned with part of a rib, which was identified as Jimmy's. Shortly after the Washington symposium, it would be placed in his empty grave in Arlington National Cemetery.

Among the Vietnamese delegates was retired Senior Lt. Gen. Nguyen Van Rinh. As a junior officer, he had marched south across the DMZ at the end of 1967 in time to take part in the Tet Offensive. His unit was part of the celebrated 320th Division, which Manus Campbell's company had confronted near the ruined village of Phu Oc. As the fighting raged in Quang Tri, Rinh was soaked by the spray from the C-123s. In the days that followed, he watched yellowed leaves drop from the trees, saw his men sicken and farm animals die. Fifteen years older than General Vinh, he had served for nine years as vice-minister of defense, and after his retirement, he'd become the president of VAVA.

Even after the cleanup of the Danang air base had begun, Rinh remained bitter. The Americans had committed war crimes, he'd said during a conversation in Hanoi in 2015, and he still wanted a formal apology, though he surely knew he would never get one. But now, with the Danang project completed, here he was on a panel chaired by Bailey, praising the cleanup of the hot spots and U.S. aid to the victims of dioxin as the keystone of the new relationship between the two countries.

This wasn't to say, however, that things had gone smoothly or moved quickly in the twelve years since Bailey had his Christmastime meeting with Tim Rieser and Bobby Muller at Noi Bai airport. Once the decision was made to clean up Danang, there was no great controversy about finding the money. It isn't cynical to say that the project was the kind of thing Americans do best, and like best: complex, expensive, but doable. It offered a story with a beginning and an end, the prospect of saying "mission accomplished." It showcased the technological mastery of the American firms who got the contracts. And it was the moral thing to do, even though it focused on protecting those who might be harmed in the future, and it glossed over those who had already been harmed in the past.

The visible symbol of the cleanup was the great white ziggurat structure that rose near the runway, the size of a football field and eight meters high, a giant oven designed to remove the dioxin by superheating hundreds of thousands of tons of contaminated soil and sediments to 330 degrees Celsius. That was a fine and honorable thing, Bailey thought, but it was only an expensive stepping-stone to addressing the real problem, which was more diffuse, less visible, and more politically sensitive and had no definable end.

There was still a fraught path to navigate with the U.S. government where humanitarian aid was concerned, although in the case of USAID, it was more a war of attrition. While Bailey was a master of diplomatic nuance, Tom Boivin, Hatfield's president at the time, would have been the first to admit that he was built differently. "We had to write twenty-seven versions of our report on Danang before it was approved," he said. "The blood and breast milk samples were the biggie. USAID tried to get us to remove all references to those because the project was only supposed to remediate the soil and sediment on the base. But I told them the human connection was critical. Did they not believe the science? And why were we doing all this anyway? We went back and forth. They'd delete stuff, I'd put it back in. I said if they didn't include what we wanted, Hatfield wouldn't put its name on the document. In the end they didn't call my bluff. But the truth is that I would have fucking pulled us out of it. Game over!"

Hatfield didn't get into the specific needs of people with disabilities; that would have strayed beyond its scientific mandate. But the logic was implicit. The United States, thanks largely to Patrick Leahy, had been helping war victims in Vietnam for close to twenty years. Ergo, didn't Danang—not to mention Bien Hoa and other hot spots—deserve the same kind of generosity? There was no longer any need to get hung up on old, unwinnable arguments about cause and effect. Was dioxin the reason for this boy's contorted limbs or that girl's balloon-like skull? It didn't matter; it should just be a question of making an informed and humane judgment. Jeanne Stellman offered an analogy. "It's like Love Canal," she said, referring to the environmental disaster in upstate New

York in the late 1970s. "Were the chemicals in the canal toxic? Absolutely. When the children became sick, was it because of the chemicals? Epidemiologically, we can't answer that question. Would I buy a house at Love Canal? No."

After plans for the joint U.S.-Vietnamese study of birth defects fell apart in 2005, the two governments had convened the first meeting of a Joint Advisory Committee on dioxin. The Vietnamese team was chaired by Dr. Le Ke Son, the head of Office 33, which marked a subtle but unmistakable shift in the political center of gravity. Bailey's support now had to be channeled through Office 33, no longer the 10-80 Committee, and both of that committee's leading figures, Hoang Dinh Cau and Le Cao Dai, were now dead. Although Le Ke Son was a physician with a Ph.D. in toxicology, the main focus was now on the science and politics of cleaning up Danang. Dealing with the impact of Agent Orange on public health would be limited to removing the immediate threat to people living close to the base.

The deeper issue of getting help to those who had already been sickened by dioxin would have to be addressed in other ways, and Bailey moved forward in two directions at once. First, he embarked on what he called "Track-II diplomacy," outside the official constraints of the Joint Advisory Committee. In the fall of 2006, shortly before he returned from Hanoi, his boss, Susan Berresford, put him in touch with Walter Isaacson, the polymath journalist, editor, and biographer, who somehow also found time to run the international not-for-profit Aspen Institute. Aspen was renowned as a place where creative thinkers came up with solutions to intractable problems. What better place to press forward with the conversation on Agent Orange?

Working with Isaacson and Ton Nu Thi Ninh, former ambassador to the European Union, Bailey put together a small group of individuals with impeccable credentials, equal numbers of Americans and Vietnamese. After visiting Ford-funded projects in Danang, they held their first formal meeting in the ballroom of the grand old Metropole Hotel in Hanoi. Isaacson opened it with a simple and overdue sentence: "We feel your pain." The group, with Aspen as its hub and Berresford as its convener, became known as the U.S.-Vietnam Dialogue Group on Agent Orange and Dioxin.

While the dialogue group devoted its considerable energies to keeping the issue in the public eye and on the agenda of officials in both governments, Bailey directed millions of Ford Foundation dollars to a dozen groups providing direct aid to people with disabilities in areas that had been sprayed or contaminated. He found three that were especially effective: Children of Vietnam, founded by retired American engineer Ben Wilson, which helped street kids in Danang; Vietnam Assistance for the Handicapped, an organization set up by Ca Van Tran, a Vietnamese-American who had fled Saigon in 1975 and worked closely in the early 1990s with Adm. Elmo Zumwalt; and the East Meets West Foundation, created by the author Le Ly Hayslip. Ford's support went to projects in half a dozen provinces, some in the South and others in the Red River Delta in the North, where there was a large population of disabled war veterans. It paid for surgery and prosthetics, rehab programs, vocational training, self-help groups, the protection of legal rights, and measures to combat discrimination.

Bailey also funded teams from the Hanoi School of Public Health to go door-to-door in Danang and Bien Hoa to survey eating habits and steer residents away from potentially risky food like locally produced fish and ducks. But from the perspective of targeting future humanitarian aid from the U.S. government, the most important initiative came in 2009, when Bailey used Danang as a kind of demographic test case, drawing on census data and family-by-family surveys in four districts to arrive at the clearest picture anyone had yet created of which people with serious disabilities were likeliest to be "victims of Agent Orange." His best estimate was that they made up 10 to 15 percent of the city's total disabled population.

As Tim Rieser had promised, Congress appropriated $3 million in 2007 for "pilot programs for the remediation of conflict-era chemical storage sites, and to address the health needs of nearby communities." Another $3 million followed in 2009. At first, every penny was earmarked for Danang, but over time the program slowly expanded to include Dong Nai and Binh Dinh provinces, home to the hot spots at the Bien Hoa and Phu Cat air bases. But Bailey was dismayed to see the money going to people with every kind of disability, "regardless of cause," which allowed USAID to stick to conditions like blindness and deafness, as well as UXO injuries, which were no longer controversial.

Nuances of wording are everything in sensitive situations like this, and the problem could be remedied, he suggested to Rieser, by chang-ing the language in the annual appropriations bill to make sure the aid would go where it was most needed. Rieser duly wrote this into the Senate staff report accompanying the 2012 bill: the money would go to "areas in Vietnam that were targeted with Agent Orange or remain contaminated with dioxin."

After a trip to Vietnam that year, Bailey recommended Quang Tri and Thua Thien-Hue as the next most urgent priorities, and the dia-logue group went on to add four more heavily sprayed provinces—neighboring Quang Nam, Kon Tum in the Central Highlands, and Tay Ninh and Binh Phuoc, both closer to Saigon.

It was possible now to use the once-taboo phrase "Agent Orange victims" in polite society, though it still couldn't be put in writing. State Department lawyers never budged from their stubborn insistence on the phrase "regardless of cause," but Bailey's work in Danang made it clear that those sickened by dioxin were most likely to have the most severe disabilities.

Finally, in the spending bill for 2015, Rieser crafted the wording that Bailey had been looking for. The priority would be "assistance for indi-viduals with severe upper or lower mobility impairment and/or cog-nitive or developmental disabilities." The following year Rieser finally fused the two concepts together: the worst-affected areas and the worst-affected people. The new budget would earmark $7 million for "health and disability programs for areas sprayed by Agent Orange and other-wise contaminated by dioxin, to assist individuals with severe upper or lower body mobility impairments and/or cognitive or developmental disabilities." No one needed to use the word *victims,* but everyone knew what was intended. The whole painful process had taken ten years.

"The spraying of Agent Orange was a terrible deed. It should never have happened," Bailey said, "but it did, and by its nature it's difficult to impossible to correct in its entirety." But by the end of the decade, he felt that a good number of the goals that the dialogue group had laid out in its 2010 road map had been accomplished.

There were still glaring disparities between the massive cost of the Danang cleanup and the money Congress was allocating to disabilities, which trickled through in the kind of amounts folks on Capitol Hill call "decimal dust." At the same time, the money was spread increasingly thin as the scope of the program broadened to eight provinces, and Bailey and Rieser still hoped to add others.

Like the aid program, the Danang project was often snarled by delays and the slow-grinding wheels of bureaucracy. Some were typical of those that tend to beset big Superfund projects in the United States. The volume of contaminated material turned out to be two and a half times greater than anticipated. It took longer than expected to train the local technical staff. There were cost overruns and an overly optimistic assessment of the risks, like the possibility of kicking up dioxin-laden airborne dust. The project also had to be shut down for four months each year during the rainy season.

When planning began in 2008, the goal was to complete the cleanup by 2013. In the end, it didn't even begin until April 2014. The original budget was $33.7 million, but by the time the project was wrapped up in November 2017, it had risen to $116 million. For the private American contractors, it was a lucrative business. More than $100 million went to TerraTherm, which devised the proprietary technology used to remove the dioxin; CDM International, which handled the site management and oversight; and Tetra Tech, an excavation and construction company. This was anything but decimal dust. It was almost exactly what had been allocated to Vietnam's presumed victims of dioxin over eight years.

The Danang cleanup was at the heart of a sweeping political realignment, more than a decade in the making. In diplomacy as in Senate appropriation bills, words are chosen with exquisite care. The language of communiqués, speeches, and public statements steadily evolved, words gaining force through repetition and fine-tuning. The seminal joint statement by George W. Bush and President Triet in November 2006 was sprinkled with words like *progress, dialogue, frank and candid discussion of differences.* As time went on, the keyword was *trust—building trust, growing trust, deepening trust*—and then the celebration of what were now described as *shared values* and *common interests.* The official texts swarmed with large, uplifting abstractions: *peace, freedom, stability, liberty, prosperity, security,* until finally the language blossomed into all-encompassing phrases like *comprehensive partner-*

ship and *strategic alliance*. And improbable as it seemed, it was the willingness to confront the legacy of Agent Orange, as much as anything else, that propelled the process.

In 2011 the United States and Vietnam signed a memorandum of understanding on defense cooperation, with General Vinh walking point on the Vietnamese side. Its goal, he told the Washington symposium, was "a future of no war, no hatred, a future of working together." It would embrace a slew of issues, both old and new: continued progress on MIAs, both American and Vietnamese, UXO clearance, dioxin removal, but also international peacekeeping operations, military training, natural disaster relief, and above all, "enhanced maritime security capabilities"—a phrase that tiptoed around the elephant in the room.

China, Vietnam's overbearing neighbor to the north, was still the millennial enemy. For Vietnamese, "the last war" didn't mean the American one but China's punitive invasion in 1979. The most recent shots Vietnam had seen fired in anger were when sixty-four sailors were killed by the Chinese navy in 1998 as they tried to plant their flag on a disputed reef in the East Sea. Now China was building out runways and military facilities on the two archipelagos of small coral islands, the Spratlys and the Paracels, over which Vietnam and several other Asian nations claimed sovereignty, as well as installing oil-drilling rigs in what Vietnam considered to be its territorial waters.

In 2016, as part of his strategic "pivot to Asia," Barack Obama had lifted the forty-one-year-old arms embargo on Vietnam and promised funding to clean up the Bien Hoa air base. This didn't necessarily mean a sudden gold rush for American arms manufacturers. Most of Vietnam's aircraft and heavy weaponry still came from Russia, and squadrons of Sukhoi fighters weren't suddenly going to be replaced by F-16s. American weapons systems and spare parts were expensive. Pilots, operators, technicians, and mechanics would all need to be retrained. And other countries—India, Israel, Japan, South Korea—were already pecking away at different parts of the Vietnamese arms market.

Plans for the Bien Hoa cleanup, which would be orders of magnitude bigger than Danang, still had to deal with one final speed bump. John McCain, now chairman of the Senate Armed Services Committee, at first objected to any Defense Department involvement, and when

Rex Tillerson became secretary of state in February 2017, he rescinded Obama's promise of funding. Ironically, it took the liberal-minded U.S. ambassador to Hanoi Ted Osius to push back successfully, cabling the State Department to insist, "Resolving dioxin as a legacy of the war is essential to the future of our defense ties with Vietnam."

The first ship to arrive under the new military agreement, that May, was a refurbished U.S. Coast Guard cutter, the *Morgenthau*, which added further layers of echo and irony to the new relationship, since the vessel had been used during the war to interdict enemy arms shipments and ferry Navy SEALs into combat.

In November, *Air Force One* landed in Danang, bringing Donald Trump to the annual summit of Asia-Pacific Economic Cooperation (APEC) at the luxurious Furama resort on China Beach. The cleanup had been completed only days earlier, and General Vinh insisted that *Air Force One* should be parked on top of what had once been the dioxin hot spot. The vets in Danang had mixed emotions about all this. Some, like the ex-Marine David Clark, held their noses and cracked jokes about Cadet Bone Spurs, recalling how Trump had told a radio shock-jock that the fight to avoid sexually transmitted diseases had been his personal Vietnam. Others, like the former airborne "warlord" Mark O'Connor, who came each year to supply bikes to kids in the A Luoi Valley, felt differently. He sped across town to the Furama on his motorbike but couldn't get past the heavy security. All he'd wanted to do, he said, was deliver a message to Trump: *Thank you for making America great again and taking our country back.* To add to his frustration, he'd left his red MAGA hat at home.

The following March, after the first of two visits by Defense Secretary Jim Mattis, the nuclear-powered aircraft carrier USS *Carl Vinson* anchored off Danang, the first American carrier to visit Vietnam in forty-three years. The ship's band played a goodwill concert, as its predecessors had done when Bob Hope's USO tours came to town, and sailors from the *Vinson* got a couple of days' shore leave. Some went to China Beach or hit the bars; others visited a care center for "Agent Orange victims," the smiling children crowding around them for photos, flashing the two-fingered peace sign.

As usual, the media entourage recycled the old saw about "three million victims," as if the more conservative numbers Charles Bailey preferred to cite—10 to 15 percent of all the disabled—were not shocking enough. But no matter: the visit of the *Carl Vinson* was about symbolism, not fact-checking. Everyone came away happy.

Mattis made his second visit that October, with the Danang project done and dusted. Ninety thousand cubic meters of soil and sediment had been superheated and decontaminated in the great white oven. Thirty hectares of land, about seventy-five acres, were now safe to use for the expansion of the airport. The U.S. ambassador, Dan Kritenbrink, was preparing for a ceremony to unveil a commemorative plaque. (His predecessor, Ted Osius, had resigned earlier in the year in protest at Trump's threat, subsequently withdrawn, to deport more than eight thousand Vietnamese immigrants in the United States, most of whom had arrived as refugees after the fall of Saigon.)

Mattis didn't stop in Danang, but after a persuasive phone call from Patrick Leahy, he drove out from Ho Chi Minh City to Bien Hoa. As Osius had proposed, the cost of the U.S. contribution to the cleanup there would be split fifty-fifty: USAID promised to put in an initial $150 million, and Mattis promised to match that sum, the first time the Pentagon had openly acknowledged responsibility for the legacy of Operation Ranch Hand.

But scale wasn't the only difference between the two projects. The Danang airport had been revamped into a glittering symbol of the new Vietnam. You could fly there direct from Tokyo, Seoul, Singapore, Hong Kong, Doha, and New Delhi. But Bien Hoa was another matter. A linchpin of the American war, it was now the most important military air base in southern Vietnam, home to the 935th Fighter Dong Nai Squadron of the People's Air Force, a cornerstone of the country's defense of its sovereign interests in the East Sea.

One of the high-ranking Pentagon officials at the symposium at the U.S. Institute of Peace said that for Mattis, the commitment to clean up Bien Hoa was about "exorcising our last ghosts and freeing our hearts and minds"—another choice of words that might have given pause, with its echoes of the war. When the time came for General Vinh to speak about Agent Orange, he expressed a similar thought, though he put it a little differently. "The worst thing in the past," he said, "is now the best thing for our future."

The Painter, the Sprinter, and the Monk

A MONTH AFTER THE SYMPOSIUM, a plane carrying a bipartisan group of nine senators, headed by Patrick Leahy, touched down in Ho Chi Minh City. The delegation was on its way to the ceremony inaugurating the cleanup of the nearby Bien Hoa air base.

Like Hanoi, Saigon remembers the war, and Saigon forgets. With its souvenir shops and food courts and duty-free area, Tan Son Nhat feels as anodyne as any other international airport. As the novelist Lawrence Osborne has written, for the present-day traveler, "Everywhere resembles everywhere else," and arrival confers a feeling of "whereverness."

If you go to 22 Gia Long Street, where helicopters airlifted the last evacuees from the rooftop offices of the CIA deputy chief of station in 1975, it looks much like any other nondescript apartment building, its walls tagged with graffiti, across the street from an H&M and an Old Navy store. The Rex Hotel, where reporters gathered for the Five O'Clock Follies, is still there, but the lobby and hallways are now a sparkling marble labyrinth of luxury brands: Rolex, Chanel, Cartier, Givenchy, Balenciaga, Salvatore Ferragamo. A Tiger beer at the rooftop bar will set you back fifteen dollars.

A block to the east, Graham Greene's Rue Catinat is now Duong Dong Khoi, Mass Uprising Street. After a spell as the Doc Lap (Independence) Hotel, the Caravelle has regained its old name, and its rooftop bar, the war correspondents' favorite, is still there, with its own proprietary craft beer and a signature cocktail that is called, perhaps inevitably, Miss Saigon. Much of the famous view is now obscured by glass-and-steel towers, but you can still catch glimpses of the city as it was in wartime, with an unobstructed view up Dong Khoi to the Cathédrale Notre Dame. Across the cathedral square, tourists mob the mustard-yellow Central Post Office, where one wing is now occupied by a McDonald's franchise. Other beauties of old Saigon, the grand mansions and custom houses and banks that didn't coin the tourist dollar, have fallen to the wrecking ball.

The waterfront has been transformed since Chuck Searcy sat on the banks of the Saigon River, drunk and stoned, listening to *Sgt. Pepper.* Now it's a six-lane boulevard with murderous traffic and no stoplights. A short way upstream there are French-Asian fusion restaurants where the seafood is flown in direct from Phu Quoc Island, where Phu Nguyen's father languished in prison. The Saigon experience is a cocktail of history, cognitive dissonance, and kitsch nostalgia, and sometimes not much more than a blur of noise, money, and motorbikes.

For most visitors, the War Remnants Museum is an obligatory stop. Though the souvenir shop is heavy on postcards of sylphlike girls in *ao dais* and farmers in conical hats, sepia-toned photos of old Saigon, and *Tintin au Vietnam* T-shirts, the galleries upstairs are still a chamber of horrors, the walls filled with stark black and white images of deformed fetuses from the Tu Du Maternity Hospital, crater fields from B-52 strikes, the corpse-filled ditch at My Lai, villages set afire by Zippo lighters, bodies incinerated by napalm, and soldiers from the First Air Cavalry waterboarding a Viet Cong prisoner.

Other than parties of schoolchildren, the people shuffling around the exhibits are mainly foreigners, of every imaginable nationality. Vietnamese visitors tend to cluster outside in the courtyard, where high school kids and young couples mug for selfies in front of captured tanks and Chinook helicopters. Sometimes you will find a middle-aged man named Quy by the entrance, hawking pirated editions of *The Quiet American* and the Lonely Planet guide. Quy lost an arm and one eye when he was eight years old, stepping on an unexploded *bom bi* in the Central Highlands. Having picked up a few words of English, he will tell customers that he feels no bitterness toward Americans. "The war is over; it was a long time ago," he says, offering his stump, amputated above the elbow. "Please shake my hand. We can be friends, yes?"

Across the river in District 2, above a coffee shop, is the airy studio of a painter named Le Minh Chau, who was born in a village close to Bien Hoa. He was what was customarily referred to as an "Agent Orange victim," though as he bounded up the narrow stairs on his knees and palms, *victim* was the last word you would ever use to describe him.

Chau's upper- and lower-body disabilities were extreme. He wore a single earring and had spiky black hair shaved in a high fade at the temples—sometimes he liked to dye it blond or flame-orange—and an impressive collection of tattoos. A big one on his back said CHAU: BEYOND THE LINES, the title of a documentary about his life. Another, on his neck, said COURTNEY MARSH, the name of the film's director. Canvases were stacked up along the walls of the studio. They were startlingly eclectic: folk art Vietnamese landscapes, self-portraits and still lifes, abstracts, a colorful underwater scene (his disabilities hadn't stopped him from learning to snorkel), and one he'd just completed that channeled Jackson Pollock. The work was very accomplished, which was remarkable, because all of it was painted by mouth.

Chau didn't have much interest in talking about his deformities; the future was more important to him than the past. He thought he might have come by them because his mother had drunk contaminated river water at a local festival, but a likelier explanation seemed to be that his parents were wartime refugees, moving southward from Quang Nam, trying to keep one step ahead of the fighting, sleeping on the ground, drinking from streams and ponds and foraging for food in areas that had been targeted by the herbicides, until finally they settled in a village in Trang Bom district, just north of Bien Hoa.

Hatfield's maps of Ranch Hand missions over the area showed a saturated grid of red lines crossing at right angles, too many to count. This was War Zone D, one of the three areas that posed the most serious direct threat to Saigon, along with Tay Ninh province, on the Cambodian border, and the so-called Iron Triangle with the adjacent Cu Chi district, whose famous tunnels are mobbed these days by tourists who crawl through sections that have been enlarged to accommodate foreigners, posing for goofy photographs with their heads sticking up out of holes in the ground. Some pay a little extra for the thrill of firing an AK-47.

Chau's two siblings were both born healthy, but when he came along in 1991, his disabilities were more than his parents could cope with.

When he was six months old, in exchange for a generous donation, a relative had him transferred to the peace village at Tu Du hospital. He learned of his parents' existence only at the age of twelve, but didn't go back to his birthplace until he was eighteen. When they pocketed his small disability stipend and gave him nothing, it triggered his rebellious streak. At Tu Du, he refused to listen to nurses who told him it was ridiculous that someone who lacked the strength in his hands and arms to hold a paintbrush should harbor ambitions of becoming an artist.

Marsh spent eight years on her movie, seeing it as a labor of love, not something that would move the needle of public policy. But as it was nearing completion, she contacted Charles Bailey, and Chau found himself a minor celebrity. The film was a finalist for the 2016 Academy Award for best short documentary, and Bailey promoted it heavily. Then-ambassador Ted Osius arranged for showings in Hanoi and Ho Chi Minh City. Patrick Leahy hosted a screening in the Senate, and Chau flew to New York for another at the United Nations. It was the first time an "Agent Orange victim" had ever spoken at the UN. Accompanied by Marsh, he wheeled himself around the Metropolitan Museum and the Museum of Modern Art, where he discovered Picasso and Pollock.

"Courtney's film brought about a sea change, another real breakthrough," Bailey said. While public attention was focused on the cleanup at Danang and the prospect of the same at Bien Hoa, the documentary gave shape to his insistence that in dealing with the legacy of the defoliants, the ultimate goal was not cleaning up the hot spots, important though that was. Chau might be a singular character, capable of pursuing his dreams through sheer force of will. But others needed more of a helping hand. If they got it, Bailey said, "they too could become like Chau, put aside any sense of victimhood, and have lives of comfort and dignity and accomplishment."

Since the war, Bien Hoa had grown into a sprawling city of 1.3 million people, ringed by new industrial parks and apparel factories where manufacturers turned out vast quantities of Nike sneakers, Samsonite luggage, and North Face outdoor wear. Ubiquitous in the markets of

Ho Chi Minh City, it was impossible to say which were real and which were knock-offs.

At the provincial office of VAVA, the director, an amiable middle-aged woman, greeted visitors in a small meeting room decorated with the flag of Vietnam, a gold hammer and sickle, the invariable portrait of Ho Chi Minh, and another that paired Marx and Lenin. She reeled off statistics: 1,055 people in Bien Hoa were classified as Agent Orange victims, and there were more than 14,000 in the whole of Dong Nai province.

A short walk from her office was the home of a man named Nguyen Kien. Born four years after the war, he lived with his widowed mother in a neighborhood a few hundred yards south of the air base and two blocks from a small, pretty lake called Bien Hung. Their cluttered living room was dominated by more portraits of Uncle Ho, a parked motorbike, and a large altar with a vase of flowers, brass candlesticks, an incense burner, and offerings that included a large tin of traditional Danish butter cookies. The altar was dedicated to the memory of Kien's late father, a senior Communist Party official, and there was a framed photograph of him as an austere-looking young man in uniform. The walls were hung with gold and silver medals on colorful ribbons that belonged to Kien himself.

He was a man made of two halves. From the waist down, his body was much like Chau's, with emaciated legs tucked beneath him at unnatural angles. Doctors had tried to straighten them when he was three years old, but the surgery had failed, and it had left long scars. But he was broad-shouldered, with a powerfully muscled torso. The medals recorded his triumphs as a wheelchair racer; his personal best for the hundred-meter sprint was eighteen seconds. Work was hard to find, because he had never learned to read or write. His disability payments amounted to about one-third of the average wage, which he supplemented by selling lottery tickets. But the real money came from his racing. A gold medal in a regional competition could be worth several million *dong,* and as his reputation grew, the government rewarded him with a small additional stipend.

Near the medals was an outsize color photograph of Kien, dressed in a shiny blue suit jacket and a red bow tie, and a pretty young woman in a lacy white dress with her head laid on his shoulder. They were seated against a bank of orange chrysanthemums, which signify love, fidelity, and domestic harmony. She was a seamstress in Ho Chi Minh City, a fellow athlete, and they'd met at a racing event. They'd just got married. "We'd love to have children," he said, "but I'm not sure we should take the risk."

Kien's father had fought for years on the Ho Chi Minh Trail. So was that the source of his disabilities? Or were they because his home was a couple of blocks from Bien Hung Lake, where the sediment had been contaminated by runoff from the chemical storage area of the air base? Eating fish from the lake, or the ducks and chickens raised in neighborhood backyards, seemed a plausible path of transmission. His mother had no idea. "We didn't even know that Agent Orange was toxic until 2003," she said. "Before that it was only a rumor."

The Hatfield team had carried out four systematic surveys, finding concentrations of dioxin in the lake sediment twelve times higher than the level regarded as safe. Indeed, the sheer scale of the contamination at Bien Hoa was hard to wrap one's head around. Danang had been the equivalent of what the EPA classifies as a Superfund "mega-site" in the United States, but Bien Hoa was four or five times larger. The volume of soil and sediments to be treated was enough to fill two hundred Olympic-size swimming pools, almost double Hatfield's initial estimate. Most of the dioxin at Danang had been concentrated in a couple of well-defined areas. At Bien Hoa it was dispersed among a slew of locations, spread out over 128 acres.

Lady Borton had identified many of them, first of all working with Le Cao Dai before his death in 2002, and later through conversations with a veteran, Jack McManus, who had served on the base as a Ranch Hand loader and later became president of Vietnam Veterans of America. Some of the contaminated sites were almost perversely random, McManus told her. High-handed commanding officers would assert their authority by ordering soldiers to shunt the barrels of defoliants around in the broiling midday sun, and their passive-aggressive protest was to pierce them "accidentally" with the teeth of their forklifts. Even in 2019, it wasn't certain that all of the contaminated areas had been identified. The footprint of the base had changed slightly since the war, and USAID officials in Hanoi were still asking veterans' groups to search their memories for other sectors that might have been affected.

Bien Hoa was also more challenging than Danang because of its topography. The base was tucked into a bend of the Dong Nai River, and the ground rose gently toward the north side of the runway, which is almost one hundred feet higher. In a notoriously flood-prone city, this was enough during the monsoon season for the runoff to flow downhill from the two most contaminated sections of the base, the hottest spots within the hot spot.

The first of these was designated Z1. This had been the main storage area for the herbicides during wartime, with three large tanks, one each for Agents Orange, Blue, and White. But in the dry language of USAID's final assessment of the contamination, "Because of wartime conditions, demobilization from former Ranch Hand sites (including the air base) was not always undertaken with adequate precautions to minimize impacts to human health or the environment." In an underground concrete sump, one of Hatfield's samples had a jaw-dropping 5.8 million parts per trillion of dioxin. From Z1, the toxin seeped invisibly downslope through drainage ditches into Bien Hung lake and the home neighborhood of the champion wheelchair racer.

At the edge of the base, you could walk up a grassy incline from the busy main road and look over the cement-block perimeter wall. There were a couple of small, muddy lakes on the other side. The same principle applied here as in A Shau and Danang: the most menacing pathway of dioxin into the human body was the fish ponds, only here they were on a vastly greater scale. A propaganda slogan after the war was "Each home, one fish pond, one orchard," and Vietnamese had always taken the pond part seriously. Freshwater fish were a staple of the diet, especially in the low-lying South, with its vast network of waterways, and consumption had risen sharply with Vietnam's growing prosperity.

Aquaculture was big business on the air base. There were more than thirty ponds and lakes of various sizes, and the Ministry of National Defense allowed them to operate freely. For decades they produced about twenty-five tons of fish a year—carp, tilapia, snakehead, and catfish, bottom-feeders that rooted around for food in the dioxin-laden sediment. Some of this harvest was destined for the twelve hundred permanent residents of the base and its thousand part-time workers, and the rest went to local markets.

In 2010, after Hatfield's research showed the gravity of the problem, the military banned fishing and put up warning signs, but enforcement was, to put it generously, spotty. "People still fish," said VAVA's provincial director. "They risk being caught, but they sneak in anyway despite the warnings. The health effects don't show up right away, so they go on eating the fish and say, 'Look, nothing happened to me!'"

People also went on fishing in Bien Hung Lake, which was set in a pleasant little urban park, with half a dozen pink paddleboats in the shape of swans. At one corner, a dirty trickle of water filtered into a concrete-lined ditch from the direction of the Z1 storage area. The government had segregated the most contaminated soil at Z1 in a temporary landfill in 2009, but there were still NO FISHING signs spaced out along the bank.

On the evening before Senator Leahy's party arrived, a family was sprawled on the grass right next to one of them, apparently unconcerned. Two of the boys were wielding cane poles, and a man was yanking out six-inch-long tilapia on a spinning rod and tossing them back. Was he worried about the dioxin? He shook his head and laughed, "Not really. They're just too small to keep."

Hatfield found the worst contamination near the southwestern corner of the base, where in 1971, during Operation Pacer IVY, the unused chemicals were collected before being shipped to Johnston Island for incineration. About eleven thousand fifty-five-gallon barrels had been scrubbed out here, and the herbicides redrummed. The heaviest concentration of dioxin Hatfield found in the soil was almost a million parts per trillion, more than eight hundred times above the level considered safe for industrial land. There were also high levels of arsenic, the distinctive signature of Agent Blue. The plume from the site migrated into a narrow canal that ran down into the Dong Nai River through a neighborhood called Buu Long.

Most people living around the base were smarter these days about what to eat and what to avoid, thanks to the team from the Hanoi School of Public Health that Charles Bailey had funded, following the model he'd established in Danang. A young Hanoi doctor, Tran Thi Tuyet Hanh, had worked on the project. "The importance of the remediation at Bien Hoa is that it will fix the situation inside the air base and prevent any further spread of the dioxin," she said. "But the problem is that it's been spreading for decades now, and we know that it has a very long half-life." It could remain, in other words, in the bodies that had absorbed it, like tar in the lungs of a smoker who quits after a lifetime habit. And people still had to eat. Hanh's team had gone door to door, handing out leaflets and asking residents to fill out questionnaires. They steered people away from free-range chicken and ducks and their eggs, from freshwater fish and aquatic snails and lotus root, but reassured them that it was okay to eat caged poultry, seafood, pork, fruit, and rice. Vegetables were safe, too, as long as people took care to wash them properly. The team followed up later to see how much consumption habits had changed, and the news was encouraging—with one exception, Buu Long.

The problem was that the full extent of the contamination of the canal that ran through the neighborhood wasn't identified until Hatfield and CDM International completed their final report for USAID in 2016. By then, Hanh's team had wrapped up its educational effort in three of the at-risk neighborhoods around the base. The fourth, Buu Long, had fallen through the cracks.

Each new study raised more alarms. The residents of Buu Long not only knew less about the risks and had done less to change their habits; they also had more dioxin in their bodies than their neighbors. The most chilling statistic of all showed how much of it was making its way into their babies. The World Health Organization stipulates a tolerable maximum daily intake of between one and four picograms—one trillionth of a gram—per kilogram of body weight per day. A 2018 study by scientists at the Hanoi Dioxin Laboratory found that the mean intake in breastfed infants in Buu Long was eighty picograms.

The greatest risk was to the firstborn child, because when a mother breastfeeds for the first time, she excretes about half the dioxin in her body into her milk. "So in the first weeks after giving birth we tell women that they should express some of the milk before they feed the baby," Hanh said. But this involved a kind of maternal Russian roulette. "Unless she's one of the few who have been tested it's hard to know whether a particular woman has high levels of dioxin, and the tests are really expensive. And without knowing, how can you tell her not to breastfeed?"

The drainage canal ran for about half a mile from the base through Buu Long before emptying into the river. On this sweltering April afternoon, with the monsoon rains still a couple of weeks away, the canal, which was no more than ten feet wide, was a stagnant greenish-brown murk strewn with garbage and choked in places with water hyacinths. It curved around some showy new mansions with red-tiled roofs, spike-tipped high walls, ornamental palms, and elaborate wrought-iron gates before passing beneath a small bridge. A middle-aged woman was washing her hands and feet in the mucky water at the foot of a short flight of rough stone steps. Outside her neighbor's house, ducks and chickens were poking around in the dirt, and nearby a fisherman, huddled in a bright-blue hoodie as protection from the fierce sun, was sitting on a low wall at the mouth of the canal, where it entered the river.

Next to the bridge there was an ornate Theravada pagoda, an eclectic complex of buildings with colorful murals, bas-relief sculptures, and a twelve-foot-high golden Buddha, in a jumble of styles that made it look as if they'd brought in architects from Thailand and India who'd left their stylistic arguments unresolved. The monk-administrator, a jolly, potbellied man in sweat-soaked saffron robes, was supervising a group of monks refinishing some teak furniture and repairing broken statuary.

"The canal often overflows its banks," he said. "Last time we had a big flood, the water came up to here." He pointed to his waist. "The government put in running water ten years ago, but before that we always used to bathe in the canal, and we drew our water from a well next to it." Asked about the contamination—the sediment in the canal had tested more than twenty times above the safe limit—he looked puzzled. *What contamination?* He'd heard the news about the air base cleanup, but the word *dioxin* was unfamiliar to him.

The problem was that Buu Long didn't yet figure in the remediation plan. The government was planning to evacuate several hundred people from their homes along the canal. Once that was done, the soil could be tested, the houses would be demolished, and the Ministry of National Defense would take charge of the land and fold it into the larger remediation project. This was all news to the monk.

He gestured toward the ostentatious new residences. "I've lived here all my life," he said. "This was all rice paddy when I was a boy. I used to tend the water buffalo here." But speculators had recently moved into the neighborhood and bought up lots for development at knockdown prices, turning huge profits. These houses were only a few months old. He didn't know who the owners were. Outsiders, he thought, maybe from Ho Chi Minh City, maybe foreigners from South Korea or Taiwan. He started to say more but stopped himself. "I'd better not say anything, in case I get in trouble with the government," he said.

But even if there was a plan to clean up Buu Long, the monk couldn't imagine it happening anytime soon. Things like that took a long time. And if the houses were razed, what would become of the pagoda and its golden Buddha? Nonetheless, he smiled. "I'm forty-three now, and in twenty years I'll be dead," he said. "So this dioxin probably won't affect me. But if they don't clean it up, who knows about the next generation?"

Unfinished Business

THE AIR BASE was a bleak place, open and flat and parched under a pitiless sun, with patches of scrubby trees and two long runways that ran parallel for a couple of miles from east to west. It was a world away from the pandemonium of wartime, when more planes had taken off and landed at Bien Hoa each day than at Chicago's O'Hare. At the Pacer IVY site, a stage had been erected under a large awning, flanked by the American and Vietnamese flags. In the front row of seats were U.S. ambassador Dan Kritenbrink and Senator Leahy, the guest of honor, at the head of his delegation of nine senators, seven Democrats and two Republicans. Tim Rieser, was there, and so was Charles Bailey. Chuck Searcy had flown down from Hanoi.

When the speeches were over, the senators lined up at a row of podiums that were joined together by red ribbons. Each of them had been given a pair of scissors, and on the count of five they made the ceremonial snip. Nearby, two yellow backhoes with the clasped-hands insignia of USAID stood ready to scoop up the first symbolic shovelfuls of contaminated dirt.

After the ribbon-cutting, a convoy of minivans whisked everyone off to the five-star Mira Central Park Hotel, the fanciest in town, where the senators mingled with Vietnamese in wheelchairs before going in to the seven-course banquet lunch. Another round of speeches celebrated a new five-year commitment of at least $65 million in U.S. assistance to the severely disabled. Although this was an increase on years past, it seemed relevant to note, at the risk of cynicism, that $65 million was almost exactly the cost, in current dollars, of a single B-52 bomber.

"Cleaning up the hot spots was only the initial step forward on Agent Orange," Bailey said. "It was a means to an end, not the end itself." But this distinction became blurred whenever journalists parachuted in to write about events like the Bien Hoa ceremony. TV reports tended to follow a fixed formula: a grainy shot of the C-123s making their low pass over the forests; the bustling streets of the new, cosmopolitan Vietnam; the beaming faces of children in the orphanages and peace villages. It all made for a simple, stripped-down moral parable. America had done wrong; America had made it right; the story had a happy ending.

Defense Secretary Jim Mattis had said that the Bien Hoa cleanup was "exorcising our last ghosts." But how much truth was there in that? The omission of Buu Long from the cleanup plan was a small but symbolic piece of unfinished business. Forty-four provinces had been defoliated, but humanitarian aid for dioxin-related disabilities was reaching only eight of them.

Many other legacies of the war might never be erased. More was becoming known about the health of those who had served in Vietnam, like a new study of 300,000 veterans that found that those who had been exposed to Agent Orange were almost twice as likely to suffer from dementia. The VA would go on processing claims and paying out benefits for sick veterans until the last of them gave up his dying breath. But many of these claims would be rejected. Alvin Young, "Dr. Orange," the air force toxicologist who had fought any suggestion that exposure to dioxin was a cause of later health problems, had turned his scientific credentials into a lucrative business, earning, in his own words, "a few million dollars" by consulting for the Defense Department and the VA, which often relied on his advice to deny benefits to vets he dismissed as "freeloaders" trying to "cash in" on the compensation program.

As for the Vietnamese, in the neighborhoods east of the Bien Hoa base, which were also not part of the cleanup plan, researchers had found unusually high levels of cancer. According to former Ranch Hand pilot Paul Frederick Cecil, if a C-123 was forced to return to base because of mechanical problems or after being hit by ground fire, it dumped the whole thousand-gallon load just short of the runway. That happened on dozens of occasions. Could that be the reason for the cancer cluster? No one had ever explored the question. Nor had anyone ever studied the long-term health consequences of the arsenical Agent Blue.

The mantra "no man left behind" meant that the costly, painstaking search for the fifteen hundred or so remaining American MIAs would continue indefinitely. The Vietnamese were still looking for theirs too. During the war, there was a small rubber plantation in the same area east of the runway. On the first night of the Tet Offensive, two Viet Cong battalions had surged out from the trees to attack the base. Cobra helicopter gunships had made short work of them, and when it was over, about 150 bodies were buried in a mass grave. The Vietnamese military had searched for them for decades, but the site wasn't identified until 2017, when a former air force MP, Bob Connor, happened to be looking at Google Earth, sifting memories of his time at Bien Hoa, and pinpointed the spot. Seventy-two bodies were eventually recovered, and almost half were positively identified. The remains were returned to the families, finally banishing their fear of unquiet wandering ghosts.

Connor was part of a long tradition in which Bobby Muller's Vietnam Veterans of America, as well as individual vets acting on their own initiative, helped the Vietnamese search for their dead. They offered hand-drawn maps of battlefields and burial sites, turning over the wallets, papers, and photographs they'd taken as souvenirs from the bodies of the dead. PAVN troops were constantly on the move, but there was always someone in each unit who carried a notebook that recorded personnel and deaths. The Pentagon had opened its archives so the Vietnamese could scour the after-action reports looking for further clues, and Ann Mills Griffiths of the League of Families was sympathetic to the effort. Now the initiative had expanded. Leahy and Rieser managed to write an additional $1.5 million into the 2021 Senate appropriations bill to upgrade Vietnam's capacity to carry out DNA analysis of human remains, and in August of that year, during a visit to Hanoi, Secretary of Defense Lloyd Austin signed an agreement that would allow archival and technical experts at Texas Tech and Harvard to give Vietnam the sophisticated digital tools to analyze millions of documents that might yield further data, from declassified military records to tattered scraps of paper found on a fallen soldier's body. These were important gestures of goodwill, though no one really knew how many Vietnamese MIAs remained to be found and identified; the most recent official estimate was 200,000.

The event at Bien Hoa had a scarcely veiled subtext: those who had contributed most to the long postwar reckoning were not getting any younger. Senator Leahy was known as a fitness fanatic; he'd jokingly told a journalist that he would retire only "if I reach the point that I can't go on scuba diving and do my somersaults." The legend was that with each birthday, he went a foot deeper, doing an underwater flip when he reached his target; the depth of his latest dive was seventy-nine feet. But everyone knew that Leahy—who had entered the Senate in 1974, the last remaining member of the generation elected during the war in Vietnam—wouldn't be around forever, and indeed he announced his retirement in 2022. The other eight senators on his delegation to Bien Hoa were mainly in their sixties, so it had the flavor of an audition, preparation for a passing of the baton.

Charles Bailey was also in his seventies now, and it was almost twenty years since he'd begun his collaboration with the 10-80 Committee and Hatfield Consultants on their hot spot study, which finally disconnected the third rail of Agent Orange. But the wheels of politics and bureaucracy turned at an excruciating crawl. There was still no single hub in Washington where all the work on the herbicides could be pulled together. This made no sense to Bailey, since the Pentagon office charged with the ongoing search for MIAs and the State Department's Office of Weapons Removal and Abatement, which dealt with unexploded ordnance, had both been created decades earlier.

After Hatfield presented the report on A Luoi to Ambassador Peterson, it had taken seven years to get the United States to do something concrete to address the problem, a further seven before work on the Danang airport began, three more to complete it, another two until the ribbon-cutting ceremony at Bien Hoa. If all went according to plan, the project would be finished by 2030, sixty years after the Z1 and Pacer IVY sites were contaminated.

No one really knew how much the cleanup would cost in the end. The initial estimate was $390 million, but USAID allowed for a 75 percent overrun in modeling its project budgets, so that could bring it up to $682 million. Given how far the original estimates for Danang had fallen short, some even thought Bien Hoa might end up topping $1 billion. And though it was the right thing to do, and some benefits would flow to people in the surrounding neighborhoods, the more politically significant beneficiary was the People's Air Force and the squadron of advanced long-range Sukhoi SU-330MKK attack aircraft based in Bien Hoa to protect Vietnam's sovereign interests in the East Sea.

Wayne Dwernychuk, Hatfield's main dioxin expert, was retired now. He lived on Vancouver Island, at the edge of a lovely provincial park that looked out across the Strait of Georgia. He drove around in a black Toyota with a vanity license plate that said DIOXIN and continued to offer advice to vets trying to get Agent Orange–related disability payments from the VA. He had spent a good chunk of his retirement funds on a roomful of classic and custom-built guitars. One of these, a Martin acoustic of his own design, was incised with the words DUTY HONOR COUNTRY and dedicated to the veterans. He had commissioned a limited edition, with all proceeds from the sale going to Guitars for Vets, a volunteer organization that provided guitars and lessons to veterans. "The pain of our Vietnam veterans has become his pain," said retired Lt. Col. James Zumwalt—son of Adm. Elmo Zumwalt—who had served as a company commander in Vietnam with the 1/4 Marines, Manus Campbell's old outfit.

Chris Hatfield himself was also long retired and was living on Salt Spring Island, a short ferry ride from Vancouver, where he shared a house with Tom Boivin, Boivin's Lao wife, and their three children. Boivin now ran his own consulting firm, and in his spare time he hosted a weekly classic rock show on the local community radio station.

Lady Borton was just two years younger than Leahy, though her energy seemed undiminished. The COVID pandemic would make it impossible for her to get back to Vietnam for more than two years, and while she fretted to return she immersed herself in her literary and historical pursuits, revising her biography of Ho Chi Minh and editing Vietnamese manuscripts for American publishers: the memoirs of Ho, Giap, and Madame Nguyen Thi Binh, the former foreign minister of the Provisional Revolutionary Government, now in her nineties; and a collection of letters by men and women who had been active in the French and American wars.

The veterans too were all in their seventies. Chuck Searcy was about to celebrate a quarter-century since his return to Vietnam, and he seemed a little weary, his hair a little whiter. Project RENEW was in excellent hands, with its all-Vietnamese staff, and he'd begun to wonder if he might go back home one day, sit on the porch of the house he still owned in Athens, Georgia, and watch another UGA Bulldogs game. Yes, he agreed, a lot had been accomplished, and perhaps he'd been fortunate enough to play a small part—his modesty was invariable. But even if Quang Tri, the most heavily bombed place in history, had become a model for the world, there was so much still to be done in all the other provinces that had suffered.

Some vets, like Manus Campbell, had come a long way toward healing their psychic wounds from the war, but many others still carried the burden. The next generation, those who'd served in the War on Terror, had to wrestle with their own demons. Searcy worried that the larger lessons of the American war in Southeast Asia had never been absorbed, that his country still seemed too often heedless of John Quincy Adams's famous injunction, "[America] goes not abroad in search of monsters to destroy."

He took comfort, however, in knowing that some of the children of the Vietnam veterans were taking up the torch. As people milled about after the ribbon-cutting ceremony in Bien Hoa, there were celebratory hugs and handshakes for an American woman in her mid-fifties, Susan Hammond. She'd just received Vietnam's Friendship Medal, its highest award to foreigners, joining a select group of Americans that included Searcy himself, Borton, Bailey, and Ted Osius, the first U.S. ambassador to receive the honor.

Hammond was an army brat, born at Camp Drum in upstate New York. In the late 1950s, the base had a vexing problem: the artillery range was littered with unexploded shells that couldn't be easily removed because of an obstinate four-square-mile stand of sugar maples. So the army sprayed them with a new, experimental defoliant, a mixture of two chemicals called 2,4-D and 2,4,5-T, that later would be known as Agent Purple, then as Agent Orange. The exercise was a great success, and the army noted that the defoliant had great potential for future military use.

Hammond's father, Prentice, was an army engineer. In 1967 he was sent to Vietnam, the first of two tours. At home in Vermont, her brothers dug out a replica of the famous Cu Chi tunnels on the sandy hillside behind the family farmhouse, with a chicken coop doing service as a Vietnamese hooch. Their father got on the phone as soon as he heard about it, the only time he was ever known to call home. *I'll give you twenty-four hours to fill that in, or I'll get on the first plane home and whup your asses.*

Posted to Saigon, Prentice Hammond oversaw facilities for the twenty thousand American and allied troops stationed there, an expansive job description that included making arrangements for the USO Christmas concert by Bob Hope that Chuck Searcy attended. During the Tet Offensive, Hammond was in a jeep near the Saigon racetrack when the vehicle ahead of him exploded and a chunk of shrapnel landed at his feet. "That almost left your mother a widow with seven kids," he told them later.

His second tour took him to Danang in 1970, the first full year of Vietnamization. He was in charge of maintaining all the roads and bridges in I Corps, as well as transferring base facilities to ARVN. Having won three Bronze Stars for meritorious service, he retired as a lieutenant colonel. He became the town manager of Chester, Vermont, a popular local figure who tapped the sugar maples on his land, hunted, fished, golfed, and played poker with his friends at the American Legion. He never spoke about the war. When he developed Parkinson's disease in 2011, he was reluctant to approach the VA for benefits, even though it was on the list of diseases associated with dioxin exposure. The money should go to others more deserving. But Susan leaned on him. His state pension would end after his death, but the VA benefits would continue to go to his widow.

Susan Hammond's passion for Vietnam began in 1991, when she and her sister took off on a round-the-world bike tour. They traveled from Ho Chi Minh City as far north as Hue, part of the first influx of tourists. She struggled to absorb the kaleidoscopic images of bomb craters, amputees, and kids grubbing for scraps in polluted canals. She ended up spending three months in Southeast Asia, her mind spinning with questions: *How does a country recover from war? Is there a role for me here?*

After that first trip, Vietnam consumed her. As the two countries took tentative steps to talk to each other about the past and the present, and how one might shape the other, she went back to graduate school to gain a deeper understanding of the economic reforms, then lived for a year and a half in Ho Chi Minh City, time enough to master the difficult language. She abandoned thoughts of a Ph.D. and took a job with the U.S.-Indochina Reconciliation Project, an outgrowth of the American Friends Service Committee, which put her in a direct line of succession to the work that Lady Borton and her AFSC colleagues had done earlier in Vietnam.

Over the next decade she commuted back and forth to Vietnam, as well as spending long periods in Laos and Cambodia. She became deputy director of the Fund for Reconciliation and Development, the project's new incarnation, working on a string of conferences where the web of connections between Americans and their Southeast Asian counterparts wove itself tighter. In the process she moved steadily closer to the center of the Venn diagram that brought together Borton, Searcy, Bailey, the Hatfield scientists, and Jacqui Chagnon and her husband, the theologian Roger Rumpf, who had for years run AFSC's postwar program in Laos.

The currents of conversation pushed her steadily closer to the problem of Agent Orange. Wayne Dwernychuk showed up for one of the conferences, at Yale, fresh from wrapping up Hatfield's study of the A Luoi Valley. Le Cao Dai of the 10-80 Committee came to another, and in Hanoi he introduced her to Maj. Gen. Nguyen Don Tu, who had been a battalion commander under General Giap at Dien Bien Phu and fought on the DMZ during the American War. Now he had a daughter who was severely disabled with cerebral palsy.

Hammond resolved that Agent Orange would be the main focus of her work. When VAVA filed its lawsuit against the chemical companies in New York in 2003, she learned how to work the press as journalists struggled to navigate an issue that many still saw as something that afflicted only American veterans. After Charles Bailey came back to the United States, she worked closely with him on the periodic reports for his "Track-II diplomacy" with the Dialogue Group on Agent Orange.

One day in 2007, out of the blue, she got a call from the wife of a vet named Bob Feldman, who had served with the Army Signal Corps at Bien Hoa and knew of chemical spills at the base that had not been officially recorded. Now he was dying of lymphoma, one of the diseases on the VA's dioxin list. He had saved about $40,000 from his disability pension and wanted it to go to Vietnam. When he died, his wife, Nancy, offered to add her widow's benefits.

The Feldmans' gift, along with a grant from the small Chino-Cienaga Foundation in California, a major backer of Project RENEW in Quang Tri, allowed Hammond to strike out on her own and found a new organization, which she called the War Legacies Project. It was a one-woman operation, run out of the old family farmhouse near the covered bridge in Bartonsville, Vermont, where she also served on the town select board and continued her father's tradition of making maple syrup.

In Vietnam, she collaborated with the forester Phung Tuu Boi on his project to plant a protective barrier of honey locust trees around the dioxin hot spot at the A Shau base. She funded a small physical therapy project in nearby Nam Dong, site of another frontier outpost of the Green Berets. But mainly she concentrated on the kind of direct aid that Project RENEW was offering in Quang Tri, where a few hundred dollars—a wheelchair ramp, a course of vocational training, a water buffalo, or a brood cow—could transform a family's life. Much of her work was in the hilly backcountry of Quang Nam. By the time she received the Friendship Medal in 2019, she'd contributed almost half a million dollars and was famous in the province for what people called the "Feldman cows."

Hammond had always kept in frequent touch with Jacqui Chagnon, and after Roger Rumpf died of leukemia in 2013, she suggested that Chagnon should become the chair of the War Legacies Project. They mulled over a new initiative, one that involved arguably the biggest of all the loose ends of the war, one of its most closely guarded secrets, forgotten even by the few people who had known about it in the first place.

After the symposium in Washington, she had talked about this idea with Tim Rieser. "Why are we doing nothing about the legacy of Agent Orange in Laos?" she asked him.

His answer was simple. "Because we don't know anything about it, and in any case we couldn't do anything unless the Lao government asked us to."

Hammond's reply was equally straightforward: "We're working on it. We'll let you know what we find."

Turning the Ho Chi Minh Trail Brown

Susan hammond's conversation with Tim Rieser actually posed two separate challenges. One was to document the magnitude of the secret spraying of Laos. The other was to find evidence of its long-term impact.

Early in 1966, an indiscreet official in Saigon had said that the United States was "turning the Ho Chi Minh Trail brown," and Ambassador William Sullivan, the "field marshal" of the war in Laos, thought this would require "massive amounts" of herbicides. But what did that mean exactly?

Congress had first asked questions about the defoliation of Laos in a closed-door hearing in late 1969. The Military Assistance Command, Vietnam gave lawmakers a classified summary of 434 sorties, which might have added up to a little more than 400,000 gallons. The first mission MACV acknowledged was in December 1965, the last in September 1969. Later, the Pentagon's Environmental Support Group gave details of a few more flights as late as October 1970.

Earlier that year, CIA director Richard Helms had sent Henry Kissinger guidance on what to say in case further inconvenient questions were asked about Laos.

Question 21: "Have we ever conducted defoliation operations in Laos?"

The Delphic answer: "So far as we are aware, the answer to this question is defensively 'no.' "

There matters rested until 1982, when a lawsuit by the National Veterans Task Force on Agent Orange, brought under the Freedom of Information Act, forced the air force to release the draft of its official history of Ranch Hand, with one twenty-page segment denied. Jacqui Chagnon and Roger Rumpf asked the author, William Buckingham, whether he planned to include anything on Laos. He told them he wasn't authorized to discuss the subject; the records were still classified. But after pressure from members of Congress, the published report contained a brief three-page summary of the campaign, with a half-page chronology, roughly matching what MACV had said thirteen years earlier. The only official comment was a statement from William Westmoreland, saying he knew nothing about the defoliation of Laos, even though he was the one who had authorized it.

Meanwhile the former Ranch Hand pilot Paul Frederick Cecil was interviewing former comrades for a book of his own. They all agreed that missions in Laos had been unusually challenging. Often the targets were on higher ground than in Vietnam, with high winds increasing the risk that the chemicals would drift miles from the location that was being sprayed. Since so many of the targets were invisible, the Ranch Hand pilots had to devise imaginative new techniques like dropping smoke grenades whenever they spotted a short section of open road and then joining up the dots by educated guesswork. The threat from the ferocious antiaircraft defenses on the Trail only added to the daredevil aura the pilots cultivated.

The original transcripts of Cecil's interviewees reveal details that never saw the light of day, accounts of many missions that went unrecorded, including flights that took off from air bases in Thailand. More intriguing still, several pilots spoke about another of the lingering mysteries of the war—the defoliation of neutral Cambodia. Cecil's book said not a word about this.

The government in Phnom Penh had accused the United States of using herbicides as early as 1964, but the only definitive evidence was the unexplained spraying of rubber plantations in Kampong Cham, across the border from Vietnam's Tay Ninh province, in 1969. A team of four government scientists inspected the site later that year, but the air force denied involvement, which left the CIA as the only plausible suspect. But at least five Ranch Hand pilots described missions they'd flown over Cambodia. Lowell Thomas, who was stationed in Danang in 1965–66, told Cecil that "ninety percent of all our sorties there were run in Laos and northern Cambodia. Primarily the Ho Chi Min [*sic*] Trail and the Sianook [*sic*] Road in northern Cambodia." Cambodia was "spookier," said Charles Hubbs, who also flew sorties over both countries at around the same time. "When we first got there, we didn't exist. We worked for the ambassador. We had no identification on us. If we went down they would not acknowledge us."

No further information on Laos came to light until 1999, when Chagnon and Rumpf went to a pool party in Vientiane with U.S. ambassador Wendy Chamberlin. The families were friends; Miranda Rumpf and Chamberlin's daughter were high-school classmates. The ambassador was on her way to Washington. Was there anything they needed? Yes, Rumpf said, you can get the data on the air force bombing of Laos—which she did, in time for Bill Clinton's visit to Vientiane the following year. While you're at it, said Chagnon, never one to be shy, how about the records on Agent Orange?

Once these were released, the numbers gradually edged upward. Jeanne Stellman's database documented 210 missions in Laos, accounting for about 470,000 gallons, although she acknowledged that her data might be incomplete. "I'm sure many of the records on Laos are missing," she said, "and my understanding is that the guys who were assigned to missions there were sworn to secrecy."

In 2002 a young researcher with the Fund for Reconciliation and Development, Andrew Wells-Dang, probed further. Hammond, who was now the group's deputy director, had conferences coming up at Yale and in Sweden. She was hoping some Lao and Cambodians would attend, and Wells-Dang's research was part of that effort. Burying himself away in the National Archives, he dug out a good number of official documents, including much of the classified correspondence between Sullivan and the State Department. He estimated that more than half a million gallons had been sprayed in Laos, though his findings never circulated widely beyond the fund's small newsletter.

Tom Boivin, too, found his attention turning to Laos, wondering, as Hatfield wrapped up its research in the A Luoi Valley, whether the same problem might exist on the other side of the border. With only a tiny community of expats in Laos, he soon encountered Chagnon and Rumpf, introduced to them by the ubiquitous Lady Borton. Before long he had put down more personal roots, opening a small Hatfield office in Vientiane, buying a house there, and marrying the daughter of a Lao security official.

Chagnon and Rumpf opened the door to some sympathetic low-level government officials, who listened as Boivin described Hatfield's work in Vietnam. Why no one had ever tried to do something similar in Laos was something of a mystery, since the secret had been hiding in plain sight for half a century, like the purloined letter of the war. But for journalists, Vietnam had always been the main event, Laos a side-show. After 1975 the country slipped off the radar altogether, and no one was inclined to devote much energy to anecdotal reports from an obscure, forgotten country by a couple of young American aid workers who had opposed the war. For firsthand accounts of the spraying, you had to look to the memoirs of Le Cao Dai or unpublished Vietnamese histories of the Ho Chi Minh Trail. In the scant English-language literature on the Trail and the war in Laos, it was impossible to find any meaningful reference to the herbicides.

But there were also more consequential reasons for this culture of silence. In 1993, when the United States finally agreed to deal with the legacy of the war in Laos, the massive problem of unexploded ordnance pushed aside all other issues. Thanks in good part to the work of Chagnon and Rumpf, Laos, saturated with cluster bombs, became a poster child for the global UXO crisis. Emerging from two decades of crippling poverty, the government was happy to accept the infusion of support that began to flow through Senator Leahy's War Victims Fund, which over the next quarter-century amounted to more than $230 million. But it had no real incentive to raise the fraught issue of Agent Orange at a time when it still poisoned relations between the United States and Vietnam.

Where Vietnam was concerned, the magnitude of the impact of Agent Orange made the issue impossible to ignore, and the Vietnamese pushed it aggressively. "The Vietnamese die of persistence," Chagnon said. "The Lao die of pride."

In the United States, it was veterans' political influence that forced the government to grapple with their rage. None of this applied to Laos. The mountainous border areas along the Trail had been controlled by the North Vietnamese, and no sick Royal Lao Army soldiers were clamoring for attention. There was no flood of refugees to the cities. The Americans who fought there had done so in secret. If they came to harm, their families were told it had happened in Vietnam.

The ethnic minorities of the Truong Son range, which the Lao call Phou Luang, were the poorest people in Laos, cut off from the rest of society by barriers of geography, language, culture, and racial prejudice. Their homeland remained largely inaccessible. These were the conditions that had allowed the Trail to exist in the first place, and they were what kept its people in isolation when the war was over. The Pacoh and the Katu, the Ta Oi and the Bru in Laos remained, as they always had been, out of sight and out of mind.

The first niche Tom Boivin saw for himself was when Laos signed on to the Stockholm Convention on Persistent Organic Pollutants, the "forever chemicals." Like every signatory, Laos was obliged to report on sources of dioxin contamination in its national territory. "It was challenging to explain the basics of sampling to Lao scientists," Boivin said. "The level of technical competence was very low." So in 2005 he took on the task himself, with a modest grant from the United Nations Industrial Development Organization (UNIDO). There wasn't much to report; the country had almost no trace of dioxin other than from forest fires and some Soviet-financed steel and cement plants. The only industry of note was the celebrated Beerlao factory.

As an appendix to his report, Boivin synthesized the data from the HERBS tapes into the most coherent list yet of the missions over Laos and their locations. He came up with a more precise figure: 527,345 gallons. But that was clearly not the whole story, and the treasure house of declassified documents on the war at Texas Tech University and in the National Archives revealed more.

Three CIA aerial surveillance photos, for example, showed PAVN installations around Xepon between November 1964 and January 1965; attached notes said they were visible only because the area had been defoliated. This was a full year before the acknowledged start of the campaign in Laos. A document from August 1969, prepared for a meeting with "SEACORD"—presumably Maj. Richard Secord, who was detailed from the air force to the CIA during the secret war and later became notorious for his role in the Iran-Contra affair—listed several big missions that didn't appear in the HERBS tapes. Involving as many as seven "ships" at a time, they probably accounted for at least another thirty thousand gallons.

There were also scattered reports of sorties in 1971 by C-123s whose only documented purpose was listed as "defoliation," and of smaller T-28 and F-4 aircraft being fitted out experimentally for spraying. Unpublished North Vietnamese diaries described the spraying of the PAVN's Base Area 611 on dates that didn't match the official records.

Another classified air force report on the first intense burst of defoliation at the end of 1965 and in early 1966 gave numbers higher than Boivin had found, but more than that, they showed that the earliest missions, targeting the critical section of the Trail between La Hap and the A Shau Valley, had used the highly toxic Agent Purple, which had been abandoned in Vietnam more than a year earlier. The average concentration of TCDD in Purple was about three times higher than the level in Orange.

Moreover Boivin, like Jeanne Stellman, was convinced that the CIA, whose records have never been declassified, had also used herbicides in Laos. This conviction seemed to be borne out by one of the few journalists to venture there during the war, Jacques Decornoy, a reporter for *Le Monde*. An American official he interviewed in 1968 told him that Air America, the CIA's passenger and cargo airline, had been contracted by the Defense Department to conduct defoliation in Vietnam, Laos, and even Thailand.

Hammond had contacted surviving veterans of Air America to see if they would say more, but their lips were still sealed. One told her that he had been obliged to sign a fifty-year nondisclosure agreement. "It makes no sense," she said, exasperated. "I mean, it's been fifty years, let's just come clean." Perhaps another Freedom of Information Act request would shake something loose.

Putting all the numbers together, 600,000 gallons seemed a more than conservative estimate of the volume of herbicides that rained down on the Ho Chi Minh Trail in Laos. That amount might sound trivial compared to the 20 million gallons that were used in South Vietnam, but the comparison was misleading. The campaign in Laos was compressed in time and space. More than ten thousand square miles were sprayed in Vietnam; in Laos, the Tiger Hound and Ranch Hand missions were tightly focused on long, five-hundred-meter-wide sections of the Trail and surrounding crop fields. More chemicals were sprayed on this narrow border strip than on the A Shau Valley in seven and a half years, and that was one of the most important targets in Vietnam. During just the first three months of the campaign in Laos, at least 150,000 gallons hit the Trail in Savannakhet and Salavan. The intensity of the defoliation was comparable to anything that was happening at the time in Vietnam, where the escalation of Operation Ranch Hand had just begun.

Boivin wondered if there might be hot spots in Laos like the one Hatfield had found at A Shau. After all, he reasoned, in addition to the heavy spraying of the border area, the CIA was known to have operated hundreds of secret bases, many with primitive airstrips and a few bigger ones that could be used by jets and cargo planes. It made sense that some might have been used for herbicide flights and chemical storage, and as Lady Borton said, it was standard practice in Vietnam to spray the perimeter of facilities like these to keep down vegetation. So Boivin followed his hunch.

Traveling in the southern panhandle was close to impossible in those days: driving to the border villages from the nearest airport took two days on some of the worst roads in the world. "I spent three weeks in Savannakhet and Salavan and Sekong provinces, knowing that I was looking for a needle in a haystack," Boivin said. But chance took a hand, near a small village in Sekong called Dak Triem.

On the outskirts of the village, Boivin noticed a strikingly flat strip of land. He asked around, seeking out village elders with long memories. Yes, they said, there had once been an air base there—Javan. The Americans had used it, as well as the Royal Lao Air Force, and before them the French. The elders told him that after the American War, like all the locals, they had gone out in search of scrap metal. They'd found some old barrels, painted with an orange stripe. "They had no reason to tell me fables," Boivin said. "They'd never heard of Agent Orange, they had no idea what the barrels were, they were just scavenging."

He took a few samples of the soil and of fish tissue from a pond. "After working in A Luoi we knew what we were looking for," he said. "At the end of the runway, we got one hit, a spot with high levels of TCDD, which could only have come from Agent Orange." Villagers told him that there was also an airplane crash site close to the village, and he flagged that for later inspection.

He came back three years later with a team of Japanese scientists, and they took more samples. "It is likely that this site has much higher contamination in some areas and should be investigated further," he wrote in his report. But that never happened; he could never find anyone to put up the money for the kind of sophisticated dioxin analysis that would be needed. Once again the borderlands of Laos slipped off everyone's radar, a forgotten sideshow to a largely forgotten war.

Technically at least, the Lao government knew about the defoliation, because Boivin had included the basic information in the three reports he wrote over a ten-year period. In the first of them, he'd appended a small-print spreadsheet listing all the known flights. In the second, completed in 2009, he elaborated on what he'd found at the Javan base. Susan Hammond worked closely with him on the third report, which he submitted to the government in 2015. The purpose of this one, which drew on aerial remote sensing and was financed in part by the European Space Agency, was to identify possible public health risks from the combination of UXO and residual dioxin. This time Boivin put the full six-year chronology of the flights over Laos into an easily digestible table, and Hammond's research added a list of more than five hundred secret CIA bases, singling out twenty-seven where there was a significant likelihood of dioxin contamination.

But all this work vanished into the bureaucratic ether. This might have seemed startling, since Boivin was presenting previously unknown data. But his reports went to midlevel officials in a scientific agency that Hammond called a "poor stepchild" of the Lao government. To be fair, Boivin said, they weren't obligated to do anything with his findings, and he had no authority to release the reports himself.

An American diplomat who had served as deputy chief of mission in Laos said she wasn't surprised by the inertia. This was just how things worked there. "We always used to say there was Third World time, and then there was Lao time," she explained. "Midlevel bureaucrats don't see any personal stake for themselves in doing anything on something like this. Only people at the highest levels of government will consider or speak about controversial topics."

Boivin concluded that there wasn't much more he could do. "One thing we always learned at Hatfield," he said, "is go high or go home."

But there was a deeper reason why the reports failed to gain traction: they filled in only half the puzzle. Yes, Boivin had estimated the huge volume of herbicides that had been sprayed in Laos. He'd found a single likely hot spot and warned there might be more. He and Hammond had pointed to the potential health risks. But they'd never set out to document how many people in the sprayed areas were sick, or what diseases they suffered from, or how much dioxin they had in their bodies, or how this might be related to the locations that had been defoliated. This was the research that had finally forced the United States to take responsibility for its actions in Vietnam. Absent this kind of data, the Lao government had no particular incentive to demand action on what might have seemed little more than an abstract set of statistics about a remote place and a faraway time.

The task that Hammond set herself was to flesh out the missing half of the puzzle, to show the lasting impact of the defoliation of Laos and to count its victims. Chagnon and Rumpf had toyed with this idea for a long time, but everything was put on hold with the onset of his final illness. After his death in 2013, Hammond revived the plan. "I think it was Jacqui's way of honoring Roger's memory," she said.

It didn't happen overnight. The War Legacies Project needed permissions from the national, provincial, and district governments, and those negotiations proceeded on Lao time. The research began in earnest only in 2017, and the following February Hammond signed a three-year memorandum of understanding to make it official.

"When we started out, I told American officials what we were doing, and that we had no idea what we would find," she said. "In fact, I hoped we would find nothing." But as it turned out, they found a lot.

The Pocket of Fire

L AOS STILL SEEMED SUSPENDED between two worlds. The dusty, unvisited national museum in Vientiane, housed in the former mansion of the colonial governor, displayed faded photographs of Pathet Lao war heroes, hair-raising paintings of French soldiers tossing babies into a well, a life-size statue of Lenin, and a portrait of the bearded father of Communism, labeled "Mr. Kakmak, the politician, economy, leadership revolution of international worker." The city's gloriously ornate *wats,* which saw few tourists, were decorated with murals of the Buddhist Hell—wrongdoers cast into pits of fire, beheaded and disemboweled, hung upside down and spit-roasted, as lurid as anything dreamed up by Hieronymus Bosch. Yet at dusk, hanggliders soared and swooped over the Mekong, and a banner over the entrance to the posh new Crowne Plaza Hotel advertised its Senses Day Spa, "A Secluded Haven of Wellness and Pampering."

Upcountry Laos, like Vietnam, was monetizing its extraordinary natural beauty. Since the late 1990s, backpackers had beaten a well-traveled trail from Vientiane to the old royal capital of Luang Prabang and the sleepy town of Vang Vieng, where they zipped up and down on motorbikes on the old runway that had once been the CIA's Lima Site 6, and drifted down the Nam Song River in float tubes with a Beerlao in one hand and a spliff in the other.

There were more and more Chinese tour groups now, and Chinese money was everywhere. The road from Vientiane's tiny airport into town was lined with billboards advertising Chinese steel and cement companies. China held almost half the nation's public debt and was financing hydropower projects on tributaries of the Mekong that would supposedly turn Laos into "the battery of Southeast Asia." By the end of 2021, a high-speed cross-border rail link would fold the landlocked country into China's Belt and Road Initiative.

At the Lao Development Center for Disabled Women in the village of Thanalang, on a bend in the river on the outskirts of Vientiane, a group of girls were measuring out dress patterns around a long table. In another room, several older women were seated at hand looms, weaving the traditional Lao skirt, the *sinh*. Two teenage girls had just had surgery to repair their cleft lips, one of the most common birth defects associated with exposure to dioxin. They stood shy and solemn-faced, getting used to the possibility of smiling. They were from villages close to the Vietnamese border, one on either side of the old Road B45, the section of the Ho Chi Minh Trail that led to the A Shau Valley. In the older girl's village, a week-old infant had recently died after being born with all its intestines hanging loose outside its body.

Off in a corner was a seventeen-year-old Ta Oi girl named Yen Ly Vongkansa. She had a radiant smile and lustrous black hair teased up in a whimsical topknot. She was sitting next to her wheelchair with one toothpick leg splayed out in an unnatural direction at the knee and the other encased in a brace after surgery to straighten her ankle. It was a severe case of arthrogryposis, another condition linked to dioxin exposure. But although her hands bent inward at right angles from the wrist, she had mastered cross-stitch, and her work was sold at the center's small gift shop, which earned her a modest stipend, enough to cover food, clothes, and a rented room.

Yen was entitled to five days of annual leave, and she was due to set off the next morning to see her family for the first time in two years. Her village, Pasia, was just a couple of miles from La Hap, the forward command headquarters of the Ho Chi Minh Trail.

Hammond and Chagnon were planning to accompany Yen to Pasia, together with Niphaphone Sengthong, a retired Lao schoolteacher and Ministry of Education official with a sly sense of humor and a shrewd understanding of the opaque workings of the government bureaucracy. She was Chagnon's neighbor in Vientiane, their adjacent wooden homes commanding glorious sunset views across the Mekong to Thailand. The three women made up the entire staff of Hammond's War Legacies Project. Sengthong was based permanently in Vientiane. Chagnon divided her time between Laos and the United States, and Hammond generally came over a couple of times a year.

The plan to document the extent of disabilities and birth defects in villages along the most heavily sprayed section of the Ho Chi Minh Trail had begun to take shape in 2014. It hadn't really been feasible until then, given the primitive state of the roads in the southern panhandle, but now there were paved highways connecting the provincial capitals and dirt roads to many of the villages that were passable during the dry season. Taking Yen home would be part of a nine-day journey down the Trail from the seventeenth parallel to the Vietnamese border at the head of the A Shau.

Next morning, at the Vientiane airport, Sengthong helped Yen swivel into her wheelchair. "Time to rock and roll," she said—a phrase she'd picked up from Tom Boivin. The girl was fretful, because the trip home involved a ninety-minute flight followed by a long, tiring drive into the mountains. She'd been on an airplane once before, and it frightened her out of her wits. She'd sat in the back row screaming, "I'm going to die, I'm going to die!" When the plane landed, a distinguished-looking elderly gentleman in an adjacent row turned to comfort her. "I'm glad you didn't die. You're too pretty to die young." The man was Thongloun Sisoulith, the future president.

Yen was anxious about going home for another reason too. She worried about what kind of reception she would get from her family. After all, she said, because of her deformities, her mother had wanted to kill her at birth.

The two main sections of the Trail that entered Laos from Quang Binh province converged a couple of miles north of the seventeenth parallel, and in the nearby village of Ban Phoukham the women stopped at the home of an elderly man named Suly Volaboud. He said he'd often seen the C-123s, sometimes flying right over the village and other times going back and forth over what he called the "gold mountain." This was a few miles away on the outskirts of the small town of Vilabouly, capital of one of the three districts in Savannakhet province that the War Legacies Project had surveyed. There was a big open-pit gold and copper mine there, formerly owned by Australians until it was sold to a Chinese company. The roads to the mine were chewed up by heavy trucks and earth-moving equipment, and the tailing pits were stained aquamarine and pea-green with chemicals. Chagnon said the Australians had always been very cooperative with UXO removal, but that had changed since the Chinese arrived.

It was always hard to judge how reliable people's memories were of events that had happened so long ago, and even to know with certainty how old people had been at the time. An old man in one village said he was 109. A wizened old Ta Oi woman said she was fifty. Asked how long she'd lived in her present home, she said sixty years. But when Suly Volaboud gave his age as sixty-six, there seemed no reason to doubt him or the clarity of his memories. He remembered distinctly that the spraying over the gold mountain had begun in 1966, because it was the year before he'd married, at the age of fourteen. As far as it went, that matched the official records, which showed four missions around Ban Phoukham that year. His account suggested, however, that this was far from the whole story. Four flights was not an inconsequential number, but he insisted that there were many more—about ten flights a month over a three-month period. It was the first of several lucid accounts from village elders that cast doubt on the completeness of the Ranch Hand records.

Hammond, Chagnon, and Sengthong had dropped in on the old man because they wanted to check up on his son Bounyan, who was on the list they had been compiling of people with disabilities that might be attributable to Agent Orange. They found Bounyan hunched over a table by the window, silently ironing a length of cloth. Despite his deformities, he had found work as a tailor. Volaboud counted off a list of his eleven children, all of them delivered in a birthing hut in the forest, which was the way of the Bru, the ethnic group to which he belonged. The first, born in wartime, had strangely shaped arms and legs, all curves and bends, and he had died. Another had no visible deformities but passed away at the age of ten. A third child was paralyzed and had feet that flopped as if they had no muscles; this one lived for only two months. Five other pregnancies had ended in miscarriages or stillbirths. That left two healthy survivors and Bounyan the tailor.

Volaboud had never connected these events to the white spray from the airplanes, and there were no doctors or hospitals to explain the disasters that had befallen the family; he and his wife sacrificed a pig each time, to appease the angry spirits.

During his 1968 visit, Jacques Decornoy of *Le Monde* recorded a startling conversation with an American diplomat. He asked the man what future prospects he saw for Laos; the reply was, "For this country finally to make some progress, everything would have to be leveled. The inhabitants would have to be reduced to zero." It was like the famous line from Vietnam about destroying the town in order to save it, but on a nationwide scale.

On the road south from Vilabouly, which followed the main axis of the Ho Chi Minh Trail, the evidence of that intent was everywhere. Fifty years on, this was still a landscape made by war. The burned-out tanks and trucks and artillery pieces had finally been cleared away, destined for the scrapyards or museums, or bought up by itinerant Thai dealers for the export market. But the road itself was a kind of museum, a living archive of the war, in which its remnants and relics had been absorbed into the fabric of everyday life.

There were bomb craters everywhere. The thousand-pounders from B-52 strikes had left holes in which you could have buried a two-story house. In someone's front yard, there was a fishing boat at least thirty feet long, made, by the look of it, from the entire fuselage of a Phantom or a Thunderchief, with the addition of blue-painted wooden gunwales and cross-struts for seats. Rusted *bom bi* mother pods did service as vegetable planters or substituted for wooden stilts to support the thatched huts that stored rice, frustrating the claws of hungry rats.

Hammond's team stopped in one roadside hamlet to check on the health of a sad-eyed young man in a broken tricycle wheelchair. Nearby, two boys played war games, dodging in and out between the bomb-stilts of a storage hut with AK-47s made from green stalks of bamboo, rearing back and aiming at the sky and looking for all the world like North Vietnamese antiaircraft gunners. One of the olive-green cluster bomb pods still bore the faded imprint of its serial number and loading date in 1972.

By the end of that year more than 400 million *bom bi* had been dropped on Laos along with some 11 million larger explosives. These numbers were not casual estimates: the air force kept meticulous records of every bombing mission, and eventually these were made public. Between 1964 and 1973, U.S. aircraft flew 580,344 sorties over Laos, which averaged out to one every eight minutes, twenty-four hours a day, for nine years.

The town of Xepon had been rebuilt from scratch since the war. It was a grubby, featureless place on Route 9, the main road to Quang Tri, with an early-morning market where you could buy fresh baguettes and black and pink sticky rice charcoal-grilled in banana leaves, and a guesthouse where a Swedish bomb disposal specialist and a Lao official were working their way through a bottle of Johnnie Walker. Old Xepon was a mile or two away, and almost nothing remained of it after the 1971 ARVN invasion but a pagoda where the monks ate their meals off aluminum trays made from airplane parts and had yet to finish patching the big bullet holes. The building had been spared only by chance; there was a big bomb crater just a few yards from the entrance, next to a row of tombs and a golden Buddha and an ancient tree where worshippers had pressed small globs of sticky rice into the wrinkles and crevices of the bark.

The museum commemorating the ARVN's defeat was in Ban Dong, a few miles nearer the border. Built on the site of a postwar Pathet Lao reeducation camp, it had a collection of captured tanks and Hueys and howitzers and the dismembered wreckage of a T-28—what the Vietnamese-American writer Viet Thanh Nguyen calls the "totems of the industrial enemy brought low." The entrance lobby had the usual bronze bas-relief of heroic soldiers, workers, and peasants, and there were maps that added more detail to the one in the Ho Chi Minh Trail Museum in Hanoi. There were more dioramas and faded photographs, a portrait of a smiling General Giap on a tour of inspection, temporarily back to a position of influence at this point in the war, and lurid paintings that showed flaming American helicopters dropping from the sky, as Michael Herr had written, like so many fat, poisoned birds.

In the early days of the Trail, the PAVN had used the nearby Xepon River to float fuel downstream for the truck depots in big, reinforced nylon bags, losing many of them to the river's treacherous currents and rapids. Now, at dusk, fishermen were at their labors under a bridge, near a small shrine with a reclining Buddha; one was propelling himself around in a small boat that was fashioned from the auxiliary fuel tank of an F-4 Phantom, which pilots often jettisoned on the way back to base or to lighten their weight when they needed to climb fast to avoid antiaircraft fire.

Hammond's team stopped at eight or ten more villages over the next few days, crossing from Savannakhet province into Salavan. As in Vietnam, everything depended on the cooperation of the local government, and some were more hospitable than others. In Vilabouly district, it was enough to pay a courtesy call on a local official, but in neighboring Phine district, the authorities had so far refused to let the War Legacies Project conduct its survey. In Salavan province, Chagnon and Hammond had to wrangle over demands that they take along a contingent of armed police. They pushed back on that, but an SUV-load of officials still insisted on tagging along, though whenever they found a signal, they spent most of their time noodling around on Facebook on their smartphones.

The CIA had operated one of its secret bases near Mouang Nong, the next district capital south of Xepon. It was a bustling little town on an elbow bend of a tributary of the Mekong, with a crowded street market where hustlers were running games of chance, vendors offered sizzling plates of deep-fried grasshoppers, and kids clamored for Spiderman masks and plastic machine guns and olive-green T-shirts that said AIRBORNE SPECIAL FORCES. During the war, Mouang Nong had been the point of entry into a massively bombed area that the PAVN called the Pocket of Fire, which extended southward for fifteen or twenty miles across the hills to La Hap. The War Legacies Project had found several more cases in the town to add to its database, mainly neurological disorders.

Sometimes the women had to abandon the attempt to reach a village on their list. Although the monsoon had ended a couple of weeks earlier, one dirt road was still blocked by a landslide; on another, a bridge was out. At a crossroads on the north-south highway, near a cobbled stretch of the Trail that had been preserved behind a rusty fence, they picked up a young woman whose symptoms suggested occult spina bifida—a doctor would have to make the diagnosis—and headed west toward a remote village called Lapid. Chagnon had been there before and described the access road as "life-threatening." The first few miles were deceptively broad and well-graded, and some herders were taking their cattle to the high pastures, where they grazed during the dry season. But after fording a shallow river where women were washing clothes, the road turned into a narrow track that twisted its way uphill. Still several miles short of Lapid, the big four-wheel-drive vehicle ground to a halt in the ridges of hardened mud.

Chagnon climbed out and paced up and down the steep slope, inspecting ruts that were deep enough to swallow a person whole. She shook her head; there was no way through. It was frustrating, because Lapid had been hit hard. The Hatfield maps showed that at least ten Ranch Hand missions targeted this stretch of the Trail in 1966, and a C-123, with its full thousand-gallon load of chemicals, was shot down in the hills behind the village in 1967, the only one ever lost over Laos. Many years later a Defense Department team searching for the wreckage and the crew of five reported that the area of the crash site was known as "the leper forest" for the high incidence of cancer and birth defects in nearby villages. No doubt most of those people were long dead, but on their previous visit to Lapid, the War Legacies Project had added several cases to their list: a paralyzed baby girl, a four-year-old with a clubfoot, a three-year-old and a seven-year-old both with too many fingers or toes, a teenager born without eyes.

South of Mouang Nong, the modern highway diverged from the original Trail, looping around a low range of mountains and hugging the river valley. Wartime maps showed that the Trail had cut through the rugged hills to La Hap, and you could still see parts of it as a faint, broken tracery on Google Earth. It ran past a village called Labeng-Khok, and that was where the women went next, approaching the most important of all the PAVN's border strongholds, Base Area 611.

Getting to Labeng-Khok meant traversing another bad road and fording a mountain stream that was choked with boulders, next to a derelict wooden bridge that looked as if it might date back to wartime. Smaller bomb craters followed the road with uncanny precision, a testament to the skill of the pilots.

The village was a tiny cluster of no more than thirty or forty homes around a central area of beaten earth. "We call this the oil-drum village," Hammond said, and it was easy to see why. They were everywhere, rusted fifty-five-gallon barrels that were now used to store rice pounders and farm tools, hammered flat to make fences for the vegetable gardens, or simply strewn around randomly beneath the stilthouses, among the pigs and chickens and half-naked children. The front end of a Soviet truck was rotting away in the weeds, and near it was a heavy-duty tire, encrusted with mud, that was stamped, in English, MADE IN USSR. An elderly man who had fought here with the Pathet Lao said the village had originally been a little farther downhill, on the headwaters of the stream. After it was destroyed, the villagers had moved here and combed the area for any metal they could make use of; now they had more oil drums than they knew what to do with.

Each of the main binh tram on the Ho Chi Minh Trail had its nearby support facilities, auxiliary storage areas, and truck parks, and it was clear that Labeng-Khok must have been one of these, providing support for La Hap, which was six or seven miles away across the hills. Narrow, overgrown footpaths led away from the village in that direction, and it was easy to imagine North Vietnamese porters moving along them with their reinforced bicycles, invisible to the forward air controllers circling overhead.

The first tendrils of prosperity had reached Mouang Nong, jarring, tawdry, and heedless of the past. But Labeng-Khok was a world away, much like the A Shau Valley must have been in the immediate postwar years. These days even the poorest rural backwaters in Vietnam had the cheap basic accoutrements of modern life, things like plastic dishes and tableware. But in Labeng-Khok the enforced ingenuity of the blacksmiths on the Ho Chi Minh Trail still sustained the entire domestic economy. The village women had laid out their kitchen goods on the wooden platforms outside their homes. Buckets, bowls, spoons, cooking pots, and oil lamps made from yellow "pineapple" cluster bombs, named for the vanes that spread out to stabilize their descent—everything here seemed to have begun life as part of an airplane. The soundtrack of Labeng-Khok was the dull clang of cowbells made from sawed-off projectiles. "These were our gifts from the villagers of America," an old man said.

The women already knew of one disabled child in the village

and they went from house to house looking for more information, although on this hot, quiet afternoon most people seemed to be out in the rice fields. They stopped at one house whose owner had replaced the wooden ladder to the living quarters with a sturdier one he'd made from pineapple *bom bi* tubes. His four-year-old son was partially paralyzed and mentally disabled and had just learned to walk. They added him to their list, which had now grown to more than five hundred cases.

Later, by chance, they met one of the child's relatives, a provincial official from a village on the road to Mouang Nong, near a North Vietnamese base that had held American POWs. "We were like a guesthouse for American prisoners, before they were taken north to Hanoi," he said. Hammond and Chagnon told him about their survey, and he said he had a great-nephew who suffered from severe birth defects. He showed them a picture. It was the boy from Labeng-Khok. He was not the only disabled child in the extended family, the old man said. The boy's cousin had been born mute and couldn't walk until he was seven. A third child had died at the age of two. "That one could not sit up," he said. "The whole body was soft, as if there were no bones."

The modern world had reached out and touched Yen's village, in a modest way. Two big stone blocks had been placed at the entrance to the dirt road that led to Pasia and La Hap to deter illegal logging trucks. A few villagers had motorbikes, and electric light had finally come to Pasia two years earlier, shortly after Yen's last trip home. Her family had built a new house since then, all of wood rather than the traditional plaited bamboo and thatch, and it had a real staircase instead of a ladder.

She'd taken pains to dress for the occasion: a red blouse, brightly flowered calf-length pants, a sky-blue sandal on her unbraced foot, a fashionable yellow shoulder bag. But if she'd hoped for a warm reception, she didn't get it. Her mother stood at the foot of the stairs, stonyfaced, arms folded, her body language seeming to block passage. She wore a purple and blue *sinh* with geomorphic designs and a striped T-shirt that said SINGLE. Older women leaned on their windowsills, puffing on metal-stemmed pipes. There was the usual cluster of inquisitive children. Their T-shirts said FLY EMIRATES and had the logos of elite European soccer teams: Manchester City, Barcelona, Paris Saint-Germain. The children gawked at Yen, this alien being from the big city, and giggled.

Niphaphone Sengthong had first heard about Yen in 2014, when they'd begun planning the survey. She'd stopped at a village on the other side of the river, where there was a small clinic. She asked, as she did routinely, if they knew of anyone in the area who suffered from birth defects. Later a teacher sent her a photograph of Yen via WhatsApp. She was one of thirteen children, the eldest of the three who survived. Since then the War Legacies Project had documented several other cases in Pasia. Sometimes when there seemed to be a reasonable chance of success, Hammond was able to scrape together a few hundred dollars to send a child to the city for treatment. The project paid for Yen to spend a week at a rehab center in Pakse, the nearest city, together with a boy from the village who had two clubfeet. Later the teacher had brought Yen to Vientiane, where she had surgery on one ankle and moved for a while into Chagnon's riverside home before getting a room of her own and learning to become self-sufficient.

She'd gone to school at the age of ten; she especially liked math and Lao, which all the children learned these days, although their parents still spoke only Ta Oi. The other kids scorned her: *Why are you wasting the teacher's time? You'll never amount to anything. You're a cripple, why don't you just go away and die?*

But Yen was agile and determined as well as bright. Though her legs splayed out in contrary directions, she could maneuver herself along the village paths, even cross the small nearby stream to gather firewood in the forest. Like Le Minh Chau, the mouth-painter in Ho Chi Minh City, and Nguyen Kien, the wheelchair racer in Bien Hoa, she was nobody's victim, except perhaps her mother's.

It was really only because of her grandparents that Yen survived. They overruled her mother, who had wanted to kill the child at birth according to ancient Ta Oi custom, which holds unnatural births to be the work of punitive spirits. These must be placated by an animal sacrifice, usually of a water buffalo, a ceremony that is also performed when the rice harvest is brought in. Stillbirths are secretly buried in the forest, because a dead baby will pollute the village. Twins also stir the anger of the spirits, and in former times they were killed and their bodies burned. The custom still persisted in some ethnic minority groups, Chagnon said, though the Ta Oi had abandoned it.

Although old habits had begun to slip away in a world of smartphones and motorbikes and logging trucks, the Ta Oi, like all the Katuic peoples, still existed in a sentient spirit universe held together by an intricate system of hierarchies, rules, and taboos. The spirits form a kind of parallel government in which human society is subordinate, and below humans are animals, birds, and fish.

At the pinnacle are what one Swedish anthropologist calls the "grand spirits of the first order"—Earth, Water, Forest, and Sky. Below them are the spirits of the second order, perhaps a tiger, or a particular hill, or a big old-growth tree in a part of the forest that is untouched by human hand. There are master hill spirits and tutelary village spirits, spirits of the outside world and domestic spirits of the inside world, perhaps ancestors who were given a proper burial and now protect the household. Though more benevolent, these must still be honored if one is to keep in their good graces.

If the elders make the right tributes and sacrifices, a village will prosper; if the spirits are harmed or offended, they will respond in kind. Many of the gravest taboos involve offenses against the natural world. Clearing and burning a patch of forest that is the domain of spirits, or killing the animals who live there, can be punished by death and disease.

It was hard not to think of all this when a group of the Pasia elders gathered to share their memories of events half a century ago. "The fighters used this road during the war against the French," one old man said. "But that was a land war, and the American one was an air war," and the natural order of the tree and forest spirits never crossed the minds of those who selected the targets and set the rules of engagement.

"The airplanes with the chemicals always came three at a time, early in the morning, but sometimes also in the late afternoon," another elder said. "If they came in the morning they didn't come in the afternoon, and if they came in the afternoon, they didn't come in the morning"—another distinct memory that was at variance with the official records.

"All the trees died, even the big ones that six people could stretch their arms around, and then they burned the forest with napalm," he went on. "The next spring they came again, after the vegetation had grown back." The villagers of Pasia split up into two groups and spent five years in the mountains, moving from place to place, taking the thatch roofs of their homes with them and cutting timber to build new walls, floors, and stilts, or often just sleeping out in the forest or digging improvised bomb shelters covered with brush, big enough to hold an entire family. Some took refuge across the hills in Labeng-Khok, but they found no respite there. They planted upland rice where they could, but when the crop was green the planes burned that too, with a brilliant fire that sounded from the elders' descriptions like white phosphorus. The village had about thirty families in those days, the first man said. Twenty people from Pasia had died in the bombing, and more than that from starvation. There were still a lot of *bom bi* in the forest, and there was an unexploded two-hundred-pounder near the village stream. They'd found it three years ago and left it buried in the mud.

The first birth defects began to appear soon after the war, babies born without arms and legs. To the elders, there was a clear chain of causation here: with their bombs and chemicals, the Americans had destroyed the domain of the spirits, and the spirits had taken out their rage on the village by deforming its children. Within the Ta Oi belief system, the logic of this was as ironclad as the proof by Western scientists of how dioxin moved up through the food chain.

By the time the elders had exhausted their memories of the spraying, Hammond, Chagnon, and Sengthong had finished their rounds. Yen was sitting disconsolate on a tree stump, surrounded by spectators, fighting back tears. Then she looked up at Chagnon and said, "I don't want to stay here; I want to go back to Vientiane." She hoisted herself into their SUV, refusing help, and they drove off. On the road, they passed an old man returning from the fields. He glanced up, scarcely making eye contact. "That was my grandfather," Yen said.

29

———

The End of the Trail

T HE WAR LEGACIES PROJECT knew of four people with disabilities
in La Hap, three miles from Pasia and twenty from the Vietnamese
border. It was easy to see why Col. Vo Bam had chosen the location
for his command headquarters. Museum maps and dioramas could
show you how geography dictates the outcome of wars, but there was
no substitute for seeing the military logic of the landscape in real life.

The two villages occupied a horseshoe-shaped valley, ringed by
forested mountains that rose two thousand feet from the valley floor.
The storage areas and living quarters, as well as a field hospital, were
dug securely into the base of the hills. Antiaircraft batteries and infantry bunkers were concealed all along the ridgelines, and although the
spraying was as intense here as anywhere in Laos, it took several days
for the defoliation to take effect, so the guns could be constantly reposi-
tioned, always one step ahead. Code-named Oscar Eight by the Americans, La Hap was "a defender's dream," said one forward air controller.

The largest arms depot outside of North Vietnam, La Hap housed
about 3,200 fighters and stored four thousand tons of war matériel
bound for Quang Tri and the A Shau Valley. Westmoreland concluded
that all military operations in I Corps were planned from here.

"It was NVA Central," said one officer who took part in American
clandestine operations inside Laos, "one of the most lethal crossroads
in military history." By 1968, it "had been worked over so many times
by B-52s and other bombers, it resembled nothing so much as a cra-

tered moonscape." But that didn't mean it could be destroyed, and more airplanes were shot down around La Hap than anywhere else in Laos.

"Every team that went in there got the shit shot out of it," said another American veteran of these operations. Sometime around June 1, 1967, listening posts picked up a sudden flurry of radio transmissions between La Hap and the high command in Hanoi. The tentative conclusion was that General Giap himself was visiting, and orders came down for a raid by two platoons out of Khe Sanh, "to attempt to kill or capture the VIP Giap in Oscar-8 and to kill all other enemy forces encountered."

But the raid turned into the worst disaster the clandestine teams ever experienced. By the time it was over, seven aircraft were down, twenty-three Americans were dead, and six were recorded as MIA. In fact, there was never any hard evidence that Giap was there, and within two days PAVN crews had repaired the bomb damage, and trucks were rolling again, headed for the A Shau Valley.

Hammond, Chagnon, and Sengthong followed the old Trail as it wound its way east into Samuoi district, where Vo Bam's first teams of regroupees had crossed into Laos in 1959. It wasn't always easy to distinguish the defoliated hillsides from those burned and cleared for upland rice, but Hammond had a sharp eye for them, and there were more here than on the Vietnamese side, with none of the acacia plantations that covered the scars there like bandages on an old wound.

In one village after another, the stories they heard from the elders were all woven from the same threads. This slope or that slope, once densely forested, had been bare of vegetation since the war. The Americans had spies on such and such a hilltop. A dozen had died in this village, twice as many in that one. The spray made them dizzy, nauseous, breathless, brought them out in a rash, made their eyes stream, as did the foul-smelling clouds that drifted from canisters the airplanes sometimes dropped, probably CS gas.

Officially, the pilots were forbidden to target populated areas, but the elders' answer to that was a furrowed brow: *What are you talking about?* This village had been flattened by bombs, that one burned to the ground with napalm. People had gone without rice for years, foraging in the mountains, digging up wild roots. Sugarcane and lemongrass survived the spraying. So did cassava and white pumpkins, although they swelled to an unnatural size and became inedible.

People lived according to the Lao proverb "Owls by day, foxes by night." To avoid the spotter planes, they never wore light-colored clothes. There were two kinds of water buffalo, one dark and one light, and in the daytime they covered the light ones under a black cloth. If they had chicken runs or pigpens, they concealed those too. They dug earthen shelters or lived in caves. Sometimes the PAVN soldiers shared their supplies of rice with the villagers; they taught them to use the *hoang cam* cookstove, an ingenious invention that carried the smoke away through tunnels so it would dissipate in the forest. Some villagers helped the North Vietnamese to clear the Trail, while others kept their distance, watching from the hills as the truck convoys made their way toward the border. The demarcation line meant nothing to them; most had family on both sides.

One man in his late seventies had headed a Pathet Lao unit of thirty-five men in a village five miles from Vietnam, and once, in 1967 he thought, they had confronted a group of MACV-SOG raiders face to face. But most villagers had seen Americans only from a distance, or high in the sky. "If I'd met one, I'd have hit him with a shovel," one old man said. An elder in a village ten miles from the border pointed up at a nearby ridgeline. "They dropped men up there at night," he said. "They were afraid they'd be shot in the daytime. Then they would pick them up again when the Vietnamese fighters were around." In helicopters? It took him a moment to understand the question. "Ah, yes, *hélicoptères*," he said, remembering the word from the time of the French War.

Arriving in a village, the three women worked according to a set protocol. After the first courtesies were exchanged, they sought out the headman, the *naiban*, and asked him to assemble everyone he knew to have a birth defect or a disability. While Chagnon stood by with her clipboard and her questionnaire, Sengthong pulled out the laminated sheet of photographs that showed people some of the most visible deformities they were looking for. They'd started off with cartoons but found that photos worked best. These depicted conditions that were rare in the general population but not along the Ho Chi Minh Trail—things like clubfeet (normally one in 1,000 live births), cleft lip, with or without cleft palate (one in 1,200), and arthrogryposis (one in 2,000). Through an interpreter, she talked about how some of these might be treatable.

The closer the Trail came to the Vietnamese border, where the spraying had been heaviest, the more cases there were. In Adorne, where one of the rusted North Vietnamese oil drums had been improbably repurposed to hold up a satellite dish, the team already knew of at least fifteen. Among the small crowd that assembled was a man with a hole in his face, a girl with an ugly row of metal staples still circling her neck from a botched surgery eight months earlier, a boy with spindly legs in an ancient wheelchair, and a teenage orphan named Bouan whose upper body was a mountain range of swellings and outgrowths of bone.

The survey had its limitations, Hammond acknowledged. They could never be sure they'd learned of all the cases in a village. It was October, and with the upland rice harvest under way, most women were out in the fields all day, sometimes accompanied by their small children and perhaps laboring with disabilities of their own. Because of the stigma attached to birth defects, afflicted children might be unacknowledged. And of course she, Chagnon, and Sengthong were not doctors, let alone geneticists—of which, in any case, there were none in Laos. But they were able to identify the most obvious conditions and sometimes their limited funds stretched to a bus trip for a few of those afflicted to one of the cities where they could receive a diagnosis and treatment. Bouan was on that list; they planned to send him to Vientiane to see a team of volunteer spinal specialists from Indiana who were arriving soon.

There were prosthetics and rehab centers in the cities of Savannakhet and Pakse, which were accustomed to dealing with victims of *bom bi,* and the district hospital in Salavan could do simpler surgeries, like repairing a cleft lip or opening an imperforate anus in an infant—another condition on the dioxin list—assuming they caught it in time. The chief surgeon in Salavan had just removed a tumor from a one-year-old with abdominal cancer, but anything more complicated, like radiation or chemotherapy, required a trip to Vientiane, where the Soviet-built Mittaphab (Friendship) Hospital had the only MRI machine in the country.

Even then, there were many obstacles, both practical and cultural. A referral for treatment might involve carrying the patient to the nearest paved road by motorbike, or even on someone's back, followed by an arduous bus journey, as long as twenty-four hours if they were going to the capital, to be poked and prodded by strangers in white coats who didn't even speak their language. Sometimes patients awoke in the night and bolted.

Yet with all these constraints, Hammond's team had managed to survey 126 villages, almost two-thirds of them in two districts of Salavan, and the rest in parts of three districts in neighboring Savannakhet, following the flight paths of the C-123s. Sengthong had spreadsheets that she updated to include the new cases they'd found on this trip. She didn't include cases that were clearly unrelated to dioxin exposure, like amputees from unexploded munitions, and there were many of those. About two-thirds of the cases were on the Vietnamese list of conditions presumptively associated with Agent Orange. Others still needed professional diagnosis or were unspecified mental disorders that the Vietnamese would also have ascribed to dioxin. More than half the cases were of children under the age of sixteen. That meant the third generation since the war, since the ethnic minority people typically marry in their teens. There were multiple cases in extended families, like that of the boy in Labeng-Khok. Chagnon said they'd been sent a photograph of five brothers, all with serious deformities, in Attapeu province, but they didn't yet have permission to extend the survey there.

There were also disturbing clusters: five babies born with missing eyes in Nong district; an inordinate number of cases of hip dysplasia in Samuoi—a condition that normally occurs in only one in one thousand live births and may leave one leg shorter than the other. It's easily treatable in infancy, but left alone it will lead to severe pain, a waddling gait, and more serious deformities. The rudimentary healthcare system meant that few if any infants were even diagnosed. With every pair of hands needed in the rice fields, caring for a disabled child was a heavy economic burden, and no one would ever know how many of them had simply died for want of medical attention, or how much effort had been made to keep them alive.

One of the biggest challenges was getting provincial officials to cooperate with the survey, for this depended on their understanding that the human tragedies afflicting their villages might be related to events half a century ago. All of them had graphic anecdotes of the horrors they'd seen during and after the war, the stillborn monsters, missing limbs, missing eyes and noses and faces, heads as big as their bodies. Others born without a head. One retired official in Samuoi knew of three who had been born with tails. They all agreed that nothing of the kind had been seen before the war, but they had never made a connection to the herbicides. The acting governor of Salavan province said he'd learned of this only five years earlier, when a visitor from neighboring Quang Tri showed him a video on YouTube. Officials in Ta Oey district knew nothing about it until Hammond, Chagnon, and Sengthong showed up with their PowerPoint presentation.

"The problem in Laos is the same as we had in Vietnam twenty-five years ago," Tom Boivin said later, "but with even less data, and the medical records are terrible. Overall awareness is next to nil. Out there in the rural areas, nobody knows about it except for the people who have worked with Susan and Jacqui and Niphaphone." Vietnam had its house-to-house surveys and commune-level clinics and local VAVA offices, its statistical tables and its public awareness campaigns. The borderlands of Laos were a world away.

The village of Lahang was the last settlement of any size before the border. It was a place rife with disabilities and birth defects. It had seventeen cases in a population of a little over five hundred, and there were double-digit numbers in many of the other villages here at the heart of what had been the PAVN's Base Area 611. Sengthong added a new case to her list, a two-year-old boy named Sodsai, whose swollen skull suggested hydrocephalus, the congenital form of which is included in the VA list of dioxin-related conditions in paternal offspring. Sodsai's father had a birth defect himself, a deformed ear.

The pattern was inescapable: the more intense the spraying, the greater the number of congenital defects. In the villages the War Legacies Project had surveyed in Ta Oey district, about one in every twelve households had a member whose disabilities made it on to the list. In Samuoi, it was closer to one in seven. In the dozen villages closest to the border in the two districts, it was almost one in every five. These levels were more than comparable with those VAVA and the Vietnamese government had logged on the other side of the mountains in the A Luoi Valley.

Rising above Lahang was an imposing 4,300-foot-high mountain named Co Ka Leuye, and the border ran along its summit. Viewed end-on, it formed an almost perfect cone, like a subtropical Mount Fuji. But on the rough road north to the nearby hamlet of Lalay Angkong, it became apparent that the summit was formed by a long razorback escarpment more than two miles long.

Lalay Angkong was a tiny hamlet. Under a thatched shelter was a battered green-baize pool table with carved legs. The crowd that assembled nearby to meet the three women included a girl of ten or eleven, naked from the waist down and with impossibly long, emaciated legs drawn up to her chin; she rocked and drooled and made small, guttural noises until her father picked her up on his back and carried her home.

A bucolic stream meandered through the village, and a long row of bomb craters of various sizes marched arrow-straight through the open field next to it, where some cattle were placidly grazing. Below the village, the stream hugged the southern slopes of Co Ka Leuye. The gap in the mountains was wide enough to have carried a spur of the Trail, and the stream itself looked deep enough for a shallow-draft sampan carrying fighters and weapons. The old PAVN maps showed that this infiltration route led to the point where the Da Krong and A Shau valleys met, and it was easy to see how meaningless the dividing line between Laos and Vietnam was in this wild, remote country.

Co Ka Leuye and its lower, flatter sister peak were the first target of the herbicide campaign on the Ho Chi Minh Trail. The first flights, in December 1965, were two of the biggest ever in Laos, dropping 8,700 gallons of Agent Purple, and the south-facing slopes of Co Ka Leuye were still scarred naked from the defoliation.

This was where the Marines made their single officially authorized incursion into Laos, during Operation Dewey Canyon I in early 1969. Taking Co Ka Leuye was one of its first objectives. From the summit, you could stand with one foot in Vietnam and the other in Laos, with an unparalleled view over the A Shau Valley and the Trail on both sides of the border. But when Company G of the Second Battalion of the Third Marines reached the thickly forested summit of the mountain, it was enveloped in the usual A Shau fog and lashing rain. Conditions stayed that way for the next five days, and having marched his men to the top of the hill, the company commander marched them down again—slipped and slithered would be more accurate—straight into an ambush that left five Americans dead and eighteen wounded. The battalion commander hailed it as "a tremendous performance in leadership and fire discipline," which was another way of saying it was a nightmare, like most things in the A Shau.

Marine commanders took advantage of a loophole in the rules of engagement that authorized them to cross the border "in the exercise of self-defense." If the trucks were carrying weapons into South Vietnam, surely that counted? The Marines crossed the border twice, just east of Lahang. The first incursion was on a small scale, a night ambush just inside Lao territory. The second was larger, involving almost an entire battalion and lasting for six days. When they withdrew, the official losses were eight dead and thirty-three wounded. The families were told that the men had died "southeast of Vandegrift Combat Base, Quang Tri Province, Republic of Vietnam." Three days after the operation ended, the PAVN trucks were on the move again, inexorable.

The border post at the foot of Co Ka Leuye marked the end point of the women's nine-day journey down the Ho Chi Minh Trail. Sengthong updated her spreadsheets. There were 517 recorded cases now, with the sprayed areas of two mountainous districts in Salavan province more or less completed, although a dozen or so villages in Savannakhet were yet to be surveyed. The project still hadn't reached Attapeu and Sekong, the other two provinces that had been heavily defoliated. They hoped to move on to these later, if their meager resources allowed, and if the provincial authorities were willing to cooperate.

The women had dinner one evening with Khampheui Phanthachone, the provincial delegate from Salavan to the National Assembly in Vientiane. He looked on intently as they traced the flight paths of the Ranch Hand missions on a map, and listened as they told him what their survey had revealed. He frowned. "The Prime Minister should know about this," he said. "But how can you prove there's a connection between these birth defects and Agent Orange?"

The simple answer, they told him, was that you couldn't. It wasn't like a leg blown off by a fifty-year-old pineapple bomb. But the deeper answer was a political one, or perhaps it was more accurate to say a moral one: you shouldn't have to. American veterans had crossed that bridge with the Agent Orange Act of 1991. Vietnamese with severe disabilities had finally been granted the same benefit of the doubt. Thanks to Charles Bailey, Tim Rieser, and Senator Leahy, and the groundwork laid by Hatfield Consultants and the 10-80 Committee, American aid was now beginning to reach them, at least in eight of the defoliated provinces.

The logic of double standards lay heavy on a conversation with the angriest person Hammond's team had met in Laos. He was a Pacoh elder named Kalod, in the village of Lahang, where so many had sickened. He was an imposing seventy-five-year-old, tall, straight-backed, silver-haired, wearing an olive-green suit with an epauletted shirt that gave him a martial bearing, even though he was barefoot. Like most Pacoh and Ta Oi, and most Katu and Bru-Van Kieu, he saw the border as an artificial construct, an arbitrary line drawn by foreigners for their own inscrutable reasons. During the war, he said, people had fled in both directions, depending on which side of the border was being bombed and sprayed at the time. He leaned forward, gesticulating angrily as half a dozen other elders nodded agreement. "Vietnamese people affected by the chemical spraying get compensation," he complained. "In Laos, we also need support from America, like they get in Vietnam."

By nature, Hammond said, she was "an optimistic realist," and working for almost thirty years in Vietnam had been a master class in patience and persistence. Rieser had told her that the Senate could do nothing in Laos without hard data and an official request from the Lao government. USAID officials in Vientiane had told her that they couldn't act without funds from Congress. Other embassy officials had dismissed the idea out of hand. "The chargé d'affaires told us that if we were so interested in what the U.S. had done wrong in Laos, why didn't we also focus on what the Soviets and North Vietnamese had done," she said, exasperated. "It was like being in a time warp, like dealing with an official in Vietnam in the 1990s. So we've been on this endless treadmill."

But Rieser seemed eager to see what the War Legacies Project had found. "We have our work cut out for us in Vietnam," he said, "but we'd also want to know what was done in Laos, since clearly those who were involved"—meaning previous generations of American political and military leaders—"have not made a point of making it widely known. I've always approached this as doing what's necessary to solve the problem, and if there's more to the problem than we know, then we need to deal with it."

"We can show clearly that the people in these villages have high levels of congenital disabilities," Hammond said. "We can show that they correspond to the areas that were sprayed, and that they're the same kind of disabilities you see on the Vietnamese side of the border, like the A Luoi Valley."

She was painfully aware of how slowly the wheels turned in Washington, and that Vietnam would always be the front-burner issue. But the smaller scale of the problem in Laos should also make it easier to deal with. Extrapolating from what they'd found, her best guess was that the total number of birth defects and disabilities attributable to the defoliation campaign would be somewhere between 5,000 and 7,500. "Even the small amounts that the U.S. started off with in Vietnam, would go a long way here," she said. Some could be used for direct humanitarian aid and some for research to see if there were still any dioxin hot spots. The affected people were running out of time. Nine of the children on her list had already died for want of medical care.

"All we need to do," she said, "is to add the language we use now for Vietnam"—the wording Bailey and Rieser had crafted to make sure that money was earmarked to reach the people who needed it most.

"Just that one little sentence," she sighed. "That's all it takes."

The wheels of bureaucracy ground on for another two years, and then in March 2022 the news finally came from Rieser. The new federal budget had been passed by the Senate. The presumed victims of Agent Orange would get $1.5 million, with more held in reserve for future research into possible dioxin hot spots. It was more decimal dust, yet it was still a big step, the first acknowledgment of responsibility for this long-guarded secret of America's lost war in Southeast Asia.

Epilogue

HILL 674

IT WAS SIX MONTHS since I'd last seen Manus Campbell, and his feet had begun to itch again. He said he missed Hanoi, his mornings at Hoan Kiem Lake, the close friends like Chuck Searcy, but the constant construction noise had grown intolerable. So he was back in Hoi An, once more seeking out a quiet neighborhood away from the clangor of the tour buses. He was spending more and more of his time around kids. He still sent his monthly checks to the Beloved School in Hue, and he was also supporting two local organizations that had been founded by foreigners. In Hoi An, he'd joined the board of the Children's Education Project, created by an Australian friend, where he was teaching the kids to swim, sponsoring their education, and documenting their lives in photographs. In a village near Danang, it was the Kianh Foundation, started by an Englishwoman, which ran a school for kids with serious disabilities. Were they victims of Agent Orange? Who could say, and why did it matter?

We met for lunch in Hue at La Carambole, a French bistro a couple of blocks from Ushi Clark's restaurant. Next door was a bar called Taboo, where the sign over the entrance said DON'T WORRY, BE HAPPY. It was a chilly, overcast day, and a steady downpour was drumming on the street outside. It always seemed to rain in Hue.

"Things have been moving quickly since I last saw you," he said. "I was taking photographs of this woman one day, an English teacher, and she said, 'There's this woman you really have to meet.' I thought, yeah, right, where have I heard that before." He'd always had a knack for meeting women.

Her name was Phan Doan Trang, and they connected through Facebook. She had a small business selling clothes online. She lived in Danang with her parents and her six-year-old son, Quoc Anh, who loved to fly kites. But she had an independent streak and did things a traditionally modest Vietnamese woman wasn't supposed to do, like holding hands in public. Campbell had asked her to marry him.

Her parents were appalled. *It's him or us, you have to choose.* Trang made her choice, and now the old couple were slowly coming around.

We planned to go up to Dong Ha together later in the week. It was only a couple of hours from Hue, and two other veterans, one of whom had served as an army officer in Quang Tri, were going to be visiting Project RENEW to see Dieu Linh's all-women UXO survey team in action. Searcy would also be in town on one of his regular visits.

First, though, we'd arranged to spend a day in the A Luoi Valley with the head of a small humanitarian group called Hearts for Hue that worked on some of the projects American vets were supporting there. The grim symbolism of the valley in the history of the war and its centrality to the story of Agent Orange had made it a magnet for these efforts over the years—Mark O'Connor with his MAGA hat and his bicycles; kindergartens built by the Vietnam Veterans of America Foundation and funded by the Boeing Company, makers of the B-52; a clinic sponsored by the evangelical group Vets with a Mission and dedicated to a comrade whose Huey had gone down in the nearby hills. This was in the commune of Hong Ha, where Charles Bailey had done his early work with Katu farmers.

The road from Hue, notorious in the war as Route 547, still began at the bridge on the Perfume River, where Campbell had been deployed on his arrival in Vietnam in June 1967. In springtime, it could be an idyllic drive, winding through green mountains in radiant sunshine, crossing placid streams, passing small villages and farmsteads with mango and jackfruit trees and fields of lemongrass and cinnamon. But it was October now, and the valley lived up to its baleful reputation. As the road became a series of hairpin bends in its precipitous descent to the valley floor, the Truong Son mountains reared up in an almost perpendicular wall of blackness that was briefly revealed and then swallowed up again behind scudding banks of mist. On the other side lay the unexamined mysteries of Laos. A cold rain beat down on the open field that had once housed the Special Forces base. Finally, after half a century, the Ministry of Defense was getting ready to launch a remediation project, to clean up 35,000 cubic meters of contaminated soil. Using low-cost technology and advice from South Korea and Japan, it would begin in 2022.

It was a place that still gave you goosebumps, as Wayne Dwernychuk had said, thinking of all the ghosts of war, though nothing remained now but some of the bomb craters and a single burned-out building. A big sign, made out of primary-color capital letters like something out of a kids' theme park, said, in English, A SO AIRPORT. The A Sap River, where soldiers had once drawn water to wash out the spray tanks on the C-123s, curved around the site of the base, swollen brown with the downpour. It was still classified as a restricted military zone, and we'd had to obtain a special permit, but there was no one around to check on it, just a few tiny Pacoh or Katu women in plastic rain slickers, herding farm animals with long sticks and puffing on their metal-stemmed pipes. A dirt road, off-limits to foreigners, led through a gap in the mountains to the border two miles away, following an old spur of the Trail, but the guardpost was locked and unattended.

A Luoi itself was a bustling little town these days, and the flat piece of ground that had once been an airstrip for the Green Berets was now used by local kids as a soccer field. West of town, on the border, was the dark, shrouded hump of Hamburger Hill. On the road through town, which was part of the new Ho Chi Minh Highway, signs promoted the valley as an ecotourist destination. An English-language brochure for a two-day tour, produced by a travel agency in Hue, offered hikes to nearby waterfalls, bike rentals, and overnight stays in thatch-roofed Pacoh and Katu villages, where visitors could observe local weaving techniques and enjoy performances of traditional music. The trip included a trek to the top of Hamburger Hill, with a local guide who knew where the unexploded ordnance was. "Allow yourself to truly relax in the comfort and peace of the mountains that this area is famous for," the brochure said, without apparent irony.

Half a century after Operation Ranch Hand, there were still one or two bald patches on the mountains where nothing grew but coarse grasses and stunted banana palms. But on the lower slopes all signs of the defoliation had vanished, the groves of bamboo and rattan replaced by the geometric monotony of acacia plantations.

In the commune of A Ngo, where the Hatfield scientists had bought samples of pork and beef for their dioxin survey, the chairman of the people's committee took us to visit an old man who was sitting cross-legged on the floor of his house under a poster of two cherubic, pink-cheeked infants that said, in English, HAPPY BABY. He was eighty years old, with a long face and a hangdog expression. A Katu, he'd grown up on the Lao side of the meaningless border, in a village in Sekong province where the mountains were honeycombed with limestone caves that served as storage areas for trucks and weapons. As a young man he had helped the PAVN build that section of the Trail, and often saw the spray planes overhead during the most intense period of the defoliation campaign.

His granddaughter was one of its presumed victims. She was clutching at the rail of her crib in a dark, cheerless inner room, bobbing up and down with a fixed manic grin. Her thick black hair was chopped short, and she had almost no shoulders. She looked to be eleven or twelve, but the old man said she was twenty-one. Outside the door was a pigpen, where a brood sow was grunting and snuffling, and half a dozen piglets were suckling under a heat lamp. The animal was a boost to the family's income, part of the program that Hearts for Hue administered for the Vietnam chapter of Veterans for Peace.

At the district office of VAVA, the old man's granddaughter was on a list of those receiving a government stipend for dioxin-related disabilities. There were 647 in all, out of the valley's population of fifty thousand. The head of the office was also a Katu who had been born in Laos. As a teenager he'd worked as a courier on the Trail, shielding himself from the spray by wetting a handkerchief and putting it over his nose and mouth. *Border?* His ancestors would have laughed at the idea.

Back at the bridge over the Perfume River, another road wound its way toward the hills northwest of Hue, leading to what had once been the command headquarters of the PAVN's Tri-Thien Military District, Base Area 114. And that raised a question I'd always hesitated to ask Campbell in all our many hours of conversation about the war and its aftermath. Would he ever consider going back to the scene of his "stream fight," where his platoon from Alpha 1/4 had walked unsuspecting into the PAVN kill zone on Hill 674? Because that was where the road led.

He thought about it and said yes.

The Marines' daily after-action reports were meticulous in their detail, recording every step the grunts had taken, with the exact time and location. The entry for October 29, 1967, read:

1430 Fwd. elements 3d plat., Co. A recd. heavy A/W [automatic weapons] fire from unknown number NVA while moving toward mouth of draw. YD509229.

The military used the Universal Transverse Mercator system, or UTM, to fix geographical coordinates, and it was a simple matter to translate this number into degrees of latitude and longitude. Google Earth showed two narrow ribbons of water running down the west side of the hill, flowing under a narrow one-lane track that connected the Co Bi-Thanh Tan Valley with the A Shau, the spur of the Ho Chi Minh Trail that the PAVN had numbered B71. A huge scarred area on the back side of the mountain was covered with worm tracks, land being cleared for another new acacia plantation, and the same area was crisscrossed by spray paths on the Hatfield maps. This had been the site of FSB Rakkasan, one of the biggest firebases of the war and the staging area for the attack on Hamburger Hill. Tucked between an adjacent fold of hills, a small river had been dammed, forming a reservoir where Charles Bailey had once gone to meet a team of Czech scientists looking to sample lake sediments for evidence of dioxin. It was a world of cross-connections, of threads wrapped together.

It was a twenty-mile drive from Hue, passing through villages that had been famous Viet Minh strongholds during the war against the French. Hill 674 rose steeply above the commune of Phong Son, a long saddleback ridge.

At the foot of the mountain there was now a five-star Buddhist-themed spa resort called Alba Wellness Valley. Posters at the entrance advertised ziplines and the biggest jungle highwire in Vietnam, and a sign, in English, described the resort as THE PERFECT PLACE TO CON-DUCT YOUR BUSINESS MEETING OR CORPORATE TEAM-BUILDING. It was owned and operated by a company called Fusion ("the leading inno-vator of wellness-inspired hotels in Southeast Asia"), which seemed appropriate since this was the kind of place where all the identities of Vietnam merged: a war, a country, a tourist attraction.

A personable young manager offered to show us around. He took us to see the Alba-Thanh Tan hot springs, which he said had been discov-ered by a French doctor in 1931, though presumably local people had known of its curative qualities long before that. We saw small, pretty lakes spanned by red-painted Japanese bridges, kids playing under fountains in the bright sunshine, and a party of matrons posing for group photos, out on a spree in their most elegant *ao dai*s.

Campbell suddenly pulled up short at a couple of replica stilt houses. He frowned: "I've been here before." This was where he'd brought par-ties of disabled kids from the Beloved School in Hue, soon after his return to Vietnam and some years before the resort was built. He'd never made the connection to Hill 674.

A swaying rope bridge crossed over a rocky stream, and beyond it a path led uphill to the zipline station. Several hundred feet below, the line passed over the resort's small organic farm, and a young Japanese tourist whizzed high above it, a speck in the sky, a high insect whine cutting through the silence of the valley.

The cheapest accommodations were the faux stilt houses, and at the high end a row of thatch-roofed bungalows looked out directly onto Hill 674. The manager said that one day the great Buddhist teacher Thich Nhat Hanh came here from Hue, now in his nineties and frail, with an entourage of twenty followers, but he had declined to stay. He had sat in his wheelchair outside one of the bungalows, looking up at the mountain, and said no, there was something unsettling here, something out of balance. But then he came again, contemplated the mountain for a second time, and said yes, now he felt a sense of peace had been restored.

The bungalows were exquisitely appointed. Each had a bamboo swing, a big walk-in rainfall shower, and a white mosquito net over the bed. Outside were quiet, winding paths and tranquil pools with flitting clouds of dragonflies, and small garden plots where you could pick your own vegetables. "You know what," Campbell said, "this is a perfect place for a honeymoon."

The manager pored over the map, showing the twists and turns that led from the village to the west side of the mountain and the narrow back road to A Luoi. It proved to be a steep climb. The road crossed one small stream, and Campbell got out to look at it. No, he said, this one didn't feel right; it wasn't much more than a trickle.

A little farther on, a larger stream ran under a bridge. This one looked more promising, although he didn't recognize the surrounding landscape. The jungle had vanished, and the slopes all around were carpeted with acacia. But the map showed no other possibilities on this side of the mountain. "I guess this must be it," he said.

We hiked uphill for a bit, following the stream through fields that had recently been planted with rubber and orange trees. Ripe fruit lay rotting on the ground. After a few hundred yards, we came to a place where you could cross on stepping stones, and Campbell did so. He quoted the famous line from Heraclitus, *No man ever steps in the same river twice, for it is not the same river, and he is not the same man.*

"The stream divides in two just up ahead, around a small island," he said. "That's where it happened."

He stood there for a very long time, staring uphill, saying nothing. Finally he took a deep breath and turned his back on the mountains.

"Ready to move on?" I asked.

"Yeah," he said, "I'm ready."

Acknowledgments

This is the story of a war and its aftermath, but above all it's a story about people, and my principal thanks go to those who allowed me into their lives, shared their deep knowledge of Vietnam and their most personal memories, and spent countless hours patiently answering my endless questions. I'm honored by their trust.

My thanks first of all to those who are at the center of the "Venn diagram" of my story—Chuck Searcy, Lady Borton, Manus Campbell, Charles Bailey, and Susan Hammond. In Vietnam, none of my eight trips felt complete unless I spent some time in Quang Tri with Hien Ngo (Ngo Xuan Hien), Phu Nguyen (Nguyen Thanh Phu), and their colleagues at Project RENEW, including Col. Bui Trong Hong, Dang Quang Toan, Ho Van Lai, Luong Toan Hung, Nguyen Dieu Linh, Nguyen Hieu Trung, and the late Ngo Thien Khiet.

For an understanding of the complex history and science of Agent Orange and the other chemical herbicides used in Southeast Asia, I'm deeply indebted to Tom Boivin, Wayne Dwernychuk, Chris Hatfield and their colleagues at Hatfield Consultants, including Grant Bruce, Andy Dean, and Dan Moats. For our lengthy conversations and extended correspondence, I'm especially grateful to Jeanne Stellman, whose work, together with the work of Hatfield and the 10-80 Committee, transformed the debate on Agent Orange. My appreciation also to Matthew Meselson and Arnold Schecter, both of whom did pioneering work on the impact of the defoliation campaign in Vietnam.

Among Vietnamese scientists, I've benefited from the insights shared by Drs. Le Ke Son, Nguyen Viet Nhan, and Tran Thi Tuyet Hanh. On the geography and natural environment of the Truong Son Mountains, I must add Nguyen Cu, a veteran of the Ho Chi Minh Trail, as well as Dang Gia Tung, Le Manh Hung, Le Trong Trai, Phung Tuu Boi, Matt Grainger, and Alain Hennache. My correspondence with the forestry expert Greg Nagle has illuminated questions related to the A Luoi Valley.

At the Vietnam Association for Victims of Agent Orange/Dioxin (VAVA), my thanks to Senior Lt. Gen. Nguyen Van Rinh, Pham Truong, and the late Col. Nguyen Minh Y in Hanoi; Le Van Dang in Quang Tri; Ho Sy Binh and Troang Anh Vinh in A Luoi; and Nguyen Dao and Nguyen Hien in Bien Hoa.

Special thanks to Hien Dao and My Ha Nguyen for helping to give me a soft landing on my first trips to Hanoi, and to Amie Alley and Todd Pollack for their friendship and hospitality on many subsequent visits. At various times, and in various places, Le Quy Minh, Nguyen Thi Nhung, and Nguyen Tuan Huy were excellent traveling companions, all of them gifted with the sense of humor that's essential for long days on the road. I've also been lucky enough to work with two superb photographers, who were also great company on the back roads of the Ho Chi Minh Trail: Justin Mott (in Vietnam) and Christopher Anderson (in Laos). I've not yet found the opportunity to work with Catherine Karnow, who also works magic with a camera, but in the meantime I'll settle for her friendship. Another friend, Nguyen Trang Thu, has given me important help with some tricky translation problems. David Black provided valuable research assistance with classified documents.

Le Minh Chau, Le Thi Mit, Nguyen Kien, Nguyen Thu, Nguyen Van Bong, Nguyen Van Loc, Tran Thi Gai, and Tran Van Tran were all, in their different ways, an inspiration. Many other Vietnamese were generous with their time and support, including Bui Thi Lan, Bui Van Toan, Cuong Tran, Dang Sy Toai, Dang Tung, Ho Thi Binh, Hoang Nam, Le Anh Tuan, Le Minh Hue, Le Ngoc Tam, Thi Bay Miradoli, Nguyen Dao Trai, Nguyen Duc, Nguyen Hong Hanh, Nguyen Hung Minh, Nguyen Ngoc Bich, Nguyen Qui Duc, Nguyen Thanh Lam, Phan Hung Ming, Phan Van Sonh, Quynh O, Toang Quach, Tran Thu

Ha, Tran Xuan Nam, Truong Cong Vinh, Truong Trong Khanh, Van Cao, Vu Le Anh, and Sister Vu Thi Vinh.

In addition to Chuck Searcy and Manus Campbell, I'm grateful to the many other American veterans who shared their stories, answered my questions, and encouraged my research. Thanks to Louis Andre, Mike Burton, David Clark, Gerry Condon, Bob Connor, David Cortright, Paul Cox, Arthur Faiella, Suel Jones, Lance Kaufman, Frank Krushin, Ron Milam, Mark O'Connor, Jeff Roy, Paul Sutton, Dick Schmitt, Greg Smith, Larry Vetter, Chuck Ward, John Ward, Rick Weidman, and David Wells. I've also appreciated my conversations with Kris Goldsmith, Garret Reppenhagen, and Neal Rickner, veterans of the wars in Iraq and Afghanistan, which will have their own long reckoning.

For introducing me to the wonders of Laos, thanks above all to Jacqui Chagnon and Niphaphone Sengthong of the War Legacies Project (two more great traveling companions), and to Sera Koulabdara, Khamsone Sirimanovong, Aleena Inthaly, and their colleagues at Legacies of War. Thanks also to Saowanee Alexander, Siphandone Boud, Bouavanh Chanthavilay, Angela Dickey, Ian Baird, Mike Boddington, Erik Harms, Steve Heder, Khumphat Hoxongluang, Phouthong Khamannivong, Vien Chien Koumman, Bounmi Liyouvanh, Dr. Tavanh Manivong, Duncan McCargo, Kit Norland, Ong Pa Ouang, Cheo Palai, Tamplo Palieng, Khampheui Phanchathone, Dr. Sonexay Rajvong, Michael Sheinkman, Phetsamone Souliyavong, Boomteuy Soulivongsa, Suly Volaboud, Kham Vuoi, and Vongphet Xaisangouane. And a special *sabaidee* to Yen Ly Vongkansa.

Chris Abrams, Eileen Fanelli, Tony Kolb, Nisha Morrissey, and their colleagues at the U.S. Agency for International Development (USAID) in Hanoi were invariably helpful, as were Lt. Col. Kenneth Hoffman and Lt. Col. Tamara Fischer Carter at the Defense POW/MIA Accounting Agency (DPAA). Sanjeev Bahl and Simon Barstow kindly hosted me on my first trip to Bien Hoa. Elizabeth Becker, one of the finest American reporters on the wars in Southeast Asia, generously passed on to me some of her collection of rare English-language books published in Hanoi in the 1960s and '70s, while her husband, retired Maj. Gen. Bill Nash, shared his memories of the 1970 Cambodia incursion. Thanks to Lien-Hang T. Nguyen of Columbia University for her warm support of my work and her groundbreaking scholarship; David

Biggs of the University of California, Riverside, for offering his expert knowledge of the war in Thua Thien-Hue; Dick Hughes, for several enlightening conversations since we appeared together some years ago in a TV documentary on Agent Orange; Tim Doling, for introducing me to some of the forgotten beauties of old Saigon on one of his inimitable walking tours; Dave Elder and Murray Hiebert, for sharing their knowledge of the work of the American Friends Service Committee and other humanitarian groups in postwar Southeast Asia; Steve Maxner and Amy Mondt at the Vietnam Center and Sam Johnson Vietnam Archive at Texas Tech University, a treasure house of digitized research materials that made it possible to work effectively during the two years of Covid lockdowns; and Judith Henchy, coordinator of the Vietnam Studies Group, which has been a source of all sorts of fascinating arcana.

In Washington, I've learned a lot from conversations with Brian Eyler at the Stimson Institute; Andrew Wells-Dang at the U.S. Institute of Peace; Michael Martin at the Congressional Research Service; Ted Osius, former ambassador to Hanoi and subsequently head of the U.S.-ASEAN Business Council; and Tim Rieser in the office of Sen. Patrick Leahy.

Whether they know it or not, many other people have left their fingerprints on this book. They include Alan Adelson, Joe Babcock, Sally Benson, James Bradley, Keith Brinton, Mike Cerre, Bill Cook, Richard Craik, Eliot Cutler, Greg Daddis, Peter Davis, Ragnhild Dybdahl, Diane Fox, Matthew Friedman, Jim Galloway, George Gibson, Marc Jason Gilbert, Jonathon Guthrie, Jenny Hourihan, Shelley Inglis, Richard Joynes, Peter Kiang, Claudia Krich, Ambassador Dan Kritenbrink, Courtney Marsh, John McAuliff, Craig McNamara, Myra McPherson, Betty Munson, Steve Nichols, Drew Pearson, Mokie Porter, Mark Rasmuson, Robert Richter, Steve Ross, Stefan Schultz, Mark Sidel, Steve Talbot, Dave Troy, Gabor Vargyas, Courtney Weatherby, Ray Wilkinson, Nadya Williams, Jonathan Winer, Eric Wright, and Andrew Wyatt.

Some passages in this book began life as magazine articles, and I'm grateful to the editors who knocked them into shape. In chronological order: Katrina vanden Heuvel and Roane Carey at *The Nation* (with a special nod to Teresa Stack and Debra Eliezer at the Nation Institute); Nicholas Thompson and Eric Lach at *The New Yorker;* Jennifer

Bogo at *Audubon;* Roger Cohn and Rene Ebersole at *Yale Environment 360;* Hamilton Fish at *The Washington Spectator;* and Mark Jannot and Lauren Katzenberg at *The New York Times Magazine.* The Pulitzer Center on Crisis Reporting is a national treasure for the beleaguered profession of journalism, and I'm deeply grateful to Jon Sawyer, Tom Hundley, Nathalie Applewhite, Kayla Edwards, and their colleagues for supporting my travels in Laos and promoting the results.

The seed that grew into this book was planted some years ago in a conversation with the historian Lorraine Patterson, as we were on our way to the My Son sanctuary in Quang Nam. At the time, I was working on a travel book called *On the Ganges,* an account of a journey from the Himalayas to the Indian Ocean. She suggested I write a follow-up: *On the Ho Chi Minh Trail.* The project has traveled a good distance since then, but it's still woven around that core idea. Thank you, Lorraine.

My old friend Henry Dunow went far beyond the call of duty in helping me shape it into a coherent narrative with an ever-expanding cast of characters. Another old friend, Wendy Wolf, pushed it a couple of important steps further. My wonderful agent, Carolyn Savarese of Kneerim and Williams, immediately decided that the perfect editor for *The Long Reckoning* would be Jonathan Segal at Knopf—to which, I confess, my immediate response was "Dream on." But her instincts were impeccable. Jon is one of those rare editors who cares equally for the grand architecture of a book, the flow of a narrative, and the rhythm of every sentence and word choice, and it's been a rare privilege to place myself in his hands. It's been a pleasure to work with his assistant, Sarah Perrin, who is a model of efficiency and gifted with boundless patience. I'm also grateful to the rest of the excellent team at Knopf, including Janet Biehl, Maggie Hinders, Chip Kidd, Nicholas Latimer, Rita Madrigal, Elka Roderick, Denise Stambaugh, Ellen Whitaker, and Kathryn Zuckerman. Joe LeMonnier, one of the finest mapmakers I know, crafted the two beautiful maps for this book.

My wife, Anne Nelson, our son, David, and our daughter, Julia, have all used their skills and passions as well as their respect for research, reporting, and writing, to make this violent world a better and safer place. They constantly add new dimensions of understanding to my life.

An Essay on Sources

By one estimate, about thirty thousand books have been written about the French and American wars in Vietnam. Given this vast literature, it's impossible for anyone to say what the "best" books are. All an author can do is to single out those that he or she found most useful. I've also relied on a large number of scholarly articles and declassified documents, some of which are cited in my notes. For the benefit of academic readers and those interested in exploring the subject more deeply, a comprehensive bibliography and additional notes, including on significant Vietnamese sources, are available on my website, https://george-black.net.

On the French War, from 1946 to 1954, and its seamless continuity with the American war that followed, Fredrik Logevall's Pulitzer Prize–winning *Embers of War: The Fall of an Empire and the Making of America's Vietnam* (New York: Random House, 2012) is indispensable. The works of Bernard Fall, who was killed near Hue in 1967, are also essential reading, notably *Street Without Joy* (New York: Schocken, 1961), which focuses on the French War in Thua Thien and Quang Tri, and *Hell in a Very Small Place: The Siege of Dien Bien Phu* (Philadelphia: Lippincott, 1966). Ted Morgan, *Valley of Death: The Tragedy at Dien Bien Phu That Led America into the Vietnam War* (New York: Random House, 2010), is an exhaustively researched account of the battle. Christopher Goscha, *The Road to Dien Bien Phu: A History of the First War for Vietnam* (Princeton: Princeton University Press, 2022) is an especially important new contribution to our knowledge of the French War.

William J. Duiker's *Ho Chi Minh* (New York: Hyperion, 2000) has long been regarded as the classic biography of the Vietnamese leader. Sophie Quinn-Judge's *Ho Chi Minh: The Missing Years 1919–1941* (Berkeley: University of California Press, 2003) contains many fresh insights. Lady Borton's concise biography, *Ho Chi Minh: A Journey* (Hanoi: The Gioi, 2017), is especially useful for its rich collection of archival images. A short biography for the general reader, published during the war, is David Halberstam's *Ho* (Lanham, Md.: Rowman & Littlefield, 1971).

A good number of the classic early studies of the American War—by which I mean those written roughly before the mid-1990s—have stood the test of time. Among those written by journalists, the most notable are Frances Fitzgerald's *Fire in the Lake: The Vietnamese and the Americans in Vietnam* (Boston: Little, Brown, 1972); Stanley Karnow's *Vietnam: A History* (New York: Viking, 1983); Neil Sheehan's *A Bright Shining Lie: John Paul Vann and America in Vietnam* (New York: Random House, 1988); and David Halberstam's *The Best and the Brightest* (New York: Random House, 1989). Among the first generation of works by academic historians, those that stand out include George C. Herring, *America's Longest War, 1950–1975* (New York: McGraw-Hill, 1979); Larry Berman, *Planning a Tragedy: The Americanization of the War in Vietnam* (New York: W.W. Norton, 1982); Berman, *Lyndon Johnson's War* (W.W. Norton, 1989); William S. Turley, *The Second Indochina War: A Short Political and Military History* (Boulder, Colo.: Westview Press, 1986); and Marilyn Young's provocatively titled *The Vietnam Wars 1945–1990* (New York: HarperCollins, 1991). Neil L. Jamieson's *Understanding Vietnam* (Berkeley: University of California Press, 1995) takes a broad view of the war in the context of Vietnamese culture and political history. An analysis of the war from a Marxist perspective is Gabriel Kolko, *Anatomy of a War: Vietnam, the United States, and the Modern Historical Memory* (New York: Pantheon, 1985).

Of the numerous accounts of the war by U.S. officials, I found it necessary to read Gen. William Westmoreland's *A Soldier Reports* (New York: Doubleday, 1976); Lt. Gen. Phillip C. Davidson's *Vietnam at War 1946–1975* (Novato, Calif.: Presidio, 1988), written by his chief of intelligence; and *Strange War, Strange Strategy: A General's Report on Vietnam* (New York: Funk & Wagnalls, 1970) by Gen. Lewis W. Walt, who commanded Marine forces in I Corps from 1965 to 1967. Gregory A. Daddis, *Westmoreland's War: Reassessing American Strategy* (New York: Oxford University Press, 2014), is an insightful recent addition to the literature, arguing that historians' focus on Westmoreland's search-and-destroy operations presents too narrow a view of his military strategy. On the civilian side are the memoirs of Robert McNamara, *In Retrospect: The Meaning and Lessons of Vietnam* (New York: Times Books/Random House, 1998); Daniel Ellsberg, *Secrets: A Memoir of Vietnam and the Pentagon Papers* (New York: Viking, 2002); and of course *The Pentagon Papers: The Secret History of the Vietnam War* (New York: New York Times Company, 1971).

The question that principally concerned this first generation of authors was "Why did we lose?" A subsequent generation, with greater access to Vietnamese publications and previously classified materials, has turned to the equally important corollary question: "Why did they win?" William J. Duiker's *Sacred War: Nationalism and Revolution in a Divided Vietnam* (New York: McGraw-Hill, 1995) was one of the first to discuss the factional divisions within the Vietnamese Workers Party and the dominant role of Le Duan in the politburo. A. J. Langguth's excellent *Our Vietnam: The War 1954–1975* (New York: Simon & Schuster, 2000) touches on some of these questions, as does John Prados's *Vietnam: The History of an Unwinnable War* (Lawrence: University Press of Kansas, 2009). The work of Christopher Goscha is especially important, and these new perspectives on the war are incorporated in his monumental *Penguin History of Modern Vietnam* (London: Allen Lane, 2016).

The landmark contribution to our understanding of the internal politics of the VWP and the complex relationship between the Democratic Republic of Viet Nam and its two main backers, China and the Soviet Union, is Lien-Hang T. Nguyen's *Hanoi's War: An International History of the War for Peace in Vietnam* (Chapel Hill: University of North Carolina Press, 2012), which draws on the author's unique access to previously closed archives. Two volumes by Pierre Asselin are a valuable complement to her groundbreaking work: *Hanoi's Road to the American War 1954–1965* (Berkeley: University of California Press,

2013) and *Vietnam's American War: A History* (New York: Cambridge University Press, 2018).

Three useful volumes of essays from this second generation of scholarship are Mark Philip Bradley and Marilyn Young, eds., *Making Sense of the Vietnam Wars: Local, National, and Transnational Perspectives* (New York: Oxford University Press, 2008); Marc Jason Gilbert, ed., *Why the North Won the Vietnam War* (London: Palgrave, 2002); and Geoffrey W. Jensen and Matthew M. Stith, *Beyond the Quagmire: New Interpretations of the Vietnam War* (Denton: University of North Texas Press, 2019).

Douglas Pike's *PAVN: The People's Army of Vietnam* (Novato, Calif.: Presidio, 1986) is a useful reference to Vietnamese military organization and strategies. *Victory in Vietnam: The Official History of the People's Army of Vietnam* (Lawrence: University Press of Kansas, 2002), in an excellent translation by the former CIA analyst Merle L. Pribbenow II, was first published in Hanoi in 1988 and then in a revised edition in 1994. While it glosses over most of the internal policy disputes, it does contain some revealing acknowledgments of mistakes made and lessons learned. A scathing critique of official policy is Bui Tin, *Following Ho Chi Minh: Memoirs of a Vietnamese Colonel* (Honolulu: University of Hawai'i Press, 1995), by a PAVN officer loyal to Ho and Vo Nguyen Giap, who eventually left Vietnam. An admiring portrait of the courage of PAVN and NLF combatants from the perspective of an American officer is James G. Zumwalt (son of Adm. Elmo R. Zumwalt, Jr.), *Bare Feet Iron Will: Stories from the Other Side of Vietnam's Battlefields* (Jacksonville, Fla.: Fortis, 2010).

Other noteworthy books on the war from an American perspective are Paul Hendrickson, *The Living and the Dead: Robert McNamara and Five Lives of a Lost War* (New York: Alfred A. Knopf, 1996), which includes the story of the Quaker Norman Morrison; David Maraniss, *They Marched into Sunlight: War and Peace, Vietnam and America, October 1967* (New York: Simon & Schuster, 2003); and Nick Turse, *Kill Anything That Moves: The Real American War in Vietnam* (New York: Metropolitan Books, 2013), which echoes the arguments presented to the Senate by John Kerry in 1971—that atrocities occurred frequently and were condoned by senior officers. A comprehensive history of the war, lavishly illustrated in coffee table book format, is Geoffrey C. Ward and Ken Burns, *The Vietnam War: An Intimate History* (New York: Alfred A. Knopf, 2017), the companion volume to Burns's 2017 PBS series.

There is a rich literature on the war in I Corps. Notably vivid accounts by journalists who were there include Michael Herr's *Dispatches* (New York: Alfred A. Knopf, 1968); Jonathan Schell's *The Military Half: An Account of the Destruction in Quang Ngai and Quang Tin,* in *The Real War: The Classic Reporting on the Vietnam War* (New York: Pantheon, 1985); and John Laurence's *The Cat From Hue: A Vietnam War Story* (New York: Public Affairs, 2002). Among the most notable memoirs of combat are Philip Caputo's *A Rumor of War* (New York: Henry Holt, 1977); W. D. Ehrhart, *Vietnam-Perkasie: A Combat Marine's Memoir* (Amherst: University of Massachusetts Press, 1983); and Frederick Downs, *The Killing Zone: A True Story* (New York: W.W. Norton, 1978), about the war in Quang Nam. John Musgrave, *The Education of Corporal John Musgrave: Vietnam and Its Aftermath* (New York: Alfred A. Knopf, 2021), is a good recent addition to the bookshelf. The environmental historian David Biggs's *Footprints of War: Militarized Landscapes in Vietnam* (Seattle: University of Washington Press, 2018) is a strikingly original study of the impact of the French and American wars in Thua Thien province. Phil Ball's *Ghosts and Shadows: A Marine in Vietnam 1968–1969* (Jefferson, N.C.: McFarland & Co., 2012) describes the author's experiences in Quang Tri, as does Suel Jones's self-published *Meeting the Enemy: A Marine Goes Home* (2008), which also recounts the story of his homecoming and eventual return to Vietnam.

Among the most important works of fiction to emerge from I Corps are Tim O'Brien's *If I Die in a Combat Zone, Box Me Up and Ship Me Home* (New York: Delacorte Press, 1975) and O'Brien's *The Things They Carried* (Boston: Houghton Mifflin, 1990); John Del Vecchio's *The Thirteenth Valley* (New York: St. Martin's Press, 1982); and Karl Marlantes, *Matterhorn* (New York: Atlantic Monthly Press, 2010). Marlantes's later work of nonfiction, *What It Is Like to Go to War* (New York: Grove Atlantic, 2011), is also vastly illuminating. From a Vietnamese perspective, Le Ly Hayslip's *When Heaven and Earth Changed Places: A*

Vietnamese Woman's Journey from War to Peace (New York: Penguin, 1989) is a devasting memoir-cum-novel of the war in Quang Nam.

The wartime experience of those who fought in Vietnam is captured well in a number of works. Vietnamese and American voices mingle in Christian Appy's exemplary oral history, *Patriots: The Vietnam War Remembered from All Sides* (New York: Viking, 2003). Appy's earlier book, *Working-Class War: American Combat Soldiers and Vietnam* (Chapel Hill: University of North Carolina Press, 1993), delivers what the title promises. Doug Bradley and Craig Werner, eds., *We Gotta Get Out of This Place: The Soundtrack of the Vietnam War* (Amherst: University of Massachusetts Press, 2015) discusses the central importance of music in the experience of the American grunt. And Richard Bernstein's *The East, the West, and Sex: A History of Erotic Encounters* (New York: Alfred A. Knopf, 2009) includes a fascinating chapter on that particular dimension of the war, "I Souvenir, You Boom-boom."

The essential work on the wartime experience of PAVN fighters is Bao Ninh's extraordinary novel, *The Sorrow of War* (New York: Pantheon, 1995). *Not Only in the Past,* the autobiography of Senior Lt. Gen. Nguyen Van Rinh, with Nguyen Duy Tuong (Hanoi: People's Army Publishing House, 2014), is especially interesting for its description of the Tet Offensive in Quang Tri. Tran Mai Nam, *The Narrow Strip of Land* (Hanoi: Foreign Languages Publishing House, 1969), is a vivid account of the war in northern I Corps by a journalist assigned to the People's Liberation Armed Forces. Truong Nhu Tang, with David Chanoff and Doan Van Toai, *A Viet Cong Memoir: An Inside Account of the Vietnam War and Its Aftermath* (New York: Vintage, 1986), is the story of Vietnam's former minister of justice, who defected to the West. Chanoff and Toai also collaborated on *Vietnam: A Portrait of Its People at War* (London: I.B. Tauris, 1987), which presents a wide range of Vietnamese voices, both military and civilian.

On the Tet Offensive, the first significant book by a journalist was Don Oberdorfer's *Tet!: The Turning Point in the Vietnam War* (New York: Doubleday, 1971). The standard work by a military historian is James H. Willbanks, *The Tet Offensive: A Concise History* (New York: Columbia University Press, 2006). Erik Villard, *The 1968 Tet Offensive Battles of Quang Tri City and Hue* (Washington, D.C.: U.S. Army Center of Military History, n.d.), focuses on northern I Corps. As the title suggests, Peter Braestrup's *Big Story: How the American Press and Television Reported and Interpreted the Crisis of Tet 1968* (New York: Anchor Books, 1978) is a critical analysis of American media coverage. Mark Bowden's *Hue 1968: A Turning Point in the American War in Vietnam* (New York: Atlantic Monthly Press, 2017) is a granular hour-by-hour account of the battle for the city. For a recent example of conservative revisionist thinking about Tet, it's worth looking at James S. Robbins, *This Time We Win: Revisiting the Tet Offensive* (New York: Encounter Books, 2010). Lien-Hang T. Nguyen's book on Tet (New York: Random House, forthcoming) promises to include many important new insights into the offensive from the perspective of Hanoi.

James Willbanks is also the author of *A Raid Too Far: Operation Lam Son 719 and Vietnamization in Laos* (College Station: Texas A&M University Press, 2014), an account of the South Vietnamese invasion of Laos in 1971. As for the 1972 Nguyen Hue, or Easter, Offensive, the most comprehensive work on offer is Stephen P. Randolph, *Powerful and Brutal Weapons: Nixon, Kissinger, and the Easter Offensive* (Cambridge, Mass.: Harvard University Press, 2007).

Accounts of a number of other significant battles and battlegrounds were also helpful in illustrating the unique levels of destruction in Quang Tri and Thua Thien. These include Jim Brown, *Impact Zone: The Battle of the DMZ in Vietnam, 1967–1968* (Tuscaloosa: University of Alabama Press, 2004); James P. Coan, *Con Thien: Hill of Angels* (Tuscaloosa: University of Alabama Press, 2004); Jack McLean, *Loon: A Marine Story* (New York: Ballantine, 2009); Samuel Zaffiri, *Hamburger Hill: The Brutal Battle for Dong Ap Bia, May 11–20, 1969* (New York: Simon & Schuster, 1988); Jay Phillips, *A Shau: Crucible of the Vietnam War* (San Francisco: Izzard Ink, 2021); Thomas P. Yarborough, *A Shau Valor: American Combat Operations in the Valley of Death, 1963–1971* (Philadelphia: Casemate, 2016); John Prados and Ray W. Stubbe, *Valley of Decision: The Siege of Khe Sanh* (New York: Dell, 1991); and Lawrence C. Vetter, Jr., *Never Without Heroes: Marine Third Reconnaissance Battalion in Vietnam 1965–70* (New York: Ballantine, 1996). Colin Powell's autobiography, *My American Journey* (with Joseph E. Persico; New York: Ballantine, 1995), recounts his experiences in the A Shau Valley and Quang Ngai. The classic account of the 1965 battle of Ia Drang is Harold G. Moore and Joseph L. Galloway, *We Were Soldiers Once . . .*

and Young: Ia Drang—The Battle That Changed the War in Vietnam (New York: Random House, 1992).

A good general history of the Marines in I Corps is Edward F. Murphy, *Semper Fi Vietnam: From Danang to the DMZ, Marine Corps Campaigns, 1965–1975* (Novato, Calif.: Presidio, 1997). The official histories of the Marines in Vietnam were an indispensable reference. I used the volumes for 1966 (*An Expanding War*), 1967 (*Fighting the North Vietnamese*), 1968 (*The Defining Year*), and 1969 (*High Mobilization and Standdown*). The most salient episodes are summarized in Willard Pearson, *The War in the Northern Provinces, 1966–1968* (Washington, D.C.: Department of the Army, 1975). The command chronologies and after-action reports of the First Battalion, Fourth Marines fleshed out many details about Manus Campbell's time in Thua Thien and Quang Tri, and Michael P. Kelley's *Where We Were in Vietnam: A Comprehensive Guide to the Firebases, Military Installations, and Naval Vessels of the Vietnam War 1945–1975* (Ashland, Ore.: Hellgate Press, 2002) is an extraordinary source of detailed information on specific locations.

I also found it useful to consult several books on the Special Forces and the secret Studies and Observations Group (MACV-SOG). These include John Stryker Meyer and John E. Peters, *On the Ground: The Secret War in Vietnam* (Oceanside, Calif.: SOG Publishing, 2007); John L. Plaster, *SOG: The Secret Wars of America's Commandos in Vietnam* (New York: Simon & Schuster, 1997); and Shelby L. Stanton, *Green Berets at War: U.S. Army Special Forces in Southeast Asia 1956–1975* (New York: Ballantine, 1985).

Given its vital importance to the conduct and outcome of the war, astonishingly little has been written in English about the Ho Chi Minh Trail. The most significant work is John Prados's minutely detailed *The Blood Road: The Ho Chi Minh Trail and the Vietnam War* (New York: John Wiley & Sons, 1999). Like his other works on the war, this one draws heavily on declassified American documents, but unfortunately it offers no details about the secret defoliation campaign. Virginia Morris with Clive Hills's *The Road to Freedom: A History of the Ho Chi Minh Trail* (Bangkok: Orchid Press, 2006), despite its title, is less a history than a colorful account of a trek down the Trail in 2003, notable for its useful maps of the Laos side and atmospheric photography. The most recent book on the subject in English is Sherry Buchanan, *On the Ho Chi Minh Trail: The Blood Road, The Women Who Defended It, The Legacy* (Chicago: University of Chicago Press, 2021).

For my account of the Trail and the experiences of those who fought on it, I've relied primarily on Vietnamese sources. Dang Phong's *Five Ho Chi Minh Trails* (Hanoi: The Gioi, 2016) has fascinating details of the oil pipeline, the maritime traffic routes, the "Sihanouk Road" through Cambodia, and the virtual trail that financed the war effort. Le Cao Dai, *The Central Highlands: A North Vietnamese Journal of Life on the Ho Chi Minh Trail 1965–1973*, translated and annotated by Lady Borton (Hanoi: The Gioi, 2004), includes descriptions of the defoliation of the Trail. The Barry Wain Collection (no. 2881) in the Vietnam Archive at Texas Tech University contains extensive interviews with former PAVN officials, including Col. Vo Bam and Col. Dong Sy Nguyen, successive commanders of Group 559, as well as unpublished English translations of several Vietnamese histories of the Trail. Wain, an Australian journalist, compiled these in the course of research for a book that sadly remained unfinished at the time of his death.

The literature on the war in Laos is also sparse, and what little there is deals mainly with the CIA's secret support for the Hmong in the north of the country. For general background on Laos, I've relied on Grant Evans, ed., *Laos: Culture and Society* (Chiang Mai: Silkworm Press, 1999). Jane Hamilton-Merritt, *Tragic Mountains: The Hmong, the Americans, and the Secret Wars in Laos, 1942–1992* (Bloomington: Indiana University Press, 1993), is a detailed and passionate account by a fervent advocate for the Hmong. The most recent book on this dimension of the secret war in Laos is Joshua Kurlantick, *A Great Place to Have a War: America in Laos and the Birth of a Military CIA* (New York: Simon & Schuster, 2016). A hawkish critique of U.S. policy in Laos, particularly the inability to cut the Ho Chi Minh Trail, is Norman B. Hannah, *The Key to Failure: Laos and the Vietnam War* (Lanham, Md.: Madison Books, 1987). Two detailed official accounts of the bombing campaign on the Trail have been published: Jacob Van Staaveren, *Interdiction in Southern Laos 1960–1968* (Maxwell AFB, Ala.: Center for Air Force History, 1993), and Bernard C. Nalty, *The War Against Trucks: Aerial Interdiction in Southern Laos 1968–1972* (Washington, D.C.: Air Force History and Museums Program, 2005). Peace activist Fred Branfman collected moving accounts of the bombing in *Voices from the Plain of Jars: Life Under an Air War* (New York: Harper Colophon, 1972).

On the consequences of the war in Southeast Asia after 1975, three early works remain essential: William Shawcross, *Sideshow: Kissinger, Nixon, and the Destruction of Cambodia* (New York: Simon & Schuster, 1979); Elizabeth Becker, *When the War Was Over: Cambodia's Revolution and the Voices of Its People* (New York: Simon & Schuster, 1986); and Nayan Chanda, *Brother Enemy: The War After the War, A History of Indochina Since the Fall of Saigon* (New York: Collier Books, 1979).

The work of Gerald C. Hickey on the wartime history of the ethnic minorities of the Truong Son Mountains remains without parallel, notably *Free in the Forest: Ethnohistory of the Vietnamese Central Highlands, 1954–1976* (New Haven, Conn.: Yale University Press, 1982); *Shattered World: Adaptation and Survival Among Vietnam's Highland People During the Vietnam War* (Philadelphia: University of Pennsylvania Press, 1993); and *Window on a War: An Anthropologist in the Vietnam Conflict* (Lubbock: Texas Tech University Press, 2002). Vatthana Pholsena, author of *Postwar Laos: The Politics of Culture, History, and Identity* (Ithaca, N.Y.: Cornell University Press, 2006), has also published several important academic papers on the ethnic minorities of Laos. Nikolas Arhem, "Forests, Spirits, and High Modernist Development: A Study of Cosmology and Change Among the Katuic Peoples in the Uplands of Laos and Vietnam" (Ph.D. thesis, Uppsala University, Sweden), was extremely helpful to my research in Laos and the A Shau Valley.

Early works on the defoliation campaign and its consequences looked mainly at the ecological impact of the herbicides. These include Barry Weisberg, *Ecocide in Indochina: The Ecology of War* (San Francisco: Canfield Press, 1970) and *Ecological Consequences of the Second Indochina War* (Stockholm: International Peace Research Institute, 1976). Thomas Whiteside's *Defoliation: What Are Our Herbicides Doing to Us?* (New York: Ballantine/Friends of the Earth, 1970) looks at what was known at the time about the toxicity of the chemicals.

The first important Vietnamese studies of the health impacts of dioxin were those of Dr. Ton That Tung, collected as *U.S. Chemical*

Warfare and Its Consequences: Dossier (Hanoi: Vietnam Courier, 1980). Charles Waugh and Huy Lien, eds., *Family of Fallen Leaves: Stories of Agent Orange by Vietnamese Writers* (Athens: University of Georgia Press, 2010), contains what the title promises.

Three very different volumes give the official perspective on the herbicide campaign. William A. Buckingham, Jr., *Operation Ranch Hand: The Air Force and Herbicides in Southeast Asia 1961–1971* (Washington, D.C.: Office of Air Force History, 1982), is the most comprehensive, although sections of Buckingham's original draft remain classified. Paul Frederick Cecil, *Herbicidal Warfare: The Ranch Hand Project in Vietnam* (Westport, Conn.: Praeger, 1986) is the story as told by a C-123 pilot, though it omits many controversial elements of the program, especially regarding defoliation in Laos and Cambodia, tantalizing details of which were revealed in his interviews with other pilots and crew members, transcripts of which are in the Vietnam Archive at Texas Tech University. Alvin L. Young, *The History, Use, Disposition and Environmental Fate of Agent Orange* (New York: Springer, 2009), was written by the air force's leading toxicologist, who has never wavered in his advocacy of the value and safety of the defoliation campaign.

By far the most impressive study of the subject is Edwin A. Martini, *Agent Orange: History, Science, and the Politics of Uncertainty* (Amherst: University of Massachusetts Press, 2012). Le Ke Son and Charles R. Bailey, *From Enemies to Partners: Vietnam, the U.S. and Agent Orange* (Chicago: C. Anton, 2017), is a useful concise overview of the dioxin problem in southern Vietnam, the situation of Agent Orange victims, American public attitudes to Agent Orange, and the evolution of U.S. policy. Evelyn Frances Krache Morris, "Into the Wind: The Kennedy Administration and the Use of Herbicides in South Vietnam" (unpublished Ph.D. dissertation, Georgetown University, 2012), is the only work I know on a topic that really deserves a book in its own right. Philip Jones-Griffiths, *Agent Orange: "Collateral Damage" in Viet Nam* (London: Trolley, 2003), is a heartbreaking photographic record of the devastating consequences of the defoliation. It includes portraits of families in Quang Tri's Cam Nghia commune, which I describe in Chapter 23. Fred A. Wilcox, *Waiting for an Army to Die: The Tragedy of Agent Orange* (New York: Random House, 1983), recounts the early struggles of American veterans for recognition.

On the broader history of the impact of the war on American culture and society, two of the most important early works were Gloria Emerson, *Winners and Losers: Battles, Retreats, Gains, Losses, and Ruins from the Vietnam War* (New York: W.W. Norton, 1976), and Myra MacPherson, *Long Time Coming: Vietnam and the Haunted Generation* (New York: Doubleday, 1984), both of which include brief vignettes of Jacqui Chagnon. Christian G. Appy, *American Reckoning: The Vietnam War and Our National Identity* (New York: Viking, 2015), traces the longer-term legacy of Vietnam through the later wars in Central America, Afghanistan, and Iraq.

The classic veteran's memoir of a traumatic homecoming is Ron Kovic, *Born on the Fourth of July* (New York: McGraw-Hill, 1976). Ellen Frey-Wouters and Robert S. Laufer, *Legacy of a War: The American Veteran in Vietnam* (Armonk, N.Y.: M.E. Sharpe, 1986), is a comprehensive study, based on 1,159 interviews, of veterans' attitudes toward the war. A more recent history of the veterans' experience is James Wright, *Enduring Vietnam: An American Generation and Its War* (New York: Thomas Dunne Books, 2017). Jerry Lembcke, *The Spitting Image: Myth, Memory, and the Legacy of Vietnam* (New York: New York University Press, 1998), uses what the author calls the "urban myth" of the spat-upon veteran as a point of entry to other distortions of postwar history. Arnold R. Isaacs, *Vietnam Shadows: The War, Its Ghosts, and Its Legacy* (Baltimore: Johns Hopkins University Press, 1997), takes on a number of issues related to the postwar "Vietnam Syndrome." In understanding the experience of Manus Campbell and others with PTSD, I've relied heavily on Arthur Egendorf's classic *Healing From the War: Trauma and Transformation After Vietnam* (Boston: Shambhala, 1986), as well as Jonathan Shay, *Achilles in Vietnam: Combat Trauma and the Undoing of Character* (New York: Scribner, 1994).

On the POW/MIA controversy, the definitive work is Michael J. Allen, *Until the Last Man Comes Home: POWs, MIAs, and the Unending Vietnam War* (Chapel Hill: University of North Carolina Press, 2009). A firsthand account of the work of "the Ranch" in Hanoi is Garnett "Bill" Bell with George J. Veith, *Leave No Man Behind: Bill Bell and the Search for American POW/MIAs from the Vietnam War* (Madison, Wis.: Goblin Fern Press, 2004). Garry L. Smith, *The Search for MIAs* (Spartanburg, S.C.: Honoribus Press, 1992), recounts details

of many of the early joint U.S.-Vietnamese missions, including to the
A Shau Valley and Quang Tri. An important study of the politicization
of the issue and the attendant disinformation is H. Bruce Franklin,
*M.I.A. or Mythmaking in America: How and Why Belief in Live POWs
Has Possessed a Nation* (Brooklyn, N.Y.: Lawrence Hill Books, 1992).
As I argue, once cooperation between the United States and Vietnam
was under way on the MIA issue, the next step in improving relations
was U.S. humanitarian aid for prosthetics and orthotics. One of the
main advocates of this was Frederick Downs, whose encounters with
Vietnamese amputees on his return to the places in I Corps, where he
saw combat, are movingly recounted in *No Longer Enemies, Not Yet
Friends: An American Soldier Returns to Vietnam* (New York: W.W.
Norton, 1991).

Perhaps not surprisingly, the postwar period in Vietnam has received
much less attention than the war itself. Several reporters who covered
the conflict recorded their impressions after going back in the 1980s.
The best are William Broyles, Jr., *Brothers in Arms: A Journey From
War to Peace* (New York: Alfred A. Knopf, 1986); Morley Safer's beauti-
fully written *Flashbacks: On Returning to Vietnam* (New York: Random
House, 1990); and Neil Sheehan, *After the War Was Over: Hanoi and
Saigon* (New York: Random House, 1991).

Studies of Vietnam's immediate postwar struggles are thin on the
ground. William J. Duiker, *Vietnam: Revolution in Transition* (Boulder, Colo.: Westview Press, 1995), is a helpful overview. Gabriel Kolko,
Vietnam: Anatomy of a Peace (London: Routledge, 1997), presents a
jaundiced view of what the author sees as the abandonment of socialist values. Nonetheless, it contains some useful material on the *doi moi*
reforms. Georges Boudarel and Nguyen Van Ky, *Hanoi: City of the Rising Dragon* (Lanham, Md.: Rowman & Littlefield, 2002) is a good portrait, both historical and contemporary, of that magical city.

In the period of normalization of U.S.-Vietnamese relations, a new
wave of journalists came to Vietnam. Inevitably the books they produced are snapshots in time and don't necessarily age well, though
all of them contain illuminating vignettes of life in Vietnam at the
time, which helped me to contextualize the stories of Chuck Searcy

and Lady Borton during those years. They include, in chronological order, Murray Hiebert, *Chasing the Tigers: A Portrait of the New
Vietnam* (New York: Kodansha International, 1996)—particularly
interesting because of the author's experience as both a reporter and
a wartime aid worker; Robert Templer, *Shadows and Wind: A View
of Modern Vietnam* (Boston: Little, Brown, 1998); and David Lamb,
Vietnam, Now: A Reporter Returns (New York: PublicAffairs, 2002),
which includes a brief encounter with Searcy. A more recent work is
Bill Hayton, *Vietnam: Rising Dragon,* 2nd ed. (New Haven, Conn.: Yale
University Press, 2020).

In a lighter vein, Andrew X. Pham's *Catfish and Mandala: A Two-
Wheeled Voyage Through the Landscape and Memory of Vietnam* (New
York: Farrar, Straus & Giroux, 1999) is a portrait of the country through
the eyes of a Viet Kieu, an "overseas Vietnamese." Catherine Karnow's
Vietnam 25 Years: Documenting a Changing Country, is a stunning collection of photographs, published as the catalog for an exhibition of
her work at the Art Vietnam Gallery in Hanoi, which I had the pleasure
of seeing in 2015.

The multiple legacies of the war are explored in a number of fascinating books. On the Vietnamese side, Heonik Kwon's *Ghosts of War
in Vietnam* (New York: Cambridge University Press, 2008) deals com-
pellingly with ghosts both literal and figurative, including the unquiet
spirits of the countless thousands of Vietnamese MIAs. Hue-Tam Ho
Tai, ed., *The Country of Memory: Remaking the Past in Late Socialist
Vietnam* (Berkeley: University of California Press, 2001), is a collection
of essays on topics including memory, museums, cemeteries, propaganda, and war-related tourism. Viet Thanh Nguyen, author of the
Pulitzer Prize–winning novel *The Sympathizer,* covers similar territory
in brilliant fashion in *Nothing Ever Dies: Vietnam and the Memory of
War* (Cambridge, Mass.: Harvard University Press, 2016). Wayne Kar-
lin's *Wandering Souls: Journeys with the Dead and the Living in Viet
Nam* (New York: Nation Books, 2009) is a beautifully written account
of the return to Vietnam of a veteran, Homer Steedly, to ask forgiveness of the family whose son he killed in battle.

There are also several useful volumes on how war legacies have
affected later U.S.-Vietnamese relations. I'd single out the outstand-
ing work of Scott Laderman and Edwin A. Martini. This includes, in

addition to Martini's book on Agent Orange, their edited collection of essays, *Four Decades On: Vietnam, the United States, and the Legacies of the Second Indochina War* (Durham, N.C.: Duke University Press, 2013); Martini's *Invisible Enemies: The American War on Vietnam, 1975–2000* (Amherst: University of Massachusetts Press, 2007); and Scott Laderman's *Tours of Vietnam: War, Travel Guides, and Memory* (Durham, N.C.: Duke University Press, 2009). Robert M. Slabey, ed., *The United States and Viet Nam from War to Peace* (Jefferson, N.C.: McFarland & Co., 1996), rounds out the list.

A more conventional political-diplomatic history of U.S.-Vietnamese political and diplomatic relations is Robert D. Schulzinger, *A Time for Peace: The Legacy of the Vietnam War* (New York: Oxford University Press, 2006). Last but by no means least is Ted Osius, *Nothing Is Impossible: America's Reconciliation with Vietnam* (New Brunswick, N.J.: Rutgers University Press, 2022), a unique insider's account of the process by a diplomat who was the first political-military officer in the embassy in Hanoi in 1997 and who later served from 2013 to 2017 as ambassador.

Notes

CHAPTER 1 GOING TO B

16 *The spectacle would have appalled:* Against Ho's wishes, the politburo began secretly planning to embalm his body in 1968 and approved the proposal for a mausoleum in November 1969, two months after his death. It was eventually completed in August 1975. Duiker, *Ho Chi Minh*, 565–66.

17 *Ho Chi Minh, "He Who Enlightens":* Ho Chi Minh was born Nguyen Sinh Cung. In childhood he was given the name Nguyen Tat Thanh ("He Who Will Succeed"), and as a young man in France he took the name Nguyen Ai Quoc ("Nguyen the Patriot"), one of many pseudonyms. For details, see Duiker, *Ho Chi Minh*, especially chaps. 1–3.

18 *Sometimes these factions:* For the fullest discussion of the DRV's complicated relationship with the Soviet Union and China and its fluctuations over time, see particularly Nguyen, *Hanoi's War*, passim. Other important analyses include Stein Tonnesson and Christopher Goscha, "Le Duan and the Break with China," *Cold War International History Project Bulletin* 12/13 (2001), 273–288; and Tuong Vu, "In the Service of World Revolution: Vietnamese Communists' Radical Ambitions Through the Three Indochina Wars," *Journal of Cold War Studies* 21, 4 (2019) 4–30.

18 *There was fierce argument:* Logevall, *Embers of War*, 597–604, gives a thorough analysis of the negotiations over the line of demarcation.

18 *the ancient imperial capital:* Hue occupies a unique role in Vietnamese politics and history, in addition to its strategic importance as a military target for the PAVN and NLF, especially during the 1968 Tet Offensive. Situated at almost the exact geographical midpoint of Vietnam, it was the seat of the Nguyen imperial dynasty from 1802 to 1945, as well as being the birthplace of Diem himself and his two brothers, Ngo Dinh Nhu and Ngo Dinh Thuc, the bishop of Hue. The city was also a center of Buddhist learning (and Buddhist protest) and of academic excellence. Those who attended Hue's elite Quoc Hoc high school included Diem himself, Ho Chi Minh, Gen. Vo Nguyen Giap, Prime Minister Pham Van Dong, Communist

Party General Secretary Tran Phu, and Dr. Ton That Tung, pioneering researcher into the effects of Agent Orange.

19 *That only fed his grievances:* According to former PAVN colonel Bui Tin, who left Vietnam in 1990 and took up residence in France, Le Duan's critique of Ho Chi Minh and Giap's policies was shot through with personal animus. After Ho's death in 1969, Bui Tin wrote, Le Duan said that Ho "opened his mouth and talked along the lines of the Confucian code of morality, like human dignity, loyalty, good manners, wisdom, and trustworthiness. What is that? It is outmoded feudalism." As for Giap, Le Duan was reported to have said in 1983 that his attitude during the American War was like that of "a frightened rabbit." Bui Tin, *Following Ho Chi Minh,* 66, 132.

20 *Some 26,000 of these "regroupees":* Gilbert, *Why the North Won,* 56, estimates the total number at between 70,000 and 80,000.

22 *"It must not be allowed":* Dang, *Five Ho Chi Minh Trails,* 56–57, citing Vo Bam's memoirs.

22 *All of them would be regroupees:* On their personal selection by Nguyen Chi Thanh, see Bui Tin, *Following Ho Chi Minh,* 42.

22 *The first targets for infiltration:* I Corps straddled what the Viet Minh, during the French War, called Interzones 4 and 5. The four tactical military zones were designated by the ARVN, with the U.S. military using the same terminology. I Corps covered the five northern provinces of South Vietnam, II Corps the Central Highlands, III Corps the area around Saigon, and IV Corps the Mekong Delta and the far south. See the map on page 3.

23 *American military strategists would:* Department of Defense Intelligence Information Report, "Organization and Activities of the 559th Transportation Group," June 13, 1968. Sam Johnson Vietnam Archive, Texas Tech University, https://www.vietnam.ttu.edu/ (no. 1071618023).

23 *originally an insulting term:* Nonetheless, *Katu* (also sometimes spelled Kotu or Cotu) is now the official ethnic category used by the Vietnamese government. Oscar Salemink, *The Ethnography of Vietnam's Central Highlanders: A Historical Contextualization 1850–1990* (London: Routledge, 2002).

23 *"All goods delivered safely":* This first group of infiltrators began their journey in Khe Ho, north of the Ben Hai River, where there is now a commemorative monument. The weapons and supplies were handed over to southern cadres at Ta Riep, two miles from the Lao border in southern Quang Tri. *Victory in Vietnam,* 52–53.

24 *As soon as the rainy season ended:* In that same month, Walt Rostow, director of the State Department's policy planning staff and an aggressive advocate of the domino theory, argued that North Vietnam would never be defeated unless the DMZ and the Lao border were sealed off against infiltration and Quang Tri province designated a "kill area"—in effect an ARVN free-fire zone. See Howard Jones, *Death of a Generation: How the Assassinations of Diem and JFK Prolonged the Vietnam War* (New York: Oxford University Press, 2003), 136.

24 *Nonetheless, in a matter of months:* The advance became possible after the PAVN's elite 325th Division seized the town of Xepon on Route 9 on April 11, 1961, airlifted supplies into the nearby Ta Khong airfield, and gained control of the highway from Xepon to the village of Ban Dong, near the Vietnamese border. *Victory in Vietnam,* 88. The following passage, as well as later descriptions of the development of the Ho Chi Minh Trail, draw on translated Vietnamese documents in the Barry Wain

collection (no. 2881), Texas Tech Vietnam Archive. These include many interviews by Wain, editor of *Asian Wall Street Journal;* official PAVN histories, books, and articles by military historian Col. Nguyen Viet Phuong; unpublished memoirs and writings by other military officers including Lt. Gen. Dong Sy Nguyen, commanding officer of Group 559, and Col. Vo Bam, original architect of the Trail; and diaries of rank-and-file PAVN fighters. Wain compiled these materials for a book on the Trail that remained unpublished.

24 *He could back up his argument:* The buildup began in 1961 with the secret "Project Beef-Up." Johnson remarked that Diem was "the Winston Churchill of Asia" during a visit to Saigon that April. Langguth, *Our Vietnam,* 131.

25 *If the politburo needed proof:* Ap Bac is dealt with at length in Sheehan's *Bright Shining Lie,* 212–265.

25 *"Some comrades tremble":* On the rivalry and schisms between Giap and Thanh, see Pribbenow, "General Vo Nguyen Giap and the Mysterious Evolution of the Plan for the 1968 Tet Offensive," *Journal of Vietnamese Studies* 3, no. 2 (2008), 1–33; Nguyen, *Hanoi's War,* 28–29, 79–80, 99; and Asselin, *Vietnam's American War,* 100.

25 *"It is the CCP":* Duiker, *Sacred War,* 164.

26 *"to a greater or lesser degree":* Logevall, *Embers of War,* 689.

26 *But Resolution 9 was an authorization:* For historical background on Nam Dong as a Communist tactical zone, see Biggs, *Landscapes of War,* 82–87 and 120–22.

27 *In a series of letters:* On February 20, Le Duan wrote to Nguyen Chi Thanh that the first priority was "attacking and shattering three or four puppet regular divisions in battle in the course of wave after wave of attacks by our forces. . . . If for some reason the uprisings in the cities run into trouble . . . that will not matter." In May, after American ground troops entered the war, he wrote to Thanh again, urging him to "seize the opportunity and incite uprisings even if we have only a seventy-to-eighty percent chance of success." Pribbenow, "General Vo Nguyen Giap."

27 *"Let's act, then see":* Langguth, *Our Vietnam,* 345 attributes the line to Napoleon; Duiker, *Sacred War,* 170–7, attributes it to Lenin.

27 *Two-ton Soviet trucks:* One celebrated porter, Nguyen Dieu, had broken all records by transporting 420 kilograms—925 pounds—on his "steel horse."

27 *"The Americans were most afraid":* Duong Mang Ten Bac (*The Road That Bears Uncle's Name*), in Wain Collection (two volumes, nos. 2881010601 and 28810111001), Texas Tech Vietnam Archive.

CHAPTER 2 OF MOUNTAINS AND MACHINES

32 *Both women had risen:* For a brief history of Road 20, see Ngo Thanh Long, "May on the Legendary Road 20," May 17, 2014, https://baoquangbinh.vn.

34 *This was the heart:* Tui Lua (The Pocket of Fire) is the title of a book by Col. Nguyen Viet Phuong. Wain Collection (no. 28810311001), Texas Tech Vietnam Archive.

35 *"a strategic unity":* Giap's ideas on military strategy are laid out in his *Big Victory, Great Task: North Vietnam's Minister of Defense Assesses the Course of the War* (New York: Praeger, 1968) and *The Military Art of People's War* (New York: Monthly Review Press, 1970).

36 *"War is death and destruction":* Quoted in Harry G. Summers, Jr., *On Strategy: A Critical Analysis of the Vietnam War* (New York: Dell, 1984), 69. A useful study of

the impact of "machines," particularly germane to my account of the war in the A Shau Valley, is Amélie Robert, "At the Heart of the Vietnam War: Herbicides, Napalm, and Bulldozers Against the A Luoi Mountains," *Journal of Alpine Research* 104 (2016): 1–17.

36 *Rising to five thousand feet:* The PAVN installed a secret radio transmitter above the Hai Van Pass to direct clandestine arms shipments by sea. *Victory in Vietnam,* 53. For a full account of the "sea trail," which was organized by the PAVN's Group 759, see Phong, *Five Ho Chi Minh Trails,* 187–307.

36 *This quirk of geology:* Westmoreland's constant fear was that the PAVN—or even the monsoon rains—could cut off the Hai Van Pass, severing Quang Tri and Thua Thien from the rest of South Vietnam. "I . . . would be unable to accept loss of those two provinces. The psychological effect on the South Vietnamese, if not on the American people, would be catastrophic." *Soldier Reports,* 167–68.

37 *The Marines took by far:* Vietnam War U.S. Military Fatal Casualty Statistics, National Archives.

CHAPTER 3   THE SUMMER OF LOVE

40 *This pseudospeciation:* Marlantes, *What It Is Like to Go to War,* 40–41.

40 *"blows away the illusion":* Ibid., 17.

41 *"We were put through every":* Erich Maria Remarque, *All Quiet on the Western Front* (1929; reprint New York: Continuum, 2004), 14–15.

43 *The Fourth Marines had a tainted reputation:* See, for example, "Honor and Dishonor: The Story of the Pacific's 4th Marine Regiment," *Stars and Stripes,* April 6, 2018.

44 *Of the 58,220:* Vietnam War U.S. Military Fatal Casualty Statistics, National Archives.

46 *the historic Saigon Morin Hotel:* Much of the hotel, the first in Hue, was reduced to rubble in 1947 when Viet Minh forces besieged the French troops barricaded inside. It was seriously damaged again during the 1968 Tet Offensive.

46 *"They come from city":* Department of the Army, "The Men From the Boys: The First Eight Weeks," available on YouTube.

47 *"A feeling is widely and strongly":* McNaughton to McNamara, May 5, 1967, in *Pentagon Papers,* 546–47.

47 *Everyone in the plane fell silent:* Three weeks before the start of Operation Rolling Thunder in March 1965, Lyndon Johnson had ordered the bombing of Quang Binh province, just above the DMZ, in retaliation for a PAVN attack on Pleiku that killed nine Americans. Herring argues that he had been seeking a pretext for bombing the North, and that Pleiku presented a convenient opportunity. "Pleikus are like streetcars," McGeorge Bundy said later—if you missed one, another would be along shortly. Herring, *America's Longest War,* 5th ed. (2014), 158–60.

CHAPTER 4   SOCKS ON AN OCTOPUS

50 *During the French War:* Such base areas were a concept developed by Mao Zedong in the 1930s. He famously described them as "the buttocks of the revolution," a safe

place to sit and rest while amassing the human and material resources needed to advance the revolutionary struggle. See R. Keith Schoppa, *The Columbia Guide to Modern Chinese History* (New York: Columbia University Press, 2000), 85.

50 *ARVN units roamed the hinterlands:* Diem's draconian Decree 10/59 authorized local military commanders to impose the death sentence without appeal for acts of treason—defined as they saw fit. Biggs, *Footprints of War,* 121.

50 *The CIA quickly saw the importance:* Stanton, *Green Berets at War,* 39–43.

50 *"The Communist will find":* Quoted in Westmoreland, *A Soldier Reports,* 41.

51 *Some believed in a python god:* Oscar Salemink, "Return of the Python God: Multiple Interpretations of a Millenarian Movement in Colonial Vietnam," *History and Anthropology* 11 (1994): 129–64.

52 *"revolutionary-minded people":* Nguyen Viet Phuong, *Official History of the Ho Chi Minh Trail,* Wain collection, Texas Tech Vietnam Archive (two parts, nos. 28810102001 and 28810103001).

52 *The program advanced more rapidly:* "Notes on Strategic Hamlets," Office of Rural Affairs, U.S. Aid Mission, Saigon, August 15, 1963, Texas Tech Vietnam Archive (no. 2130303013).

52 *Their young men:* The Katu "blood hunts" are discussed in detail in Arhem, "Forests, Spirits, and High Modernist Development," 139–80.

53 *"The Katu eat our flesh":* Nguyen Viet Phuong, *Official History, Part 1.*

53 *"have tried to establish":* U.S. Army Intelligence School, Fort Holabird, Md., "Montagnard Tribal Groups of the Republic of Vietnam," July 1964. "This tribe is very important because of their location along the 17th Parallel and along the Laos border," the report continued. "It is reported by special forces returnees that many of the Katu have been sent to North Viet Nam for more training by the Communists."

53 *His name was Colin Powell:* Powell's stint at the A Shau base is described in detail in *My American Journey,* 78–98. He served a second tour in 1968–69 in Quang Ngai province, first at the Duc Pho base and then at Chu Lai as chief of operations for the Americal Division, a company of which had carried out the My Lai massacre shortly before his arrival. In addition to his exposure to Agent Purple at A Shau, these two bases would have been routinely sprayed with herbicides. The conditions from which he suffered before his death—Parkinson's disease and multiple myeloma—are both on the VA list of those presumptively associated with service in Vietnam. See George Black, "The Legacy of Colin Powell, and the Legacy of Vietnam," *Washington Spectator,* October 26, 2021.

53 *"an absurd quality":* White House senior aide Michael V. Forrestal to Kennedy, May 1963, *New York Times,* July 1, 1971.

55 *"teaching simple people":* "This southern effort, generally referred to as the Kha program, now has 2,000 armed tribals, helping defend a population of 60,000. Once we begin work with tribals in a selected area it is essential to arm them as quickly as possible." "CIA Rice-Roots Programs in Vietnam and Laos" (classified "secret"), August 25, 1965. https://www.cia.gov/readingroom/docs/CIA -RDP79T00827A000200060003-7.pdf.

55 *The United States was not a signatory:* The signatories to the Geneva Accords were France and the Democratic Republic of Viet Nam. The People's Republic of China, the USSR, and the United Kingdom also took part in the talks but did not sign the agreement.

55 *McNamara shared those doubts:* He never admitted as much in public, however, until 1983, when he opened up to—of all unlikely places—Andy Warhol's *Interview* magazine.

56 *The first operation:* The name of the operation was Leaping Lena, in honor of a West German racing pigeon that was lost for days over Czechoslovakia before eventually returning with a message tied to her leg: "We plead with you not to slow down in the fight against Communism because Communism must be destroyed." As the MACV-SOG operations in Laos intensified, a number of designations were used for the outfits involved, including Spike teams, Hornet Forces, Hatchet Forces, and company-size missions (Search, Locate, Annihilate, Monitor) missions. These are described in detail in Plaster, *SOG*.

56 *"Buddhist monks were able":* The note concludes, "This was considered a small price to pay for continued utilization of a $181,000 aircraft." CHECO (Contemporary Historical Examination of Current Operations), Report no. 142, MAP Aid to Laos 1959–1972, Texas Tech Vietnam Archive (no. 0390122001).

56 *The bombing had limited impact:* The CIA's alarm is evident in three secret intelligence memoranda: "Communist Activity in the Laos Panhandle," October 15, 1965; "Communist Road Development in Laos," December 9, 1965; and "Road Construction and Trail development in Laos During 1965," January 11, 1966. The last of these specifies seventeen miles of improved road and eight miles of improved trails from La Hap to the border with the A Shau Valley. CIA Electronic Reading Room, Vietnam Collection.

57 *"Sprayed two [hectares]":* Information on these eight missions, Ranch Hand missions 52–59, is drawn from Agent Orange Data Warehouse, https://www.worker veteranhealth.org/milherbs/new/. Buckingham, *Operation Ranch Hand,* says that the herbicide used for this hand-spraying in the A Shau Valley was Agent Pink (81), but this is contradicted by the HERBS tapes, which specify Agent Purple.

58 *"would violate every Christian ethic":* Cited in Buckingham, *Operation Ranch Hand,* 82. The early debates about crop destruction in the Kennedy administration are discussed in detail in Morris, "Into the Wind."

58 *"If you live with":* "The Ambassador admitted that authorities in the province had almost totally ignored the psychological warfare aspect, but he assured Washington that he would not approve the operations until he was satisfied with their efforts in this regard." Buckingham, *Operation Ranch Hand,* 81. Retired Sgt. Maj. Herb Friedman has compiled an extraordinary collection of documents on the psychological operations associated with Operation Ranch Hand, including more than twenty leaflets distributed to the civilian population in advance of spraying missions. "Defoliation Psyop of Vietnam," https://www.psywarrior.com/DefoliationPsyop Vietnam.html.

59 *In June 1963 General Giap:* "Herbicide Operations in the Republic of Vietnam," report classified "secret," undated but probably 1965. National Archives, RG472, Records of the United States Forces in Southeast Asia, Headquarters MACV Secretary of the Joint Staff (MAC J03), Military History Branch. As early as the spring of 1962, the DRV had denounced aerial crop destruction as an integral part of the strategic hamlet program, although there is no documented evidence that U.S. planners saw it this way. *Vietnam* magazine (in French), Hanoi, May 1962; Morris, "Into the Wind," 237–38.

59 *A dozen areas of South Vietnam:* South Vietnam Administrative Boundaries, Recommended Areas for Crop Destruction, Saigon, 1543, December 1963 (classified "secret"), map in the Alvin L. Young Collection on Agent Orange, National Agricultural Library Special Collections, USDA.

59 *When his plane prepared for takeoff:* Westmoreland described the incident in *Soldier Reports*, 60–61. On his demand for defoliation of the airstrip, see Phillips, *A Shau*, 10–11.

59 *By the time the campaign wound down:* Dr. Tran Manh Hung of the 10-80 Committee estimated a total of 527,345 gallons. Dr. Le Ke Son, head of the committee's successor, Office 33, gave the figure of 1,197,420 gallons, but this likely includes the surrounding hills that were regarded in military terms as part of the A Shau area of operations. Route 547 between the A Shau Valley and Hue was very heavily sprayed, but this is not technically part of the watershed—which corresponds to present-day A Luoi District. Son and Bailey, *From Enemies to Partners*, 24, and Le Ke Son, personal communication to author.

CHAPTER 5   "SADDLE UP, COWBOYS!"

60 *Ranch Hand had begun:* For a concise summary of the various rainbow herbicides and their chemical properties, see Buckingham, *Operation Ranch Hand*, 195–200.

61 *In December 1964, Saigon saw:* Johnson's aide Jack Valenti said that South Vietnam's coat of arms should be a turnstile. See George C. Herring, "Fighting Without Allies," in Gilbert, *Why the North Won*, 80.

61 *Hitler was his only hero:* Ky interview with London *Sunday Mirror*, as reported in *Washington Post*, July 14, 1965.

61 *"These are your colors":* Cecil, *Herbicidal Warfare*, 65.

61 *"Flying the one-twenty-three":* Cecil, ibid. 49.

62 *"Meetings usually terminate":* Twelfth Air Commando Squadron briefing paper, undated. CHECO report no. 115, support document, Texas Tech Vietnam Archive (no. F031100320267).

62 *"monumental in scope":* The pilots composed at least half a dozen of these parodies, including of "Blowing in the Wind" ("How many hectares can a Ranch Hand spray, before it all blows away? And how much rubber can a Ranch Hand kill, before Uncle Sam has to pay?").

63 *For demonstration purposes:* Twelfth Air Commando Squadron briefing document.

63 *In this organic form:* See, for example, Ronald Eisler, "Arsenic Hazards to Fish, Wildlife, and Invertebrates: A Synoptic Review," *Containment Hazard Review* Report 12 (1988).

64 *The problem was that it contained:* Jeanne Mager Stellman et al., "The Extent and Patterns of Usage of Agent Orange and Other Herbicides in Vietnam," *Nature* 422 (April 17, 2003): 681–87. On concentration as much as ten times greater, Stellman personal communication to author, February 21, 2015.

64 *"People would have sprinkled":* Stellman, personal communication to author, February 2021.

64 *"I am convinced that our efforts":* U.S. Embassy in Vientiane to Department of State,

(telegram), November 30, 1965, cited in Andrew Wells-Dang, "Agent Orange in Laos: Documentary Evidence," unpublished research paper, August 2002.

65 *"a weight of effort"*: Capt. Melvin F. Porter, CHECO report 238, *Tiger Hound*, September 6, 1966 (classified "top secret"), Texas Tech Vietnam Archive (no. 0390137001).

65 *Even flying over it slowly*: U.S. Embassy in Laos to Department of State (telegram), June 21, 1965, in *Foreign Relations of the United States (FRUS) 1964–1968*, vol. 28, *Laos*, doc. 187.

65 *Westmoreland himself was said*: Van Staaveren, *Interdiction in Southern Laos*, 96.

65 *"massive amounts"*: U.S. Embassy in Laos to Department of State (telegram), August 9, 1965, *FRUS 1964–1968*, vol. 28, *Laos*, doc. 194.

65 *An indiscreet source in Saigon*: R.W. Apple, Jr., "U.S. Planes in Action," *New York Times*, February 16, 1966.

66 *Once the effects of the defoliation*: CHECO *Tiger Hound* report.

67 *"Silver wings upon their chest"*: This at least is Sadler's version of the story, in a 1968 interview with *Soldier of Fortune* magazine. Marc Leepson, *Ballad of the Green Beret: The Life and Wars of Staff Sergeant Barry Sadler* (Guilford, Conn.: Stackpole Books, 2017), 29.

68 *"You will kill ten"*: In his *Vietnam: A History*, Stanley Karnow rendered this as "You can kill ten of my men for every one I kill of yours. But even at those odds, you will lose and I will win." Karnow does not provide a source for this version, which has passed into legend as one of Ho Chi Minh's most celebrated quotes. In his memoir, French politician Jean Sainteny describes Ho telling former Minister of the Colonies Marius Moutet, a supporter of Vietnamese independence, "If we must fight we will fight. You will kill ten of my men while we will kill one of yours. But you will be the ones to end up exhausted." Sainteny, *Ho Chi Minh and His Vietnam: A Personal Memoir* (Chicago: Cowles, 1972), 89. Even so, Giap made clear his opposition to seeking out such large-scale confrontations with American forces. "We do not believe in big-unit battles, for this favors the strategy of our enemy," he wrote in 1966. Giap, *Big Victory, Great Task*, 17.

68 *Half of the camp's Vietnamese defenders*: In the course of the war, the ARVN lost 254,256 dead, more than four times as many as the United States. Jeffrey J. Clarke, *United States Army in Vietnam: Advice and Support: The Final Years, 1965–1973* (Washington, D.C.: Center of Military History, U.S. Army, 1988), 275. When desperate local fighters mobbed the relief helicopters at A Shau, the retreating Americans opened fire on them, killing thirteen. "It was a hell of a thing to have to do; some of them had to be shot to maintain control," said Lt. Col. Chuck House, commanding officer of the helicopter squadron. "I know of no other answers in a case of this nature. It was either that or sacrifice everybody." House interviewed by John Laurence in *Cat from Hue*, 306–8.

68 *It has been said*: News of the attack on the A Shau base was a huge story for the Saigon press corps, who flocked to Danang and Phu Bai looking in vain for a ride to the valley only to be told flights were too dangerous, and "trying to get there by road was suicide." Laurence was eventually able to fly over the camp when the battle was over. Laurence, *Cat from Hue*, 360–368.

68 *The answer came without hesitation*: "As the ancient imperial capital, Hue was the symbol of a united Vietnam. Taking it would have a profound psychological impact on the Vietnamese in both the North and the South, and in the process the North

Vietnamese might seize the two northern provinces as bargaining points in any negotiations. . . . The loss in March 1966 of the CIDG-Special Forces camp in the A Shau Valley, opening the valley to the enemy, made a North Vietnamese move on Hue all the more likely." *Soldier Reports,* 167.

CHAPTER 6 GRUNT

71 *"Let the chips fall":* For almost half a century, the story of the Pentagon Papers was that Daniel Ellsberg collaborated actively with Neil Sheehan to have the seven thousand leaked documents published. But in an interview before his death, Sheehan revealed that he had deceived Ellsberg about his editors' plans and copied the documents without permission, and that Ellsberg had been blindsided by their publication. Janny Scott, "Now It Can Be Told: How Neil Sheehan Got the Pentagon Papers," *New York Times,* January 7, 2021.

71 *Though patrician in his manners:* After Bunker's arrival, the old pacification strategy was replaced by a new joint military-civilian effort to win hearts and minds, the Office of Civil Operations and Rural Development Support, or CORDS. This in turn spawned the Phoenix Program, run by the CIA, which set out to gather intelligence and "neutralize" Viet Cong operatives and gained a grim reputation for torture and targeted assassination.

72 *The core of their fight:* Douglas Pike identifies this militant spirit of resistance to outside domination, or *dau tranh,* as the key to understanding the Vietnamese struggle. See Pike, *PAVN,* especially 215–22.

72 *The statistics tended to favor him:* According to MACV studies, between 80 and 90 percent of encounters were initiated by PAVN or NLF forces. See Jeffrey Record, "How America's Military Performance Aided and Abetted the North's Victory," in Gilbert, *Why the North Won,* 125.

72 *"We'll just go on bleeding":* Ibid, 124.

72 *"We will entice the Americans":* Peter G. Macdonald, *Giap: The Victor in Vietnam* (New York: W.W. Norton, 1993), 210.

73 *"In effect, we are fighting":* Westmoreland speech in New York City, April 1967, cited in "William C. Westmoreland Is Dead; General Led U.S. Troops in Vietnam," *New York Times,* July 20, 2005.

74 *"You can't defend a place":* Jack Schulimson and Charles M. Johnson, *U.S. Marines in Vietnam: The Landings and the Buildup, 1965* (Washington, D.C.: U.S. Marine Corps, 1978), 29.

74 *Westmoreland had no philosophical objection:* On tensions between Westmoreland and Krulak's view of pacification and the "inkblot theory," see Sheehan, *Bright Shining Lie,* especially 631–638. Cabot Lodge's comment on the "little man" is quoted in Schulimson, *An Expanding War,* 44.

76 *Like the U.S. government, the politburo:* An especially valuable analysis of the debates leading up to Tet is Pribbenow, "General Vo Nguyen Giap."

76 *But Giap, to whom that accusing:* The Party and the PAVN clearly took pains to portray the two generals as being of one mind by releasing a photograph of them discussing plans for the Tet Offensive just before Thanh's death. See the photo at the bottom of page 2 of Insert 1.

76 *He was stricken after a send-off:* At the time MACV viewed the official version of Thanh's death as a cover-up, concocted to conceal the embarrassment of losing the PAVN's top commander on the battlefield. See Oberdorfer, *Tet!,* 42–44. MACV's baseless assertion that Thanh had died in an air raid near COSVN on the Cambodian border proved remarkably resilient. It is repeated, for example, in Sheehan, *After the War Was Over,* 89, to illustrate the Communists' terror of B-52 strikes. The long-standing debate about the cause was put to rest, however, by Lien-Hang T. Nguyen, whose account is based on testimony by Thanh's wife. Nguyen, *Hanoi's War,* 87–88.

76 *Though Giap was blameless:* Nguyen discusses the "Revisionist Anti-Party Affair" in detail in *Hanoi's War,* 102–7. There is still no published account of the failed assassination attempt on Ho Chi Minh.

76 *The most radical elements:* The PAVN committed four of its main-force infantry divisions to the Tri-Thien Military District—the 304th, 320th, 324th, and 325th—as well as five artillery regiments. *Victory in Vietnam,* 215.

77 *In the fifteen months:* Collectively known as Operation Pirous, these actions are detailed in Phillips, *A Shau,* 73–87.

78 *"Make mud, not war":* Embassy in Vientiane to Department of State (telegram), May 29, 1967. in *FRUS 1964–1968,* vol. 28, *Laos,* doc. 289. "We might be able to make enemy movement among the cordillera of the Annamite chain almost prohibitive" Sullivan wrote. "In short, chelation may prove better than escalation. Make mud, not war!"

79 *So did another secret:* The program ran from 1968 to 1972. See Eleanor Cummins, "With Operation Popeye, the U.S. Government Made Weather an Instrument of War," *Popular Science,* March 2018. The goals of the operation were laid out in Deputy Assistant Secretary of State Foy D. Kohler to Secretary of State Dean Rusk, secret memo, January 13, 1967, *FRUS 1964–1968,* vol. 28, *Laos,* doc. 274. On the "limited and unverifiable" results of Operation Popeye, see "Weather Modification," Hearings Before the Subcommittee on Oceans and International Environment of the Committee on Foreign Relations, United States Senate (Washington, D.C.: U.S. Government Printing Office, 1974).

81 *Lt. Gen. Robert Cushman:* The failed preparations for Operation Cloud are described in Vetter, *Never Without Heroes,* 166–74.

82 *The operation, code-named Granite:* For a full account of Operation Granite, see Gary L. Telfer, Lane Rogers, and V. Keith Fleming, *U.S. Marines in Vietnam: Fighting the North Vietnamese, 1967* (Washington, D.C.: U.S. Marine Corps, 1984), 172–74.

86 *"The forests protect our soldiers":* Interview with Giap in the television documentary *Vietnam After the Fire* (London: Acacia Productions, 1988), cited in Laderman and Martini, eds., *Four Decades On,* 247.

CHAPTER 7   ORPHANS OF CREATION

89 *One of Searcy's first assignments:* The handbook is available online at the Ike Skelton Combined Arms Research Library, https://cgsc.contentdm.oclc.org.

90 *"Over 95% of the refugees":* Human Sciences Research, Inc., Refugee Study Program, "Memorandum for the Record: Preliminary Data on the Refugee Population of

Cam Lo Government Resettlement Camp, Quang Tri Province," October 1967. This report was part of a larger study of eleven resettlement camps in I, III, and V Corps, Texas Tech Vietnam Archive (no. 2223216001).

90 *CICV's upbeat reporting:* For an excellent analysis of RAND's work on the defoliation campaign, see Martini, *Agent Orange,* 62–69 and 81–92.

91 *an intelligence failure:* James J. Wirtz, *The Tet Offensive and Intelligence Failure in War* (Ithaca, N.Y.: Cornell University Press, 1994).

91 *In the minds of the American media:* Perhaps the clearest symbol of this was the cover image on *Time* magazine's edition on the Tet Offensive: a dark and menacing portrait of Giap. "Days of Death in Vietnam," *Time,* February 9, 1968.

95 *Westmoreland's response was Operation Hastings:* These two operations are recounted in detail in Jack Schulimson, *U.S. Marines in Vietnam: An Expanding War, 1966* (Washington, D.C.: U.S. Marine Corps, 1982), 137–98.

95 *Some of the Marines found it:* Vietnam Veterans Against the War, Winter Soldier Investigation, Testimony Given in Detroit, Michigan, January 31–February 2, 1971 (Third Marine Division). See especially testimony by Bill Hatton and Walter Hendrickson. Vietnam Veterans Against the War, *The Winter Soldier: An Investigation into American War Crimes* (Boston: Beacon Press, 1972); Richard Stacewicz, *Winter Soldiers: An Oral History of the Vietnam Veterans Against the War* (Chicago: Haymarket Books, 2008).

96 *Con Thien was a battlefield:* On July 2, 1967, 86 men in a single company of the First Battalion of the Ninth Marines died in an ambush near the base, the worst single-day losses of the entire war. Members of the unit were known thereafter as the Walking Dead.

97 *Its baby-faced correspondent:* Laurence's vivid description of the siege of Con Thien in the fall of 1967 is in *Cat from Hue,* 439–473.

CHAPTER 8 "THIS IS NOT A PRACTICE"

98 *"the cream of the scholarly":* The McNamara Line was variously code-named Project Practice Nine and Dye Marker. The basic concept was proposed by Roger Fisher, a professor at Harvard Law School, and fleshed out by the scientists. Since they convened under the auspices of the Jason Division of the private Institute of Defense Analyses, they were known as the Jasons. The electronic surveillance program was code-named Igloo White and run out of the Nakhon Phanom air base in Thailand ("Naked Fanny" to those who served there).

99 *Although Westmoreland was a creature:* For more on the 1969 speech in which he outlined his vision of the future army, see Antoine Bousquet, *The Scientific Way of Warfare: Order and Chaos on the Battlefields of Modernity* (New York: Columbia University Press, 2010), 125–126.

99 *"We wire the Ho Chi Minh Trail":* An air force officer in *Armed Forces Journal,* 1971, cited in John T. Correll, "Igloo White," *Air Force Magazine,* November 1, 2004—an excellent short overview of the project.

101 *Yet buried away in the papers:* Young Collection, USDA.

103 *If there was a serious threat:* Westmoreland, *Soldier Reports,* 338. This was neither the first nor the last time the United States discussed using nuclear weapons in

Vietnam. Eisenhower considered their use to support the French at Dien Bien Phu in 1954. See "When Ike Was Asked to Use Nukes in Vietnam," *Washington Post,* August 22, 1982. On discussions of the nuclear option by Nixon and Kissinger in 1969 and again in 1972, see William Burr and Jeffrey Kimball, eds., "Nuclear Weapons, the Vietnam War, and the 'Nuclear Taboo,'" National Security Archive Electronic Briefing Book no. 195, July 31, 2006. https://nsarchive2.gwu.edu/NSAEBB /NSAEBB195/index.htm.

103 *But National Security Adviser Walt Rostow:* On February 10, 1968, Westmoreland shared details of Fracture Jaw with Adm. Grant Sharp, commander in chief, Pacific, and Gen. Earle Wheeler, chairman of the Joint Chiefs of Staff. Rostow informed Johnson the following day, and according to notes taken by a White House aide, "When [the president] learned that planning had been set in motion, he was extraordinarily upset and forcefully sent word through Rostow, and I think directly to Westmoreland, to shut it down." Sharp sent a terse cable to Westmoreland on February 12, ordering him to "discontinue all planning for Fracture Jaw. . . . There can be no disclosure of the content of the plan or knowledge that such planning was underway or suspended." See David E. Sanger, "U.S. General Considered Nuclear Response in Vietnam, Cables Show," *New York Times,* October 6, 2018.

105 *"in the nature of a reflex":* For Sheehan's account of the Tet Offensive in Saigon, see *Bright Shining Lie,* 709–19.

106 *The internal postmortems were devastating: Victory in Vietnam,* 21; also Ngo Vinh Long, "The Tet Offensive and Its Aftermath," in Jayne Werner and David Hunt, eds., *The American War in Vietnam,* Southeast Asia Program Series (Ithaca, N.Y.: Cornell University Press, 1993), 23–45.

106 *"The people, some of whom":* CIA Intelligence Information Cable, "Situation Appraisal of Post-VC Offensive Problems in Quang Tri Province and Anticipated Enemy Actions," February 29, 1968. https://www.cia.gov/readingroom /document/06786477.

106 *"If we get out of Vietnam":* Kissinger quoted in Ken Waltz, interview by Fred Halliday and Justin Rosenberg, *Review of International Studies* 24, no. 3 (1998): 371–86.

106 *Right-wing military leaders:* The stab-in-the-back theory has persisted for decades, with the Tet Offensive at its heart. A striking recent example is Robbins, *This Time We Win.* The paramilitary Oath Keepers take much of their inspiration from a 2015 essay "Tet, Take Two," by former Navy SEAL Matthew Bracken, which uses Tet as a template for America's betrayal by forces sympathetic to Islamist extremism. For a general discussion of military veterans and post-Vietnam conspiracy theories, see George Black, "All Enemies, Foreign and Domestic: The Road from Vietnam to the Capitol Steps," *Washington Spectator,* April 27, 2021. Kathleen Belew's *Bring the War Home: The White Power Movement and Paramilitary America* (Cambridge, Mass.: Harvard University Press, 2019) discusses the role of Vietnam veterans in the development of the modern militia movement.

CHAPTER 9 "TONIGHT YOU DIE, MARINE"

109 *In the latter part of the war:* Retired Sgt. Maj. Herb Friedman's account of Operation Wandering Soul, accompanied by audio of the broadcast, can be found at http:// www.psywarrior.com/wanderingsoul.html.

110 *"The best way"*: Nguyen Xuan Duy, interview by Barry Wain, Hanoi, January 2, 1990, Wain Collection, Texas Tech Vietnam Archive (no. 28810439001).

110 *"It was the thoughts"*: Song Tung, interview by Barry Wain, Hanoi, January 5, 1990, Wain Collection, Texas Tech Vietnam Archive (no. 28810431006).

110 *One porter carried a copy:* Larry Rottman, *Voices from the Ho Chi Minh Trail: Poetry of America and Vietnam, 1965–1993* (Desert Hot Springs, Calif.: Event Horizon Press, 1993), 145. "I wondered," the porter told Rottman, "how a nation that gave birth to Walt Whitman could also produce napalm and Agent Orange."

111 *"Rightist thoughts, pessimism, and hesitancy"*: For the PAVN's assessment of the successes and failure of the Tet Offensive, see *Victory in Vietnam*, 217–224.

112 *After a ferocious three-day battle:* The battle of Dai Do involved the Second Battalion, Fourth Marines, "the Magnificent Bastards." See Keith Nolan, *The Magnificent Bastards: The Joint Army-Marine Defense of Dong Ha, 1968* (Novato, Calif.: Presidio, 2009).

112 *Some of the bodies had been:* After being cut out of his chest, the Marine's tattoo was nailed to a tree. His body was skinned. Campbell's encounter was the fourth major battle at Phu Oc in 1967. The third one, on September 21, also involved "the Magnificent Bastards." See Coan, *Con Thien*, 82–85, 234–38, 259–62, and 298–302.

112 *It was the action:* ibid., 300.

114 *He dubbed the operation Pegasus: The Defining Year*, 238.

115 *"the most important VC war zone"*: Department of Defense Intelligence Information Report, "Organization and Activities of the 559th Transportation Group," June 13, 1968.

116 *Alpha 1/4 arrived in the area:* An account of the PAVN attack on LZ Torch from an artillery lieutenant's perspective is in Coan, *Con Thien*, 217–42. The battle of LZ Loon, which immediately preceded it and was part of the same operation, is vividly described in McLean's *Loon*, another of the best Marine memoirs of the war in Quang Tri.

CHAPTER 10 SCAVENGERS

123 *On May 4, 1963:* Diem had ordered Buddhist flags to be taken down, denounced the protests as the work of the Viet Cong, and said the violence had been started by a Communist throwing a hand grenade. But widely circulated home movies made it clear that soldiers had opened fire without warning. Among the dead were two children crushed by the treads of armored vehicles. See Langguth, *Our Vietnam*, 211–12.

124 *She fought for the next three years:* The weapons Hanh transported would likely have been destined for the PAVN's Base Area 101, in the Hai Lang forest, straddling the foothills in southern Quang Tri and northern Thua Thien. See the map at the top of page 4 of Insert 1.

125 *The new offensive:* Nguyen Thi Nhan, ed., *Collected Party Documents* 33 (Hanoi: National Political Publishing House, 1972), cable 119, 27.

125 *After a decade of war:* The following passage on conditions in Quang Tri after Hanh's return is drawn from reports by Western visitors including Arthur Westing, *New York Times*, September 29, 1973; T. G. S. George, *Far Eastern Economic Review*, July 30, 1973; and Steve Talbot, *International Bulletin*, March 25, 1974; as well as

analyses of postwar Quang Tri from official Vietnamese sources. Figures on villages destroyed are from *Viet Nam Destruction War Damage* (Hanoi: Foreign Languages Publishing House, 1977).

127 *By 1978 the transformation:* Official Vietnamese reports on economic, social, and political conditions in the new Binh-Tri-Thien province include Bui San, "Bin-Tri-Thien Is Determined to Advance to Become a Prosperous and Strong Province," *Tap Chi Cong San* (Hanoi), July 1977; and Vu Thang, "Binh-Tri-Thien's 10 Years of Reform, Construction," *Nhan Dan* (Hanoi), March 25, 1985; both as transcribed and translated by the Foreign Broadcast Information Service (FBIS).

128 *Phu Quoc was notorious:* For details, see Phu Quoc Prison, https://phuquocprison .org/. Phu Quoc island is now a major tourist center, famed for its beaches, and the prison is a popular destination for visitors.

131 *"These Chinese hegemonists":* On Le Duan's turn against China in the 1970s, see Asselin, *Vietnam's American War,* 189–90 and 219–20.

131 *Richard Nixon wrote a secret letter:* "Nixon Note on Aid to Hanoi Disclosed," *Washington Post,* August 20, 1977.

132 *"The destruction was mutual":* While Carter's comment is frequently cited as evidence of his hostility to Vietnam, the context is often omitted. At a press conference on the eve of Secretary of State Cyrus Vance's trip to the Soviet Union, Carter said he favored the normalization of relations with Vietnam. A reporter asked, "Do you still feel that if that information on those American servicemen who are missing in action is forthcoming from the Vietnamese, that then this country has a moral obligation to help rebuild that country, if that information is forthcoming?" Carter made the comment in response. See President's News Conference, March 24, 1977, at https://www.presidency.ucsb.edu/documents/the-presidents-news-conference-116.

132 *The Vietnamese were "naughty children":* Asselin, *Vietnam's American War,* 242.

132 *China began radio broadcasts:* Between 60 and 70 percent of the "boat people" were ethnic Chinese, although only a few thousand fled the former South Vietnam in the early postwar years. The first major exodus was in response to the elimination of capitalist trade in March 1978, but most of those refugees left for mainland China. The number rose dramatically after the February 1979 Chinese invasion, when the Vietnamese government launched a propaganda campaign denouncing ethnic Chinese communities as nests of spies and fifth columnists. For a moving account of conditions in a refugee camp in Malaysia, see Lady Borton, *Sensing the Enemy: An American Woman Among the Boat People of Vietnam* (New York: Dial Press, 1984).

CHAPTER 11   THE SMOKY LANDSCAPE

136 *The Marines had already made:* For the connoisseur of irony, Nixon, a lapsed Quaker, had been sworn in for his second term with his hand placed on the Milhous family Bible, open to Isaiah 2:4. "They shall beat their swords into plowshares, and their spears into pruning hooks."

137 *the whole operation in the valley:* The 101st Airborne Division gave the number of sixty-three, with 367 wounded. The military historian Jay Phillips calculated the higher figure. See his *A Shau,* 318 and 325.

137 *"For a time," said a classified report:* Col. Bert Aton and William Thorndale, CHECO

report no. 2, *A Shau Valley Campaign December 1968—May 1969*, Texas Tech Vietnam Archive (no. 0390126001).

140 *They shut down the school:* Anthony Depaul Sadler, "We Want Fred! UGA's Reaction to Kent State, 1970," *Source Athens*, March 26, 2014.

141 *Vietnam Veterans Against the War:* See VVAW, *The Winter Soldier*, and Stacewicz, *Winter Soldiers*.

143 *Scott Camil, yet another Marine vet:* Scott Camil, interview by Stuart Landers, October 20, 1992, University of Florida Oral History Program.

144 *Vietnam's chief negotiator:* In his letter to the Nobel Committee, Tho wrote, "The Saigon administration, aided and encouraged by the United States, continues its acts of war. Peace has not yet really been established in South Vietnam. In these circumstances it is impossible for me to accept the 1973 Nobel Prize for Peace which the committee has bestowed on me." He did not mention Kissinger. For the full text of the letter, see "Tho Rejects Nobel Prize, Citing Vietnam Situation," *New York Times*, October 24, 1973.

145 *Hollywood had steered clear:* Renata Adler, " 'Green Berets' Viewed by John Wayne," *New York Times*, June 20, 1968.

147 *Egendorf came to the problem:* Egendorf, outtake interview from Stanley Karnow, *Vietnam: A History*, PBS, 1983. "Healing is not a process" is from the preface to his *Healing from the War*.

147 *Numbed by alcohol:* For a provocative recent analysis of PTSD and the veteran experience, see Joseph Darda, "Like a Refugee: Veterans, Vietnam, and the Making of a False Equivalence," *American Quarterly* 71, no. 1 (March 2019): 83–104.

CHAPTER 12 BENEFIT OF THE DOUBT

152 *The loudest voices at this early stage:* The most detailed account of the AAAS's work is David Zierler, "Inventing Ecocide: Agent Orange, Antiwar Protest, and Environmental Destruction in Vietnam," Ph.D. thesis, Temple University, 2008. I've also relied on telephone interviews with Matthew Meselson and the unpublished papers of Arthur Westing, kindly made available to me by his estate. See also "Herbicides in Vietnam: AAAS Study Finds Widespread Devastation" and "AAAS Convention: Radicals Harass the Establishment," *Science* 171 (January 8, 1971); and Institute of Medicine Committee to Review the Health Effects in Vietnam Veterans of Exposure to Herbicides, *Veterans and Agent Orange: Health Effects of Herbicides Used in Vietnam* (Washington, D.C.: National Academies Press, 1994), chap. 2.

152 *The Pentagon replied: Veterans and Agent Orange:* Part 2, "History of the Controversy over the Use of Herbicides," https://www.ncbi.nlm.nih.gov/books/NBK236351/.

153 *If the mangrove forests:* Walter Sullivan, "Zoologist, Back From Vietnam, Notes Defoliants' Value and Toll," *New York Times*, April 4, 1969.

153 *In April 1970, the Department of the Interior:* The EPA announced its ban on 2,4,5-T on February 28, 1979.

154 *Later these were analyzed:* Robert Baughman and Matthew Meselson, "An Analytical Method for Detecting TCDD (Dioxin): Levels of TCDD in Samples From Vietnam," *Environmental Health Perspectives*, September 1973.

155 *Kinnard told him that he knew:* Meselson, interview by author. For his book, *The*

War Managers, Kinnard surveyed the opinions of 173 general officers who had commanded forces in Vietnam, the great majority of whom responded to his detailed questionnaire. Of these, 21 percent felt that the herbicides were "not worth their value considering physical damage they caused," and another 20 percent believed that "more controls should have been imposed."

156 *"exceptionally toxic":* On March 23, 1965, Dow brought together representatives of the four largest producers of Agent Orange to discuss the contamination of the defoliant with TCDD. They discussed whether to inform "the appropriate federal government agencies" of the problem, but it appears that this never happened, and Ranch Hand moved into its full operational stage six days later. See Martini, *Agent Orange,* 146–48.

157 *The question now was:* The most detailed discussion of Operations Pacer IVY and Pacer HO is in Young, *History, Use, Disposition,* 123–58.

158 *Agent Purple, which had been:* The use of Agent Purple in Laos between December 1965 and March 1966 is described in CHECO, *Tiger Hound.* The last use of Agent Purple in Vietnam, according to the HERBS tapes, was at the mouth of the Saigon River on March 18, 1965.

158 *In 1980 scientists gathered:* For basic information on POPs, see Environmental Protection Agency, "Persistent Organic Pollutants: A Global Issue, A Global Response," December 2009, https://tinyurl.com/bdhvuvdv.

159 *"You have to know":* Bobby Muller, interview by Stephen McKiernan, Binghamton University, July 8, 2019.

160 *Maj. Jack Spey, president:* John Spey to Rep. Douglas Applegate (Correspondence Concerning the Agent Orange Controversy), December 6, 1982, Texas Tech Vietnam Archive (no. 2520401014).

161 *Starting with a random selection:* American Legion Vietnam Veterans Study, report no. 1, USDA Special Collections, Columbia University.

161 *"CDC study oversight":* Jeanne M. Stellman and Steven D. Stellman statement, November 2, 1993, in National Academy of Sciences Agent Orange Committee Report, Hearing Before Committee on Veterans Affairs (Washington, D.C.: U.S. Government Printing Office, 1993), 178–188.

163 *More than three thousand rural villages:* To assemble these data, Stellman used the demographic information in MACV's Vietnam's Hamlet System files (HAMLA/HES).

163 *But the brick wall at the VA remained:* Pamela A. MacLean, "Judge Reinstates Vietnam Vets' Agent Orange Health Claims," UPI, May 8, 1989.

164 *Admiral Zumwalt's report:* Report to the Secretary of the Department of Veterans Affairs on the Association Between Adverse Health Effects and Exposure to Agent Orange, May 5, 1990. The full text can be found at http://www.vvacalsc.com/files/zumwalt_agent_orange.pdf. See also Elmo Zumwalt, Jr., and Elmo Zumwalt, III, with John Pekkanen, *My Father, My Son* (New York: Macmillan, 1986). A Vietnamese version of the Zumwalt book was published later, in a translation by Le Cao Dai and Nguyen Thi Ngoc Toan.

164 *Among the sources he drew on:* Nguyen Thi Ngoc Phuong et al., "An Estimate of Reproductive Abnormalities in Women Inhabiting Herbicide-Sprayed and Non-Herbicide-Sprayed Areas in the South of Vietnam, 1952–1981"; Nguyen Thi Ngoc Phuong et al., "An Estimate of Differences Among Women Giving Birth to

Deformed Babies and Among Those with Hydatidiform Mole Seen at the Ob-Gyn Hospital of Ho Chi Minh City in the South of Vietnam"; and Le Diem Huong et al., "An Estimate of the Incidence of Birth Defects, Hydatidiform Mole, and Death in Utero Between 1952 and 1985 at the Obstetrical and Gynecological Hospital in Ho Chi Minh City, Republic of Vietnam," all in *Chemosphere* 18, nos. 1–6 (1989).

165 *For the vets, the clinching proof:* Clary was a government scientist in the Chemical Weapons Branch, Biological and Chemical Warfare Division, U.S. Air Force Armament Development Laboratory, Eglin AFB, Florida, where he worked on the design of the herbicide spray tanks aboard the C-123s. He also prepared the final Air Force report, *Ranch Hand: Herbicide Operations in Southeast Asia,* July 1971. CHECO report no. 171, Texas Tech Vietnam Archive (no. F031100030169). Clary to Sen. Tom Daschle, September 9, 1988. 2013 House Standing Committee Minutes, South Dakota House Government and Veterans Affairs Committee HB 1405, January 31, 2013, https://www.ndlegis.gov/files/resource/63-2013/library/hb1405.pdf.

165 *Anyone who had served in the country:* Current updated lists of the conditions "presumptively associated" with service in Vietnam and a summary of benefits available—"Veterans Diseases Associated With Agent Orange" and "Birth Defects in Children of Women Vietnam Veterans" (which does not specifically mention Agent Orange)—are available on the VA website, https://www.publichealth.va.gov /exposures/agentorange/conditions/ and https://www.publichealth.va.gov/expo sures/agentorange/birth-defects/children-women-vietnam-vets.asp, respectively.

165 *Eventually benefits were even extended:* The Blue Water Navy Vietnam Veterans Act of 2019 (PL 116-23) extends to those who served up to twelve nautical miles from the coast of Vietnam.

CHAPTER 13 UNTANGLING THE TANGLE

168 *"Chuck has a Zelig-like ability":* Pete McCommons, editor's letter, *Flagpole,* December 15, 2009.

170 *Gen. John W. Vessey, Jr.:* For Vessey's participation in the march, I'm indebted to conversations with retired Maj. Gen. Bill Nash. Vessey's role in preparing the ground for normalized relations with Vietnam is well covered in Schulzinger, *Time for Peace,* 33–50.

171 *One of the society's founders:* Kornfield had also served in the Peace Corps with a tropical medicine team in the Mekong Delta in 1967. See "About Jack Kornfield," https://jackkornfield.com/bio.

172 *He explored new forms of therapy:* Gallegos describes his Personal Totem Poll Process as "spontaneously meeting the alivenesses that were rooted in my energy centers and that presented themselves primarily as animals, but they had to be approached through the knowing of the deep imagination. I realized that the teacher I had sought for my entire life was in fact deep within my imagination and had always been there." See "About," https://esgallegos.com/about-steve/.

175 *Lawyers have become:* Chuck Searcy, "Don't Abandon Justice," *Atlanta Journal-Constitution,* September 10, 1992.

175 *George H.W. Bush had laid out:* The complete text of the road map is in the Texas Tech Vietnam Archive (no. 11272307027).

176 *The first vets to return:* Bernard Weinraub, "Vietnam Invites 4 U.S. Veterans to Visit Hanoi," *New York Times,* December 13, 1981.

176 *"It was an emotional roller coaster":* Terzano, remarks at University of Dayton Vietnam Legacies Symposium, October 23, 2020.

179 *the Black Patches:* Recordings of several of Hershel Gober's songs, including "Six Klicks," "Saigon Warrior," "Picture of a Man," and "An American's Dream," can be found on YouTube.

CHAPTER 14 "BRING OUR DADDY HOME"

180 *Right-wing conspiracy theories:* An especially lurid picture of these conspiracies is in the memoir by James "Bo" Gritz, *Called to Serve* (Sandy Valley, Nev.: Lazarus, 1991). Generally see Belew, *Bring the War Home,* and Black, "All Enemies, Foreign and Domestic."

181 *"Kill, kill, kill":* Gritz, interviewed in *Erase and Forget,* documentary film, dir. Andrea Luka Zimmerman.

181 *"to buy time and divert":* Neil Sheehan, "Prisoners of the Past," *New Yorker,* May 24, 1993.

182 *fiercely conservative views:* For a discussion of Sybil Stockdale's political opinions, see Allen, *Until the Last Man Comes Home,* 24–29.

183 *A House Committee on Missing Persons:* The final report of the select committee is available on the Library of Congress website, at https://tile.loc.gov/storage-services/service//frd/pwmia/486/155747.pdf.

183 *"They're still there to this day":* Recorded telephone call for an appeal by Republican Congressman John LeBoutillier to raise funds for his Skyhook II Project, a private initiative to rescue imagined POWs in Southeast Asia. See Isaacs, *Vietnam Shadows,* 127.

183 *Funded by Ross Perot:* Gritz's house was in Nakhon Phanom, where the giant computers of Igloo White had once processed the torrent of electronic data from the Ho Chi Minh Trail. His team included fellow veterans of the Special Forces and Navy SEALs and anti-Communist Lao rebels who had previously worked for the CIA. His right-hand man, David Scott Weekly, was known as Dr. Death for his expertise in weaponry and explosives. Gritz led their operations wearing a POW/MIA bracelet inscribed with the name Jimmy Mills, the airman brother of the League of Families' president, Ann Mills Griffiths.

184 *Someone else suggested:* The driving force behind the creation of Rolling Thunder was Ray Manzo, a veteran of the Seventh Engineer Battalion of the First Marine Division in Quang Nam province. See Roger L. Vance, "The Man Who Made Rolling Thunder Roar," Historynet.com, May 5, 2012. Another of the notable founders was the controversial POW/MIA activist Ted Sampley, who served with the Special Forces and the 173rd Airborne Division. He was a fierce critic of John Kerry and John McCain, who called him "one of the most despicable people I have ever had the misfortune to encounter." Michael Janofsky, "The 2004 Campaign: McCain Fights Old Foe Who Now Fights John Kerry," *New York Times,* February 14, 2004.

184 *The Rolling Thunder event continued:* On Bikers for Trump, see Perry Stein, "Meet

the Biker Hosting the Biggest Pro-Trump Demonstration at the Inauguration," *Washington Post,* January 13, 2017. Several of the larger veteran bikers' groups, including Leatherneck MC, for former Marines, are profiled in Jon R. Anderson, "A New Surge Is Fueling Membership in Military Motorcycle Clubs," *Military Times,* July 12, 2015.

185 *"These men are all dead"*: As quoted by Ted Schweitzer in testimony before the Senate Select Committee on POW/MIA Affairs, December 1992, *Oversight Hearings: Department of Defense, POW/MIA Family Issues, and Private Sector Issues* (Washington, D.C.: Government Printing Office, 1994).

186 *It turned out to be yet another hoax:* Laderman and Martini, *Four Decades On,* 283.

187 *"a Desert Storm style roll"*: Bell, *Leave No Man Behind,* 382. According to Bell, Christmas appears to have believed that the problem could be solved by seizing and excavating a small number of clearly identifiable burial sites.

187 *"Bring on Rambo"*: *Wall Street Journal,* August 2, 1991.

187 *"some of the most craven"*: Editorial, "The POW Scams," *Washington Post,* December 4, 1992. McCain's comment came after POW/MIA militants accused him of having been brainwashed by the North Vietnamese during his captivity in Hoa Lo prison, the "Hanoi Hilton." When he ran for president in 2008, the same activists described him as "the Manchurian Candidate." See "John McCain: The Manchurian Candidate," *Vietnam Veterans Against John McCain,* June 15, 2020, https://vietnam veteransagainstjohnmccain.com/cin_tedmancurin/.

187 *"American businessmen"*: Bell, *Leave No Man Behind,* 433.

187 *"the mark of the beast"*: Gritz goes into considerable detail about "the Beast," supposedly housed in a giant computer in Brussels. Under the "New World Order," he explains, citizens will be marked with an invisible tattoo on their right hand or forehead, readable with an infrared scanner. *Called to Serve,* 603–4.

188 *"No more lies!"*: Five minutes into Bush's speech, said dissident board member Jeff Donahue, "the place just turned into bedlam." Donahue and the president got into a shouting match. Ann Mills Griffiths appealed for order, and Bush finally exploded, "Would you please shut up and sit down." The "Rambo faction" was soon selling T-shirts that said, "SHUT UP AND SIT DOWN: GEORGE BUSH'S POLICY ON POW/MIAs." Allen, *Until The Last Man Comes Home,* 279–281.

188 *"Mr. Perot has shown"*: Michael Kelly, "The 1992 Campaign: Candidate's Record, Perot Shows Penchant for Seeing Conspiracy," *New York Times,* October 26, 1992.

188 *He held raucous mass gatherings:* One reporter who covered a Perot event called it "the Jerry Lewis Telethon of politics: an interminable rally at which thousands of decent citizens trying to do good had to indulge the high-pitched ravings of an egomaniacal clown." Frank Rich, "Robertson: The Other Perot," *Baltimore Sun,* August 18, 1995.

188 *"If Donald Trump is"*: Quoted in Jonathan Martin, "Ross Perot and Donald Trump, Presidential Candidates and Outsiders Looking in," *New York Times,* July 9, 2019.

190 *She felt like a keeper:* "New Women of the New South," *Atlanta Journal-Constitution,* September 9, 1996.

190 *"the Clintonistas might as well"*: Jim Auchmutey, "Soldier of Conscience," *Atlanta Journal-Constitution,* June 21, 1998.

190 *"an unconscionable insult"*: Statements opposing Searcy's nomination were entered into the *Congressional Record* by Sens. Bob Smith and Strom Thurmond, Veterans

of Foreign Wars, the League of Families, Jewish War Veterans of the United States of America, and AMVETS. Texas Tech Vietnam Archive (no. 11272210079).

191 *"as an outsider"*: "I recognize the problems associated with my opposition to the war after I came back from military service in Vietnam. I believe it was the right thing to do, and an act of patriotism. You disagree, as do others. That question we may not resolve, but we can at least acknowledge that we shared the same goals: to bring American servicemen and women home to their families safely, if possible, with as few injuries as possible and, in the case of POWs and MIAs who had not returned, to account for them as fully as possible. The last challenge we still face." Searcy to Mills Griffiths, May 31, 1994. Texas Tech Vietnam Archive (no. 1440312016). Mills Griffiths herself described the meeting as "very direct but cordial."

192 *Of those who went down:* Author's calculation from declassified lists of active cases in 1992 and 1993 supplied by the Defense POW/MIA Accounting Agency.

193 *Twelve thousand choppers:* "Helicopter Losses During the Vietnam War," compiled by Gary Roush, Vietnam Helicopter Pilots Association, updated December 31, 2018. Texas Tech Vietnam Archive, Gary Roush Collection (no. 805).

193 *The last of them was in June 1972:* This was during operations to prevent further PAVN attacks on Hue from the A Shau Valley during the Nguyen Hue Offensive, which also included heavy fighting for control of the old American firebases on Road 547, Bastogne and Birmingham, occupied at this point by ARVN troops. See Randolph, *Powerful and Brutal Weapons,* 257, 273–78.

193 *The first American search teams:* Early missions to the A Shau Valley and Quang Tri are described in detail in Smith, *Search for MIAs,* 130–40.

194 *One of the first of the new wave:* Case 0784 declassified mission reports July 1, 1993; December 12, 1993; and April 25–May 4, 1994. All human remains were returned on June 8, 1994, although positive DNA identification was not made until July 2001.

196 *But by early 2022:* Of the 1,584 who remained unaccounted for, 1,244 were lost in Vietnam, and of those 470 were classified as "nonrecoverable." Defense POW/MIA Accounting Agency Factsheet, Progress in Vietnam, April 13, 2022. https://www.dpaa.mil/Resources/Fact-Sheets/Article-View/Article/569613/progress-in-vietnam/.

CHAPTER 15 THE THIRD RAIL

197 *When Vietnam and the United States:* The most complete discussion of Holbrooke's Vietnam diplomacy is George Packer, *Our Man: Richard Holbrooke and the End of the American Century* (New York: Knopf, 2019), 23–139.

198 *Tung was born into:* Ton That Tung, outtake interview from Stanley Karnow, *Vietnam: A History,* PBS, 1983.

198 *His specialty was diseases of the liver:* Ton That Tung and Nguyen Duong Quang, "A New Technique for Operating on the Liver," *Lancet* 281 (1963): 179–232; Ton That Tung et al., "Immunostimulants in Primary Hepatomas," *Lancet* 305 (1975): 471–534.

199 *This was startling:* Ton That Tung describes herbicide flights between July 1969 and May 1971 over several villages around Hue, on the road from Hue to Phu Bai, and in other parts of Thua Thien, none of which appear in the HERBS tapes. He also enu-

merates flights in twenty-seven other provinces during this period, many of which are also missing from the official records. An additional appendix contains details of extensive CS gas use in Thua Thien, Quang Ngai, and several other provinces. Tung, *U.S. Chemical Warfare*, 109–51, 151–61.

201 *Cau's report focused:* Hanoi International Service in English, FBIS, June 15, 1983.

201 *"the Albert Einstein":* "Le Cao Dai, 74, Top Vietnamese Expert on Agent Orange's Effects," *Los Angeles Times*, April 19, 2002. "He had a wonderful gift," Schecter said, "for knowing where to look, where to sample people. And he had a historic knowledge of the actual spraying of Agent Orange."

201 *In Danang, they found:* Schecter et al., "Recent Dioxin Contamination from Agent Orange in Residents of a Southern Vietnam City," *Journal of Occupational and Environmental Medicine* 43, no. 5 (2001): 435–43.

203 *in 1992 a "Friendship Village":* For the full story of George Mizo and the Friendship Village, originally conceived as a "peace pagoda," see https://vietnamfriendship.org.

206 *"it became necessary to destroy the town":* Journalist Peter Arnett reported this comment from Ben Tre, perhaps the most memorable to come out of the war in Vietnam. He has insisted on its authenticity and accuracy, but it has been widely questioned. See, for example, Stephen L. Carter, "Destroying a Quote's History in Order to Save It," *Bloomberg*, February 9, 2018.

CHAPTER 16 THE THINGS THEY CARRIED BACK

211 *"The families of our men":* Frederick Downs, Jr., "Making a Real Peace With Vietnam," *Washington Post*, December 25, 1988.

212 *"it was as if a bomb":* Downs remarks at U.S.-Vietnamese symposium "Overcoming War Legacies," U.S. Institute of Peace, March 26, 2019.

213 *"is largely responsible":* "Bush Visits U.S. Vietnam Veterans' Hanoi Clinic," Reuters World Service, September 6, 1995.

214 *Honoring those who had:* Having been a platoon commander in Vietnam, North served in 1974 in Okinawa as commander of Manus Campbell's old unit, Alpha Company of the First Battalion, Fourth Marines. North recounted his travels in Vietnam with Vets with a Mission in his memoir, *One More Mission: Oliver North Returns to Vietnam* (New York: HarperCollins, 1993), esp. 258–61. North notes his personal identification with the group's motto, from 2 Corinthians 5:18, "Called to a Ministry of Reconciliation." The group's more recent work, including projects in the A Luoi Valley, is detailed at *Vets with a Mission,* https://vetswithamission.org.

215 *In those early days in Hanoi:* For an interesting profile of Bangert, see Kevin Dennehy, "The Odyssey of Joe Bangert," *Cape Cod Times*, August 6, 2006.

216 *Clinton chose Pete Peterson:* Searcy's friend Hershel Gober was on Clinton's shortlist for the ambassadorship. Osius, *Nothing Is Impossible,* 28–29.

216 *There was a memorial:* Downs, *No Longer Enemies,* 168.

217 *Since its publication, Bao Ninh:* For an absorbing account of Bao Ninh's life since publication of *The Sorrow of War* (which was banned by the Vietnamese Communist Party from 1991 to 2006), see Rohit Inani, "The Long Silence of Bao Ninh," Diasporic Vietnamese Artists Network, December 14, 2018, at https://dvan.org/2018/12/the-long-silence-of-bao-ninh/.

CHAPTER 17 A VIETNAMESE IN DISGUISE

219 *Her uncle, Hugh Borton:* Borton was the author of *Japan's Modern Century* (New York: Ronald Press, 1955) and *Spanning Japan's Modern Century: The Memoirs of Hugh Borton* (Lanham, Md.: Lexington Books, 2002).

220 *Some individuals were more radical:* Norman Morrison's story is told in detail in Hendrickson, *Living and the Dead,* 187–240. His wife, Anne, had no advance knowledge of his plan for self-immolation and learned about it only with a phone call to a reporter.

220 *The Quang Ngai program:* My description of AFSC's wartime work in Quang Ngai draws heavily on the Richard (Dick) and Cynthia W. Johnson Collection (no. 2699) in the Texas Tech Vietnam Archive, as well as my interviews with Dave Elder and Lady Borton.

220 *"independent by tradition":* Tim O'Brien, "The Vietnam in Me," *New York Times Magazine,* October 2, 1994.

221 *AFSC's New England office:* Minutes of New England Peace Committee Endorsed by the New England Executive Committee, October 20, 1967, Johnson Collection, Texas Tech Vietnam Archive.

221 *Before they let her go:* Nelson tells the story of her time in captivity, as well as her work with AFSC in Quang Ngai, in her memoir, *To Live in Peace in Midst of the Vietnam War* (independently published, 2019).

222 *She took a* Newsweek *reporter to My Lai:* The story of the massacre was broken by the investigative reporter Seymour Hersh in Dispatch News Services after being rejected by *Life* and *Look* magazines. But Hersh did not, as commonly believed, go to Vietnam or visit the site. His reporting was based on examining Pentagon records and gathering testimony from returning veterans. CBC Radio, "How Reporter Seymour Hersh Uncovered a Massacre, and Changed the Vietnam War Dialogue," *Current,* June 14, 2018.

222 *After the 1973 Paris Peace Accords:* Dave Elder, interview by author, Kennett Square, Pennsylvania, September 28, 2021, and Murray Hiebert, interview by author, Washington, D.C., November 8, 2021.

224 *In February 1980, on the eve:* The journey is described in Borton, *Sensing the Enemy,* 3–4.

225 *For years she avoided mirrors:* On her visit to Tu Du, see Borton, "Ambushed by Memory," *New York Times,* January 28, 1988, and a later interview with NPR's Terry Gross, https://freshairarchive.org/segments/aiding-civilian-survivors-vietnam-war.

225 *The result was a second book:* Lady Borton, *After Sorrow: An American Among the Vietnamese* (New York: Viking, 1995).

225 *"Chiefly she seems to be":* Pike served in Vietnam for several years for the U.S. Information Agency before moving to the State Department. His scholarly work is primarily of value for its analysis of the PAVN and NLF's organizational structure and military strategies. His memorandum goes on to disparage Borton's writing on Vietnam as "simplistic stereotyping, often with implied indictment—the noble Vietnamese vs. wretched Americans." In fact, neither of her books, other than brief descriptions of her experiences in Quang Ngai during the war, says anything about Americans other than AFSC staff and includes nothing about U.S. policy other than noting the frequent indiscriminate killing of civilians. Pike memorandum

to the MacArthur Foundation, December 9, 1996, Texas Tech Vietnam Archive (no. 2360109050).

226 *She spent the next:* See https://douglasibell.com/2012/07/17/stuck-in-the-middle -international-voluntary-services-and-the-humanitarian-experience-in-vietnam -1957-1971/.

227 *"A pretty, sturdy young woman":* Emerson, *Winners and Losers,* 352–54. Chagnon's work during this period is also described in MacPherson, *Long Time Passing,* 451–55.

227 *In Missouri, she met Rumpf:* For more on Rumpf, see Emily Langer, "Roger Rumpf, International Peace Activist, Dies at 68," *Washington Post,* May 11, 2013.

228 *"The war in Vietnam":* King's speech, delivered on April 4, 1967, is reprinted in full in American Rhetoric Online Speech Bank, https://americanrhetoric.com.

228 *Irrigation pumps were assembled:* Murray Hiebert, interview by author.

228 *When a "yellow rain" fell:* Chagnon and Rumpf, "Search for 'Yellow Rain,'" *Southeast Asia Chronicle,* no. 90 (June 1983).

228 *The Reagan administration claimed:* "I based this conclusion on the basis of my field studies in Thailand, review of declassified U.S. government documents, corroborating evidence by a Defense Department/State Department team, and CIA interviews with defecting North Vietnamese chemical officers. Although the Hmong people may well have experienced some unexplained illness, there is no reliable evidence that it was caused by what was described as 'yellow rain.'" Meselson personal communication with author. See Matthew Meselson and Julian Perry Robinson, "The Yellow Rain Affair: Lessons from a Discredited Allegation," in A. L. Clunan et al., eds., *Terrorism, War, or Disease?* (Stanford, Calif.: Stanford University Press, 2008), 72–96; and Merle L. Pribbenow, "Yellow Rain: Lessons from an Earlier WMD Controversy," *International Journal of Intelligence and Counterintelligence* 19 (2006), 737–745.

229 *It took the Europeans:* Angela Dickey and Kit Norland, interview by author, November 9, 2020.

230 *Rumpf took Arnold Schecter:* Schecter et al., "Dioxin, Dibenzofuran, and Coplanar PCB Levels in Laotian Blood and Milk from Agent Orange–Sprayed and Nonsprayed Areas, 2001," *Journal of Toxicology and Environmental Health* 66 (2003): 2067–75.

CHAPTER 18 POLICING THE BRASS

239 *Searcy and Borton traveled:* The site visit found an estimated 62 metric tons of CS in powder or crystal form in bags and rusted, leaking fifty-five-gallon barrels. Quaker Service Vietnam and Hatfield Consultants, "Field Reconnaissance of Da Nang and Quy Nhon Chemical Contamination Sites," June 2002. On the complex chemical footprint of the war in Vietnam, see David Biggs, "Vietnam: The Chemical War," *New York Times,* November 24, 2017.

240 *"Nothing like this had ever":* Malcolm W. Browne, "Vietnam Is Said to Harass American Medical Aid Team," *New York Times,* July 13, 1995.

240 *His views on Vietnam deepened:* Waltz, *Man, the State, and War: A Theoretical Analysis* (New York: Columbia University Press, 2001).

242 *This time he did so without:* See also Osius, *Nothing Is Impossible*, 42–43, on his participation in the ride.

242 *How would disabled riders cope:* Although the journey time from Hue to Danang has been cut by a new tunnel through the mountain, the scenic route over the Hai Van Pass remains a favorite with tourists, who can clamber on a graffiti-covered watchtower built by the nineteenth-century Nguyen emperor Minh Mang to protect the city of Hue and later used by both the French and the Americans. The nearby gift shop offers souvenir bottles of "Minh Mang wine," purportedly crafted for the emperor as an aphrodisiac from a recipe named either *nhat da luc giao sinh ngu tu* (to have sex six times a night and father five sons) or *nhat da ngu giao sinh tu tu* (to have sex five times and father four sons).

245 *A smallholding might bring:* Bru Van-Kieu fisherman Mr. Bo, interview by author, Ho Rau Quan, Quang Tri, May 10, 2017. On acacia plantations and deforestation, see James Morgan and Justin Woolford, "Vietnamese Smallholders Help End Deforestation," *Guardian*, July 24, 2017.

245 *When the wars were over:* See George Black, "In Search of the Stunning—and Possibly Extinct—Edwards's Pheasant," *Audubon*, Winter 2017. On the saola, see "Saola," World Wildlife Fund, https://www.worldwildlife.org/species/saola.

245 *Pangolins, once ubiquitous:* See "Chinese Medicine and the Pangolin," *Nature* 141, no. 72 (1938); and Jonathan Watts, "China Still Allowing Use of Pangolin Scales in Traditional Medicine," *Guardian*, October 12, 2020.

248 *Searcy went with them:* PeaceTrees worked entirely in Quang Tri from 1995 to 2020, when it opened an office in Quang Binh and began projects on the legendary Road 20 on the Ho Chi Minh Trail.

248 *Though Nam was born in the North:* Both of Nam's paternal uncles served in the PAVN and both were killed, one in Da Krong and the other on the Ben Hai River, in the heart of the DMZ. Hoang Nam, interview by author, Da Krong, February 2015.

250 *Clinton spent much:* "When Katherine Harris, Florida's secretary of state, certified results that showed Bush ahead of Gore by more than seven hundred votes, President Clinton was apoplectic. Believing that the election had been stolen, he wanted to make a statement. His traveling staff prevailed on him to remain publicly silent." Osius, *Nothing Is Impossible*, 49.

251 *But in his historic speech:* William J. Clinton Presidential Library recording of the speech is available on YouTube.

CHAPTER 19   MILK THAT GLOWED IN THE DARK

252 *What brought this about:* The bulk of this chapter draws on my extended interviews with Tom Boivin, Wayne Dwernychuk, Chris Hatfield, and Grant Bruce of Hatfield Consultants and the reports Hatfield and the 10-80 Committee issued on their research in the A Luoi Valley: "Preliminary Assessment of Environmental Impacts Related to Spraying of Agent Orange Herbicide During the Viet Nam War" (1998); and "Development of Impact Mitigation Strategies Related to the Use of Agent Orange Herbicide in the Aluoi [*sic*] Valley in Viet Nam" (2000). The full text of these, together with many other Hatfield reports and associated scientific literature, is archived on the company's website, https://www.hatfieldgroup.com.

253 *The Vietnamese standard for cropland:* A table of Vietnamese, Japanese, and U.S. standards is in Son and Bailey, *From Enemies to Partners,* 21. The Health Canada guidelines are discussed in Hatfield, "Development of Impact Mitigation Strategies."

254 *a Ph.D. thesis on birth defects:* Nguyen Viet Nhan, "Evaluating Some Kinds of Congenital Malformations in Camlo District, Quangtri Province, Vietnam," Hue Medical School, ca. 1998. English translation provided to author by Dr. Nhan.

260 *In the end, in 2006:* See Christie Aschwanden, "Through the Forest, A Clearer View of the Needs of a People," *New York Times,* September 18, 2007; Phung Tuu Boi, personal communication to author.

CHAPTER 20 THE END OF OUR EXPLORING

263 *"When you travel somewhere new":* Among Ricard's writings is *The Quantum and the Lotus: A Journey to the Frontiers Where Science and Religion Meet* (New York: Broadway Books, 2004), a dialogue with Vietnamese physicist Trinh Xuan Thuan.

264 *He visited the secluded:* Thich Nhat Hanh entered the Tu Hieu temple as a novice in 1942, at the age of sixteen. After visiting the United States in 1966, he became closely allied with Rev. Martin Luther King, Jr., who nominated him for the Nobel Peace Prize the following year. As a result of his opposition to the war, he was denied permission to return to Vietnam and lived in exile in France until his return in 2005. He died at Tu Hieu in January 2022 and was cremated there.

268 *As Campbell's fellow ex-Marine:* Suel Jones, interview by author, Danang, November 2014.

272 *But his humanitarian impulses:* O'Connor, interview by author, Danang, April 21, 2019.

273 *Vietnam's tourist boom on steroids:* In 2022, TripAdvisor listed 653 hotels and guesthouses in Hoi An, as well as 459 vacation rentals. Hoi An's population is 150,000.

273 *"the manufacture of nostalgia":* Laurel B. Kennedy and Mary Rose Williams, "The Past Without the Pain: The Manufacture of Nostalgia in Vietnam's Tourist Industry," in Tai, *The Country of Memory,* 135–63; David Lowenthal, *The Past Is a Foreign Country* (New York: Cambridge University Press, 1985). For a broader discussion, see Laderman, *Tours of Vietnam.*

274 *empire of Champa:* On the Champa empire, see Goscha, *Penguin History of Modern Vietnam,* especially chaps. 1 and 14. The Danang Museum of Cham Sculpture contains an extraordinary collection that mingles Hindu and Buddhist iconography.

275 *The residents of Hue:* In addition to the Exposition Coloniale, the political context for the escape to the hill stations was the "Red Terror," the Communist uprising in 1930, and the brutal French response in 1931, the "White Terror." See the fascinating Ph.D. thesis by Lawrence Raymond Fife, "Bach Ma, Historical Archaeology at a French Colonial Hill Station, Central Vietnam, 1930–1991" (University of New England, 2009).

275 *There were more than 330 species:* Richard Craik, "Birdwatching Areas: Bach Ma National Park, Vietnam," *Oriental Bird Club Bulletin* 33 (June 2001).

278 *This marked the site of Hang Tam Co:* For a brief history, see "A Sacred Venue: The Cave of Eight Women," *Tuoi Tre News,* March 18, 2014.

CHAPTER 21   THE ROAD TO DAMASCUS

283 *The Red Cross appealed:* Nguyen Trong Nhan, "Message to the President Bill Clinton," November 18, 2000. Clinton's response was sent on February 12, 2001, after he left office. "Thank you for your moving letter expressing your thoughts regarding the Vietnamese victims of Agent Orange," he wrote—language that no U.S. official had ever previously used. "I share many of your concerns about the medical and psychological difficulties they face, and I agree with the need for scientific research and joint humanitarian efforts between our two nations." https://www.holycross .edu/faith-service/mcfarland-center-religion-ethics-and-culture/agent-orange.

284 *Since fish were now known:* On the "catfish wars," see Seth Mydans, "Americans and Vietnamese Fighting over Catfish," *New York Times*, November 5, 2002.

285 *"I thought at the time":* Jason Grotto, "Bickering Blocks Search for Causes of Congenital Deformities," *Chicago Tribune*, December 8, 2009.

285 *"to counter the Vietnamese propaganda":* "Joint Research on Environmental/Health Effects of Agent Orange—An Assessment of Vietnamese Attitudes," February 16, 2003 (marked "sensitive but not classified"). https://agentorangerecord.com /us-embassy-memo-joint-research-on/. The same memo accuses Vietnam of a similar propaganda effort on UXO: "The government makes every attempt to use this to generate sympathy and funding, especially with the international community, and often links the two issues of AO/dioxin and UXO together to maximize the effect of demonizing the U.S. for the 'holocaust' of the Vietnam War. . . . The GVN never mentions that much of the UXO resulted from their own military and guerilla [*sic*] operations in the affected provinces." This part of the memo is especially startling since the U.S. government had by this time been involved in funding UXO removal operations for several years, and the amount of UXO generated by U.S. operations was orders of magnitude greater than by the Vietnamese. The two issues, because of the operational combination of spraying and bombing, were indeed symbiotically related, as I discuss in Chapters 22 and 23.

287 *A few months after it was published:* Martini gives a good summary of the VAVA lawsuit in *Agent Orange*, 222–37.

288 *Call it enlightened self-interest:* Sen. John McCain may have been the first to recognize the need for this shift. When relations were normalized, he remarked on Vietnam's historic animosity toward China, noting that this made it the most natural ally for the United States to contain future Chinese expansionism. "Good Morning, Vietnam," *Time*, July 24, 1995, cited in Gilbert, *Why the North Won*, 22. Vietnamese attitudes toward China remain ambivalent, however. On one hand, Vietnam has the traditional anxiety about Chinese threats to its national security, especially in the contested South China Sea, while on the other the conservative Communist Party leadership still feels an ideological kinship with its Chinese counterpart because of its wartime support.

290 *But the worst of the hot spots:* On the hot spot theory, specific locations, and the implications for U.S. policy, see Wayne Dwernychuk, "Agent Orange/Dioxin Hot Spots—A Legacy of U.S. Military Bases in Southern Viet Nam" (a summary of conference papers and presentations, 2002–5); Dwernychuk et al., "The Agent Orange Dioxin Issue in Viet Nam: A Manageable Problem," paper presented at the Oslo dioxin conference, 2006; Dwernychuk, "Dioxin Hot Spots in Vietnam," *Chemo-*

sphere 60 (2005): 998–99; and Hatfield Consultants/10-80 Committee, "Identification of New Agent Orange / Dioxin Contamination Hot Spots in Southern Viet Nam," January 2006. All papers archived at https://www.hatfieldgroup.com /agent-orange/.

291 *a joint project:* The partners in this initiative were the gynecologist Nguyen Thi Ngoc Toan; John Constable, who had worked in Vietnam with Matthew Meselson and Art Westing; the Joslin Diabetes Center, an affiliate of Harvard Medical School; and the Viet Nam War Veterans Association.

292 *Now that everyone knew:* The core literature includes two early studies by Arnold Schecter et al, "Recent Dioxin Contamination from Agent Orange in Residents of a Southern Viet Nam City [Bien Hoa]," *Journal of Occupational and Environmental Medicine* 43, no. 5 (2001): 435–43; and "Food as a Source of Dioxin Exposure in the Residents of Bien Hoa City, Viet Nam," *Journal of Occupational and Environmental Medicine* 43, no. 8 (2003): 781–88. Hatfield Consultants has produced several detailed reports: "Assessment of Dioxin Contamination in the Environment and Human Population in the Vicinity of the Danang Airbase, Viet Nam" (April 2007); "Evaluation of Contamination at the Agent Orange Dioxin Hot Spots in Bien Hoa, Phu Cat and Vicinity, Viet Nam" (June 2009), "Comprehensive Assessment of Dioxin Contamination in Danang Airport, Viet Nam: Environmental Levels, Human Exposure, and Options for Mitigating Impacts" (November 2009); "Environmental and Human Health Assessment of Dioxin Contamination at Bien Hoa Airbase, Viet Nam" (October 2011); and "Environmental Assessment of Dioxin Contamination at Bien Hoa Airbase" (USAID/Hatfield, May 2016). All are archived at https://www.hatfieldgroup.com.

293 *Bailey would eventually invest:* A list of all Ford Foundation Agent Orange–related grants is included in Son and Bailey, *From Enemies to Partners,* 181–88.

294 *Faiola's story checked all the boxes:* Anthony Faiola, "In Vietnam, Old Foes Take Aim at War's Toxic Legacy," *Washington Post,* November 13, 2006.

CHAPTER 22 GREAT LOSS AND CONFUSION

296 *"the bastards have never been bombed":* Operation Linebacker, which was launched on May 9, 1972, was Nixon's direct response to the Easter Offensive. One motivation for the much more intense Linebacker II—the Christmas bombing—was his anger at North Vietnamese efforts to improve their position in the Paris peace talks, including the continued infiltration of PAVN forces into Quang Tri to strengthen "leopard spot" areas of control that could be maintained after a ceasefire as liberated zones. The relationship between the Easter Offensive, the bombing, and the approaching peace talks is analyzed in detail in Nguyen, *Hanoi's War,* and from a narrower military perspective in Randolph, *Powerful and Brutal Weapons.*

296 *In Quang Tri, the greatest tonnage:* All data on the bombing of Quang Tri and its impact are as officially made available by the U.S. Air Force, summarized in Hoang Nam/Project RENEW, "A Study of Explosive Remnants of War Accidents and the Knowledge—Attitudes—Practices—Beliefs of People in Quang Tri, Viet Nam (2011)," which includes a map of bombing sorties.

296 *"Never were we out of sight":* Arthur H. Westing, "Sifting the Ashes of Quang Tri,"

New York Times, August 14, 1973. See also David Bird, "U.S. Scientist, Back From Hanoi 'Numbed' by Raid Devastation," *New York Times,* August 24, 1973.

299 *A humanitarian initiative:* The work of Norwegian People's Aid in all three countries is detailed at its website, https://www.npaid.org.

301 *Britain's Princess Diana:* Diana famously dramatized her commitment to the issue by an iconic televised walk through a minefield in Angola, wearing protective gear. See Suyin Haynes, "Prince Harry Is Honoring His Mother's Work in Angola. Here's What to Know About Princess Diana's Landmines Walk," *Time,* September 23, 2019 (with video).

305 *After a series of failed harvests:* Estimates of deaths during the famine range from 700,000 to 2 million; Goscha says "over a million," *Penguin History of Vietnam,* 199.

307 *Napalm, a mixture:* Napalm was the product of "Anonymous Research Project #4," headed by Louis Fieser, a professor of organic chemistry. It was first tested on Independence Day 1942 on a lawn behind Harvard Business School. The story is told in Robert M. Neer, *Napalm: An American Biography* (Cambridge, Mass.: Harvard University Press, 2013). The distant ancestry of napalm dates back to the Persians and the Romans and the defenders of Constantinople, who experimented with sulfur and burning pine resin. The use of arsenic as a weapon, as in the herbicide Agent Blue, had a similarly long history; it was first used by the Spartans to produce a noxious smoke to disable their Athenian enemies during the Peloponnesian War.

309 *By coincidence, it was:* Tom Vitale, "When Anthony Bourdain Invited Obama to Dinner . . . in Hanoi," *Daily Beast,* October 4, 2021. Their table at the Bun Cha Huong Lien restaurant, which now offers an "Obama Combo" of *bun cha* plus a fried seafood roll plus a Hanoi beer, is preserved behind glass, complete with two empty beer bottles.

310 *A new American ambassador:* Minh Nga, "U.S. Ambassador Pays Respects at Vietnamese Military Cemetery," *VN Express International,* August 27, 2019.

CHAPTER 23 ANGRY GHOSTS

313 *Also, about 80 percent:* Author's calculation from declassified U.S. Air Force statistics, broken down by specific agents used in each year of Operation Ranch Hand.

313 *The timing of crop destruction:* A November 22, 1965, memorandum from Maj. Gen. Nguyen Van Chuan, commander of ARVN First Infantry Division, Young Collection, National Agricultural Library, spells out in detail the targets for Ranch Hand project 1/2/1/66—crop fields in mountainous rural areas of Quang Tri and Thua Thien. The project, using Agents Orange and Blue, began in February 1966 and continued until late 1968.

314 *Le Van Dang, the provincial head:* Le Van Dang, interview by author, Dong Ha, February 2015.

315 *Small-scale Vietnamese:* Nhan, "Some Kinds of Congenital Malformations"; Dang Duc Nhu et al., "A Study of Dioxin Contamination in Herbicide Sprayed Area in Vietnam by GIS," in Andreas Kortekamp, ed., *Herbicides and Environment* (London: IntechOpen, 2003); Michael G. Palmer, "The Legacy of Agent Orange: Empirical Evidence From Central Vietnam," *Social Science and Medicine* 60 (2005): 1061–70; Asian Development Bank, "Pilot Rehabilitation of Agent Orange Affected Forest-

lands in Quang Tri Province of Viet Nam," 2007, unpublished, copy in author's possession. In addition to this research in Cam Lo district, Hatfield Consultants did a small study of the site of Firebase Charlie 1, at the northeast corner of the old Leatherneck Square, "Provisional Assessment of Environmental Contamination in Gio Linh, Quang Tri, Viet Nam," May 2000.

319 *at Mai Loc:* Local residents refer to Mai Loc as "the Ham Nghi place," alluding to the eighth emperor of the Nguyen dynasty. He joined a rebellion against the French in 1885, hid out in the mountains of Quang Tri, then was captured and exiled to Algeria.

322 *"Hunger Winter":* See, for example, Laura C. Schulz, "The Dutch Hunger Winter and the Developmental Origins of Health and Disease," *Proceedings of the National Academy of Sciences* 107 (2010): 16757–58.

322 *Published in 2018:* Cristina Giuliani et al., "First Evidence of Association Between Past Environmental Exposure to Dioxin and DNA Methylation of CYP1AI and IGF2 Genes in Present-Day Vietnamese Population," *Environmental Pollution* 242 (2018): 976–85. Another study, Karl T. Kelsey et al., "Serum Dioxin and DNA Methylation in the Sperm of Operation Ranch Hand Veterans Exposed to Agent Orange," *Environmental Health* 18, no. 91 (2019): 1–11, based on a sample of thirty-seven veterans, found alteration in the H19 gene, which plays a role in early development.

CHAPTER 24 THE WORST THING, THE BEST THING

324 *Now he was deputy chair:* Vinh retired in April 2021 and was succeeded by Lt. Gen. Hoang Xuan Chien.

326 *This wasn't to say:* U.S.-Vietnamese cooperation on Agent Orange is detailed in the periodically updated reports to Congress by the Congressional Research Service, prepared by Michael S. Martin: "Vietnamese Victims of Agent Orange and U.S.-Vietnamese Relations," and "U.S. Agent Orange/Dioxin Assistance to Vietnam."

328 *"Track-II diplomacy":* The work of the Dialogue Group and "Track-II Diplomacy" is described in detail at https://aspeninstitute.org. "Addressing the Legacy of Agent Orange in Vietnam: Declaration and Plan of Action 2010–2019," copy provided to author by Charles Bailey.

329 *Bailey also funded teams:* Their findings were published in Tran Thi Tuyet Hanh et al., "Environmental Health Risk Assessment of Dioxin in Foods at the Two Most Severe Dioxin Hot Spots in Vietnam," *International Journal of Hygiene and Environmental Health* 218 (2015): 471–78; and Hanh et al., "Sustainability of Public Health Interventions to Reduce the Risk of Dioxin Exposure at Severe Dioxin Hot Spots in Vietnam," *Journal of Community Health* 40 (August 2015): 652–59.

331 *The original budget was:* USAID staff, interview by author, Hanoi, April 22, 2019.

332 *For Vietnamese, "the last war":* Tens of thousands of soldiers on both sides died in the February–March 1979 invasion, along with thousands of Vietnamese civilians. In addition to Vietnam's invasion of Cambodia and its treatment of ethnic Chinese, China cited Vietnam's occupation of the disputed Spratly Islands. On the long-term effect on relations between the two countries, see Nguyen Minh Quang, "The Bitter Legacy of the 1979 China-Vietnam War," *Diplomat,* February 23, 2017.

333 *"Resolving dioxin as a legacy":* Osius, *Nothing Is Impossible,* 249–50.

333 *The first ship to arrive:* The official purpose of the gift of the *Morgenthau* was "to improve the Vietnam Coast Guard's maritime domain awareness, increase its capacity to perform maritime law enforcement operations and conduct search and rescue and other humanitarian response operations." Sam Lagrone, "Former U.S. Cutter Morgenthau Transferred to Vietnamese Coast Guard," *U.S. Naval Institute News,* May 26, 2017.

334 *His predecessor, Ted Osius:* Osius had considered resigning in 2017 after Trump withdrew from the Trans-Pacific Partnership (TPP) and the Paris Climate Agreement. His first encounter with Trump was when he accompanied Prime Minister Nguyen Xuan Phuc to a meeting in the Oval Office. Trump asked the prime minister's name and was told it "rhymes with book." "You mean like 'Fook You'?" Trump replied. "I knew a guy named Fook You. Really. I rented him a restaurant. When he picked up the phone, he answered, 'Fook You.' His business went badly." Osius, *Nothing Is Impossible,* 238–39.

334 *USAID promised to put in:* George Black, "50 Years Later, A Daunting Cleanup of the Vietnam War's Toxic Legacy Continues," *Yale Environment 360/PBS Newshour,* May 29, 2019.

CHAPTER 25 THE PAINTER, THE SPRINTER, AND THE MONK

335 *"Everywhere resembles everywhere":* Osborne, *The Naked Tourist: In Search of Adventure and Beauty in the Age of the Airport Mall* (New York: Farrar, Straus & Giroux, 2007), 8.

336 *Other beauties of old Saigon:* Tim Doling, *Saigon & Cho Lon Heritage Tours.* www .historicvietnam.com, n.d., is a beautiful collection of vintage and contemporary images and maps of the city.

340 *Danang had been the equivalent:* The EPA uses the term "mega-site" to refer to Superfund sites with actual or expected cleanup costs of at least $50 million.

340 *Jack McManus, who had served:* McManus was in the U.S. Air Force from 1965 to 1969; he was assigned to Operation Ranch Hand in 1967–68. He was elected president of Vietnam Veterans of America in 2022.

340 *The footprint of the base:* E-mails from USAID, October 2018, shared confidentially with author.

342 *"The importance of the remediation":* Tran Thi Tuyet Hanh, interview by author, Hanoi, April 22, 2019.

CHAPTER 26 UNFINISHED BUSINESS

346 *It was a world away:* Thomas S. Snyder et al., *Air Force Communications Command 1938–1991, An Illustrated History* (Scott AFB, Ill.: AFCC Office of History, 1991). Danang was even busier than Bien Hoa in one month, May 1968.

346 *Although this was an increase:* Three models of B-52 were used in Vietnam. The B-52D and B-52F each cost $66.6 million in current dollars. The B-52G, used during Operation Linebacker II (the 1972 "Christmas bombing" of Hanoi) was more expensive, at $77.8 million. Cost at the time of production was $6.58 million,

$6.48 million, and $7.69 million, respectively. Marcelle S. Knaack, *Post-World War II Bombers* (Washington, D.C.: Office of Air Force History, 1988).

347 *More was becoming known:* This was the researchers' estimate "even after adjusting for medical and psychiatric comorbidities and other variables." Steven Martinez et al., "Agent Orange Exposure and Dementia Diagnosis in US Veterans of the Vietnam Era," *JAMA Neurology* 78, no. 4 (2021): 473–77.

347 *Alvin Young, "Dr. Orange":* Charles Ornstein and Mike Hixenbaugh, "Dr. Orange: The Secret Nemesis of Sick Vets," *Pro Publica,* October 26, 2016.

347 *As for the Vietnamese:* Tran Thi Tuyet Hanh, interview by author, Hanoi, April 22, 2019.

347 *According to former Ranch Hand pilot:* Cecil estimates that there were about ninety emergency dumps of herbicides. An emergency release valve in the tank allowed the entire load, weighing five tons, to be dumped in thirty seconds. See *Herbicidal Warfare,* 72, 102. At an Institute of Medicine meeting in 1992, Fred Schirley, a Department of Agriculture scientist, described one thousand-gallon dump over Bien Hoa from an altitude of eighteen hundred feet. Institute of Medicine Committee to Review the Health Effects in Vietnam Veterans of Exposure to Herbicides, Scientific Workshop on Exposure Assessment, Washington, D.C., December 8, 1992.

348 *Nor had anyone ever studied:* The most thorough analysis of Agent Blue is Kenneth R. Olson and Larry Cihacek, "The Fate of Agent Blue, the Arsenic Based Herbicide, Used in South Vietnam During the Vietnam War," *Open Journal of Soil Science* 10 (2020): 518–77, although the discussion of the impact on human health is limited to general comment on the toxicity of arsenic.

348 *The mantra "no man left behind":* The annual budget of the Defense POW/MIA Accounting Agency increased from $112.478 million in 2017 to $169.532 million in 2020. Lt. Col. Tamara R. Fischer Carter, DPAA, personal communication to author, October 2020.

348 *The Vietnamese military had searched:* Stephanie Farr, "A Grave Mission Back to Vietnam," *Philadelphia Inquirer,* September 20, 2017; Bob Connor, personal communication to author, March 2020.

348 *Leahy and Rieser managed:* The U.S. Institute of Peace launched its Vietnam War Legacies and Reconciliation Initiative in August 2021, following Austin's visit to Hanoi, bringing work on Agent Orange, UXO, and the identification of Vietnamese MIAs together in a single program.

349 *These were important gestures:* The true number of Vietnamese MIAs will never be known. According to Sr. Col. Doan Quang Hoa, head of the government's Steering Committee 515 for Search, Collection, and Verification of Fallen Soldiers' Remains, 200,000 remain unaccounted for. However, an estimated 300,000 are buried in cemeteries but unidentified, and there may be some overlap between these two categories.

349 *"if I reach the point":* Paul Kane, "How the Oldest Senate Ever Is Taking a Toll on the Business of Washington," *Washington Post,* December 17, 2017.

349 *The other eight senators on his delegation:* The other members of the delegation included six Democrats—Tammy Baldwin (Wisconsin), Mazie Hirono (Hawai'i), Tim Kaine (Virginia), Debbie Stabenow (Michigan), Tom Udall (New Mexico), and Sheldon Whitehouse (Rhode Island); and two Republicans, Lisa Murkowski (Alaska) and Rob Portman (Ohio).

350 *The initial estimate:* Chris Abrams, USAID, interview by author, Hanoi, April 22, 2019.
350 *"The pain of our Vietnam veterans":* Zumwalt's endorsement of Dwernychuk's announcement of his Limited Edition Vietnam Veterans Commemorative Guitar, 2016.
350 *Chris Hatfield himself:* Hatfield died on Salt Spring Island on July 4, 2022.

CHAPTER 27 TURNING THE HO CHI MINH TRAIL BROWN

356 *a classified summary of 434 sorties:* Wells-Dang, "Agent Orange in Laos."
356 *Earlier that year, CIA director:* "Laos Questions," Secret Memorandum, Helms to Kissinger, March 5, 1970. https://www.cia.gov/readingroom/docs/CIA-RDP80 R01720R000600050020-5.pdf.
357 *There matters rested until 1982:* The State Department blocked the release of these twenty pages of Buckingham's five-hundred-page typescript on the grounds that their release "would cause identifiable damage to the national security." Richard Severo, "Secret History of U.S. Spraying in Viet War," *New York Times,* January 25, 1982.
357 *Often the targets were on higher:* Cecil interviewed more than a hundred Ranch Hand pilots and crew for an oral history project. Several described the difficulty and dangers of missions over the Ho Chi Minh Trail in Laos as well as secret missions over Cambodia. These missions are not reported in the HERBS tapes. See Paul Frederick Cecil, oral history project, box 4, folders 5–12, Paul Cecil Collection (no. 252), Texas Tech Vietnam Archive.
357 *A team of four government scientists:* Undated confidential memorandum, "Herbicide Damage to Rubber and Fruit Trees in Cambodia," National Agricultural Library, USDA. The team—composed of four representatives of USAID, one from the Department of Defense, and one from the Agricultural Research Service—found extensive damage to trees over some seven hundred square kilometers. They concluded that one defoliated area was the result of spray drift from operations in Tay Ninh province on the Vietnamese side of the border, while the other was "probably caused by a direct spray application by an unknown party."
358 *"ninety percent of all":* The Sihanouk Trail, named for Prince Norodom Sihanouk, ran from the port of Sihanoukville in Cambodia to the "tri-border" region of Cambodia, Laos, and Vietnam. It is described in detail in Phong, *Five Ho Chi Minh Trails,* 311–32.
360 *Three CIA aerial surveillance:* CIA documents CSD/NPIC 345/64 (Military Area Ban Na Hi, Laos), November 23, 1964; CSD/NPIC 2/65, January 7, 1965 (Military Area Ban Na Hi, Laos); and CDS/NPIC 4/65, January 14, 1965 (Ban Thay Military Area, Laos); all classified "secret" with portions redacted on release. CIA Electronic Reading Room. Annotations attached to aerial photographs produced by the U2 spy plane operations Trojan Horse and Lucky Dragon.
361 *Involving as many as:* Agenda Item for SEACORD meeting, August 19, 1969 (classified "secret"). It describes four missions between October 17, 1968, and January 18, 1969, using both Agents Orange and Blue, with a total of at least thirty-two sorties.

361 *The average concentration of TCDD:* For a detailed discussion of estimates of mean TCDD levels in Agents Orange and Purple, see Stellman, "Extent and Patterns of Usage."

361 *This conviction seemed to be borne out:* Jacques Decornoy, "Laos: The Forgotten War," *Bulletin of Concerned Asian Scholars* 2, no. 3 (1970).

362 *During just the first three months:* Author's calculations from the HERBS tapes and from metadata compiled by Hatfield Consultants for their maps of Ranch Hand missions in Laos.

362 *The Americans had used it:* The area had a certain notoriety because it had been targeted by one of the last big SOG Hatchet Force raids of the war, Operation Tailwind—an episode that caused a minor scandal in 1998 when CNN and *Time* magazine made the accusation, subsequently retracted, that the attackers had used sarin nerve gas and tried to kill some Americans who had defected to the North Vietnamese.

363 *"It is likely that this site":* Hatfield Consultants/Environment Research Institute, Water Resources and Environment Administration, Lao PDR, "Assessment and Mitigation of an Agent Orange Dioxin and Landmine/UXO Hot Spot I Sekong Province, Lao PDR," October 2009.

363 *Susan Hammond worked closely:* Hatfield Consultants, "Site Prioritization for Risk Assessment: Screening Former Military Sites in Lao PDR From the Second Indochina War for Potential Human Health Risks," May 2014.

364 *"We always used to say":* Angela Dickey, interview by author, November 9, 2020.

CHAPTER 28 THE POCKET OF FIRE

366 *"the battery":* Kearrin Sims, "On China's Doorstep, Laos Plays a Careful Game of Balancing," *Diplomat*, July 7, 2021. China is Laos's largest provider of development financing, its second-largest trading partner (after Thailand), and its second-largest source of tourist arrivals.

370 *Between 1964 and 1973:* This figure is often incorrectly reported as 580,344 *missions.* However, a *sortie* refers to the flight of one individual aircraft, and missions were often made up of multiple sorties. A B-52 Arc Light mission, for example, might include as many as twenty-seven aircraft. For the official U.S. Air Force data, see Channapha Khamvongsa and Elaine Russell, "Legacies of War: Cluster Bombs in Laos," *Critical Asian Studies* 41, 2 (2009), 281–306. The intensity and timing of the bombing during these years is made vivid in a time-lapse video, "Bombing Missions over Laos from 1965 to 1973." See Fatima Bhojani, "Watch the U.S. Drop 2.5 Million Tons of Bombs on Laos," *Mother Jones*, March 26, 2014.

370 *Built on the site:* Vatthana Pholsena, "A Social Reading of a Post-Conflict Landscape: Route 9 in Southern Laos," in Pholsena and Oliver Tappe, eds., *Interactions With a Violent Past: Reading Post-Conflict Landscapes in Cambodia, Laos, and Vietnam* (Singapore: National University of Singapore Press, 2013), 157–85. Pholsana identifies no fewer than eleven reeducation camps along Route 9 in Laos between the Mekong and the Vietnamese border.

370 *"totems of the industrial enemy":* "This tank, these planes, these guns, these inhuman things have more purchase on the collective memory of the human species

than 99.9 percent of the human beings who lived through, or died in, the war." Nguyen, *Nothing Ever Dies*, 164.

374 *"We were like a guesthouse"*: Vongphet Xaisangouane, interview by author, Savannakhet, October 29, 2019.

376 *"grand spirits of the first"*: Arhem, "Forests, Spirits, and High Modernist Development."

376 *"The fighters used this road"*: Ong Pa Ouang, interview by author, Pasia Village, October 23, 2019.

376 *"The airplanes with the chemicals"*: Tamplo Palieng, interview by author, Pasia Village, October 23, 2019.

CHAPTER 29 THE END OF THE TRAIL

378 *"a defender's dream"*: For an American perspective on the strategic importance of La Hap and the dangers it presented to clandestine operations, see Plaster, *SOG*, 71–76.

379 *"to attempt to kill"*: Target Oscar-8, https://macvsog.cc. This is the detailed account of the operation by Sgt. Maj. Billy Waugh, the forward air controller (FAC) who first revealed the assassination attempt on Giap. Yarborough gives the date of the raid as June 1967 (*A Shau Valor*, 91), but Waugh says that he surveyed the target at four a.m. on the morning of May 4 and that the Hatchet Force team were infiltrated three hours later. A firsthand account by a PAVN officer is Col. Hong Ky, "Defending Storage Depots on the Ho Chi Minh Trail," Wain Collection, Texas Tech Vietnam Archive. He told his troops that La Hap "had to be defended at all costs. 70% of them destroyed would mean we lose; 50% a draw; and 30% would mean a victory for us." He did not specify the date and made no mention of Giap being present.

380 *So did cassava and white pumpkins*: Madame Kumphat Hoxongluang, interview by author, Salavan, October 22, 2019.

380 *"If I'd met one"*: Boun Kuang, interview by author, Lalay Angkong, October 24, 2019.

380 *"Ah, yes, hélicoptères"*: Chouey, interview by author, Adorne, October 23, 2019. In contrast to the war in Algeria, the French did not use combat helicopters in Laos, so he is likely referring to relief helicopters used during military operations. Fall, *Street Without Joy*, 265.

381 *teenage orphan named Bouan*: A team of visiting American doctors later diagnosed Bouan as suffering from two rare conditions: Maffucci syndrome, characterized by multiple growths of cartilage within the bones, and Ollier's disease, a skeletal disorder characterized by abnormal bone growth.

381 *The chief surgeon in Salavan*: Drs. Sonexay and Tavanh Manivong, interview by author, Mittaphab Hospital, Vientiane, October 21, 2019, and Dr. Kheooudone, interview by author, Salavan district hospital, October 22, 2019.

383 *One retired official*: Vien Chien Koumman, interview by author, Samuoi, October 23, 2019.

383 *The acting governor of Salavan*: Phouthong Khammanivong, interview by author, October 22, 2019.

383 *Officials in Ta Oey*: Gov. Bouavanh Chanthavilay, interview by author, Ta Oey, October 22, 2019.

383 *It had seventeen cases*: For a full analysis of these statistics, see War Legacies Project,

2021 Report on the Laos Agent Orange Survey: State of Health and Livelihood. www .warlegacies.org/research-and-reports.

383 *Sengthong added a new case:* Congenital hydrocephalus may be the result of inherited genetic abnormalities that block the flow of cerebrospinal fluid or developmental disorders resulting from birth defects in the brain, spine, or spinal cord.

384 *This was where the Marines:* The official account of Dewey Canyon I and the attack on the PAVN's Base Area 611 is in USMC, *High Mobility and Standdown,* 38–51.

384 *But when Company G:* Marc D. Bernstein, "Vietnam War: Operation Dewey Canyon," *History Net,* June 5, 2007, includes a vivid account of the disaster on Co Ka Leuye.

386 *"Vietnamese people affected":* Kalod, interview by author, Lahang, October 24, 2019.

387 *"We have our work":* Tim Rieser, interview by author, Washington, D.C., November 14, 2019.

387 *The presumed victims of Agent Orange:* Provision for future dioxin assessments would "include environmental testing in villages close to multiple spraying runs and locations where Agent Orange may have been stored and loaded onto aircraft." Foreign Operations and Related Programs Appropriations Act 2022.

EPILOGUE HILL 674

390 *Finally, after half a century:* "Thua Thien-Hue Reviews Trial Dioxin Remediation," *Viet Nam News,* November 15, 2017; Phung Tuu Boi, personal communication to author.

390 *A dirt road, off-limits to foreigners:* This was the connection between the PAVN's Base Area 607 on the Lao border and the southern end of the A Shau Valley.

391 *There were 647 in all:* Documentation provided to author by Ho Sy Binh, chairman of A Luoi district office of VAVA, October 16, 2019.

392 *Tucked between an adjacent fold:* Dekonta A.S./Ministry of the Environment of the Czech Republic, "Rehabilitation of Thua Thien-Hue Province Affected by AO/Dioxin Contamination," Development Assistance Project Between the Czech Republic and the Socialist Republic of Vietnam, 2006–8. Document provided to author by Charles Bailey.

392 *Hill 674 rose steeply:* The Vietnamese call the mountain Ma Yen, the Horse's Back. To the French, it was the Pie du Midi, named for a celebrated nineteenth-century mountaintop observatory in the Pyrenees.

393 *He took us to see:* Other sources say 1928. Dr. Albert Sallet was one of the most prominent physicians in French Indochina, with a special interest in indigenous medicine. An expert on the Champa empire and director of the Tourane (Danang) Museum of Cham Sculpture, he was also the author of a history of the Ba Na hill station.

Index

ILLUSTRATION CREDITS

Insert 1
Chuck Searcy in Saigon. Courtesy of Chuck Searcy
Manus Campbell at Con Thien. Courtesy of Manus Campbell
Ho Chi Minh and Le Duan. Archives of Ministry of Foreign Affairs
Giap and Thanh. Vietnam Military History Museum
Bicycles on Ho Chi Minh Trail. U.S. Army Center of Military History
Elephants on Ho Chi Minh Trail. U.S. Army Center of Military History
PAVN soldiers in Quang Binh. U.S. Army Center of Military History
PAVN base area map. U.S. Air Force, CHECO Division
Tunnel system. U.S. Army 519th Military Intelligence Battalion
Ranch Hand helicopter. U.S. Department of Veterans Affairs
Khe Sanh Cartoon. Courtesy of Witness Collection and © 1968,
    estate of Pham Thanh Tam
William Dykes. Vietnam Veterans Memorial Foundation Virtual Wall
Larry Havers. Vietnam Veterans Memorial Foundation Virtual Wall
Earnest Hinsley. Vietnam Veterans Memorial Foundation Virtual Wall
Lady Borton at Buddha Mountain. Courtesy of Lady Borton
Chuck Searcy at Dewey Canyon III. Courtesy of Steve Talbot
Dong Ha ruins. Estate of Arthur H. Westing PhD
Quang Tri schoolhouse. Estate of Arthur H. Westing PhD
Boivin with samples. CBS *60 Minutes*
Katu villagers with fish. CBS *60 Minutes*
Katu woman giving blood. Thomas Boivin

Insert 2
Ton That Tung. Heritage Center for Scientists and Scholars of Vietnam
Nguyen Thi Ngoc Toan and Cao Van Tranh. Courtesy of Van Cao
Hoang Dinh Cau. National Center for Health Communications and Education
Le Cao Dai and Vu Giang Huong. Courtesy of Lady Borton
Bailey in Nepal. Courtesy Jerry Rogoff, Peace Corps Nepal Photo Project, 1962–1975
Charles Bailey with Le Thi Hoa. Courtesy of Charles Bailey
Phuong An 2 family. Project RENEW
Tran Thi Gai. Author photo
Quy Nhon CS gas site. Hatfield Consultants

Rockpile unexploded ordnance. Project RENEW
Colonel Hong and Hien Ngo. Project RENEW
Phu Nguyen. Author photo
Women's team. Project RENEW
Le Minh Chau. Author photo
Dan Kritenbrink and Hoang Nam. *Toan Vu, Dan Tri*
Indochine poster. Author's collection
Bach Ma. Justin Mott
Hamburger Hill. Vina DMZ Travel
Susan Hammond. Photograph by Michael Moore, reprinted with permission
    from *The Keene Sentinel,* all rights reserved
Roger Rumpf. Roger Arnold
Prosthetic limbs. Christopher Anderson/Magnum
Yen Ly Vongkansa. Christopher Anderson/Magnum
Co Ka Leuye. Author photo
Chagnon and Hammond. Christopher Anderson/Magnum
Searcy and Tran Tuyet Mai. Author photo
Campbell on Hill 674. Author photo

A NOTE ABOUT THE AUTHOR

Born in Scotland, author and journalist George Black has spent most of his adult life in New York City. His award-winning writing on international political issues, often focusing on the human and environmental consequences of violent conflict, has appeared in *The New York Times Magazine, The New Yorker,* and many other publications. His previous books include works on the Chinese democracy movement, the River Ganges in India and Bangladesh, and the nineteenth-century exploration of the American West. *The Long Reckoning,* his eighth book, is the result of eight research trips to Vietnam and two to Laos and his travels on the Ho Chi Minh Trail in both countries. https://www.george-black.net

A NOTE ON THE TYPE

This book was set in Minion, a typeface produced by the Adobe Corporation specifically for the Macintosh personal computer, and released in 1990. Designed by Robert Slimbach, Minion combines the classic characteristics of old-style faces with the full complement of weights required for modern typesetting.

COMPOSED BY NORTH MARKET STREET GRAPHICS, LANCASTER, PENNSYLVANIA

PRINTED AND BOUND BY LAKESIDE BOOK COMPANY, HARRISONBURG, VIRGINIA

DESIGNED BY MAGGIE HINDERS